D1507917

Decisionmaking
in Criminal Justice

Decisionmaking in Criminal Justice:

Toward the Rational Exercise of Discretion

Michael R. Gottfredson
State University of New York at Albany

Don M. Gottfredson
Rutgers, the State University of New Jersey

Ballinger Publishing Company • Cambridge, Massachusetts
A Subsidiary of Harper & Row, Publishers, Inc.

This book is printed on recycled paper.

Copyright © 1980 by Ballinger Publishing Company. All rights reserved. No part of this publication may be reproduced, stored in a retrieval system, or transmitted in any form or by any means, electronic, mechanical, photocopy, recording or otherwise, without the prior written consent of the publisher.

International Standard Book Number: 0-88410-234-3

Library of Congress Catalog Card Number: 80-18909

Printed in the United States of America

Library of Congress Cataloging in Publication Data

Gottfredson, Michael R
  Decision-making in criminal justice.

  Includes bibliographical references and indexes.
  1. Criminal justice, Administration of—United States—Decision making. 2. Sentences (Criminal procedure)—United States—Decision making. I. Gottfredson, Don M., joint author. II. Title.
HV8138.G67   364   80-18909
ISBN 0-88410-234-3

To Karol and Betty

Contents

List of Figures

List of Tables

Acknowledgments

Although mere thanks will not discharge the debts we owe to the many people who assisted us in the preparation of this book, we would be seriously remiss in not giving special mention to those who lent their time and talents to improve our work. Portions of the manuscript were critiqued by John Goldkamp, Michael Hindelang, Maxine Schmalenberger, and Eileen Allen. We are grateful for their many helpful suggestions. Marjorie Jones helped with the manuscript preparation and made many editorial comments. Ann Pastore's excellent graphic skills are represented in many of the figures and tables in the book; we appreciate her talent and are grateful for her assistance. Our gratitude also goes to Diane Sager and Margaret McGuire who typed portions of the manuscript. To Harriet Spector, who typed, edited, and kept track of the whole thing, a special note of thanks. Our task was much simplified because of her fine work.

Our deepest debt is owed to two of our colleagues—Michael J. Hindelang and Leslie T. Wilkins. We have had the privilege of enjoying a lengthy collaboration with these two scholars over the years. Our concepts and analyses have been greatly influenced and improved by them. Of course, it would be difficult for anyone to write a book about criminal justice and not be stimulated and enriched by the work of Michael Hindelang and Leslie Wilkins—their research is too pervasive and important and their concepts are too compelling. We are delighted to acknowledge their contributions to our thought and work.

Finally, we each want to thank the other for accepting the responsibility for the errors in the book.

The law is written by legislators, interpreted occasionally by appellate courts, but applied by countless individuals, each acting largely for himself. How it is applied outweighs in importance its enactment or its interpretation.

N. Baker, "The Prosecutor—Initiation of Prosecution," *Journal of Criminal Law, Criminology and Police Science* 23:770 (1933).

Preface

It will be argued in this book that the study of decisions in the criminal justice process provides a useful focus for the examination of many fundamental aspects of criminal justice. Indeed, an understanding of the decisions made by victims of crime, police, prosecutors, judges, corrections administrators, and paroling authorities is critical to an understanding of the criminal justice process. These decisions are not always highly visible. They are made, ordinarily, within wide areas of discretion. The objectives of the decisions are not always clear; and indeed, the principal objectives of these decisions are often the subject of much debate. Usually they are not guided by explicit decision policies. Often the participants are unable to verbalize the basis for the selection of decision alternatives. Adequate information for the decisions usually is unavailable. Rarely can the decisions be demonstrated to be rational.

By a "rational decision" we mean "that decision among those possible for the decisionmaker which, in the light of the information available, maximizes the probability of the achievement of the purpose of the decisionmaker in that specific and particular case."[1] This definition, which stems from statistical decision theory, points to three fundamental characteristics of decisions. First, it is assumed that a choice of possible decisions (or, more precisely, of possible alternatives) is available. If only one choice is possible, there is no decision problem, and the question of rationality hardly will arise. Usually, of course, there will be a choice—even if the alternative is to decide not to decide, a choice that, of course, often has profound consequences. Choosing to do nothing (report a crime, make an arrest) has its impact; and the prison inmate whose case is "continued" for later parole consideration would no doubt agree that "delay is the deadliest form of denial."[2] Second, it is assumed that some information is available for use in arriving at the decision. Again, the idea of a rational decision made wholly without information would hardly occur to us. Ordinarily it is expected that if a decision is to be made, some information will be available. Third, there is assumed to be a goal or a set of goals, purposes, or objectives to be achieved (or maximized or minimized). If it is not known what is sought to be achieved, then it is not possible to assess the rationality of any particular decision choice.

There is no requirement that we prefer rationality, but we assume that rational decisions generally are preferred and sought in the criminal justice system. We admit the preference and the assumption.

It will be argued that available methods of diagnosis, classification, and prediction are inadequate at present to provide much useful guidance to law enforcement, prosecutorial, judicial, or correctional decisionmaking. Much has been learned, however, that can contribute to such guidance, and we seek to summarize some of this knowledge and to point to areas of ignorance requiring research on these topics.

It is clear that increased rationality in criminal justice is likely to be achieved only after it has become possible to identify more explicitly, with adequate operational definitions, the specific objectives of each phase of the apparatus intended to reduce, control, or at least cope with problems of delinquency and crime (or in some other sense to provide justice). A second requirement must be the identification, adequate description, and perhaps the elaboration of additional alternative decision choices at each step. The third necessity, of course, is the requirement of information. By the term "information," we do not refer to mere data, no matter how carefully collected or how reliable, but to those data that, by demonstrable relevance to objectives, reduce uncertainty in the decision under consideration. Thus, having information implies having knowledge of the relation of the datum in question to the decision objectives; and such knowledge often is wholly lacking in the criminal justice system.

If the decisionmaker, whether victim, policeman, or, judge, is unclear about the objectives of a given decision, that person hardly can be expected to behave rationally in the sense of maximizing the probability of achieving that undefined purpose. Of course, people do have objectives in making decisions, but often they are only vaguely felt and difficult to express. A profound lack of clarity of definition and of adequate measurement of objectives abounds in the criminal justice system.

Moreover, these objectives are sometimes conflicting. Given a mixed set of criminal justice goals, including such possibly conflicting aims as retribution, deterrence, rehabilitation, reintegration, or desert, it is not surprising to find absent a clear consensus on objectives within or among criminal justice agency personnel. At each step in the processes of these systems, which require decisions with remarkably profound impact on the subsequent lives of the persons involved, fundamental conflicts may be readily perceived. The most basic, perhaps, is a conflict between perceived essentials of justice that require provision of just desert (punishment or reward) and various utilitarian perspectives that stress crime reduction. In this book we emphasize utilitarian aims; these are compatible with the rational, pragmatic, and probabilistic frame of reference that we have sought to employ.

We may briefly justify our focus on utilitarian aims. Among juvenile justice procedures, what are the objectives, for example, of taking a child into custody by law enforcement personnel? Setting aside the due process issues raised subsequently to (what amounted to) the arrest of Gerald Gault,[3] one may ask whether the objectives of the decision problem confronting the sheriff's officer in a like situation are clear, reasonably well agreed upon, and hence permit assessment of the rationality of the decision. Was the purpose to ensure Gerald's availability to the juvenile court? Was the "arrest" or the subsequent detention thought to be required to prevent Gerald's harming of others or himself or his running away? Much attention has been given to the constitutional issues stemming from this famous case and to the potential impact of the decision of the Supreme Court of the United States on the philosophy and practice of the juvenile courts. Little attention, however, has been given to the fundamental questions that must be asked when the *rationality* of the decisions (of the officer or the juvenile court judge) is examined. This is not to minimize the importance of the legal issues involved. It is, rather, to assert that the legal questions may have little to do with whether or not decisions are taken in such a way as to maximize the probability of achieving the presumed objectives of those decisions.

When the postadjudication decision for placement of the young offender is considered, the situation is analogous to the sentencing of adults and the objectives are no more clear. To argue the relative merits of *parens patriae* and criminal sanctions adds little to the needed clarification. If this is correct and if, for example, the philosophy of the juvenile courts leads to assignment of a greater degree of importance to rehabilitative or other utilitarian aims and less to desert, this does not negate the importance of specifying when and how the assessment of rehabilitation (or crime reduction generally) is to be made. Only when such criteria are developed can we ask whether boys in Gerald Gault's circumstances rationally ought to be placed in custody, in detention, or in the training school—in addition to asking whether constitutionally correct procedures are followed.

With this example from the area of juvenile justice, we should point out that only occasional and cursory discussion of some aspects of that system appear in this book. Authors who set out to describe and to analyze major decisions in the criminal justice process are confronted quickly with a critical decision themselves: which decisions, among the scores that occur between the initial definition of conduct as illegal and the decision to release a punished person from state control, should serve as examples for the inquiry? Compelling arguments could be made that nearly every decision in the juvenile and criminal justice processes ought to be regarded as critically in need of careful study. Most juvenile and criminal justice decisions can be regarded rightly as vitally affecting both the lives of those about whom the decisions are made and the welfare of the community. In part, our decisions were made pragmatically: we assumed the juvenile justice system decisions generally to be beyond a reasonable scope for our efforts, and the decision points to be discussed are those about which most recent research has been concerned (and, consequently, about which most is known). It was our further aim, however, to select those decisions made by individual actors in the criminal justice system that have the greatest impact on the system as a whole.[4] For that reason, we begin in Chapter 2 with a discussion of the decision to report a crime to the police.

The decision of the victim of crime as to whether or not to report the offense to the police is of such a critical nature that the victim may be regarded fairly as a principal gatekeeper to the criminal justice system. Yet if we ask how much is known of the objectives of the victim (in calling or not calling the police), we find that the answer is, "surprisingly little." How often, and in what circumstances, does the victim seek mere retribution? When, in reporting a crime, is the victim concerned to achieve the offender's incapacitation? Is deterrence sometimes an aim in crime reporting, as it is, apparently, in sentencing or parole decisions? What objectives are sought by the victim when an event perceived as a crime is *not* reported?

The decisions made by police are similarly complex and not yet well understood, although more research has been done on this topic. If a crime is reported to them or discovered by them, it is they who ordinarily must decide what is to be done next. Generally, they must decide whether or not to invoke the law. This involves deciding whether or not a crime apparently has occurred. It may involve deciding on legal issues such as "reasonable suspicion" or "probable cause." In deciding whether or not to make an arrest, the police officer may have various discretionary choices—for example, arrest, issue a citation, refer to a social agency, offer counsel, do nothing. Again, the objectives may be diverse. General goals are subject to debate. Information to guide general policy or individual decisions may be lacking.

The discretion in decisionmaking exercised by prosecutors has perhaps been less noticed in the past, less in the public eye, than that of police or judges. Nevertheless, it is very broad, and the decisions have profound consequences for the rest of the criminal justice system. Prosecutors too must decide whether or not to invoke the law. Is the defendant to be charged? If so, what specific offense or offenses will be alleged? Shall the accused be brought to trial or should a plea of guilty to a lesser offense be negotiated? What resources should be brought to bear on the necessary investigation? Again, the prosecutor may have a variety of goals—increasing convictions, winning cases, "cracking down" on specific kinds of offenses, or more generally, aims of deterrence, incapacitation, rehabilitation, or desert. Some recent research has focused on the information needs of the prosecutor to aid in the selection of alternative courses of action in pursuit of diverse objectives.

Should an accused person be held in custody before trial? A foundation of American law traditionally has been the presumption of innocence before trial. Bail may be used to help ensure the availability of the defendant in court, but the Constitution of the United States prohibits that it be excessive. Some have advocated, nevertheless, the preventive detention of some accused—not for what they may have done but for what they may do. Within this context, we seek to examine the goals and information needs of the court for decisionmaking on bail and "release on recognizance." Again, both general policy and individual case decisions are involved. Fundamental issues of liberty and crime control are at stake.

The judge, in passing sentence, traditionally has had much autonomy and much discretion. Yet he or she is dependent upon the police, the prosecutor, and the probation officer (among others) as sources of information. The often conflicting goals of the entire criminal justice system are those typically expressed by individual judges: desert, rehabilitation, incapacitation, deterrence—in short, the provision of both deserved punishment and crime control. Thus, the aims may be derived from moral principles or from utilitarian purposes of crime reduction. Alternative dispositions, once the determination of guilt has been made, are increasingly complex. They generally must be selected within legal constraints that vary markedly among jurisdictions. And these decisions generally must be made in the absence of clear consensus on the aims of sentencing, without an explicit, clearly articulated policy guiding the exercise of discretion. They are made also in the absence of a systematic procedure for feedback on the consequences of decisions, even in terms of the later criminal careers of those sentenced. Also absent, therefore, is convincing evidence of the relationship of a given disposition to deterrence, incapacitation, or rehabilitation. Furthermore, there is no demonstrated consensus on deserved punishment. In short, most present sentencing decisions involve complex goals, much data, little information, diverse alternatives, considerable discretion, and little structured policy.

The correctional institution administrator must run a distinctive type of hotel facility without benefit of a reservation service. Typically, the jail or prison administrator has little to say about who comes to stay or for how long. Within the institutional confines, however, there are many decisions to be made. These, as elsewhere in the system, are of two general types—policy decisions and individual decisions. General policy decisions may involve, for example, the development of appropriate (effective?) programs of treatment for differing kinds of offenders. Individual decisions may be required with immediacy—for example, assign to suicide prevention watch or place in protective custody—or they may appear more mundane— select work assignment; place where beds are available; decide initial custody classification—or they may be critical to rehabilitative aims—place in educational programs or in vocational training; recommend counseling; place in institution nearest family. The aims are similarly complex. Often, they appear to conflict—as when custody and security concerns and those of treatment are at odds. Some correctional research may help to inform these decisions, but much remains to be done to sort mere data from useful information to guide correctional decisions to greater rationality.

Probation, although typically an "arm of the court," also may be considered to be a part of corrections—namely, corrections in the community. Parole, which generally refers to supervision in the community after a period of incarceration (rather than in lieu of it) may be regarded in the same way. Probation decisions do not end with the placement by the judge of the convicted offender in that dispositional category. Rather, a process of decisions by probation staff is then initiated. Some of these have to do with placement—for example, in case loads of varying size, methods, or levels of intensity of supervision or surveillance. Others, of course, address whether or not an assertion of probation violation (to the court) or parole violation (to the paroling authority) is to be made. The objectives, alternatives, and information needs are, in general, similar to those that obtain in other parts of the system.

Paroling decisions are highly visible, much discussed, and widely debated. Goals of parole board members tend to reflect a variety of differing perspectives—sanctioning, treatment, fairness, citizen representation, and gatekeeping (reservation service). Like judges, parole boards have been subject to much criticism for alleged arbitrary and capricious decisionmaking, for disparity in the granting or denial of parole, and for ineffectiveness. As with sentencing decisions, much research has been done, and much remains to be learned. Similar needs for consensus on goals, for structured policies governing the exercise of discretion, and for information demonstrably relevant to both policy and individual decisions are apparent.

These are all complex decisions, and our title, given both this complexity and the importance of the topic, is presumptuous. Our goals are more modest: to examine some of this complexity, to discuss some of the recent research relevant to the concept of rationality in decisionmaking, and to point to some areas in which further inquiry is most needed. We do not claim expertise in all the areas discussed. Each of the critical decision points examined involves a large topic in itself.

Some large topics are omitted, or nearly so, altogether. General deterrence and incapacitation provide two closely related examples.[5] The empirical evidence bearing on these two important traditional utilitarian aims of the criminal justice system has obvious importance for decisions—of both policy and individual focus—discussed throughout this book. Similarly, we have not attempted to provide a comprehensive review of evidence bearing on rehabilitation; a number of recent overview discussions are available.[6] And although we focus on decisions, a large body of literature on decision theory generally has been ignored—not because it is perceived as irrelevant, but because it would extend the scope of the discussion beyond the tolerance of even the most sympathetic reader.

When the criminal justice system is considered from a perspective of decisions, it is apparent immediately that decisions are the stuff of that system. Thus, few aspects of criminal justice are found to be outside the plausible scope of discussion. It might be argued that the greatest omission in this book is a chapter on the decision of the offender to commit a crime. There is a reason, however, for omitting such a chapter, in addition to the obvious one that the topic involves much of criminology, sociology, psychology, psychiatry, and related disciplines. It is that we have sought to focus on information needs, objectives, and choices within the criminal justice system, toward the end of more reasoned and logical dealing with the problem of crime after it has occurred.

Even within the criminal justice system, additional large areas of inquiry have been ignored. Examples include the entire process for determination of guilt or innocence, the subject of plea bargaining, the topic of disciplinary hearings in confinement, and in general, issues of determination of probation or parole violation. Issues related to decisions of competency to stand trial are little discussed, and those concerning the insanity defense are ignored. Concerning these and related important topics not given their fair and proper share of attention, we plead guilty but ask that others address them.

We do not deal sufficiently, either, with the question of the nature of a decision. What, after all, is a decision? Is it a process or an end state—that is, a termination of a process? Are decisions of different kinds, such that information is processed differently in different cases? Are there different kinds of decisionmakers—for example, persons who process information, to arrive at decisions, in different ways? If so, does this have significance for the forms of presentation of information to the decisionmakers? These, too, are important issues, little discussed in this book.[7]

We stress *rationality* throughout this book, but that is not because we believe it to be the only, or even the most important, concern of criminal justice decisionmakers. Obviously, concerns of fairness, justice, legality, and even symbolism are essential features of most of these decisions. Each could provide themes to be scrutinized in respect to any of the decisions discussed in this book. Rather, our stress on the rational exercise of discretion derives from our belief that it is an understudied and yet a critical aspect of criminal justice decisionmaking.

This book differs from many discussions of criminal justice decisionmaking not just because of its emphasis on rationality, but for its primary emphasis on scientific social research. To be sure, some legal analysis is undertaken, principally in the context of discussions of decision goals. But our concern with the idea of *information* leads us to examine research that attempts to discover how decisions actually are made in the criminal justice system and whether they are made in ways compatible with purported aims. Traditionally, these areas of inquiry have fallen into the realm of social science.

We stress rationality, and we urge a scientific outlook, but we trust we will not be mistaken as propounding these as a sole driving force for progress toward criminal justice. Rather, in agreement with Bertrand Russell, we would note that "The impulse toward scientific construction is admirable when it does not thwart any of the major impulses that give value to human life, but when it is allowed to forbid all outlet to everything but itself it becomes a form of cruel tyranny."[8] Science increases knowledge, and knowledge brings power. It is apparent that the increased rationality through social science that is sought may be exercised safely only in a context of values beyond the scope of discussion here. That suggests a further limitation of this book; but, indeed, it stems from a limitation of science. Russell concluded his essay on science and values by stating, "The dangers exist, but they are not inevitable, and hope for the future is at least as rational as fear."[9]

We have not attempted to review all of the research bearing on the important areas of decisions discussed. On the contrary, we have been selective in our attempt to review those studies that best inform about the concepts of information, goals, and alternatives. And we limit our analyses to studies of routine cases in the system; all too often discussions of decisions in criminal justice focus on the unique, exceptional cases, to the detriment of an understanding of how decisions typically are made. Despite these omissions, we have sought to deal with areas of particular importance to criminal justice if the decisions of significant actors in that system—and hence procedures and programs—are to be made more rationally.

We have tried to write for our colleagues in criminal justice research and in criminal justice administration, at the same time hoping that the book will be found useful to students. These are in some respects diverse audiences, and we are aware that going down the middle of the road may disrupt traffic both ways. We have sought, however, to refer the reader elsewhere for more detailed, more technical, or more thorough discussion of critical points.

In the final chapter we identify ten requisites for increased rationality in criminal justice decisionmaking. These requisites are derived from our analyses of the decisions discussed in this book. We also attempt a reconciliation among the apparently conflicting goals that seem to abound in the criminal justice system. In this final chapter we assert that the application of scientific methods to criminal justice decisionmaking offers the greatest hope for improvement of our system of justice. We are well aware that to argue in favor of a central role for facts in a world of values will be seen as short sighted by some, naive by others—a dangerous revision to an inglorious and thoroughly discredited earlier era or an embarrassingly optimistic faith in the potential for change. Our consolation lies in our belief that the alternative position rests on the implicit supposition that progress will be made when presumptions are regarded as facts, when untested hunches are acted upon with vigor, when goals are unspecified, and when trendy alternatives are accepted for their novelty alone.

The theme of the book involves goals, alternatives, and information as three legs of the stool on which the decisionmaker sits. If goals are unclear or confused, if alternatives are unrelated to them, or if information is irrelevant—if any one leg is weak—he or she who sits upon the stool must sit with trepidation.

Michael R. Gottfredson
Don M. Gottfredson

NOTES

1. L. Wilkins, "Perspectives on Court Decision-making," in D.M. Gottfredson, *Decision-making in the Criminal Justice System: Reviews and Essays*, Crime and Delinquency Issues: a Monograph Series (Washington, D.C.: Government Printing Office, 1975), p. 70. This discussion, and indeed our analytic framework, draws heavily upon Wilkins' argument. See also, L. Wilkins, *Evaluation of Penal Measures* (New York: Random House, 1969).

2. C.N. Parkinson, *The Law of Delay*, 2nd ed. (Boston: Houghton Mifflin, 1971), p. 119.

3. *In re* Gault, 387 U.S. 1 (1967).

4. The frame of reference that stresses the interdependence of the decision points that make up the criminal justice system is stated in F. Remington, D. Newman, E. Kimball, M. Melli, and H. Goldstein, *Criminal Justice Administration* (Indianapolis: Bobbs-Merrill, 1969). See especially Chapter 1.

5. See, for example, National Research Council, *Deterrence and Incapacitation: Estimating the Effects of Criminal Sanctions on the Crime Rate* (Washington, D.C.: National Academy of Sciences, 1978).

6. See, for example, L. Sechrest, S. White, and E. Brown, eds., *The Rehabilitation of Criminal Offenders: Problems and Prospects* (Washington, D.C.: National Academy of Sciences, 1979).

7. See, for discussion of these and related issues, Wilkins, *Supra* note 1 at 59-81.

8. B. Russell, *The Scientific Outlook* (New York: W.W. Norton, 1962), p. 260.

9. *Id.* at 269.

❋ *Chapter 1*

Overview

This chapter presents an overview of the decisions in the
criminal justice system—what they are, who makes them,
how they are made, and with what consequences. Its
aims are to identify the themes that will serve as the focus of detailed discussions in subsequent chapters, to familiarize the reader
with the decisionpoint frame of reference, and to highlight our
analytical method. Later, we put flesh on these bare bones; our
purposes here are to provide the context for our later detailed
investigations, to define our terms, and to give a glimpse of our
conclusions. The justification for these conclusions comes, we
believe, in the remainder of the book.

When a crime occurs, that event may or may not be reported
to the police or other law enforcement officials. If the victim or
other observers do not report the crime, the criminal justice system
is not invoked; but when a crime is reported, a complex sequence
of decisions may ensue. These decisions are critical events in the
lives of the persons affected, and they are the central features of the
criminal justice system.

The report to police of a bicycle theft, a rape, or a robbery may,
for example, be the stimulus to decisions such as:

Should a police car be dispatched?
Should the event be regarded as an offense?
Should an arrest be made?
Should an alleged offender be held or released?
Should a citation be issued?
Should an alleged offender be prosecuted? With what priority?

Is the offender guilty?
If guilty, what should be the sentence? Fine, jail, or prison? Should the offender be placed on probation? Any special conditions?
If sentenced to confinement, where? For what purpose? How long? What degree of custodial security is required?
To what programs should the person be assigned?
Should the offender be paroled from custody?
Should parole be revoked?
Should the offender be discharged?

These, of course, are but a few of the decisions (although they are important ones) made at every step in the criminal justice process. Many obviously are extremely important to the individuals affected. They deal with loss of liberty and other serious intrusions and interventions in individual lives. They are obviously critical to the efficient, effective, and humane functioning of the criminal justice system. If that system is to serve society well, such decisions should be made rationally, ensuring the fair, efficient, effective, and humane system widely sought for the control and reduction of crime.

Although some general agreement might be found with the statements just preceding, the obtained degree of consensus might diminish with serious efforts to define their central concepts in specific terms. What, indeed, is a "decision"? When may decisions be said to be "effective" and in what sense? It is not to be expected that the definitive answers to these fundamental questions, which are sure to be with us for a long time, will be found in these pages. Decisions made in selected major areas of the criminal justice system will be considered, however, such as decisions made by the victims of crime, police, prosecutors, judges, and correctional officials.

These decisions are of two general kinds. Some are made about persons—that is, individual decisions. Others are agency or institutional decisions.[1] Agency decisions, including questions of general policy, of course raise many important questions, but many of these are thought to be beyond the scope of this book. As will be seen, however, it is not easy to separate the two general kinds of decisions, since decisions as to general policy provide the context, including constraints, within which individual decisions are made.

THE NATURE OF A DECISION

Any decision has three main components. There is first a *goal* (or a set of goals) that the decisionmaker would like to achieve. It is reasonable and useful for analysis to assume that the decisionmaker (such as police officer, prosecutor, or judge) has some objective or objectives that may be specified. That is, if there is a decision problem, the decisionmaker wishes to bring about some change in the state of affairs or has a desire to optimize some result. For example, the prosecutor may wish to achieve a conviction of the alleged offender in court; the judge may desire an optimal sentence for both the protection of society and the rehabilitation of the offender.

Second, there are some *alternatives*. If there is no choice, there is no decision problem. Ordinarily, the decisionmaker in the criminal justice system has a variety of alternative choices, although he or she may often wish for more or better ones. It is very important to note that the decisionmaker usually has, within the law and agency rules or regulations, considerable *discretion* in choosing decision alternatives.

Third, the decisionmaker has some *information* to guide the selection among alternatives. In order to qualify as information in this sense, the data available about alternatives must be related to the goals of the decision—that is, the data must be relevant. The definition of relevance in this context is that the data must reduce uncertainty about the consequences of the decision.

It is clear that decisions may not be evaluated very thoroughly if the goals of the decisions are unknown. Similarly, it is difficult to see how decisions might be improved in the absence of clear and explicit specification of those goals, because no means for assessing the information value of data about alternatives would be available. The information value of a datum is determined by the relation of that datum to the consequences of the alternative choices; if there is no relation, then there is no information. We shall see that decisions about offenders and alleged offenders often are made with much data but little information.

Increased rationality in the criminal justice system thus requires the improvement of information available for decisions. This is a central theme of this book. In one of his *Unpopular Essays*, Bertrand Russell said:

Man is a rational animal—so at least I have been told. Throughout a long life, I have looked diligently for evidence in favor of this statement, but so far I have not had the good fortune to come across it, though I have searched in many countries spread over three continents.[2]

Citing Aristotle as perhaps the first to proclaim man as a rational animal, Russell did not find Aristotle's reason for this view very impressive—"it was that some people can do sums."[3]

Rationality in decisionmaking about persons caught up in the criminal justice system may be assumed to be a requirement to "improved," "more efficient," or "more effective" decisions. If this is accepted, then there will be further requirements. There must be some agreed upon objectives for the decisions, relevant information about the person, decision alternatives, and knowledge of the probable outcomes when alternatives are chosen. In the criminal justice system now, however, clear agreement on objectives is not found easily. Usually, little information is available to the persons with decision responsibility, and often evidence on the likely consequences of alternatives is lacking entirely. Given these difficulties, it may not be expected that Russell's observation may be refuted easily or that we will readily find much better support for Aristotle's claim of man's rationality than his own. Nevertheless, the analysis of decisions, including an assessment of the sometimes conflicting, usually poorly articulated goals in this field, and of information needs, may provide a basis for progress toward a more rational system.

The concept of rationality is, of course, a complex one. Philosophers have discussed and debated its definition from many points of view. However, for the purposes of this book, the concept of a rational decision may be defined more readily. We assume that "a rational decision is that decision among those possible for the decision-maker which, in the light of the information available, maximizes the probability of the achievement of the purpose of the decision-maker in that specific and particular case."[4]

This definition again calls attention to the three main components of a decision—goals, alternatives, and information. The definition of information, as distinct from data, is critical: information is that data that reduces uncertainty (that is, provides guidance as to the probabilities) of achievement of desired decision objectives.

These concepts are central to the analyses of decisions presented in this book. We seek to examine, for each of the decision problem areas discussed, aspects of these three decision components—goals, alternatives, and information—and to review selected empirical studies pertinent to them. From this examination, we then seek to identify some requisites for increased rationality in decisionmaking.

It is important also to define at the outset our use of the terms diagnosis, classification, and prediction. These concepts often are used in discussions of decisionmaking in criminal justice. They are related but not identical.

DIAGNOSIS

The word diagnosis, which originally meant a distinguishing or a discrimination, refers in medicine to a decision concerning the nature of a diseased condition. Initially, it carried a similar meaning in psychiatry, clinical psychology, and social work. By analogy with physical illness, patients were sorted into categories of mental disorder. Later, the application of the word was extended: a diagnosis was said to refer not only to the identification of an appropriate nosological category but also to a full understanding of the patient. This paralleled other developments in clinical psychology and social work that resulted in emphasis upon both individual uniqueness and the need to treat the whole person.

Some disenchantment with the idea of diagnosis as it is applied to offenders and is thought to be relevant to decisions concerning their placement or disposition may now be discerned in criminal justice agencies and among their critics. The diagnosis-treatment model carried over from medicine undergirded the rehabilitation philosophy that became increasingly popular in criminal justice agencies in the last half century. Prisons often were renamed as correctional institutions. Rather than places for reform, penitence, or mere isolation from the community, the rehabilitation of the convicted offender was regarded widely as a major objective of the criminal justice enterprise. Tied to this concept was the development of the indeterminate sentence. If the offender's term of imprisonment was not definitely set for a fixed period of time, this would allow (it was argued) the offender's diagnosis, appropriate treatment, and release "when ready." There has been, however, a repeated and frustrating failure to demonstrate effectiveness in reducing recidivism—that is, repeated offending—by application of this model.[5] There has also been an increasing rejection of the "medical model" as an inappropriate guide to interventions applied to all who are defined as "delinquent" or "criminal."[6]

The terms "delinquent" or "criminal" do not necessarily refer aptly to any state of the person, as would be expected to be the case with diagnosis of physical or mental disorder. Rather, they refer also to the state of the social system with which the person is involved as a result of his or her acts. The term "criminal" may be defined operationally as an act of the person and a societal response—for example, offense and conviction—but such definition is not limited to the description of the person and his or her acts. It does not seem reasonable, therefore, that they define a need for treatment of the person. It is more reasonable to assume that there are social, medical, and psychological states that may be ascribed to individuals and that some of the states may be associated with a higher probability of criminal acts. We might seek to modify these states by appropriate treatments. Clearly, however, such states cannot be defined adequately, as is commonly done, by identification of a stage in the criminal justice process.

A "diagnosis" thus refers to some state of the person that may or may not be related to present or future events defined as delinquent or criminal. Since we may group together, for purposes of analysis, persons with similar diagnoses or may use the datum of a diagnosis together with other data about the person, diagnoses may (or may not) be useful in classifications of persons. Such classifications may (or may not) be relevant to decision problems in criminal justice. They may (or may not) be useful for prediction of the outcomes to these decisions.

CLASSIFICATION

The concept of classification refers to the allocation of entities to initially undefined classes in such a way that individuals in a class are in some sense similar or close to each other.[7] It should be distinguished from "identification" or "assignment," concepts that refer to the process of choosing, for a new entity, which of a number of already defined classes should be selected for the allocation. There recently has been a growing literature in statistics, ecology, and biology concerning methods sometimes referred to as "numerical taxonomy," related to this general problem, some of which have found application in criminal justice.

Generally, however, the concept of "classification" has been used in criminal justice agencies to refer to "assignment" or else to refer to various methods of categorization or typing. The latter may be clumped under the headings of "empirical" and "theoretical" methods. The "empirical" methods include the taxonomic ones but also any method that proceeds by grouping together individuals such that each group contains members as similar as possible to each other and as different as possible from all other groups—with the selection of features to be considered not dictated by any particular theory. The "theoretical" method, however, begins with theory, from which the bases for classification are deduced. Thus, criminal justice programs may be based on classifications of persons derived from psychiatric, psychological, sociological, or other theories.

PREDICTION

The concept of prediction refers in criminology to an assessment of a person's expected future behavior (or an expected future state of the criminal justice system). Some criterion of future performance (such as delinquent or criminal acts or parole violation behavior) must be defined. This definition must be independent of any steps performed in arriving at the prediction; and thus prediction involves two independent assessments of persons, separated over time. On the basis of a first assessment, "predictors" may be established by any means whatever—including any data from diagnostic procedures, any classification scheme, or indeed, any attribute or measure related to the individual. Commonly, items pertaining to the person's life history, successes and failures, psychological test scores, or family situation are employed as candidates to become predictors. Thus, any data constituting information (as already defined—that is, reducing uncertainty with respect to the expected behavior) may provide the predictors. The second assessment establishes the classifications of performance to be predicted. The predictions provide estimates of the expected values for these criterion categories, and these estimates should be determined from earlier empirical investigations of the relations between the predictors and the criterion. Those predictor candidates found not to be useful in improving prediction are discarded. Thus, on the basis of previously observed relations between predictor and criterion classifications, one seeks to determine, for each category of persons, the most probable outcome in terms of the criterion.

The predictor categories may, as already asserted, represent any attribute or measure concerning the individual. They may be defined by what the person says about himself, others, ink blots, or other stimuli—the variety of which is limited only by investigators' imaginations. They may be established by what others say—that is, by the observations or judgments of others, singly or in groups—and this may include assessments of the person's abilities, interests, or perceptions. They may be defined by what the person has done previously, whether these be laudable achievements or criminal acts. They may be defined by what is done to or with the person, including exposure to specific treatment programs—that is, by placement decisions at any stage of the criminal justice system.

INTERRELATIONS OF THE CONCEPTS OF DIAGNOSIS, CLASSIFICATION, AND PREDICTION

The relations among these concepts may now be identified. One may, by many methods, make an assessment of an individual in order to help describe some state of that person. Such diagnoses may be relevant to his or her health or well-being. They may provide information useful for classifications for a variety of purposes. Persons may be classified in various ways to serve any number of objectives. One common aim is that of prediction. Thus, data from diagnostic procedures and from classification efforts may provide information useful for prediction of some single criterion or of various criteria. If they do not, this does not imply that such data are useless for other purposes; but the nature of criminal justice decisions is such that a predictive value of the information used for decisionmaking often is implied. The point to be stressed is that diagnostic and classification data may or may not constitute information for decisionmaking. The same is true for data with predictive utility, depending upon the decision problem.

The concepts of reliability and validity are central to critical assessments of diagnostic, classification, or prediction procedures. Reliability refers to consistency or stability of repeated observations, scores, or classifications. A procedure is said to be reliable to the extent that repetitions of the procedure lead to similar observations or classifications. The concept of validity has reference to the purposes of the procedures; the question of validity asks how well the method works in achieving those purposes. In the case of diagnoses, validity refers to the aptness of description of the state of the person when that may be assessed by some external, independent standard. Classifications, too, are by themselves merely descriptive, so the same may be said with respect to groupings of persons. When it comes to prediction, however, validity refers to the degree to which earlier assessments are related demonstrably to later classifications in new samples.

The criminal justice literature includes many reports of "prediction" studies in which the crucial step of testing the methods developed by application to new samples is missing. Such studies must be viewed very critically. They may provide useful preliminary work helpful to later prediction studies more worthy of that name, but even the cautious interpretations of validity often made in this circumstance may be quite unwarranted. A careful assessment of prediction studies is required to see how much reliability and validity they contain and how much baloney.[8]

No estimate of future behavior can be made with certainty, so statements of degree of probability are appropriate. Predictions properly are applied not to individuals but to groups of persons that are similar with respect to some set of characteristics. Thus, persons are classified, and then statements are made about the expected performance of members of the classes. The performance outcomes to be expected for specific classes of persons are those that provide the most probable values for the population as a whole.

Any prediction method may be regarded as having, or lacking, not one but many validities of varying degrees. Since validity refers to the relation between a specific criterion measure and some earlier assessment, it is dependent upon the particular criterion used. Thus, a prediction method has as many validities as there are criterion measures to be predicted. Just as a test of scholastic achievement taken after high school might provide valid predictions of grade point average in college but could be invalid for estimating marital stability, a delinquency prediction method might have some validity for judging the likelihood of, say, adjudication as a delinquent before age eighteen but might provide no information concerning the probability of adult crime, high school completion, or conviction for car theft. And it must be recognized that the issue of validity is one of degree; prediction methods are not sufficiently described merely as "valid" or "invalid." Rather, statistical statements of the relative validity—for example, in terms of accuracy of predictions in test samples—are in order.

When there is a predictive purpose, all diagnostic and classification procedures—whether they be interview assessments, results of projective testing, expert judgments, or codifications of life history variables—are bound together by the concept of validity. The proof of the pudding is in the degree to which the method is valid with respect to specific criterion classifications, and individual stylistic preferences of research workers, clinicians, judges, administrators, or others cannot logically enter the argument.

CRIMINAL JUSTICE DECISIONS

The concepts of diagnosis, classification, and prediction will be encountered repeatedly as critical decision points throughout the criminal justice system are examined. Issues of classification and prediction in particular are fundamentally involved, for example, in many decisions by police, prosecutors, judges, and correctional functionaries. Some persons pass through all these sets of decisions in their career from arrest to final discharge, and many, unfortunately, go around again. The ways in which they are diagnosed and classified and in which predictions are made about them are of central importance.

The system of criminal justice may be portrayed schematically quite well by a flow diagram showing the series of points at which decisions may be triggered by a report of a crime. Police officers, prosecutors, judges, wardens, and parole board members have in common that they all make decisions about offenders or alleged offenders against the law. They have in common also the fact that the decisions they make have consequences for other parts of the system. Thus, decisions by police affect the workload of the prosecutors, whose decisions in part determine cases to be tried in court. The correctional administrator must make numerous decisions about inmate placements, although he or she has no control over intake or discharge—these critical workload requirements being determined by decisions of judges and paroling authorities. The complex tree of decision points that may be envisioned thus also depicts the interrelated nature of the component parts of the system, such as police, prosecution, the courts, and corrections.

Examined in Chapter 2 is the trigger event for the entire system—the reporting of crime. The decision by a victim as to whether or not to report the crime is critical to the entire system of criminal justice, and it is known that many or most crimes are not reported. Yet this decision represents a rather neglected area of study, and therefore we seek to examine available evidence concerning it before considering the decisions made by functionaries of the system.

Police decisions are addressed in Chapter 3. It is the police who first decide, in any person/event that is allegedly, apparently, or actually a crime, whether or not to invoke the law. It has been asserted that police officers "have, in effect, a greater degree of discretionary freedom in proceeding against offenders than any other public official."[9] They decide, for example, whether or not an offense has occurred, whether to arrest, whether to issue a citation, whether to hold persons in custody, and whether to refer persons to other social agencies. They decide whether to press for the invoking of the criminal law or to forget it. The police do not merely apply and enforce the law; rather, and to a great extent, they use discretion in invoking the law.[10]

If a person is arrested and accused of a crime, the tradition in the United States is that he or she is presumed innocent until proven guilty. But what is to be done pending trial or some other disposition of the case? In these circumstances, regarding accused adults, the last decade has seen an expansion of interest in extending release, while trial is awaited, to large numbers of persons while maintaining assurance of the defendant's availability for trial. Traditionally, release on money bail has been the principal, and often the only, method for avoiding confinement of the accused while awaiting trial (despite its obvious discrimination against the poor).

In many parts of the United States programs of release on the person's "own recognizance" have now been added. The decision as to the disposition of the alleged offender now thus commonly includes alternatives to financial bail. The presumption of innocence, together with a concern for community security, provide a context of conflict of aims typical of many critical criminal justice decisions. The issue is joined by the need for striking a balance between the concern for the protection of society and the desire to guarantee maximum freedom for the person. The desire to prevent future crimes opposes the desire to allow the suspect to be free before trial. Thus, the analysis of this decision (Chapter 4) poses many problems of diagnosis, classification, and prediction, and the general problem provides a particularly challenging setting for the examination of the concept of rational decisionmaking.

Indeed, the intertwining of issues of law with those of diagnosis, classification, and prediction is well illustrated by problems surrounding the general concept of "preventive detention." This concept refers to the idea of pretrial confinement aimed at the prevention of crimes by an accused but not convicted person. A former Attorney General of the United States argued against challenges that a federal proposal providing for preventive detention violates the Eighth Amendment, the due process clause of the Fifth Amendment, and the presumption of innocence.[11] He argued that there is no alternative to detention of persons who will commit additional serious crimes if released pending trial, if the community is to be protected.

Setting aside legal issues, the frame of reference that stresses rationality suggests that one must ask how such offenses are to be predicted, by what classification methods, with what degrees of reliability and validity, and at what costs of incorrect predictions. Since some persons argue for the detention of the "most dangerous" defendants on the basis of the experience of trial judges, it is necessary to point out that the question of the validity of such predictions by trial judges is a question to be answered empirically. Evidence so far with such prediction problems must raise a very considerable skepticism. The present-day prognosis for violence prediction is discouraging. Even with improved prediction, the problem of erroneously confining defendants expected to be "dangerous" raises very serious moral issues. Recognizing the predictive nature of these decisions and the validity questions that then arise helps, we argue, to raise these moral issues.

A closely related problem is that of deciding whether a defendant is competent to stand trial. Confusion concerning the concepts of diagnosis, classification, and prediction also reigns notably around this issue, which again illustrates the common mixture of legal and scientific problems intertwined in criminal justice decisionmaking. Competency in this context is a legal concept referring to a person's ability to appreciate the nature of the proceedings against him and to participate adequately in his or her own defense. The concept thus concerns a state of the person—that is, a diagnosis. The diagnosis, however, must address the issues of pretrial competency that are essentially legal, not psychiatric, concerns. The criteria of competency focus essentially upon the protection of due process rights of the accused to a fair trial: the person must understand the nature of the proceedings and their consequences and must be able to cooperate with counsel. Otherwise, proceedings are suspended until the person is seen as able to participate in the defense. Diagnoses of physical or mental illness, which often are provided to the court ostensibly to assist in the competency determination, are thus not necessarily relevant to the legal questions asked. Descriptions of states of the persons involved or assignments to traditional psychiatric categories of mental illness may have little or no bearing on competency as legally defined. As a remedy, McGarry and his colleagues have developed more objective procedures for measurement of competency, seeking more adequate assessment of the specific areas of psychological functioning that are pertinent to the specific diagnosis required by the legal issues.[12] Evidence from his study suggests that such procedures can help avoid costly, often lengthy, unnecessary confinement due to hospitalization for competency determinations.

Once a person has been arrested, a variety of decisions may be made before that person leaves the adjudicatory system or is sentenced. These decisions focus on whether or not to press the case—that is, to file charges (and the specific nature of the charges) and, if the decision is to prosecute, on the degree of vigor with which to prosecute. Generally, across the country, too little is known of the criteria that provide the basis for these decisions. Even careful descriptions of the processes in various jurisdictions are lacking. Worse, there is even less information available concerning the effects of these decisions, either in terms of impact elsewhere in the criminal justice system or in respect to the later criminal careers of the persons accused.

Prosecution decisions are discussed in Chapter 5. Typical decisions include the prosecutor's decision whether or not to file charges at all and, if it is decided to do so, the selection of the specific charge. The latter decision includes the issue of "plea bargaining"—that is, a negotiated plea. Prosecutors may be involved also in decisions by a lower court, such as the need for a municipal judge to determine whether or not a defendant should be held to answer to a higher court (for example, to a superior court on a felony charge), tried on a misdemeanor charge, or dismissed. If there is "plea bargaining," are inducements offered by the prosecutor or the court to encourage guilty pleas? If so, what inducements are involved?

A related decision is that taken by the defendant: does he or she decide to plead guilty or to go to trial? If the latter, is the choice that of a trial by the court (that is, by the judge) or by a jury? Finally, of course, there is the finding of the court as to guilt.

If the defendant is found guilty, then there is the problem of sentencing. That central feature of criminal justice decisionmaking is discussed in Chapter 6. The sentencing decision is at present guided unsystematically by often conflicting goals of retribution, rehabilitation, community protection, deterrence, and equitable treatment. It is a decision that must be made within constraints imposed by law and by resources (that is, alternatives). It is a decision that typically must be made in the absence of data provided systematically to assist the judge in making equitable sentencing decisions, assuring that similarly situated offenders are similarly treated in the selection of sentencing alternatives. Moreover, it is a decision that must be made with little systematic knowledge of the consequences of previous decisions in similar cases.

The problem of equity implies a classification problem. Whatever meanings are assigned to the concept of "justice," it appears that there may be general agreement that the concept of "equity" is an included but not synonymous concept. Thus, justice must include equity; equity does not ensure justice. But how is equity to be determined? If it means that similar offenders, in similar circumstances, are given similar sentences, then it is clear that the concept of equity requires a statistical concept of classification. As decisions become less variable with respect to a given classification of offenders, they may be said to be more equitable.

Equity, of course, is not the only goal of sentencing decisions. Sentencing also implies a number of prediction problems. The courts at present, however, typically lack information about offenders that demonstrably is related to goals of changing the offender, deterring that person or others, or community protection. Such information can be provided only by follow-up studies to determine the consequences of sentencing decision alternatives. Such studies require information systems providing careful record keeping on offenders' characteristics, the sentencing dispositions, and the results (in terms of the various goals of the criminal justice system).

The attention given thus far to analyses of sentencing does not match the importance of the problem. It would be difficult to find other decision problems critically affecting the liberty and future lives of large numbers of people in which decisions are made with so little knowledge of their results.

Presentence reports, usually completed by probation officers, are employed in most jurisdictions when penalties of more than one year may ensue and in some jurisdictions when lesser penalties may result. Typically, these reports follow from an investigation by the probation officer. Ordinarily he or she has talked to the defendant and, possibly, to family, friends, employers, or others. The report usually is intended to present a comprehensive assessment of the defendant and that person's life situation. It usually includes a recommendation concerning the court's disposition. Commonly, some identifying and demographic information is included, and official and defendant's versions of the offense are summarized, as in the prior criminal record. Frequently, the report includes a brief life history; descriptions of the defendant's home and work situations; assessments of interests, attitudes, aptitudes, and physical and mental health; and other personality assessments. All are intended to clarify the factors resulting in the defendant's present difficulty and to assist in the court's disposition decision.

The judge may be presented in this way with a great mass of data concerning the offender before him; and this may provide him or her with an increased feeling of confidence in the decision. But although the courts typically keep records of decisions taken, they ordinarily do not keep score on the outcomes. As a result, information on the relevance of most of the assembled case data to rational decisionmaking for disposition (placement) of the offender is unavailable. Thus, presented with a wealth of data never assessed for its empirical relevance to his or her decision problem, the judge may have exhaustive data but little information.

After sentencing, the next critical points of decision depend, of course, upon the outcome of the sentencing process. Typically, these will include placement decisions affecting the offender's program in jail, under probation supervision, or in prison; they may include the decision whether or not to parole, and they often include determination of the length of time to be required in custody or under supervision. In each case, the decisionmakers are confronted with the usual, sometimes conflicting, demands of the criminal justice system for punishment, societal protection, and rehabilitation of the offender.

Decisions on the offender's program are made by probation officers, correctional classification officers, wardens, parole board members, parole officers, and others. Like the judge, these decisionmakers typically lack the basis from painstaking record keeping, analysis, and feedback that is requisite to a truly informed decision process. Analysis of these correctional decisions are discussed in Chapters 7 and 8.

Little work has been done toward developing classification methods for use in jails, and little systematic study has been completed that could give probation administrators an increased confidence that their charges will be provided the kind and degree of treatment most appropriate for the individuals assigned. To the extent that each jail inmate and each probationer is unique, no amount of experience can assure such confidence; but to the extent that similar persons respond similarly to differential program placements, that experience could guide future decisions and thus could improve the results of jail and probation programs.

Much more research has been done with persons sentenced to prisons or to correctional facilities for youth, and much of that has relevance to classification problems in the area of jail and probation. Except in those research studies, the term "classification" typically refers to procedures for the assignment of persons to institutions or to institutional programs. In some systems (for example, in California) the newly arrived prisoner is observed and studied intensively for a period of two or three months, in specially designed reception-guidance center facilities. Such study may include interveiws with the inmate that, together with materials assembled from inquiries of others (usually including the presentence report), provide a basis for a social history. Vocational counseling may be provided, and recommendations may be made concerning offender needs for education and training. Group and sometimes individual psychological testing may be included in the assessment procedures. Sometimes they include observations of behavior in housing units, recreational facilities, and counseling sessions. And (more rarely) they include psychiatric evaluations or individual psychological diagnostic study.

The objectives typically are determination of the institution in which the prisoner will serve at least the first part of his or her term, the degree of custody (that is, physical security and surveillance) required, and the treatment program judged appropriate in terms of rehabilitative aims. In correctional systems with sophisticated treatment resources, program placement alternatives may be diverse—each with ardent advocates with respect to rehabilitative value. For example, they may include educational regimes, vocational training for numerous occupations, group and individual counseling and psychotherapy from diverse theoretical frames of reference, occupational therapy, forestry or road camp programs, and work furlough placements. The data collected to aid in these decisions sometimes are compiled with painstaking accuracy. Ordinarily, however, even when such data are collected carefully, there is little evidence of their validity in terms of any objectives of the correctional process. Hence, again, much data, little information.

There are, indeed, beliefs among correctional staff responsible for these decisions in the validity of certain kinds of data in predicting program outcomes. Such beliefs are regarded most usefully as hypotheses to be tested through follow-up studies. Those found valid can be retained and used in educating other decisionmakers to increase the likelihood of helpful program placements. Those not supported by the evidence can be rejected. Without such a process of systematic study and feedback to the decisionmakers, improvement in the decisions cannot be expected. Rather, that which was "reasonably supposed," "assumed," or "thought likely" is apt to be accepted increasingly as if it were supported by evidence—indeed, to be mistaken for "fact." Presumptions concerning relations of offender data to desired outcomes thus may in time achieve the status of folklore. These concepts then may provide a basis for implicit classification models. In this way, implicit classification methods based on tradition and folklore may become the chief tools of the correctional decisionmaker.

Many useful starts toward more explicit and reliable classification methods have been made, and validation studies—with respect to a variety of correctional purposes—have begun to be reported. These classification methods, from psychological, sociological, or psychiatric perspectives, are not equally valuable for all purposes. Some have more direct treatment implications than others. Some are demonstrably more reliable than others. Some are more helpful in generating testable hypotheses than others. In only a few instances has the relevance of the classification for treatment placement been demonstrated clearly. The need is great for development of theoretically sound, clinically useful, testable classification systems, with enunciation of the probable etiology, for proposed treatment or control measures and for demonstration of the effectiveness of differential treatment placements.

Offenders are not the only proper subjects for classification efforts. Other components of intervention strategies may be classified as well. These may include environmental settings, workers (treaters), and treatment methods. One then may proceed to seek to sort out the optimal "matches" for greatest effect in terms of desired outcomes.

Parole decisions, discussed in Chapter 9, may be broken into three generic classes. First, there is the decision of when to release from custody (the discretionary release component). Second, there is a series of decisions relating to release that must be made—what size case load, what conditions, and so forth (the supervision component). Third, parole also at times involves decisions about return to custody (the revocation component). Parole is an area of corrections that provides a good basis for discussion of our present knowledge of decisionmaking and of the contributions and limitations of classification and prediction methods. Related to each of these components has been a long line of research efforts, many of which have had their principal focus on classification studies with a predictive purpose.

IMPORTANCE OF DECISION STUDY

It is claimed that increased rationality in criminal justice is likely to come about only after it has become possible to identify explicitly, with adequate operational definition, the specific objectives of each phase of the various parts of the apparatus designed to reduce, control, or at least cope with problems of crime. A second requirement must be the identification and adequate description of the alternative decision choices at each step. The third necessity, about which we have perhaps the least evidence, is the requirement of information.

It is far easier to conceptualize the information needs for more rational decisionmaking than to achieve them in practice. One reason is the present lack of consensus on objectives at each of the decision points that define the flow of persons through the process. Another is lack of knowledge generally of the relative effectiveness of the available alternatives—in terms of the objectives chosen—especially as measures of effectiveness may differ for different classifications of persons. The third reason is that agency information systems with appropriate interfacing with other agencies in the system do not exist to provide the follow-up studies of persons that are essential to estimation of the branching probabilities of objective achievement along the tree of decisions.

The definition and improved measurement of objectives is an obvious requisite to improved effectiveness and efficiency, but these latter values still can be attained only in terms of those definitions. The meanings assigned to the more global concept—justice—justifiably could be assigned a logically higher priority for research and search for consensus, setting the stage for derivation of intermediate objectives to be sought in its pursuit. Even in the absence of such guidance, however, it seems clear that the concept of equity may be regarded as a necessary though insufficient condition of justice. Examples will be given throughout the book to illustrate the formulation of rules for decisions with respect to specific classifications of persons in order to provide a plausible means for increased equity in decisionmaking.

Knowledge that an alternative choice exists does not by itself provide the decisionmaker with information. That is, the availability of the alternative does not reduce his or her uncertainty about the probable consequences of selection; that requires knowledge of the relation of that choice to the decision objective. This is a principal reason for the need for program evaluation at each stage in the criminal justice processes, and it is why such research is critical to the improvement of individual decisionmaking. In the final chapter we outline a system that permits the evaluation of these many decisions in light of their central components—goals, information, and alternatives.

TOWARD MORE RATIONAL DECISIONS

How are the criminal justice decisions presented in subsequent chapters to be evaluated or assessed? On what grounds can useful judgments be made about the quality of these decisions, aside from issues of the clarity of goals, the availability of suitable alternatives, and the relevance of information? Ten criteria for a pragmatic assessment of the decisions discussed in this book may be proposed. Clearly, they reflect values of the authors, yet we assume that they are shared with many others.[13]

Visibility. How open to public scrutiny, to open debate (by both specialists and the general public) are the decisions?

Simplicity. Are the procedures parsimonious and efficient? Can the decisions, and their bases, be understood by ordinary citizens?

Concordance. Are the bases for decisions reflective of community values? Are the decisions consistent with aims throughout the criminal justice system, or are they in conflict with the purposes found in other areas of criminal justice decisionmaking?

Accountability. Are there procedures for feedback on decision consequences to the persons responsible for the decisions, to others in the criminal justice system, and to the general public?

Effectiveness. Are the decisions made in such a way as to achieve, demonstrably, their stated objectives? It will be clear that, for any of the decisions discussed, modesty will be required in claiming effectiveness; yet if improvement is sought, the critical issues of "what works" are central to any assessments from utilitarian perspectives.

Symbolic Value. It is important that justice is "seen to be done," in order to promote the credibility and respectability of the law and the criminal justice system. Are decision consequences perceived as commensurate with the gravity of harms done by offenders? Is allowance for mercy included?

Fairness. Are decisions made within a context of procedural regularity, due process, and reasonable notice? Are there elements of arbitrariness or capriciousness or indications of invidious factors leading to decisions?

Equity. Are allegations of unwarranted disparity in decisionmaking supported by careful analysis? Are systems or procedures in place to reduce such disparities?

Flexibility. Is there allowance in the decisionmaking structure for reasoned discretion, consistent with the decision aims, in atypical cases for dealing with the unexpected?

Evolution. Are procedures in place to enhance progress, through experience, toward greater rationality in the decision?

Asking questions such as these leads, in our final chapter, to the identification of ten requisites for increased rationality in criminal justice. Thus, we claim that rationality can be more nearly approached by increased attention to the specification of clear, consistent purposes; by the identification or invention of adequate alternatives; by the identification of more relevant information; by using adequately flexible decision policy structures; by mechanisms for the control of unbridled discretion; by differentiation of policy and case decisionmaking; by development of explicit policy and decision rules; by provision of adequate feedback systems; by improved measurement and classification processes; and by the insistence on decision policy and procedures within a system for evolutionary development toward more rational decisions.

NOTES

1. L. Cronbach and G. Gleser, *Psychological Tests and Personnel Decisions* (Urbana: University of Illinois Press, 1957).

2. B. Russell, "An Outline of Intellectual Rubbish," in *Unpopular Essays* (New York: Simon and Schuster, 1962), p. 71.

3. *Id.* at 72.

4. L.T. Wilkins, "Perspectives on Court Decision-Making," in D.M. Gottfredson, ed., *Decision-Making in the Criminal Justice System: Reviews and Essays* (Washington, D.C.: Government Printing Office, DHEW Publication No. (ADM) 75-238, 1975), p. 70.

5. See, for example, L. Sechrest, S. White, and E. Brown, eds., *The Rehabilitation of Criminal Offenders: Problems and Prospects* (Washington, D.C.: National Academy of Sciences, 1979).

6. T. Sarbin, "On the Futility of the Proposition that Some People be Labelled as 'Mentally Ill'," *Journal of Consulting Psychology* 31:447 (1967); S.L. Sharma, ed., *The Medical Model of Mental Illness* (Woodland, California: Majestic, 1970); T. Szasz, *The Myth of Mental Illness* (New York: Harper and Row, 1961); T. Szasz, *Psychiatric Justice* (New York: Macmillan, 1965); T. Szasz, *The Manufacture of Madness* (New York: Harper and Row, 1970).

7. R. Cormack, "A Review of Classification," *Journal of the Royal Statistical Society* 3:321 (1971).

8. E. Cureton, "Validity, Reliability, and Baloney," in D. Jackson and S. Messick, eds., *Problems in Human Assessment*, pp. 372-73. (New York: McGraw-Hill, 1967).

9. E. Bittner, *The Functions of the Police in a Modern Society* (Chevy Chase, Maryland: Center for Studies in Crime and Delinquency, Public Health Service Publication No. 2059, 1970), p. 107.

10. J. Goldstein, "Police Discretion Not to Invoke the Criminal Process: Low Visibility Decisions in the Administration of Justice," *Yale Law Journal* 69: 543 (1960); H. Packer, "Two Models of the Criminal Process," *University of Pennsylvania Law Review* 113:1 (1964); S. Kadish, "Legal Norm and Discretion in the Police and Sentencing Process," *Harvard Law Review* 75:904 (1962).

11. J. Mitchell, "Bail Reform and the Constitutionality of Pretrial Detention," *Virginia Law Review* 55:1223 (1969).

12. A. McGarry et al., *Competency to Stand Trial and Mental Illness, Final Report on NIMH Grant R01-MH 18112* (Boston: Harvard Medical School, Laboratory of Community Psychiatry, 1972).

13. Some of these criteria are taken from J. Hogarth, "Alternatives to the Adversary System," in Law Reform Commission of Canada, *Studies on Sentencing* (Ottawa: Information Canada, 1974); pp. 40-44; similar criteria have been offered by F. Remington et al., *Criminal Justice Administration* (Indianapolis: Bobbs-Merrill, 1969), ch. 1.

✳ *Chapter 2*

Victim Decisions to Report a Crime

The occurrence of a crime signals the potential involvement of the criminal justice process. It is the trigger mechanism for discretionary actions on the part of victims and possibly of criminal justice functionaries—and these discretionary actions are the very basis of the criminal justice system.[1]

The occurrence of a crime is not a sufficient condition for the involvement of the criminal justice system. A series of decisions must take place before the criminal justice system becomes involved. First, the behavior in question must be noticed, and the decision to define it as a crime must be made. This discovery and definition may be made by a citizen (as a victim or as a witness) or by the police. Second, someone must decide that the behavior in question is properly in the realm of the criminal justice system. Third, the decision to enter the behavior into the criminal justice process must be made.

This chapter is concerned principally with the last of these decisions—the decision to report a crime to the police. Only recently have studies become available that permit an examination of this decision. The earlier decisions of discovery and definition, although of great interest, have received almost no research attention.[2]

VICTIMS' DECISIONS TO INVOKE THE CRIMINAL JUSTICE SYSTEM

The victims of criminal behavior may be the most influential of all criminal justice decisionmakers. Perhaps they typically are not viewed as such, but by virtue of the decision whether or not to _eport a criminal victimization to the police, the victim is a principal "gatekeeper" of the entire criminal justice process. This is true especially for the crimes of common theft and assault.[3] In the overwhelming majority of cases, if the victim does not report the crime to the police, the event will not be dealt with by the criminal justice system. This generalization is supported both by observational research on police behavior and by victimization survey data. In a study of a large urban police department, for example, Reiss found that about 95 percent of the criminal incidents known to the police came to their attention through citizen initiative.[4] The fact that the vast majority of crimes were not discovered by the police, but rather were reported to them, suggested to Reiss that urban policing is much more a reactive than a proactive process. Results from victimization surveys (discussed subsequently) also support the notion that victim behavior is the main determinant of input to the criminal justice system. When representative samples of the population were interviewed about their victimization experience, only 3 percent of the victimizations they reported as known to the police came to the attention of law enforcement because the police were on the scene.[5]

Victims thus serve as a preliminary filter for the crimes of common theft and assault with which the criminal justice process will be concerned. The cases that they report to the police have a chance (though not a certainty) of proceeding through the system. Numerous later decisions, each of which serves in turn as the filter for later decisions, are made about the case. But those cases not reported by victims to the police have virtually no chance of proceeding through the process.

It is therefore difficult to overestimate the influence that these victim decisionmakers have over the nature of the criminal justice process. The decisionmaking of the victim obviously is bound inextricably to the major questions and issues that confront the whole of society about the criminal justice system.

A moment's reflection will indicate that the victim's decision whether or not to report a crime may have considerable impact on the goals of the criminal justice system. One of the principal aims of the system, for example, often is thought to be general deterrence—the prevention of crime in the general population by the imposition of penalties on those committing criminal acts. Deterrence theorists typically argue that there are two important components to deterrence—the certainty and the severity of punishment. Clearly, the victim plays a vital role in relation to the concept of certainty. If the victim decides not to report a crime to the police, the probability of a sanction for the offender is reduced to nearly zero. Similarly, victims' discretion may influence critically the equity of the criminal justice system. If, all things being equal, some types of offenders are more likely to be brought to the attention of the police by victims than are other types of offenders, then, because all future decisions (for example, to arrest, to convict, to punish) are predicated on the victim's decision, equity is reduced. Thus, a study of how victims exercise their discretion to report crimes to the police has important implications for the attainment of this goal of the criminal justice process.

Other overall aims commonly ascribed to the criminal justice process might be analyzed similarly. Are victim's decisions made consistently with these goals? What factors appear to influence these decisions, and are they compatible with the goals of the process?

Apart from the gatekeeping influence of the victim's decision to report a crime, affecting the nature of the entire criminal justice process, the decision has critical implications also for the key participants in the system. For the victim, the decision has obvious importance. A report to the police clearly and authoritatively (although not irrevocably since the victim can decide later not to press charges) indicates that a situation has arisen in the life of the victim that is perceived as demanding official state recognition and action. It may be motivated by a desire by the victim for officially sanctioned retribution, by a more general sense of social obligation, or by a hope for restitution. For many victims it signifies the beginning of an involvement with the various agencies within the criminal justice system—an involvement that may make substantial demands on the victim's time and resources.

Alternatively, the decision to report a crime to the police may be simply the perceived solution to an immediate crisis. In many cases a call to the police in and of itself may terminate a victimization in which the victim's only desire is to find a peaceful resolution (for example, in a domestic assault). Thus, rather than necessitating full processing through arrest and conviction, the consequence desired by the victim may be only the cessation of victimization. For still other victims, the decision to report to the police may be more a matter of practical concerns. Many theft insurance policies, for example, require that the police be notified prior to awarding a claim.

Thus, a report to the police may reflect a feeling of societal obligation, a desire for retribution, or an effort to deal with a crisis. It may be a result of a dispassionate assessment of the financial benefits that will accrue. It may be a combination of these.

The consequences of the decision, then, for the victim, include the issue of how well these objectives actually were met: Was retribution satisfied? Was the immediate crisis resolved? Was the social obligation seen as fulfilled? The ultimate determination of the consequences important to the victim may turn, in part, on the activities and decisions of still other criminal justice actors: Did the police decide to proceed with the case? Was the accused convicted? Was the disposition seen by the victim as a just one? It may readily be seen that the question of the importance of the decision to victims is a complicated one, and it is one that might require a number of answers depending on the individual circumstances of the victim and the goals he or she is seeking to attain. It may also be seen that the research issues that are posed are formidable.

No less complex and difficult are the questions that may be raised by considering the societal consequences of victims' decisions. What are the implications for crime prevention, justice, and equity of this highly discretionary and extremely low visibility decision? Can a society that seeks lower levels of crime be satisfied by less than full reporting of crimes by victims when an unreported crime necessarily means an unapprehended offender? If crimes committed by some offenders—or some classes of offenders—usually are reported while others tend not to be, does this imply a corresponding reduction in equity and in justice?

Consider, however, the implications of full reporting of criminal victimization. Can an already overtaxed system of justice accommodate such an increase in the numbers of crimes reported to the police? Is justice truly better served if all events that can be brought to the attention of the police are reported to them?

As with the consequences of the victim's decision for the victim and for the criminal justice system, the potential consequences to society depend in large part on the characteristics of these decisions as they now are made. That is, in order to assess the consequence of these decisions for the victim, for the criminal justice system, and for society, it is necessary first to understand how these decisions are made.

CHARACTERISTICS OF THE DECISION TO REPORT A CRIME TO THE POLICE

Until quite recently the victim's decision to report a crime was not regarded widely as a central component in the criminal justice process. Rather, considerable emphasis was placed on the police as initiators of the system.[6] Perhaps the single most important influence on viewing the victim, rather than the police, as the principal invocator of the process was a development in the field of crime statistics—the victimization survey.

Although it has been long realized that not all crimes come to the attention of the police, until the advent of victimization surveys there were no systematic data available by which either the extent or the characteristics of crime unknown to the police could be assessed. In 1967, researchers working under the auspices of the President's Commission on Law Enforcement and Administration of Justice undertook a series of studies to determine the utility of assessing this "dark figure" of crime. They interviewed representative samples from the general population about criminal victimizations that they had experienced, whether or not the persons interviewed had reported them to the police.[7] These early surveys and subsequent similar ones revealed that a very large proportion of the victimizations reported to the interviewers had not been reported to the police. For many crimes, over half had not been reported. These early surveys demonstrated that, for whatever reason, a vast number of victims of crimes of theft and assault decided not to invoke the criminal justice process.

Since these early victimization surveys there has been a good deal of developmental work on the method. In 1972 the United States Bureau of the Census began a program to produce annual estimates of criminal victimization for the nation.[8] This project is referred to as the National Crime Panel (NCP).

In these surveys a multistage cluster sampling is used to select representative samples of Americans twelve years old or older. They are asked questions about common assault and theft victimizations that they may have experienced during the six months before the interview. About 130,000 persons are interviewed twice a year. The responses are then weighted (according to a commonly used procedure) to yield national estimates for the year. Similarly, a national probability sample of businesses is drawn, and questions about business burglaries and business robberies are asked, from which national estimates of these business victimizations are derived. These data give the basis for the best available estimates of the extent to which victims of certain crimes, in exercising their discretion, decided not to invoke the criminal process. Also, they provide some clues to the ways in which this discretion is exercised.

Some results from the National Crime Panel for 1976 are displayed in Table 2-1. For each type of crime surveyed, the estimated number of victimizations and the proportion of crimes that the victims said were reported to the police are shown. These data

Table 2-1. Estimated Number of Personal, Household, and Business Victimizations, by Reporting to Police and Type of Victimization, United States, 1976.

Type of Victimization	Total		Reported to Police		Not Reported to Police		Don't Know Whether Reported to Police	
	Number	Percent	Number	Percent	Number	Percent	Number	Percent
Personal victimizations								
Rape and attempted rape	145,193	100	76,499	53	67,549	47	1,145	1
Robbery	1,110,639	100	591,829	53	510,261	46	8,549	1
Robbery and attempted robbery with injury	360,700	100	227,057	63	130,026	36	3,617	1
Serious assault	175,660	100	116,266	66	57,000	32	2,394	1
Minor assault	185,041	100	110,791	60	73,027	39	1,223	1
Robbery without injury	453,867	100	269,428	59	182,070	40	2,369	1
Attempted robbery without injury	296,071	100	95,344	32	198,164	67	2,563	1
Assault	4,343,261	100	2,064,042	48	2,240,127	52	39,092	1
Aggravated assault	1,694,941	100	989,489	58	689,960	41	15,492	1
With injury	588,672	100	364,901	62	216,066	37	7,705	1
Attempted assault with weapon	1,106,269	100	624,588	56	473,894	43	7,788	1
Simple assault	2,648,320	100	1,074,553	41	1,550,167	59	23,600	1
With injury	691,534	100	315,858	46	368,390	53	7,287	1
Attempted assault without weapon	1,956,786	100	758,695	39	1,181,777	60	16,313	1
Personal larceny with contact	497,056	100	180,127	36	314,489	63	2,440	0
Purse snatching	91,595	100	62,598	68	28,997	32	0	0
Attempted purse snatching	55,535	100	13,483	24	42,052	76	0	0
Pocket picking	349,926	100	104,046	30	243,440	70	2,440	1
Personal larceny without contact	16,021,110	100	4,208,940	26	11,657,785	73	154,385	1
Household victimizations								
Burglary	6,663,422	100	3,208,108	48	3,390,025	51	65,290	1

Forcible entry	2,277,063	100	1,595,940	70	665,214	29	15,909	1
Unlawful entry without force	2,826,599	100	1,096,250	39	1,697,853	60	32,496	1
Attempted forcible entry	1,559,760	100	515,917	33	1,026,958	66	16,885	1
Larceny	9,300,854	100	2,515,780	27	6,731,873	72	53,201	1
Under $50	5,601,954	100	841,462	15	4,731,277	84	29,214	1
$50 or more	2,745,097	100	1,440,278	52	1,286,152	47	18,667	1
Amount not ascertained	299,350	100	60,564	20	233,466	78	5,320	2
Attempted	654,454	100	173,476	27	480,977	73	0	0
Vehicle theft	1,234,644	100	857,553	69	370,650	30	6,441	1
Completed	759,816	100	673,026	89	81,570	11	5,221	1
Attempted	474,828	100	184,526	39	289,081	61	1,221	0
Business victimizations								
Robbery	279,516	100	243,980	87	32,763	12	2,773	1
Burglary	1,576,242	100	1,148,424	73	400,731	25	27,087	2

Note: These estimates are based on data derived from surveys of households and businesses that were undertaken in connection with the Law Enforcement Assistance Administration (LEAA) National Crime Survey program. In these surveys, conducted by the U.S. Bureau of the Census for LEAA's Statistics Division, representative national samples of households and businesses were drawn. In the personal and household portion of the survey, victimization data were collected for all household members who were at least twelve years of age; therefore, victimizations of those under twelve years of age were not counted in the surveys. Because the survey focused on crimes of common theft and assault, some crimes (such as homicide) were not counted. In addition, the business portion of the survey only counted burglaries and robberies; crime such as shoplifting and employee theft proved not feasible to include.

Source: N. Parisi, M. Gottfredson, M. Hindelang, and T. Flanagan, eds., *Sourcebook of Criminal Justice Statistics 1978* (Washington, D.C.: GPO, 1979).

indicate quite clearly that vast numbers of crimes are not reported. For the crime of rape and attempted rape, for example, there were 145,193 victimizations, of which 67,549, or nearly half, were not reported to the police. For every type of crime, sizable proportions of the victimizations were not reported to the police.

There are marked differences in reporting by type of crime. Among those listed, the crime most likely to be reported to the police was vehicle theft, with about nine out of ten reported. The least likely crime to be reported was larceny—either from the person or from the household. In general, victimizations of businesses were more likely to be reported to the police than were either personal or household victimizations. And completed crimes were more likely to be reported than were those merely attempted.

Given the vast number of unreported crimes and the critical role of the victim's decision, the question of the major influences on the decision is of considerable importance. Studies of victim discretion have used essentially two methods in seeking answers to this question. The first has been to ask victims directly why they did or did not report their victimization to the police. The second has been to study various aspects of the victimization—characteristics of the victim, the offender, and the event—as they relate to whether or not the victimization was reported to the police.

REASONS FOR NOT CALLING THE POLICE

Data from the National Crime Panel on the reasons that victims gave for not reporting their crime to the police are summarized in Table 2-2. The reason most often given for not reporting a crime to the police was that "nothing could be done"; next most often was "victimization not important enough." One third of the survey reported rapes, two-fifths of the robberies, three-fifths of the personal larcenies with contact, one-half of the household burglaries and larcenies, and three-tenths of the business victimizations that were not reported to the police were not reported, according to the victims, because the victims believed that "nothing could be done."

There is some revealing variation in the reasons that people gave for not reporting their victimizations to the police. For some types of crime—most notably rape, assault, and vehicle theft—a large proportion of victims who did not report the event to the police explained that the victimization was "a private matter." "Fear of reprisal" (although infrequently given as a reason for not reporting to the police generally) was cited in nearly one in six rapes and in one in ten robberies as a reason for not reporting the crime to the police.

Clearly, it would be easy to infer too much from these reasons given by victims for not calling the police. The data reflected in Table 2-2 are subject to the numerous limitations involved in the survey method used, including problems in sampling, in the accuracy of recall, issues concerning the willingness of respondents to participate, and the sensitivity of the subject matter.[9] These categories of reasons for not reporting a crime are, in addition, rather broad and ambiguous. For example, "nothing could be done" has several possible interpretations. After an assault, for instance, giving this reason may reflect the victim's belief that the physical harm done cannot be rectified. Alternatively, it may be based on his or her belief that an unknown assailant—whom the victim may not be able to identify—could not be apprehended. The response "police wouldn't want to be bothered" may mean that the victimization was so minor that the victim was reluctant to request police involvement; on the other hand, it could mean that the victim believed that the police would simply be uninterested in his or her victimization, even if it was relatively serious. Also, "victimization was reported to someone else" may mean that it was reported to a different official agency, such as a private security guard, a teacher, or a friend or relative who will take matters into his or her own hands. Finally, the "other" category contains a large proportion of the reasons given, indicating that more refinement of the response categories would be informative.

These data on the reasons given by victims of crime for not reporting the event to the police are nevertheless informative as to how this discretion may be exercised. Many victims apparently believed that the crime was not worthy of official state action, either because it was seen by the victim as not being important or because the victim perceived the police as being uninterested. Thus, it may be that victims frequently divert from the criminal justice system what they perceive as relatively trivial victimizations. The fact that attempted crimes were less often reported to the police than were completed crimes is consistent with this interpretation. Many other victims claimed that they did not report their victimizations to the police because it was not appropriate to do so; the event was not seen as one falling properly into the realm of official recognition and sanction. Many victimizations were "reported to someone else," or they were considered to be "private matters." Thus, in dealing with many of these events, the victims chose either to ignore them (an important decision outcome) or to use nonlegal mechanisms. Included were a sizeable proportion of the rapes and attempted rapes and assaults that were not reported to the police. Thus, although the data reviewed thus far suggest that victims' discretion

Table 2-2.   Estimated Number of Personal, Household, and Business Victimizations Not Reported to Police, by Reason Given for Not Reporting to Police and Type of Victimization, United States, 1976.

		Reason for not Reporting Victimization to Police					
Type of Victimization	Total Victimizations Not Reported	Nothing could be done		Victimization not important enough		Police wouldn't want to be bothered	
		Number	Percent	Number	Percent	Number	Percent
Personal victimizations							
Rape and attempted rape	67,549	23,007	34	9,611	14	6,143	9
Robbery	510,261	206,397	40	122,705	24	67,308	13
Robbery and attempted robbery with injury	130,026	53,372	41	15,832	12	19,096	15
Serious assault	57,000	28,592	50	4,929	9	7,305	13
Minor assault	73,027	24,780	34	10,904	15	11,791	16
Robbery without injury	182,070	79,953	44	41,215	23	28,342	16
Attempted robbery without injury	198,164	73,072	37	65,658	33	19,871	10
Assault	2,240,127	453,304	20	695,773	31	181,040	8
Aggravated assault	689,960	149,758	22	163,513	24	59,200	9
With injury	216,066	48,601	22	38,110	18	17,808	8
Attempted assault with weapon	473,894	101,158	21	125,404	26	41,392	9
Simple assault	1,550,167	303,546	20	532,260	34	121,840	8
With injury	368,390	67,341	18	77,966	21	27,358	7
Attempted assault without weapon	1,181,777	236,204	20	454,294	38	94,482	8
Personal larceny with contact	314,489	185,660	59	74,251	24	31,448	10
Purse snatching	28,997	15,638	54	10,196	35	2,573	9
Attempted purse snatching	42,052	18,123	43	12,608	30	3,861	9
Pocket picking	243,440	151,899	62	51,446	21	25,014	10
Personal larceny without contact	11,657,785	4,990,957	43	4,202,748	36	982,640	8
Household victimizations							
Burglary	3,390,025	1,696,894	50	1,048,226	31	413,673	12
Forcible entry	665,214	311,164	47	160,098	24	109,251	16
Unlawful entry wihout force	1,697,853	864,806	51	536,917	32	174,787	10
Attempted forcible entry	1,026,958	520,923	51	351,211	34	129,635	13
Larceny	6,731,873	3,285,251	49	3,100,344	46	856,367	13
Under $50	4,731,277	2,205,914	47	2,611,301	55	600,960	13
$50 or more	1,286,152	747,084	58	202,680	16	163,819	13
Amount not ascertained	233,466	122,679	53	88,631	38	25,878	11
Attempted	480,977	209,573	44	197,733	41	65,711	14
Vehicle theft	370,650	162,433	44	127,584	34	28,977	8
Completed	81,570	10,915	13	19,090	23	1,327	2
Attempted	289,081	151,518	52	108,495	38	27,650	10
Business victimizations							
Robbery	32,763	9,864	30	9,238	28	5,956	18
Burglary	400,731	109,376	27	118,287	30	145,033	36

Note: Because respondents may have given more than one reason for not reporting the victimization to the police, the row sum of the "reasons for not reporting victimization to the police" may exceed "total victimizations not reported."

Source: N. Parisi, M. Gottfredson, M. Hindelang, and T. Flanagan, eds., Sourcebook of Criminal Justice Statistics 1978 (Washington, D.C.: GPO 1979).

Did not want to take time		It was a private matter		Did not want to get involved		Fear of reprisal		Victimization was reported to someone else		Other		Not ascertained	
Number	Percent	Number	Percent	Number	Percent	Number	Percent	Number	Percent	Number	Percent	Number	Percent
0	0	15,632	23	7,401	11	10,024	15	11,273	17	14,922	22	0	0
34,154	7	39,936	8	28,216	6	30,934	6	64,043	13	122,937	24	3,894	1
6,197	5	11,136	9	18,198	14	12,442	10	14,162	11	37,632	29	1,431	1
1,208	2	6,509	11	10,968	19	4,937	9	3,433	6	19,592	34	0	0
4,989	7	4,627	6	7,230	10	7,505	10	10,729	15	18,040	25	1,431	2
14,577	8	12,294	7	6,117	3	13,261	7	25,999	14	31,666	17	0	0
13,380	7	16,505	8	3,901	2	5,232	3	23,883	12	53,639	27	2,463	1
72,773	3	547,068	24	76,415	3	108,510	5	344,671	15	434,549	19	31,922	1
18,935	3	196,159	28	38,749	6	40,929	6	115,849	17	139,301	20	6,318	1
6,472	3	67,770	31	13,415	6	8,399	4	48,149	22	41,307	19	0	0
12,463	3	128,389	27	25,334	5	32,531	7	67,700	14	97,995	21	6,318	1
53,838	3	350,909	23	37,666	2	67,580	4	228,822	15	295,248	19	25,604	2
8,981	2	121,654	33	16,663	5	25,671	7	68,358	19	67,412	18	6,243	2
44,858	4	229,255	19	21,003	2	41,909	4	160,464	14	227,836	19	19,361	2
17,752	6	4,944	2	4,824	2	6,622	2	47,803	15	61,624	20	2,865	1
1,112	4	0	0	0	0	1,087	4	0	0	5,925	20	1,248	4
5,226	12	0	0	0	0	1,278	3	5,037	12	12,216	29	0	0
11,414	5	4,944	2	4,824	2	4,257	2	42,766	18	43,482	18	1,616	1
461,804	4	403,423	3	63,168	1	30,021	0	2,726,704	23	1,556,600	13	111,197	1
88,195	3	272,825	8	43,488	1	23,344	1	261,323	8	746,516	22	26,780	1
29,001	4	68,344	10	8,402	1	6,752	1	47,492	7	187,685	28	3,721	1
36,376	2	188,990	11	23,524	1	15,427	1	123,370	7	311,848	18	17,214	1
22,818	2	15,490	2	11,562	1	1,165	0	90,461	9	246,983	24	5,845	1
218,040	7	462,627	7	44,373	1	26,875	0	222,975	3	1,011,485	15	53,063	1
133,514	3	268,243	6	23,887	1	19,189	0	162,650	3	540,229	11	30,169	1
60,425	5	153,206	12	11,105	1	6,592	1	37,439	3	305,860	24	19,314	2
8,345	4	18,969	8	4,855	2	0	0	7,127	3	35,291	15	0	0
15,756	3	22,209	5	4,526	1	1,094	0	15,759	3	130,105	27	3,580	1
15,806	4	39,514	11	2,140	1	2,450	1	17,019	5	94,738	26	3,638	1
0	0	33,487	41	2,140	3	1,180	1	6,949	9	30,201	37	0	0
15,806	5	6,028	2	0	0	1,271	0	10,069	3	64,537	22	3,638	1
2,641	8	1,517	5	883	3	505	2	2,291	7	9,105	28	0	0
13,733	3	9,131	2	1,272	0	252	0	18,751	5	62,097	15	0	0

operated largely on the basis of the perceived worthiness of bringing the event to the attention of the police, a sizeable proportion did not do so because it was seen as an inappropriate response.

Hindelang studied the ways that these reasons given for failing to report a crime to the police were related to the nature of the crime, to the characteristics of the victim, and to the victim-offender relationship.[10] For crimes between strangers, compared with those between nonstrangers, the reason for not reporting the crime was more likely to be that "nothing could be done." For crimes between nonstrangers, the reason given for not reporting was more likely to be that it was a "private matter." Victims of completed crimes (and victims of crimes involving weapons) were less likely than victims of crimes only attempted to give as a reason for not reporting that it was "not important."

It might reasonably be expected that such characteristics of the victims as age, race, sex, or income would be related to the reasons given for not reporting the crime to the police. Hindelang found, however, that once the type of victimization was taken into account, they generally were not. The implication seems to be that the nature of the harm suffered by a victim of crime is more determinative of the victim's decision than are these classifications. He did find, however, that the victim-offender relationship conditions, to some extent, the reason for failing to report. Not surprisingly, people victimized by acquaintances are more apt to view the event as a private matter than as a public concern; but people victimized by strangers often believe that the police will be unable to do anything about it anyway.

Unfortunately, most research on the reasons for the invocation of the criminal justice process by victims is based on the reasons given for not calling the police. Seldom have victims who have reported the event to the police been asked why they did so. One exception is a study by Smith and Maness who, in a telephone survey of eighty-eight burglary victims, found that the reason most frequently given for reporting the burglary was that it was an "obligation."[11] The authors interpret this as a "sense of civic duty," citing some of the responses placed in this category as: "It's just the first thing you do"; "It's the proper thing to do"; "It's the natural thing to do"; and "It's the only way we can have law and order."

Other responses in the same survey had more distinctively personal utilitarian implications. About a third (32 percent) said they called the police in order to "catch the person," 23 percent to "recover property," and 27 percent for "personal protection."

These data suggest that for many victims, the decision to report a

Table 2-3. Robbery Victimizations Reported and not Reported to the Police, by Insurance Coverage, United States, 1973-1977.

Theft Insurance[a]	Reported to Police	
	No[b]	Yes
No	49% (1,163,564)	51% (1,810,863)
Yes	15% (53,705)	85% (304,347)

[a]Excludes victims who responded "don't know" to the question, Was there any insurance against theft?
[b]Includes victims who responded "no" and "don't know" to the question, Were the police informed of this incident in any way?
Source: Analysis of data tapes from the National Crime Survey, Household Portion, 1973-1977.

crime to the police may be influenced more by a sort of personal cost-benefit analysis than by a more general sense of social obligation. Is the time and energy required by reporting the event worth the benefit received by way of insurance money, freedom from continued victimization by the offender, or personal retribution? National Crime Panel robbery data on the relation between reporting to the police and whether the victim was covered by theft insurance, displayed in Table 2-3, lend some support to this cost-benefit notion. There is clearly a strong association between insurance coverage and reporting to the police. Eighty-five percent of the robbery victims with theft insurance reported it to the police, but only 51 percent of those without it did so.

There is another category of events that may fall within such a "cost-benefit" explanation, but here few data are available. These are crimes for which the victim either shares some culpability or was breaking a law or social norm at the time of victimization. In these cases, the victim may be subject either to legal action or to great embarrassment should the crime be brought to the attention of the authorities. Some "victim-precipitated" assaults may fall into this category, as may some victimizations that take place during a "victimless crime." Examples of the latter would include "johns" robbed by prostitutes, homosexuals assaulted by their partners, drug dealers robbed and beaten by their customers, and illegal abortions resulting in harm to the woman. It frequently has been suggested that the low probability of the victim reporting such crimes to the police, which makes the offender virtually immune from the law, increases the frequency of their occurrences.[12]

CORRELATES OF THE DECISION TO CALL
THE POLICE

There now have been several studies of the correlates of calling the police using victimization survey data, in particular the National Crime Panel. The survey approach to studying this problem probably is preferable, for the crimes of common theft and assault, to alternative methods for several reasons.

First and foremost, the general population survey has the goal of obtaining representative samples of the population upon which to base estimates. Of course, such a goal is an ideal seldom achieved fully in practice. For the National Crime Panel surveys, some sampling biases are known to exist,[13] but they probably are much less severe than the biases typically encountered in other procedures such as observational methods.

Second, with the survey method it is possible to ensure that standard instruments are used, in order to enhance the reliability of responses. For the National Crime Panel surveys, the reliability of responses is known to be very high.[14]

Third, given the relative infrequency of victimization, extremely large sample sizes are required to obtain sufficient numbers of victimizations so that the correlates of calling the police can be determined reliably. For example, for 1976, it is estimated that the rate (per 1000 persons twelve years old or older) for the United States for rape was 0.84, for personal robbery 6.46, and for assault 25.27. Clearly, large retrospective samples using general survey techniques are required to study the correlates of such statistically rare phenomena.

The survey method studies of the ways that victims exercise their discretion to call the police are, however, certainly not without some shortcomings. These problems fall into two rather general categories related to potential response biases and to the scope of coverage.

Response bias refers to the circumstances in which, for a variety of reasons, the answers given by the respondent are not valid. The various response biases, which include such phenomena as memory effects and questionable veracity of responses, involved in the National Crime Panel have been reviewed by Hindelang, Gottfredson, and Garofalo.[15] Perhaps the most important known bias is the apparent inability in these surveys to elicit many instances of assault. The evidence suggests that this inability is related to the victim-offender relationship. Assaults between nonstrangers are less likely to be identified in the survey than are other types of crime.

The victimization surveys are limited in their scope of coverage to the personal crimes of rape, robbery, assault, and theft; to the household crimes of burglary and theft; and to the business crimes of burglary and robbery. Other forms of crime—such as employee crime, consumer fraud, and victimless crimes—are not feasible targets for the survey approach, because the victim either will not or cannot report the event to an interviewer. For example, many consumer fraud victims are unaware of their victimization, a situation that makes the survey approach unsuitable. As a consequence, the best available information on the ways victims use their discretion to notify the authorities of crime is for the crimes of common theft and assault, and very little is known about this for other forms of crime.

One of the major dimensions on which reporting to the police varies is the nature of the offense suffered by the victim. In general, Table 2-1 indicates that the more serious the crime, in terms of greater bodily harm or financial loss, the more likely is the event to be brought to the attention of the police. Thus, victims of completed crimes are more likely to call the police than are victims of attempted crimes, victims of aggravated assault are more likely to call the police than are victims of simple assault, and so on. That the gravity of the harm done to the victim serves as a major determinant in the decision to invoke the criminal justice process can be inferred from most of the studies that have investigated the issue. For example, Gottfredson analyzed data on an estimated 208,000 personal victimizations in the NCP city surveys and found that factors associated with the concept of gravity of harm were the best predictors in the data of whether the police were called.[16] When a weapon was involved in the incident (particularly, a gun), when the victim was injured (particularly, seriously), and when there was financial loss to the victim (particularly, great), the likelihood of a call to the police increased. And when these factors were found to be present in a victimization in combination, the probability of a report to the police was very great.

Regardless of the type of crime, elements of the offense that increased the gravity of the harm to the victim were found by Hindelang to be associated with the decision to call the police.[17] He analyzed victim reporting to the police within specific crime categories, and this general result held not only for personal victimizations but for the household crimes of burglary and larceny and the business crimes of burglary and robbery as well. And as was found in Gottfredson's study, when elements that increased the gravity of the harm to the victim (such as weapons, amount of loss, or assault) were present in an offense in combination, the probability of a call to the police increased within each type of crime.

Schneider and associates reported similar findings on the relation between the seriousness of the victimization and the probability that it will be reported to the police.[18] Using data from a small victim survey in Portland, Oregon, conducted in 1974, Schneider and her associates scaled the victimizations according to the Sellin-Wolfgang (1964) seriousness index. (This index was derived, using magnitude estimation procedures, to permit the ranking of crimes according to consensually defined estimates of their seriousness.) They reported that "the seriousness of the crime is one of the most important factors explaining why some crimes are reported and others are not."[19] Of the crimes categorized as "low seriousness," only 24 percent were reported to the police, whereas of those classified as "high seriousness," 80 percent were reported. Similar results have been reported by Ennis[20] and Bloch[21] from their analyses of the survey data from the President's Commission on Law Enforcement and the Administration of Justice and by Sparks and his colleagues in a survey conducted in London.[22] An exception is a study by Hawkins,[23] who found an inverse association between seriousness and reporting to the police based on a small victim survey in Seattle. It is possible that Hawkins' results were influenced by the extremely small numbers of serious events uncovered in his survey.

Aggregating three years of the National Crime Panel national survey data on personal crimes, Gottfredson and Hindelang classified all of the victimizations reported in the survey according to the Sellin-Wolfgang seriousness scale.[24] They found an association between seriousness and whether or not the event was reported to the police (gamma = 0.30). For the four categories of seriousness used, the percentage of victimizations reported to the police ranged from 38 percent for the least serious events to 74 percent for the most serious.

CHARACTERISTICS OF THE VICTIM

Other things being equal, are some victims more likely to notify the police than are others? This question bears directly on the issues of victim decisions and general criminal justice system goals. Are some kinds of victims—perhaps because of fear or distrust of the police or because of an inability or unwillingness to take the time to comply with the demands made by the criminal justice system that attend reporting a crime—substantially less likely to invoke the criminal process by calling the police? If so, is equity, from the standpoint of these victims at least, reduced? Does differential access to the criminal justice system imply a differential general deterrent effect? Because the decision to call the police determines so substantially the nature and the effects of the entire criminal justice process, it is clearly important to know whether some classes of victims are less likely to invoke the law when victimized. Two broad groups of victim characteristics have been studied to determine whether they are associated with the decision to report a crime. Thus, in this section we may examine some results of studies of demographic variables such as age, sex, and race. In the next section, attitudinal variables, such as attitudes toward the police, will be discussed.[25]

Hindelang's study of the National Crime Panel city data showed that there were slight associations between demographic characteristics of the victim and reporting to the police. For personal crimes, whites were slightly less likely to report the offense to the police than were blacks and other minority group members (44 versus 50 percent), and younger persons were less likely to report the offense than were older persons (54 percent for persons sixty-five or older versus 33 percent for persons twelve to nineteen years old). And males were less likely to report the offense than were females (42 versus 51 percent).

Hindelang recognized that these differences in reporting may be a result of differences in the types of victimization experienced by these groups. He therefore analyzed his data for the relations between demographic characteristics and the decision to report the crime, controlling for the type of crime experienced by the victim. The relation between the victim's age and reporting to the police generally maintained when this was done. That is, the proportion reported to the police increased as age increased. When age and type of victimization were controlled, however, racial differences in reporting behavior were inconsistent. Where racial differences did exist, sometimes whites and sometimes blacks and other minority group members were more likely to call the police.[26] On the other hand, when controls for age and type of victimization were introduced, males generally were less likely to call the police then were females—often markedly so.

Gottfredson and Hindelang analyzed the relation between victim characteristics and the decision to report a crime using the NCP national data aggregated for the years 1974-1976.[27] These data provided an estimated eighteen million personal victimizations for analysis. This study involved an examination of victim characteristics at both the individual and the community level, controlling for the seriousness of the victimization.

They found little relation between the victim's family income and reporting to the police. That is, roughly the same proportion of crimes were reported to the police for the poor as for the wealthy. The same was found to be true on the community level. They categorized the respondents according to the wealth of the neighborhood in which they lived and found little difference in the proportions of crimes reported to the police in wealthy compared with poor neighborhoods. Similarly, there was only a slight difference in the proportions of crimes reported to the police according to whether the victim was victimized by a stranger or by someone known to the victim (48 versus 42 percent, respectively).

They also examined the proportions of crimes reported to the police across differing levels of urbanization. Again, little difference in the rate of reporting was found, although as population density increased, the proportion reported decreased.

Various other associations were studied. Married victims were more likely than the never married to call the police. Employment status was not related to the decision. There was a slight association between education and reporting: the more education, the more likely the event was to be reported to the police.

By far the strongest correlate of the decision to call the police was the seriousness of the crime experienced by the victim. Across all victim characteristics studied, the seriousness of the crime (as measured by the Sellin-Wolfgang seriousness scale) maintained a moderately strong relation to reporting to the police. This effect can be seen clearly in Table 2-4, which presents national crime panel data for the United States on the proportion of personal crimes reported to the police, analyzed by the victim's family income, by whether the offender was known to the victim, and by the Sellin-Wolfgang seriousness score classification. Although these data do not show much of an "income effect" or much of a "victim-offender relationship effect," they do reveal a considerable "seriousness effect." For every income group, regardless of the victim-offender relationship, as the seriousness score increases (from one to four) the proportion of crimes reported to the police increases.

ATTITUDES TOWARD THE POLICE AND THE DECISION TO REPORT A CRIME

If the victim of a crime of common theft or assault does not report the event to the police, it is unlikely that the crime will be processed through the criminal justice system; and we therefore have stressed that the victim is an important "gatekeeper" to the system. The studies

Table 2-4. Proportion of Victimizations Reported to the Police by Seriousness Level, Family Income, and Prior Relationship Between Victim and Offender, United States, 1974-1976.

Seriousness Level		Under $3,000	$3,000-7,499	$7,500-9,999	Family Income $10,000-14,999	$15,000-24,999	$25,000 or Over	Total
1	Nonstranger	36% (262,625)	41% (421,641)	42% (190,624)	31% (383,929)	35% (270,605)	22% (90,419)	36% (1,619,843)
	Stranger	38% (335,356)	36% (652,578)	42% (346,009)	43% (636,467)	41% (614,159)	25% (224,422)	38% (2,808,991)
2	Nonstranger	39% (306,874)	39% (529,671)	38% (252,849)	35% (414,426)	30% (391,541)	29% (144,283)	36% (2,039,644)
	Stranger	37% (604,138)	40% (1,083,722)	42% (531,223)	43% (1,136,758)	39% (968,581)	40% (376,329)	40% (4,700,751)
3	Nonstranger	47% (274,164)	53% (533,587)	51% (199,253)	47% (310,515)	46% (231,362)	51% (67,720)	49% (1,616,601)
	Stranger	44% (374,626)	52% (838,025)	56% (402,595)	60% (891,118)	57% (693,694)	58% (209,135)	55% (3,409,193)
4	Nonstranger	60% (100,851)	73% (132,599)	62% (60,141)	82% (64,054)	72% (35,211)	68% (14,778)	72% (407,634)
	Stranger	68% (277,000)	74% (482,534)	76% (168,782)	79% (291,148)	79% (228,859)	72% (85,769)	75% (1,534,092)
Total	Nonstranger	44% (944,514)	47% (1,617,498)	45% (702,867)	40% (1,172,924)	37% (928,719)	34% (317,200)	42% (5,683,722)
	Stranger	44% (1,591,120)	48% (3,056,859)	50% (1,448,609)	52% (2,955,491)	48% (2,505,293)	44% (895,655)	48% (12,453,027)

Source: M. Gottfredson and M. Hindelang, "A Study of the Behavior of Law," *American Sociological Review* 44:3 (1979).

discussed thus far suggest that this critical reporting decision depends substantially upon the nature of the harm suffered by the victim and to a lesser extent upon some characteristics of the victim.

An important concern of the criminal justice system is embedded in the concept of equal access to the law. The studies thus far reviewed can be regarded as preliminary assessments of the extent to which equal access to the police is achieved. From this perspective it is reassuring to find that there is relatively little variability in reporting to the police that is associated with victim characteristics studied thus far (although there is some). Where differences exist, further research is needed to determine their origins, but some plausible hypotheses might be advanced. For example, the disproportionate underreporting by males relative to females might be explained by differential sex role socialization that encourages males in our society to handle their own problems. And the inverse relation between age and reporting to the police may be a result of the availability of alternative social control mechanisms for handling disputes among younger people, such as school authorities and parents.

One important victim characteristic that may have some bearing on the notion of equal access to the law is the victim's attitude toward the police. Do people who fear or mistrust the police or those who have had negative experiences with the police fail to report their crimes more often than those without these attitudes or experiences? The issue was posed directly by the President's Commission on Law Enforcement and Administration of Justice: "People hostile to the police are not so likely to report violations of the law, even when they are victims . . . yet citizen assistance is crucial to law enforcement agencies if the police are to solve an appreciable portion of the crimes that are committed."[28] If some segments of society are markedly distrustful or suspicious of the police or simply believe them to be ineffective and if these attitudes are manifested in lower rates of reporting to the police, then clearly, the goal of equal access will not be met.

Garofalo analyzed the National Crime Panel city data for the ways in which the attitudes of victims of personal crimes were associated with the decision to report the crime.[29] He focused on the responses given to the question, "Would you say, in general, that your local police are doing a good job, an average job, or a poor job?" The findings were similar to those of other public opinion surveys. There was little variation in responses to this question, with most people giving their local police favorable ratings. (The exceptions to this general finding are that blacks and other minority group members

Table 2-5. Proportions of Personal Victimizations Reported and not Reported to the Police by the Victim's Rating of the Police, 1975 NCS City Surveys.

Rating of Police[a]	Reported (percent)	Not Reported (percent)	Estimated Number[b]
(Positive) 1	51[c]	49	(71,671)
	8[d]	7	
2	49	51	(279,608)
	31	29	
3	46	54	(362,257)
	38	40	
(Negative) 4	47	53	(223,173)
	24	24	
Estimated number[b]	(446,709)	(490,000)	(936,709)

[a]Respondents who did not express an opinion on the evaluation of police performance question were not given a scale score.
[b]Estimated number of victimizations.
[c]Row percentages.
[d]Column percentages.
Source: J. Garofalo, *The Police and Public Opinion*, U.S. Department of Justice, National Criminal Justice Information and Statistics Service (Washington, D.C.: Government Printing Office, 1977), Table 16.

and young people tend to give somewhat less favorable ratings.) Garofalo found that these evaluations of the police were not related to recent victimization experiences. Moreover, it was found (as seen in Table 2-5) that the overall ratings of police performance in the cities studied were not strongly related to whether or not a victim reported the crime to the police. As Table 2-5 shows (row percentages), Garofalo found only minor variation in the proportion of crimes reported to the police being associated with the victim's ratings of the police. Referring to the similarity in the column percentages for each level of police rating, Garofalo reported: "[g]iven the close correspondence between these two response distributions, apparently we can discount the possibility that the experience of contact with the police, that results when a victimization is reported to them, has any significant effect on subsequent ratings of the police."[30]

Because he had found that ratings of police varied systematically by race and age, Garofalo analyzed these same data within age and race categories. His results were much the same. When, however, the data were analyzed according to the seriousness of the crime (as measured by the Sellin-Wolfgang scale), an interesting pattern was revealed. For victimizations of moderate and great seriousness there was no association between the victim's attitude toward the police and whether or not the victim reported the incident to the police; but for victimizations with low seriousness scores, there was a consistent increase in the proportion of events reported to the police as the rating of the police grew more favorable.

When the victims' ratings of the police were cross-tabulated with the reasons victims gave for not notifying the police of their victimization, there did not appear to be much of a relation (see Table 2-6). Those with negative ratings were somewhat more likely to give as a reason for not reporting that the police would not want to be bothered. Overall, however, the distribution of reasons for not reporting was just about the same in each police-rating category.

A somewhat different approach to the assessment of the relation

Table 2-6. Reasons for not Reporting Personal Victimizations to the Police by Victim's Rating of the Police, 1975 NCS City Surveys.

Reasons for not Reporting[b]	Rating of Police[a] (Percent)			
	(Positive) 1	2	3	(Negative) 4
Nothing could be done; lack of proof	41	42	42	40
Did not think it important enough	32	26	31	25
Police would not want to be bothered	7	5	9	13
Did not want to take time; too inconvenient	7	6	8	5
Private or personal matter	11	13	10	16
Did not want to get involved	6	4	3	3
Afraid of reprisal	6	5	5	3
Reported to someone else	9	8	5	5
Other	12	13	11	12
Estimated number[c]	(35,183)	(143,042)	(194,145)	(117,630)

[a]Respondents who did not express an opinion on the evaluation of police performance question were not given a scale score.

[b]Percentages sum to greater than 100 because some respondents cited more than one reason.

[c]Includes only victimizations that were not reported to the police and for which the respondent gave a reason for not reporting.

Source: J. Garofalo, *The Police and Public Opinion*, U.S. Department of Justice, National Criminal Justice Information and Statistics Service (Washington, D.C.: Government Printing Office, 1977), Table 20.

between attitudes and the decision to report a crime was taken by Schneider and her associates.[31] They administered a series of opinion questions in conjunction with a victimization survey in Portland. Unlike the NCP survey (which provided the data analyzed by Garofalo), the questions asked were quite specific. Thus, for the scale they named "trust in police" they asked the victims whether the police would give serious attention to their complaints, treat them as well as others, believe them, and try to find out who committed the crime, and they also asked victims about their general attitude toward the police. They also collected data on their respondents' perceptions of police-community relations, police effectiveness, and attitudes toward the courts.

Schneider, too, found a substantial relation between the seriousness of the victimization and reporting to the police. Furthermore, this relation generally was maintained regardless of the victim's reported trust in the police or perception of police-community relations, police effectiveness, or attitude toward the courts. Also, as Garofalo found, the attitudinal items were slightly more correlated with the reporting decisions for the least serious crimes than for the most serious crimes.

Thus, it consistently has been found that, overall, demographic characteristics of victims (whether measured at the individual or the aggregate level) are less strongly correlated with the decision to report a crime than is some measure of the gravity of the crime. Similarly, a consistent finding has been that the influence of attitudes on reporting may depend on the nature of the crime experienced by the victim. The implication is that for the victim of a crime of relatively low "seriousness," factors other than the nature of the harm itself may become influential in the decision to report to the police, whereas when the harm done to the victim is grave, then characteristics of the victim play a much less influential role.

REPORTING DECISIONS FOR OTHER FORMS OF CRIME

Victimization surveys, which provide the best available data about the reporting decisions of victims, unfortunately do not include many important forms of criminal activity. In large part this is a limitation of the method. It is simply not feasible to employ the retrospective survey method to uncover victimizations of certain types. The method has been applied in an attempt to discover employee theft, but was found not to be feasible.[32] And for crimes of which the victim is unaware of victimization (for example, consumer fraud), the method obviously is not valid. Thus, for many forms of crime, we do not have the essential basis needed for study of this crucial decision—that is, we may know how many and what types of events are reported to the police, but we lack data on those that occurred but were not reported. In view of the vast numbers of crimes that do go unreported (as indicated by victimization surveys), inferences about the decisionmaking process made only from data on the reported group are extremely hazardous.

One exception to this bleak state of ignorance is found in the case of shoplifting, about which some clever and interesting research has been done. Shoplifting differs from the crimes already discussed in that the victim is an organization rather than an individual. It is also a crime of extremely low visibility. It often is not known whether inventory losses are due to shoplifting, employee theft, delivery fraud, or simply poor inventory accountability.

It might be thought that when an organization rather than an individual is the victim of criminal behavior there would be less discretion exercised about informing the police. Studies of police referral of apprehended shoplifters indicate, however, that this is not the case. Hindelang obtained the records of a security firm that serviced retail stores by keeping track of the persons apprehended for shoplifting in the area.[33] Staff of the participating stores filled out a form that included information about the person shoplifting, about the type of goods stolen and their value, and whether a police referral was made. By studying these records, Hindelang was able to determine the factors most predictive of a call to the police once an apprehension was made by store employees. Studying the records of more than 6000 apprehended shoplifters during a three year period, he found that only 26 percent were reported to the police. Thus, even for the case of organizational victims, these data indicated that discretion about invoking the criminal justice process is vast.

A large array of factors about the shoplifter (such as age, sex, race), the merchandise stolen (for example, type, retail value), and the method of shoplifting (including under clothing, price switching, professional) were available for analysis. By far the apparently most influential variable in the decision to call the police was the value of the stolen property. Of secondary importance were what was stolen (stealing liquor tended to be reported more often), who stole it (males and older persons were more likely to be reported), and how it was stolen. The ability of these few factors to discriminate between those who were referred to the police and those who were not was remarkable. Hindelang's multivariate analyses show, for example, that shoplifters who stole nonliquor articles of small value (less than $1.90) under their clothes were referred to the police only 10 percent of the time, whereas those who stole fresh meat of a large value under their clothes were referred to the police 85 percent of the time.

The possible emphasis on the value of the shoplifted merchandise as a criterion for referral to the police is consistent with the importance of offense seriousness as already discussed. That is, the "value of the merchandise" may be taken as an indicant of the gravity of the harm. Hindelang offered some plausible explanations for the other apparent criteria:

> It is likely that the interpretation placed on the act of theft by the store personnel plays an important role in moderating the probability of referral to the police. For example, if the items stolen are those which the store personnel believe are to be re-sold—liquor, cigarettes, and perhaps fresh meat—they may take a firmer position in favor of referral. Similarly, if the items stolen are viewed by the store personnel as items which are not essential to survival. . . .
>
> Likewise, the method of shoplifting may be used by the store personnel to verify intent. For example, although one may absent-mindedly or temporarily place a small object in his coat pocket while he continues to shop, or happen to pick up an object that has an incorrect price tag affixed to it, it is unlikely that placing an object under one's clothes or into another bag could be construed as accidental.[34]

In a similar study of shoplifting referrals, Cohen and Stark studied 371 case history records completed by store detectives in a large department store in Los Angeles.[35] (This study thus differed somewhat from Hindelang's work. Whereas the referrals to the police in Hindelang's data were made largely by store employees, such as clerks and managers, the Cohen and Stark data were derived from private security guards.) Again, the question investigated was whether or not the apprehended shoplifter was turned over to the police or released. The amount of discretion exercised was again vast, with over half the apprehended shoplifters not reported to the police. A wide range of attributes of the shoplifters and of the offenses was studied in an effort to determine the principal determinants of the police referral decision. For the most part the characteristics of the shoplifter (such as sex, race) were not found to be strongly related to the decision. The one major exception was employment status—unemployed shoplifters were more often referred, other things constant, then were those who were employed. The interpretation of this finding offered by Cohen and Stark was that the store detectives might perceive that unemployed shoplifters are more apt to be persons who steal for a living, and hence pose threats in the future, whereas the employed may be only occasional thieves.

The value of the shoplifted merchandise again proved to be a strong correlate of the decision to call the police. Shoplifters stealing less than $30 worth of goods were referred to the police only a third of the time, whereas those stealing more than $30 worth were referred three-fourths of the time.

Recently, Hindelang's study was replicated by Lundman on a sample of 664 shoplifting cases from the records of a nationwide department store chain.[36] In these stores, as in the Cohen and Stark study, the referrals were made by security personnel rather than regular store employees. Similar data about the shoplifters, their methods, and the merchandise stolen were collected. Again, the retail value of the shoplifted goods was the single strongest correlate of the decision to call the police. When the amount of the theft was taken into consideration, the shoplifter's sex was unrelated to police referral, but the shoplifter's age and race were associated with the decision to report. Older persons and nonwhites were more likely to be referred than younger persons and whites. Lundman's conclusion was that "[a]lthough offender characteristics are important, the seriousness of the alleged offense is clearly the most critical determinant of whether or not an apprehended shoplifter is referred to the police. Whatever the exact magnitude of the contributions of offender characteristics to the decision to refer, they occur within limits imposed by the seriousness of the offense."[37]

Perhaps the earliest study of the decision to refer shoplifters to the police was Cameron's study of shoplifters apprehended between 1943 and 1949 by the private security force of a large Chicago department store.[38] She found that both sex and race of the apprehended shoplifters were related to the police referral decision. Ten percent of the females but 35 percent of the males and 11 percent of the whites compared with 58 percent of the blacks apprehended for shoplifting were referred to the police. It has been suggested that the strong influence of offender characteristics in the referral decision found by Cameron may have been due to a lack of controls for the value of the merchandise stolen.[39] Or the differences between her results and those cited above may have been due to the different time periods studied. Alternatively, it has been suggested by Hindelang that private police force members, the source of police referral in Cameron's study (and in Lundman's), may have biases in dealing with shoplifters that the general store employers do not.[40] Lundman, on the basis of these findings and his own data, argued that "policing, both public and private, encourages reliance upon stereotypical images of the kinds of persons deserving formal actions. It would appear, then, that the greater the distance between lay decision-makers and the occupation of policing, the less the apparent reliance upon offender characteristics."[41]

There are, of course, many plausible interpretations for the consistent finding that the single strongest correlate of the decision of shoplifting victims to call the police is the value of the stolen merchandise. It may reflect the desire to focus on professional thieves, who may be expected to shoplift items of larger value. Or it may be believed that the occasional shoplifter will be deterred by the apprehension itself, and it may be thought that the costs to the store in time and money associated with prosecution might therefore be avoided. The number of persons apprehended for shoplifting would make universal referral and prosecution prohibitively costly. Thus, there is a practical need to screen the cases and refer only those thought necessary. The value of the shoplifted articles may be a useful indicant of "necessary" in the sense of preventing professional thefts:

> If the arrested shoplifter is likely to be a person stealing merchandise in order to sell it or return it for a refund of the "purchase" price, he is almost certain to be formally charged. The evidence pointing toward "commercial" theft that interrogators look for includes a catalogue of items such as inadequate or inaccurate personal identification. . . . The thief who gives an out-of-town address or a hotel address may well be a *professional* thief. . . . The nature and value of the stolen merchandise and special equipment for stealing or concealing merchandise is considered in determining whether the detective is confronted with commercial theft.[42]

Other decision criteria can be inferred from these studies. There appears to be a clear reluctance to refer young offenders to the police for shoplifting, and a preference to refer those with a prior record of shoplifting. Also, the fear of lawsuits apparently leads some stores to refer all those apprehended shoplifters who refuse to sign a confession. And Cameron reported that the store in her study sometimes referred in order to get a severely disturbed neurotic to a source of medical care.

Apart from these few studies, knowledge about how nonstreet crime victims decide to invoke the law is very meager. A large gap in knowledge exists in the area of consumer fraud. The lack of reliable data about consumer fraud generally, not even indicating the scope and characteristics of the problem, contributes to our ignorance of the factors influencing victims' decisions to invoke the law.[43] Furthermore, consumers may complain about suspected

Table 2-7. The Twenty Most Frequent Consumer Complaints, United States, 1976.

1	Automobile	11	Advertising
2	Home Repairs	12	Mobile Homes
3	Appliances	13	Utilities
4	Mail Orders	14	Insurance
5	Furniture and Carpeting	15	Food
6	Credit	16	Clothing
7	Landlord-Tenant Relations	17	Books and Magazines
8	Business Practices	18	Home Solicitations
9	Housing and Real Estate	19	Health Products and Sources
10	TV and Radio	20	Health Spas

Source: "Top 20 Consumer Complaints" (Washington, D.C.: Department of Health, Education and Welfare, Office of Consumer Affairs, November 1976).

fraudulent activities in diverse arenas (such as to the police, to better business bureaus, to newspaper columns, or to consumer complaint offices of attorneys general), and this makes compilation of accurate data difficult. Perhaps the best available data are those published by the Office of Consumer Affairs in Washington, D.C., which simply lists the ranking of the twenty most frequent complaints received (see Table 2-7). These data unfortunately shed little light on decisions to report consumer frauds, since the proportions of these types of complaints that consumers had but did not report to anyone are unknown and because not all of these complaints constituted fraud (but rather may have been general complaints about product quality).

Undoubtedly, one of the major difficulties faced by victims of consumer fraud is that they, like the law, may have great difficulty distinguishing fraud from aggressive business practices. Thus, the victim of consumer fraud may face an ambiguity (that is not as likely for victims of armed robbery) in deciding whether an event was a crime and thus merited reporting to the police or other agencies. There is some evidence that among those who do report fraudulent business practices, the desire for restitution rather than punishment predominates.[44] That is, complaining consumer fraud victims generally want their money back or the product repaired satisfactorily, rather than wanting the offending business punished in some way. Also, there are indications that knowledge or ignorance of the appropriate legal channels play a large role in who reports consumer frauds. Thus, studies generally find that it is the middle class who most often report consumer fraud to the authorities,[45] although some have suggested that the poor are most often its victims.[46]

Victims of crimes that occur within the context of the victim's participation in criminal activity may be the least likely to be reported to the police. Obviously, however, few data are available that permit study of the question. It is not uncommon for police departments to receive reports of robbings and assaults from customers of prostitutes or from prostitutes themselves, but most such occurrances undoubtedly go unreported due to the victim's fear of embarrassment or criminal prosecution. (Similarly, it is not uncommon for such complaining victims to fail to follow up on prosecution.)

The interesting issue of those persons who suddenly decide to report the ongoing criminal activities in which they themselves or their colleagues are engaged—the so-called "whistle blowers"—is also in need of study. There are documented cases of such activities in many walks of life: government bureaucrats involved in kickback schemes, organized crime figures, doctors involved in organized medicaid fraud, and the "customers" of illegal gambling and drug operations. The forces that lead to notification of the police of ongoing criminal activity in which the person reporting is implicated are in need of study.

THE DECISION TO REPORT A CRIME—SOME IMPLICATIONS OF THE EVIDENCE

The studies reviewed in this chapter demonstrate quite convincingly that citizen input, in the nature of their exercise of discretion whether to notify the police of crimes, profoundly circumscribes the cases that will serve as the basis for all of the subsequent criminal justice decisions.[47] All of these data strongly reinforce the assertion at the beginning of this chapter of the impact of the victim's decision to report a crime. The vast discretion exercised by citizens in invoking the law plays a central role in the definition of the goals of the criminal justice process and in their achievement. It is clear from the evidence reviewed here that the criminal justice system depends on the selection, accomplished by the victims of crime, of the cases and persons that will flow through the system and that a good deal of selection does go on. For many forms of criminal processing, the criminal justice system begins with victim initiative. Thus, all of the issues of interest in this book that may be raised about criminal justice decisionmaking need to be raised also about this fundamental trigger event to the application of the law.

It is important therefore that the limitations of our knowledge about victim decisions be underscored. Although the victimization surveys provide us with some hitherto unavailable information about how victim discretion to report a crime is exercised, there are many problems in using the results from that method for this purpose. Not all victimizations that occur are reported to the survey interviewers, and it is known that some types may be less likely to be reported to the interviewers than others. Crimes between people known or related to each other (such as child abuse and assaults between spouses) are probably underrepresented in such surveys. Also, some events reported to the interviewers may not in fact be crimes, and there is undoubtedly some degree of invalidity in answers to the question about whether the event was reported to the police. Although there has been some study of the reasons victims give for not invoking the law, there is very little evidence that bears directly on why victims did choose to call the police. And less yet is known about whether, after calling the police, they were satisfied with their decision. Finally, it must be stressed that the information available about the decisions of victims of common theft and assault is very great when compared to the nearly absent information about the decisions of victims of other forms of criminal activity.

The issues raised by the vast exercise of victim discretion are fundamental to the criminal justice system. As Reiss puts it, "citizens may be regarded as enforcers or non-enforcers of the law and its moral order . . . . at issue, are the questions of when is one obligated to call the police and what are the consequences of citizen discretion for moral order."[48] An answer to these questions might best be addressed by an analysis of the victim's decision in terms of the three essential components of rational decisions discussed in Chapter 1— goals, information, and alternatives.

DECISION GOALS

The evidence suggests that the goals sought by victims in relation to their decisions to report a crime are many, that any one decision may embody several of them, and that there is a considerable likelihood that many of these goals may conflict with those of other key criminal justice decisionmakers. Subsequent chapters will demonstrate that a growing body of literature exists addressing the goals of others in the system, but almost no attention has been given either to the theoretical goals of the victim as a decisionmaker or to the ways that these goals may be compatible or in conflict with the goals of other criminal justice decisionmakers.

In attempting to identify the salient goals of victim reporting it might first be useful to examine the criteria apparently used in the decision. Victims of crime, at least partially, appear to operate along a "seriousness dimension." Most studies suggest this interpretation, where "seriousness" is defined by monetary loss or physical harm. Both individuals and organizations appear to decide to call the police partly on the basis of the gravity of their loss. Hence, it may be that the first "filter" for the entire criminal justice process tends to screen out the less serious events from further processing.

The substantial nonreporting by victims raises the important issue of whether a system of justice can operate fairly (or achieve other goals set for it) when it is able to process only those cases selected for it by individual citizens. Obviously, for a large body of crimes the offenders never will be held accountable in the criminal justice system. If not all offenders are formally processed by the criminal justice system, is there necessarily a reduction in equity?[49] If one function of the justice system is to acknowledge and reaffirm, in a formalized fashion, the legal values of society, and yet it is denied that opportunity due to a reluctance of citizens to inform the legally constituted authorities that they have been a victim of a transgression of those legal values, can the system realistically be expected to fulfill that function?

Clearly, these questions have profound implications for fundamental purposes of the criminal justice system. Although their answers are bound to be complex and cannot be answered entirely with the data studied here, the data available on reporting to the police may begin to address them. For example, although it may be thought that full reporting is a requisite for an efficient and equitable criminal justice system, there may be distinct and proper advantages in a citizen-based discretionary system for invoking the criminal process. The burden that full reporting (more than doubling the number of offenses now reported) would place on an already overtaxed system of justice should be noted. Were an effort to be made to involve the full machinery of the criminal justice system (or even that of the police stage) in every victimization, the system would be less able (with its limited resources) to deal efficiently, effectively, and fairly with the more serious cases. In any case, given the low visibility of the decision, it never would be possible to ensure full reporting.

Of more concern is not whether all crimes should or should not be reported to the police, but rather, whether the reporting process operates fairly and in a way compatible with the central aims of the criminal justice system. It is possible to have less than full reporting and still have an equitable decision process. This requires, however, that criteria used in the decision by victims do not include invidious discrimination on the basis of offender characteristics unrelated to criminal justice aims; and equity requires also that no groups of victims are systematically shut off from the criminal justice system because of fear or mistrust of the police.[50] By and large, the nature of the harm suffered by victims appears to be more important than are the characteristics of the offender or attitudes toward the police in explaining variation in reporting behavior. This fact suggests that it may be possible to achieve equity without full reporting.

Some of the studies reviewed, however, do suggest inequity in reporting to the police. Nonstranger offenders, for example, are less likely, other things equal, to be reported to the police. Several explanations, of course, may be offered. For some, the victim may believe (perhaps correctly) that resolution of the victimization problem would best be achieved outside the context of the criminal justice system. Calling the police, when someone within the household is involved, may aggravate the situation later on. Or, alternative social control mechanisms—a call to the parents of the offender, for example—may be sufficient.

Of more concern are the victims of nonstrangers who suffer serious physical or psychological harm yet are afraid to involve the police lest the situation become aggravated. Spouse and child abusers may fall disproportionately into this category. In recent years attempts have been made, through special units of police departments and various "crises lines," to alleviate this problem. The problem may be seen as one of expanding the decision alternatives available to these crime victims in a way that is compatible with their goals. These often emphasize simply the cessation of the victimization, rather than retribution or general crime prevention. Unfortunately, adequate evaluations of these programs are lacking, and such evaluations are a pressing research need. The fact that one in six rape victims who failed to report to the police say that they did not because they were afraid of reprisals is evidence of the need for demonstrably effective alternatives for the victim.

Various other arguments would support the use of a "seriousness criterion" by victims in their decision to report. For example, many trivial offenses may be resolved best by the parties involved, and the invocation of the criminal justice process would be both wasteful of scarce resources and even dysfunctional to an amenable settlement of the dispute. Examples might be an assault between playmates over a bicycle or a youngster who shoplifts candy from the neighborhood drug store.

The emphasis in victim decisionmaking on the gravity of the harm suffered cannot be interpreted in light of any single goal. Depending on the circumstances, it may reflect a concern for general deterrence, since the greater the harm done, the more important the victim may believe it to be that the offender should be caught and punished in order to prevent others from the same criminal act. Many street robbery victimizations may fall into this category. It may, on the other hand, reflect an incapacitative aim. For example, the personnel of the stores in the shoplifting studies clearly desired that the professional shoplifters be given special attention. Reporting to the police as a means of stopping an ongoing victimization between nonstrangers may be seen also as pursuit of an incapacitative goal. The more serious the personal harm, the greater may be the likelihood that the victim seeks personal revenge or retribution for the crime by calling the police.

Available studies strongly imply that for many victims the decision to report a crime is made for personal utilitarian reasons. The relation between the victim's status of theft insurance and frequency of reporting to the police, the high rate of reporting stolen automobiles, and Reiss' finding that many businessmen said they reported crimes for insurance purposes, all clearly suggest a personal gain motive.[51] This raises some important issues relative to the goals of the criminal justice process. For example, Reiss argues that:

> These data on insurance coverage strongly suggest that one's civic obligation to mobilize the police against crimes of property is often subverted by question of personal gain. . . . These relationships are based on conceptions of personal gain, generally monetary gain or the avoidance of loss in time and effort. The effort is not worth the cost. . . . Given the absence of a sense of civic responsibility to mobilize the public, and the essentially reactive character of much policing of everyday life, the citizenry has enormous power to subvert the system by its decisions to call the police or not.[52]

The characterization of the goals sought by many victims in their reporting decision as one of personal gain can be supported in a number of other ways. It finds support in the factors associated with nonreporting: the greater the personal financial loss, the more likely the event will be reported to the police, and the greater the gravity of the injury, the more likely it will be to be reported. The fact that school children have been found to have a very low rate of reporting[53] may be a function of a social code that warns against informing on one's peers and, hence, may also be viewed as a personal gain decision. Additionally, the reasons most commonly given in the National Crime Panel surveys for not reporting a crime to the police ("nothing could be done" and "victimization not important enough") may be interpreted under a personal gain model of decisionmaking: it may be perceived that the effort and time (cost) involved in dealing with the police are just not worth the results, personally (gain).

The victim decision goals best suited for the achievement of the traditional aims of the criminal sanction are far from clear, and they may be expected to vary according to the specific aim in question. As Reiss suggests, there may be a profound contradiction between those goals and the personal gain goal. Under the classical deterrence position, for example, the ultimate goal is thought to be achieved if punishments are administered both certainly and severely. However, if no part of the criminal justice system is notified of a crime, there can be no opportunity to administer the penalties, and thus the certainty of punishment is diminished. If the victim sees no personal payoff in reporting a crime, perhaps because the personal loss is not substantial, then the goals of the two decision models will conflict. On the other hand, there might be substantial compatibility between such personal utilitarian victim goals and other aims of the criminal justice process. One is the already discussed initial screening on the basis of "seriousness," which may be functional for an overtaxed system of justice. Alternatively, if a retribution aim is thought to be a major goal served by the criminal sanction, and if the victim is seen as the important focus of a retributive philosophy, there may be little conflict between the aims of the criminal sanction and the personal gain decision model, at least for some types of victimizations.

The question therefore arises as to how victim decisions are to be evaluated. Are they to be evaluated by the proportion of victimizations that are reported to the police, as a deterrence purpose would seem to indicate? Or should some measure of personal satisfaction be developed that allows for a considerable degree of victim discretion?

Suppose, for example, that the extent of victim reporting were to be selected, as adoption of a deterrence aim would suggest, as the measure of "successful" victim decisions. Furthermore, suppose that an active effort were made to increase substantially the level of reporting in furtherance of the deterrence goal. Given the low levels of the current ability of the police to "do something" about many victimizations, as measured by clearance rates that approximate 20 percent for many property crimes, then it is probable that victim satisfaction would decrease with a successful increase in reporting. This may be true particularly if the victims were led to believe that by reporting their crime to the police there would be a meaningful personal gain.

DECISION ALTERNATIVES
AND INFORMATION

Currently, the decision alternatives available to the victims of crime are quite limited. The major choice, of course, is either to report to the police or to do nothing. However, the importance of such decision alternatives should not be minimized; the power vested in victims is fundamental. It is the power to invoke the law and its corresponding sanction and the power not to do so. In many respects, the decision not to call the police is the most fundamental exercise of control over the criminal justice process.

The victim as a criminal justice decisionmaker is in some ways in a position analogous to the police as decisionmakers. Neither has complete control over the consequences of their decisions. As Reiss and Bordua pointed out, the police do not have command over the output of their decisional alternatives.[54] If the main concern is justice, in using their discretion not to arrest a suspect, the police may feel, based on the individual characteristics of the case, that justice has been served. If, however, the decision is to arrest, then control over the decisional output is taken from the hands of the police and placed in the hands of the prosecutor, the judge, or both. Thus, if the latter's decision is not to proceed with the full impact of available criminal sanctions, then the police may believe that justice has not been served and, hence, that their decision has been "subverted."

A similar analysis may be relevant to the victim's decision. In deciding not to notify the police about a crime, many victims may believe that justice is better served. But when the decision is made to notify the police, the victim loses control over the decisional output, as the disposition of the case is taken from the victim's control. The fact that victims do not control the output to the process may have important implications, not necessarily consciously recognized in the individual case, for the ultimate purposes thought to be served by reporting a crime to the police. It may be that this inability to control directly the decision ouptut is a main factor in the victim's use of what may best be termed a "personal gain goal" in decisionmaking, rather than one or more of the classic criminal law goals.

The issue of the time and effort that may be involved in reporting a crime and the requirements of other significant criminal justice goals, such as general deterrence, are, in the context of this analysis, information requirements. Victim decisionmakers, like many of their counterparts in the rest of the criminal justice system, lack information about the consequences of their decisions. And in relation to many of the potential consequences, such information simply does not exist, because the relevant studies have not been undertaken.

The large proportion of crimes that go unreported may have implications for the expansion of decision alternatives for the victim. Those who fail to report, for example, because it is a "personal matter" or because of fear of reprisal may profit by the existence of nonlegal dispute resolution mechanisms (such as neighborhood counseling centers). Or it may be useful to establish strong incentives for those who have a probability of coming into contact with victims who are seriously injured (physically or psychologically) but who do not report to call the incident to the attention of the authorities. Doctors, dentists, clergy, and others provide examples but may require structures that are designed to avoid the violation of patient-client confidence.

Further studies of the ways that victim decisions may affect the goals of the criminal justice process and studies of the personal requirements of victims (many of which may conflict sharply with the goals of crime prevention and even justice) are needed both to understand the decision more fully and to design suitable alternatives. Probably no criminal justice participant has a greater amount of discretion or is in a role more capable of influencing the character of the entire system of justice. Substantial gains have been made in recent years in our basic knowledge about the role and influence of victims as decisionmakers, but still lacking is a firm basis for the design of programs to enhance the rationality of these decisions.

NOTES

1. See F. Remington et al., *Criminal Justice Administration* (New York: Bobbs-Merrill, 1969), ch. 1.

2. One major exception involves studies of police decisions to file a report of behavior as crime. These are discussed in Chapter 3. How some behaviors become defined as criminal has received some attention. See especially, J. Hall, *Theft, Law, and Society*, Second Edition (New York: Bobbs-Merrill, 1955); and W. Chambliss, "A Sociological Analysis of the Law of Vagrancy," *Social Problems* 12:67 (1969). Conversely, how some previously illegal behavior becomes legal is receiving some attention. See, for example, J. Skolnick and J. Dombrink, "The Legalization of Deviance," *Criminology* 16:193 (1978).

3. This chapter will focus mainly on crimes of common theft and assault, since it is on these crimes that most research has been done and for which the victim is the principal initiator of the criminal justice process. For many other types of crime (such as many forms of consumer fraud or victimless crimes), the victim probably is less active as the initiator of the process. There are several possible reasons for criminal justice functionaries rather than victims playing the role of activator of the criminal justice system for these other crimes: (1) for

many consumer fraud and white collar offenses the victim may be unaware of the victimization; (2) there may be more uncertainty on the part of the victim over the definition of the questionable behavior as crime; (3) there may be less certainty as to the proper authority to receive the report (e.g., police, consumer fraud bureaus, better business bureaus); (4) in the case of victimless crimes (e.g., gambling, narcotics or prostitution), if there is indeed a victim he or she might be implicated in criminal activity if a report were to be made. Portions of the text discussion draws upon M. Hindelang and M. Gottfredson, "The Victim's Decision Not To Invoke the Criminal Process," in W. McDonald, ed., *Criminal Justice and the Victim* (Beverly Hills: Sage, 1976).

4. A. Reiss, *The Police and the Public* (New Haven: Yale University Press, 1971). Reiss was one of the first researchers to recognize that citizens are the principal initiators of the process—i.e., that victim decisions are fundamental to an understanding of the criminal justice process.

5. See Hindelang and Gottfredson, *supra* note 3.

6. See, for example, F. Miller, R. Dawson, G. Dix, and R. Parnas, *Criminal Justice Administration and Related Processes* (Mineola, New York: The Foundation Press, 1971), ch. 1.

7. For a thorough discussion of these early victimization surveys see M. J. Hindelang, *Criminal Victimization in Eight American Cities: A Descriptive Analysis of Common Theft and Assault* (Cambridge, Massachusetts: Ballinger, 1976), chs. 1 and 2.

8. For a discussion of the procedures used in the National Crime Survey, see Hindelang, *supra* note 7; and U.S. Bureau of the Census, *National Crime Survey: National Sample Survey Documentation* (Washington, D.C.: U.S. Department of Commerce, 1975).

9. For a discussion of the limitations of these survey data see M. Hindelang, M. Gottfredson, and J. Garofalo, *Victims of Personal Crime: An Empirical Foundation for a Theory of Personal Victimization* (Cambridge, Massachusetts: Ballinger, 1978), ch. 10.

10. Hindelang, *supra* note 7.

11. A. Smith and D. Maness, "The Decision to Call the Police" in McDonald, *supra* note 3.

12. See, for example, L. Humphreys, *Tearoom Trade* (Chicago: Aldine, 1970).

13. See Hindelang, *supra* note 7; and Hindelang, Gottfredson, and Garofalo, *supra* note 9.

14. For a discussion of the reliability data concerning the National Crime Panel, see Hindelang, Gottfredson, and Garofalo, *supra* note 9 at ch. 10.

15. *Supra* note 9.

16. M.R. Gottfredson, "The Classification of Crimes and Victims" (Ph.D. dissertation, State University of New York at Albany, 1976).

17. Hindelang, *supra* note 7.

18. A. Schneider, J. Burcart, and L. Wilson, "The Role of Attitudes in the Decision to Report Crimes to the Police," in McDonald, *supra* note 3.

19. *Id.* at 97.

20. P. Ennis, *Criminal Victimization in the United States*, Field Surveys II, President's Commission on Law Enforcement and Administration of Justice (Washington, D.C.: Government Printing Office, 1967).

21. R. Bloch, "Why Notify the Police?: The Victim's Decision to Notify the Police of an Assault," *Criminology* 11:555 (1974).

22. R. Sparks, H. Genn, and D. Dodd, *Surveying Victims: A Study of the Measurement of Criminal Victimization* (New York: John Wiley and Sons, 1977).

23. R. Hawkins, "Determinants of Sanctioning Initiations for Criminal Victimization" (Ph.D. dissertation, University of Michigan, 1970).

24. M.R. Gottfredson and M.J. Hindelang, "A Study of the Behavior of Law," *American Sociological Review* 44:3 (1979).

25. As noted above, Hindelang, *supra* note 7, found that demographic characteristics of victims were unrelated to the reasons given for not calling the police once the type of crime and the victim-offender relationship were taken into account.

26. *Id.* at 381.

27. Gottfredson and Hindelang, *supra* note 24.

28. President's Commission on Law Enforcement and Administration of Justice, *The Challenge of Crime in a Free Society* (Washington, D.C.: Government Printing Office, 1967), p. 144.

29. J. Garofalo, *The Police and Public Opinion*, National Criminal Justice Information and Statistics Service (Washington, D.C.: Government Printing Office, 1977).

30. *Id.* at 30.

31. Schneider et al., *supra* note 18.

32. See Hindelang, *supra* note 7, for a review of victimization surveys attempting to measure other forms of criminal behavior.

33. M. Hindelang, "Decisions of Shoplifting Victims to Invoke the Criminal Justice Process," *Social Problems* 21:580 (1974).

34. *Id.* at 590-91.

35. L. Cohen and R. Stark, "Discriminatory Labeling and the Five-Finger Discount," *Journal of Research in Crime and Delinquency* 11:25 (1974).

36. R. Lundman, "Shoplifting and Police Referral: A Re-examination," *Journal of Criminal Law and Criminology* 69:395 (1978).

37. *Id..* at 400.

38. M. Cameron, *The Booster and the Snitch* (New York: The Free Press, 1964).

39. Cohen and Stark, *supra* note 35; Hindelang, *supra* note 33.

40. Hindelang, *supra* note 33.

41. *Supra* note 36 at 400.

42. Cameron, *supra* note 38.

43. One estimate places the loss to consumers of consumer fraud at $1350 million annually, as compared with a cost to the public of $27 million for robbery, $251 million for burglary, and $150 million for auto theft (President's Commission, *supra* note 28).

44. E. Steele, "Fraud, Dispute, and the Consumer: Responding to Consumer Complaints," *University of Pennsylvania Law Review* 173:1107 (1975).

45. *Id.*

46. D. Caplovitz, *The Poor Pay More* (New York: The Free Press, 1967).

47. The influence of the victim in the police decision to arrest once a complaint has been made has also been found to be considerable, as will be discussed in the next chapter.

48. Reiss, *supra* note 4 at 65, 70.

49. For a novel discussion of equality in relation to other decision aims, see N. Morris, "Punishment, Desert and Rehabilitation," in U.S. Department of Justice, *Equal Justice Under Law*, Bicentennial Lecture Series (Washington, D.C.: Government Printing Office, 1976), pp. 137-67. He argues that the principle of equality is not a limiting principle but only a guiding one "which will enjoin equality of punishment unless there are other substantial utilitarian reasons to the contrary, such as those that favor exemplary punishment—or in situations where there are inadequate resources for or high costs attached to the application of equal punishments" (at 158). His argument, of course, does not suggest any value to the circumstance that unequal treatment is unwittingly applied due to the fact that crimes are not reported.

50. It should be stressed that the victims' discretion does not rest solely with calling the police. Perhaps more important is the decision to regard some behavior as criminal in the first place. Most of the evidence suggests that it is the victim, rather than the police, who must apply the criminal law to behavior in the first instance (the police can, of course, decide later not to regard some behavior as a crime). Variability in this decision demands a good deal of study, as it might bear directly on the equity of the process.

51. Reiss, *supra* note 4, also suggests that insurance coverage may inhibit some victims from reporting for fear that their policies will be cancelled.

52. *Supra* note 4 at 68-69.

53. Gottfredson, *supra* note 16.

54. A. Reiss and D. Bordua, "Environment and Organization: A Perspective on the Police," in D. Bordua, ed., *The Police: Six Sociological Essays* (New York: John Wiley, 1967).

Chapter 3

The Decision to Arrest

Police decisions have not been a neglected area of study and commentary for social scientists and legal scholars.[1] On the contrary, the literature about police work is vast, diverse, and impossible to summarize briefly without violating its complexity.[2] Our purposes, however, do not require a thorough review. Rather, we seek to investigate the information requirements, goals, and alternatives of the decision to arrest; to review studies bearing on the ways that arrest decisions are made routinely; and to offer some comments on directions for the enhancement of rationality. This itself is no small task, for no single aspect of police work has received more scholarly attention recently than has the decision to arrest.[3] Our review therefore must be selective, including only the most informative studies and commentaries.

The focus of this chapter is on arrest—the decision by a police officer to take physical custody, by virtue of the authority of the law, of a person who is suspected to have violated a law.[4] The focus is restricted further, initially, by considering only arrests made in the absence of warrants (that is, by officers acting without prior specific authorization by a court). This latter restriction does not preclude the vast majority of arrests,[5] although it does exclude investigation of issues unique to the warrant situation.

A focus on the decision to arrest excludes from consideration most of what the police do routinely. As Bittner tells us on the basis of considerable observation: "when one looks at what policemen actually do, one finds that criminal law enforcement is something that most of them do with the frequency located somewhere between virtually never and very rarely."[6] Similarly, Reiss has noted, on the basis of sustained observation of patrol practices, that for a policeman "the modal tour of duty does not involve an arrest of any person."[7] Studies of calls to the police for assistance discover uniformly that the vast majority of citizen requests for police help do not involve crime-related matters.[8] Accordingly, this is not a chapter about police work; rather, it is a chapter about a narrow slice of routine police work, albeit a critically important slice—the decision whether to invoke the law of arrest.[9]

An appreciation, however, of the routine daily activities of police work—the context within which arrest decisions are made—facilitates a study of the goals that may be pursued by arrest decisions. In this respect, two aspects of routine police work that are particularly critical in shaping the aims of arrest merit comment at the outset— the dependency of the police on citizen demands and cooperation, and the "order maintenance" function of most routine police work. We will describe these "contexts" of the arrest decision here briefly, developing their significance to arrest decisions throughout the chapter.

In our discussion of victims' decisions to report crimes to the police, we stressed that the evidence documented the assertion that it is the victim of crime rather than the police officer who is the principal initiator of the criminal law. That is, of the crimes that come to the attention of the police, most do so as a result of citizen initiative. This observation of how criminal events generally become police business led Reiss to characterize police involvement as a great deal more reactive than proactive.[10] As described in more detail later in this chapter, Reiss has also discovered that citizens control arrest practices not only in calling the police in the first instance, but also through their preference about arrest once the police arrive.[11] As a matter of empirical reality, it appears that the arrest decision is largely circumscribed by citizen initiation.[12] Thus, whatever goals are pursued by the decision to arrest, their achievement must be measured within a context that is principally police reactive—or citizen initiated.[13]

Students of the police role also have asserted repeatedly the dominance of the police responsibility for "order maintenance" in relation to that of enforcing the law.[14] Arrest decisions are thus seen as one of the available techniques for carrying out the task of preserving order; in this respect the decision to arrest is one of several possible responses to threats to the public order and one that is the least often employed. Other techniques that fall under the rubric of order maintenance include hospitalization, talk, traffic direction, physical presence, issuing an order to move on, requesting that a radio be turned down, and so forth. Each technique has the central aim of restoring "order" where there is disorder.[15]

Bittner has developed this conceptualization of the context of arrest decisions most fully. It is the capacity of the police (and the expectation of them) to intervene in pressing problems and to compel a resolution that defines the context of police work. Bittner's thesis is thus:

> that the police are empowered and required to impose, or, as the case may be, coerce a provisional solution upon emergent problems without having to brook or defer to opposition of any kind, and that further, their competence to intervene extends to every kind of emergency, without any exceptions whatever.[16]

Bittner summarizes the special competence of the police as being responsible for events characterized as "something-that-ought-not-to-be-happening-and-about-which-someone-had-better-do-something now!"[17]

Throughout the following discussion of arrest decisions these "contexts" within which these decisions are made must be kept in mind. Arrest decisions are, to a large degree, constrained by citizen input; the police, like every subsequent actor in the criminal justice system, are dependent upon earlier decisions for input. Their information, goals, and alternatives are thus influenced strongly by the cases made available by others for their decisions. In addition, these decisions take place as a part of a larger role played by the police, the central feature of which is dealing with a wide range of problems, with authority, that have eluded alternative resolution. Solving pressing interpersonal crises involves the invocation of numerous tools, the ultimate of which is arrest.[18] And much evidence suggests that arrest is the tool of last resort; at least one observer concludes: "and no policeman who is methodical in his work uses it in any other way."[19]

The nature of these "contexts" within which routine arrest decisions are made most certainly does not denegrate the importance of these decisions. Indeed, the decision to arrest involves a fundamental application of the coercive power of the state, one with considerable consequences for both the accused and society. To whom and for what purposes such power is applied are issues of paramount importance not only to the efficient, effective, and just administration of justice, but to the whole of society. It is a decision, like the others considered in this book, with profound implications for the rationality of the entire criminal justice process.

These "contexts," however, have a critical general influence on the decision to arrest.

THE DISCRETIONARY NATURE OF ARRESTS

We noted in Chapter 1 that in the absence of alternatives, there is no decision problem. That is, there must be a choice of actions available, even if that choice is only to decide not to take any form of action. Do the police indeed have a decision problem with respect to arrest? Is discretion at this phase of the criminal justice process permissible?

Only relatively recently has the discretionary nature of the arrest decision been acknowledged widely. Historically, statutes, police administrators, and scholarly commentary all have been in agreement with the position that the police were not empowered to decide whether or not to enforce the law in all cases that come to their attention. Full enforcement, it was asserted, was both desirable and the legal requirement. Accordingly, there was no discretion involved in arrest—if the circumstances fit the letter of the statute then an arrest must be made.[20]

Admittedly, this is something of a caricature of the "no discretion" position. Although it is argued subsequently that discretion in arrests is both inevitable and proper if adequately controlled, a well-reasoned position can be sustained to strive for extremely limited discretion in these decisions. The arguments of J. Goldstein are especially noteworthy in this respect.

Goldstein stressed that police decisions not to invoke the criminal law are of low visibility—that is, if the decision is made not to arrest, the decision is not known publicly. This circumstance prohibits the possibility of review on a regular basis to ensure that this discretion is not abused. Goldstein does not argue for "total enforcement" in all situations. "Total enforcement" is precluded by due process restrictions regarding searches, arrests, and so forth. These constraints, however, define an area of "full enforcement" in which the police are authorized and expected to enforce the law. Thus, within this area, according to Goldstein, the police have not been delegated discretion.

Practically, such a position creates problems (for example, legal ambiguities, personnel and time constraints, and outmoded statutes). These are acknowledged by Goldstein. His recommended solution, however, focuses on the legislature, rather than the police. Legislatures should redefine the common areas of selective enforcement in such a way that the police not be delegated discretion not to invoke the criminal law. The statutes should be cleared, by elected representatives, of obsolete laws, and the situations in which it is preferable not to arrest should be written explicitly in law. Such a solution, it is argued, removes the power of the criminal law from the "whim" of each police officer and puts it with elected representatives.[21]

Considerable progress undoubtedly could be made in the control of police discretion were legislatures to revise the criminal codes substantially, deleting obsolete statutes and specifying more precisely the acts that are not intended to fall within the purview of the criminal law. Greater specificity is needed particularly in the realm of the so-called "victimless" crimes. But is is both unrealistic and ill-advised to argue that discretion in arrest decisions be eliminated. It is unrealistic, given the complexity and variability of behavior that, under any circumstances, can be considered criminal. It is ill-advised because individualized judgement, taking account of the immediate circumstances of the behavior in question, is a necessary component to just decisionmaking.[22]

By way of illustration, consider a case of assault between spouses. A neighbor calls the police to the scene, where they witness a physical assault and heated argument. Should they make an arrest? Of both parties? As an alternative should they seek to engage the couple in professional counseling? Does the presence of children matter? What if the victim refuses to sign a complaint? Does the presence of a weapon matter? Suppose the parties reconcile on the spot? What if one of them turns to attack the officers?[23]

Quite obviously the contingencies surrounding the event (as well as the available alternatives) may have a lot to do with the appropriateness of an arrest. Countless other examples could be constructed that illustrate essentially the same point: discretion is a central and important feature of arrest decisions. An awareness of this has led, in H. Goldstein's words, to "a steadily growing recognition of police discretion and increasing support for the contention that it is not only necessary and desirable, but should be openly acknowledged, structured, and controlled."[24] Similarly, the President's Commission on Law Enforcement and Administration of Justice argued for the legitimacy of arrest discretion:

> the police should openly acknowledge that, quite properly they do not arrest all, or even most, offenders they know of. Among the factors accounting for this exercise of discretion are the volume of offenses and the limited resources of the police, the ambiguity of and the public desire for

nonenforcement of many statutes and ordinances, the reluctance of many victims to complain and, most important, an entirely proper conviction by policemen that the invocation of criminal sanctions is too drastic a response to many offenses.[25]

Only when the "false pretense of full enforcement," to use Davis' words,[26] is put to rest and the acknowledgement made that the police do have a decision problem (that is, a choice) with respect to arrest, can the goals, alternatives and information requirements of arrest decisions be defined clearly.

GOALS AND ALTERNATIVES FOR ARREST DECISIONS

If it is agreed that police do not serve a purely mechanistic function of invoking law whenever they have the opportunity to do so, then the question arises as to the decision goals that are pursued by arrest or its alternatives (including doing nothing) in individual cases. A moment's reflection demonstrates that each of the classic aims of criminal law—desert, incapacitation, treatment, and general deterrence—often can be the aim of the decision.[27] Adding to the complexity of decision goals are the requisites of practicality, personal utility, and efficiency. Wilson describes the often conflicting goals and the immensely difficult balancing problem in an arrest decision as a cost-benefit analysis:

> his actual decision whether and how to intervene involves such questions as these: Has anyone been hurt or deprived? Will anyone be hurt or deprived if I do nothing? Will an arrest improve the situation or only make matters worse? Is a complaint more likely if there is no arrest, or if there is an arrest? What does the sergeant expect of me? Am I getting near the end of my tour of duty? Will I have to go to court on my day off? Will the charge stand up or will it be withdrawn or dismissed by the prosecutor? Will my partner think that an arrest shows I can handle things or that I can't handle things? What will the guy do if I let him go?[28]

Ignoring for the moment the idiosyncratic aims of the decision, the achievement of both utilitarian aims (crime control) and desert aims clearly are involved in many arrest decisions. That is, the general questions posed by Wilson may be analyzed according to the specific aim of intervention. Concern for the future behavior of the suspect if no arrest is made might be construed as the pursuit of the goal of incapacitation. If the suspect is not taken into custody, will he continue to offend? Consider again the case of a domestic assault.

A principal concern in the police intervention typically is whether an arrest is needed to preclude future (perhaps imminent) violence by the offender.

Treatment (rehabilitation) might similarly be a crime control aim of specific arrest decisions. Does the officer's observation indicate that, as an alternative to arrest, family counseling will reduce future domestic disturbances? Should a young person be arrested so that the family court can take appropriate treatment intervention? Should a youth apprehended for shoplifting be arrested, or will a talk with his parents suffice to prevent future occurrences?

General deterrence—the prevention of crime in the general population by means of sanctions applied to offenders—commonly is regarded as a dominant aim of the criminal law. Certainly it has been central to many analyses of arrest decisions and police work generally.[29] It clearly is an aim in many arrest decisions, as when an officer decides to arrest a youth for vandalism in an area with recent widespread vandalism. A deterrence aim may be pursued more generally as one component in most arrests for serious crimes.

Although most of the commentary on the goals of arrest decisions has focused on these crime reduction, or utilitarian aims, desert is surely a major aim as well. Put simply, people should not be arrested unless they deserve it on the basis of their behavior.

But what does it mean to "deserve" an arrest? Part of the meaning of desert in this context must reflect the fact that an arrest is, in itself, a type of sanction. Fundamentally, it deprives a person of liberty and the freedom of action. It connotes a stigma that derives from the circumstance that a person's behavior was seen by someone—a police officer—as violative of commonly ascribed legal norms. Certainly it does not take extended argument to demonstrate that an arrest, analogously to but to a lesser extent than conviction and sentencing, is a negative sanction. Thus, a concern for the goal of desert in arrest decisions is a concern that the sanction not be applied to the "unworthy"—those whose behavior does not justify the deprivation of liberty and the initiation of the criminal process against the suspect.

The concern with the goal of desert is perhaps most apparent in the legal standards that must be met before an arrest can be made. Thus, "probable cause" and "reasonable grounds to believe" are phrases that seek to justify the sanction of arrest in a specific case on the basis of the *behavior* of the suspect.[30] To some degree, desert is thus seen as a threshhold requirement for an arrest.

Concern about the goal of desert in arrest decisions, however, is not confined to the standards predicating an arrest. This goal is involved also when an arrest is not made, when an officer decides that the consequences of an arrest to the offender would be too severe given the nature of the criminal behavior. Consider again the case of a youth convicted of shoplifting; if it is a first offense and a relatively trivial event, an officer may decide that arrest and possible prosecution is too severe a penalty. Or consider again a domestic assault. In some such events it may be clear that the "victim" may share culpability with the "offender" for the behavior, and as a consequence, the officer on the scene may decide not to arrest, perhaps for reasons of desert. Thus, nonarrest decisions often may be attempts to serve the aim of deserved justice.[31]

Our focus on these goals of arrest decisions is intended to raise the requirements of rationality outlined in the first chapter. Certainly it would be an oversimplification to assert a single aim for any such decision or to claim that goals other than those described may not be critically influential. Moreover, these aims are not easily separable in a given specific situation. The identification of common decision aims, however, serves the purpose of raising for discussion and analysis the two other requisites of rational decisionmaking—alternatives and information.

The decision not to arrest is one major alternative; but "not arresting" has many forms, ranging from doing nothing,[32] to referral to a private third party (for example, parents), to referral to a public agency (such as a social service agency), to issuing a citation. Each alternative may embody a distinct set of goals and, if rationality is desired, requires study to ascertain whether or not they are achieved.

The range of alternatives available are obviously quite variable, and some will be discussed subsequently when the need for custody is considered. In many jurisdictions, however, for many of the problems that arise from their order maintenance functions, police may be faced only with the alternatives of arrest or doing nothing. One consequence of this may be, as Goldstein has observed, that "For many of these situations the system is clearly inappropriate and, even when appropriate, often awkward in its application. But in the absence of alternatives it is used, and often perverted in its use, in order to get things done."[33]

Quite clearly, the task of deciding whether or not to arrest becomes a much more complicated one once the legitimacy of discretion, the diversity of goals, and the range of alternatives are realized. Problems of diagnosis, classification, and prediction become apparent. Furthermore, the police officer's need for information that links the decision alternatives to the decision goals becomes paramount. Goldstein makes the same point: "Little skill and talent are required to crudely apply a uniform solution (like the criminal justice system) to an array of different problems. Diagnosing a situation and selecting an appropriate method for dealing with it are much more challenging tasks."[34]

Before we investigate the requirements of rationality further, it is important that we pause to consider in some detail how arrest decisions are made. What are the correlates of the decision to take a person into custody, and what do these correlates tell us about the goals, alternatives and information requirements of the arrest decision? Abstract considerations of arrest issues may be most helpful when grounded in an understanding of how the law of arrest is put into practice.

THE DECISION TO ARREST—THE VIEW FROM THE DATA

Social scientists have generated a considerable empirical literature concerning the correlates of arrest. The range of methods used, of the variables considered, and of the levels of abstraction is vast, and it reflects the diversity of approaches found within the disciplines of political science, sociology, psychology, and criminal justice. As a consequence, it is extremely difficult to summarize briefly studies that might bear on the issue of the correlates of arrest decisions.[35] Consequently, this review is restricted by two criteria. First, studies of individual arrest decisions (as opposed to aggregate comparisons of agencies with differing political cultures, for example[36]) should be most informative to our focus in this book on decisionmaking. Second, only systematic empirical research in which an assessment of the relative contributions of various factors on the decision to arrest has been attempted will be reviewed. The latter criterion is in keeping with our focus on the rationality requirements for routine case decisionmaking.

It is convenient to classify the research to be discussed into three generic groups according to methods—observational, simulation, and archival. Studies employing each method have contributed to our knowledge of arrest correlates. Each method has limitations that qualify the inferences that can be made about arrest decisions. Taken together, they tell us a great deal about the principal concerns in arrest decisions. Furthermore, there is some consistency of findings that, given the different methods of study used, increase our confidence about how well the correlates of arrest are known.[37]

Three major observational studies have generated data about how police decide to make an arrest in police-citizen encounters. One of the earliest was undertaken by Piliavin and Briar.[38] They studied the arrest decisions of thirty officers in a juvenile bureau, riding with them on patrol. They discovered that these specialized police officers encountered young people in one of three ways, in increasing order of frequency: (1) the officers discovered a "wanted" youth; (2) an offense was reported to police headquarters; and (3) the officers directly observed youths committing an offense or in "suspicious circumstances."[39] They noted that the alternatives available to the officers in their study were: (1) outright release; (2) release, but with the submission of a report; (3) release to parents or guardian; (4) citation; and (5) arrest.

Piliavin and Briar found that considerable discretion was exercised by the officers in the study. All of the alternatives were employed among the sixty-six cases studied. Their general findings may be summarized succinctly: among the "serious" offenses in their study (about 10 percent of the encounters)—robbery, homicide, aggravated assault, grand theft, auto theft, rape, and arson—police discretion was affected little by factors other than the offense. For "minor" offenses, characteristics of the offender, such as prior record and demeanor (coded as cooperative and uncooperative), seemed to influence the decision to a considerable degree.[40]

Although this study is important for its demonstration of the utility of the observational method and the findings that offense behavior, prior record, and personal characteristics of the offender all influence arrest decisions, inferences from it should be drawn carefully. The police studied were in a specialized unit concerned with the prevention of delinquency, a unit whose mandate included making disposition decisions contingent on the "character" of the youth. Also, the small sample size virtually precludes multivariate analyses of the relative contributions of situational and offender characteristics once the demonstrably relevant variable, "gravity of the behavior" is taken into account.

A similar observational study of police arrest decisions has been reported in a series of articles by Black and Reiss.[41] They placed observers with the police in three cities during the summer of 1966 to record a sample of police-citizen encounters. A large variety of data was collected about the encounters, including how they were initiated (for example, by citizens or by the police) and characteristics of the officers, complainants, and suspects. The police observed were regular uniformed patrolmen.[42]

In their analysis of 281 encounters between police and juveniles (suspects under eighteen years of age) Black and Reiss discovered several correlates of arrest decisions. (This is apart from their discovery of the exercise of considerable discretion: of these 281 encounters only 15 percent resulted in arrest.) First, the legal seriousness of the alleged behavior of the accused youth was correlated strongly with the decision to arrest; "the disposition pattern for juvenile suspects clearly follows the hierarchy of offenses found in the criminal law, the law for adults."[43] Second, they discovered that arrest decisions for nonfelony cases were correlated with the complainant's preference regarding arrest, with the presence of evidence linking the suspect with the crime, and with the suspect's degree of respect for the officer (with the very respectful and the very disrespectful more likely to be arrested.)[44]

Quite similar findings, based on considerably fewer cases, were reported from this observation study by Black for adults.[45] Again, the legal seriousness of the alleged behavior was an important correlate of the arrest decision. Felonies that were citizen initiated were nearly twice as likely to result in an arrest, as were misdemeanors that were citizen initiated.[46] The preference of the complainant was found again to be correlated with the arrest decision. For felonies in which the police-citizen encounter was initiated by citizens, only 10 percent resulted in an arrest when the complainant preferred no arrest, compared to 74 percent when an arrest was preferred.[47] Arrests were also less likely to be made when the victim and offender were known to one another than when they were strangers. For felonies, blacks were more likely to be arrested than were whites, a correlation that seemed attributable to the amount of "respect" shown to the police during the encounter—that is, Black and Reiss concluded that blacks were more likely to show "disrespect" and the "disrespectful" were more likely to be arrested.

Friedrich, in a reanalysis of some of these same observational data using multivariate techniques, added further findings to the correlates of the arrest decision.[48] Combining the juvenile and adult cases, Friedrich again demonstrated the influence of seriousness on the arrest decision.[49] Furthermore, he found a sizeable correlation between arrest and the type of evidence present in the encounter; as the "strength of the evidence" varied from "none" to "citizen testimony" to "reasonable evidence" to "police witness," the likelihood of arrest generally increased.[50] Friedrich did a multiple regression analysis, treating arrest as the dependent variable and entering as independent variables the seriousness of the alleged behavior, evidence, citizen characteristics (race, class, sex, and age), citizen behavior (for example, preference about arrest), and the number of persons present. By far the strongest correlate when these factors were considered simultaneously was the seriousness of the offense. (Friedrich comments that the "coefficient for this factor—greater than that for any other—reveals it to be the primary determinant of whether or not an offender is taken in."[51]) Characteristics of the suspects demonstrated virtually no multivariate relation to arrest; the only variable with an appreciable effect other than seriousness was the preference of the complainant.

A third body of systematic observational data was collected and analyzed by Sykes and his colleagues.[52] The basic correlates of the arrest decision described in the Black and Reiss data were in evidence also in the data presented by Sykes.

In a sample of 3000 police-citizen encounters observed during the course of their research Sykes and his colleagues found that in only 520 nontraffic offenses was an alleged violator present when the police arrived. Again, considerable discretion concerning arrest was found; in less than one-third of the encounters in which an arrest could have been made was an arrest actually made. The influence of offense seriousness was again demonstrated. When a felony was involved, an arrest almost always was made.[53] Among those cases not involving felonies, Sykes and his colleagues found that several other factors were correlated with the decision to arrest—among which were the suspect's politeness and anger.

In a study with these data that focused only upon drunkenness offenses, Lundman again found considerable arrest discretion. Of such encounters that could have ended in arrest, only 31 percent did. The "disrespectful," native Americans, and those who were drunk in public places were found more likely to be arrested.[54]

Lundman, Sykes, and Clarke reported a replication study of the Black and Reiss study of juvenile arrests. The consistency of the results between the two pieces of research is remarkable: most police encounters with juveniles are in response to citizen initiative; most such encounters are "legally minor"; the probability of such an encounter resulting in arrest is quite low (of the 200 encounters studied, only 16 percent ended in arrest); legal seriousness is a strong predictor of arrest (for example, all of the felony encounters, but only 5 percent of the "rowdiness" encounters ended in arrest); the presence of evidence increased the probability of arrest; the preference of the complainant was associated with the probability of arrest; arrest differences by race appeared to be a function of the preference of the complainant; and suspects who are either unusually respectful or unusually disrespectful are more likely to be arrested.[55]

The consistent finding in these observational studies that the seriousness of the alleged behavior is a strong correlate of the arrest decision may come as no surprise.[56] As we argue later in this book (see Chapter 10), the gravity of the behavior facing decisionmakers in the criminal justice system is a factor seen to be relevant to each of the common major aims of these decisions (desert, deterrence, incapacitation, and rehabilitation). As shown in Chapter 2, it largely conditions victim's decisions to report an offense to the police. Subsequent chapters demonstrate that "offense seriousness" influences greatly the decisions of each of the other major decisionmakers in the system as well.

That the complainant's preference appears to have a large effect in arrest decisions underscores the point made earlier that citizens play a major role in decisions about what types of cases will proceed through the criminal justice system. A major reason for this influence here undoubtedly derives from the requirements of subsequent processing; police are aware that successful prosecution of suspects requires the active participation of complaining witnesses. There is little to be gained by an arrest for an offense when the complainant prefers to drop the matter, because prosecution will be futile. This does not deny the importance of this factor, however; citizens may request police service in a variety of situations in which an arrest is possible but not desirable. The complainant may desire only the cessation of the offending behavior, for example, and this is a circumstance that underscores the need for discretion and alternatives.

The role played by suspect characteristics and suspect demeanor, judging by these observational studies, is smaller in its influence on arrest than are the seriousness of behavior and the requirements of subsequent processing. The influence of these "extralegal" attributes seems confined to the less serious events (a finding that parallels what was found about victim decisions to report to the police).[57] Nettler has made a similar observation:

> For those localities in which the matter has been studied, official tallies of arrests do not seem to be strongly biased by extralegal considerations. These studies confirm common sense. They indicate that if you are apprehended committing a minor offense, being respectful to the police officer may get you off. If, on the other hand, you are apprehended for a minor violation and you talk tough to the "cop," the encounter will probably escalate into arrest. However, if you are caught in a more serious crime—if, for example, you are found robbing a bank—being respectful to the police is not likely to keep you from being arrested.[58]

Despite some consistency with which these observational studies portray the major correlates of the arrest decision, they must be interpreted cautiously. The observational method has well-known limitations, including potential bias associated with the presence of an observer, potential problems of interobserver and intraobserver reliability, the difficulty in achieving very large samples for rare events (such as an arrest), and problems associated with the interpretation of the factors most determinative of the decision and the control of extraneous variance in natural "experiments."

Some of these problems are overcome by a second type of research study that has examined the correlates of arrest by means of simulation exercises. (Simulations can better control some forms of extraneous variance, since all decisionmakers may be exposed to the same factors, but they may involve other problems, including generalizations beyond the confines of the experiment to natural settings. Unfortunately, very few high quality simulation studies have been reported.) In one such study, Sullivan and Siegal presented twenty-four police officers with data items about the offense and offenders to determine which specific items were most often seen to be relevant to the arrest decision.[59] The items were selected sequentially by specific headings; thus both the number of items requested and the order in which they were requested could be observed.

They found that the number of individual data items requested by the police officers was small (five, on the average). Furthermore, the type of offense was the single most sought after item; twenty-three of the twenty-four officers selected it first. Sullivan and Siegal also concluded that the next most important item was the attitude of the offender. These results are certainly compatible with the findings from the observational research cited above.[60]

A third type of study that bears on the police exercise of discretion uses archival data to track the cases in which an arrest has been made (or in which a complaint has been made) and attempts to discover what happens to them and why.[61] Although several studies of this type have been undertaken that focused exclusively upon youth, data recently have become available for some criminal justice systems as a whole.[62]

Two studies especially pertinent to the problem of rationality in arrest decisions attempted to determine the reasons why some arrests never resulted in prosecution. Forst, Lucianovic, and Cox used data from the PROMIS system in Washington, D.C., to trace arrests through to conviction.[63] They found a sizeable amount of attrition from arrest to prosecution. Of the 17,500 arrests in 1974, only 30 percent resulted in some conviction. Forst and colleagues studied the factors associated with arrests that did and did not result in conviction. They discovered that those cases that tended not to result in conviction were supported by less evidence at the time the case was brought to the prosecutor. In other words, arrests were more likely to result in conviction if evidence was obtained by the police, and the evidence obtained by the police tends to be the most critical evidence in terms of conviction. Forst and colleagues also discovered that convictions were more probable for those arrests in which the police found witnesses to the crime.

Not surprisingly, the Forst data revealed also that the amount of delay between the offense and an arrest was related to subsequent conviction. The shorter the delay, the greater the chance of conviction, a relation that appeared to result from the enhanced ability of the police to recover tangible evidence when the delay was short.[64] But a perhaps unexpected result of their study was the discovery that convictions were more likely to result from offenses occurring between strangers than in similar offenses between nonstrangers. This finding held for both violent crimes and nonviolent property offenses.[65]

Forst and colleagues also studied the characteristics of officers whose arrests tended to result in conviction. They discovered considerable variability among officers in the rates with which their arrests led to conviction—that is, 15 percent of the officers who made arrests accounted for over one-half of all arrests that led to conviction. Although experienced officers tended to have higher "conviction rates" for their arrests, these rates were not found to be tied closely to the officer's age or sex but somewhat to their residence and marital status.[66]

This study by Forst and his colleagues is in a sense prototypical of the kinds of studies that are needed routinely if rationality is to be enhanced in police decisions. That is, a goal needs to be identified (in this case the "goal" might be considered to be conviction), and data need be studied that relate decisions in specific cases with the "goal."[67] The results of such research can then be "fed back" to decisionmakers for use in future decisions. Such research, of course, is not likely to resolve all of the questions and issues pertaining to the decision to arrest. For example, conviction is certainly not the only "goal" involved in these complex decisions. And, the Forst data suggest that much remains to be learned about the correlates of even this "goal." But consider for a moment the wealth of ideas that are both addressed and stimulated by their research, all of which relate to the concept of rationality in relation to the "goal" of conviction:[68]

- Should more or less effort be expended by police officers at the scene in gathering evidence and discovering witnesses?
- Are the alternatives to arrest for nonstranger crimes adequate?
- Are residence requirements for police related to an optimization of convictions?

- Should a major effort be expended in follow-up investigations that attempt to secure evidence?
- Can the procedures and techniques used by the small group of officers who seem to make a disproportionate share of the arrests that end in conviction be identified and generalized?

Research, such as that accomplished by Forst, Lucianovic, and Cox, that measures the relation between data items and goals (and, hence, produces information) is sorely needed to assess and to enhance the rationality of arrest decisions.

A similar study, with some consistent findings, was undertaken by the Vera Institute of Justice.[69] The outcomes of 1888 felony arrests in New York City in 1971 were studied. The probability that a felony complaint made to the police will result in arrest appeared to be about one in five; of the 501,951 felonies reported to the police, there were 100,739 felony arrests. (Of course, as these authors note, this probability should not be interpreted too literally. For example, one arrest may "clear" numerous complaints, and some arrests made in later years may "clear" some complaints.) As shown in Figure 3-1, the Vera study found considerable variability in the ratios of reported felonies to arrests according to the type of offense under consideration. Thus, the ratio is relatively small for homicide and relatively large for burglary.

In their examination of the "attrition" of these felony arrests (for example, by police dismissing charges, the prosecutor deciding not to charge, subsequent *nolle prosequi*, and acquittals) the Vera workers discovered several things comparable to the findings reported by Forst, Lucianovic, and Cox and added some others. A major influence of the suspect's prior record was found,[70] and the relation between the suspect and the victim again was demonstrated to play an important role. With respect to the latter finding, the Vera study reported that in half the felony arrests for crimes against the person and in a third of the crimes against property, the victim had some prior relationship with the arrestee. These cases tended disproportionately to be shunted from further processing. The authors infer from these results that:

> At the root of much of the crime brought to court is anger—simple or complicated anger between two or more people who know each other. Expression of anger results in the commission of technical felonies, yet defense attorneys, judges and prosecutors recognize that in many cases conviction and prison sentences are inappropriate responses. . . . Because our society has not found adequate alternatives to arrest and adjudication for coping with inter-personal anger publicly expressed, we pay a price.

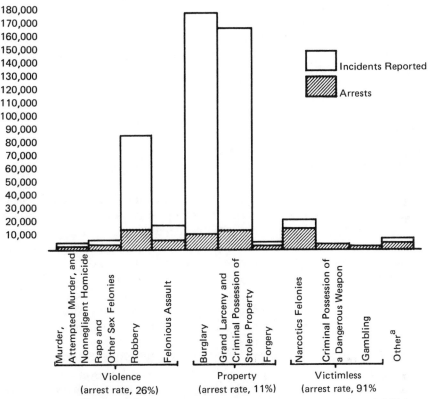

aIncludes kidnapping, coercion, arson, perjury, bribery, bail jumping, falsifying records, and so forth.

Source: New York City Police Department, "Crime Comparison Report" (for December 1971), and NYPD Crime Analysis Section, "Key Sheets" (for December 1971). Vera Institute of Justice, *Felony Arrests: Their Prosecution and Disposition in New York City's Courts* (New York, 1977).

Figure 3-1. Felonies reported to the police and persons arrested for felonies, by type of felony.

The price includes large court caseloads, long delays in processing and ultimately, high dismissal rates. . . . The congestion and drain on resources caused by an excessive number of such cases in the courts weakens the ability of the criminal justice system to deal quickly and decisively with the "real" felons, who may be getting lost in the shuffle.[71]

Systematic empirical studies such as these of the Vera Institute and of Forst and his colleagues can suggest where alternatives to arrest are most needed. They can help to discover also the reasons for the outcomes of arrest decisions, and such reasons often can be useful in the design of programs to enhance rationality (see Chapter 10). Clearly they are preferable to bald statements about inherent and irreducible goal conflict among decisionmakers (for example, between the police and the courts). The potential gains in rationality that may attend such interagency feedback are substantial.

ALTERNATIVES TO ARREST—ASSESSING THE NEED FOR CUSTODY

One common feature of all arrests is the taking of the suspect into custody. In large part, this is simply a by-product of the way in which the criminal justice process is initiated against an accused person in the typical case. But it is certainly possible to separate, for purposes of analysis, two common features of arrest decisions—the taking of custody and the initiation of the criminal justice process. Then the issue of custody may be used as the subject of an analysis of the requirements of rationality, in which the relation of goals, information, and alternatives may be assessed in some detail.[72] The problem of custody is particularly informative in this respect because it has stimulated important work concerning alternatives to arrest decisions.

Technically, the standard that guides the decision to arrest is silent with respect to custody concerns. The "reasonable grounds to believe" criterion may reflect a concern for desert (as noted above), but it gives no guidance about the need for custody.[73] How, then, is the decision about custody to be made? On the basis of what criteria?

Raising these questions helps make it clear that decisions about custody in the arrest situation are predictive decisions. As such, the requisites of prediction (discussed in Chapter 1), particularly with respect to validity, apply. That is, predictive judgements imply a criterion (for example, appearance at later proceedings or the cessation of an ongoing victimization) and a relation between this criterion and elements of the case. The test of validity is in how well these elements are related to the criterion.

The objectives (criteria) of taking a suspect into custody (apart from initiation of the process) are many. One study that investigated the objectives of custody in the arrest decision identified four generic functions—preventive, demonstrative, administrative and investigative, and social-medical.[74] Among the "preventive" objectives are ensuring the presence of the accused at later proceedings and ensuring that future crimes are avoided. The latter objective would include arrests made with the specific aim of stopping an ongoing victimization, as well as the prevention of crimes other than the one for which the police became involved in the first instance. "Demonstrative" functions of custody involve the use of arrest as a specific deterrent—that is, to impress the arrestee of the seriousness of his behavior and to warn of the consequences if it continues. Administrative and investigative functions of custody may involve the needs to gather evidence, search, or conduct line-ups. Finally, the social-medical functions involve the taking of custody to provide treatment services or medical attention.[75]

With the possible exception of the administrative and investigative functions, these objectives of custody all imply an estimate of future events. Would the suspect fail to appear later if an arrest were not made? Would the assault between husband and wife continue (or escalate) if one of the parties were not physically removed? If some sanction, if only temporary detention, is not applied now will the suspect continue to offend? Will the treatment alternative be helpful in diminishing repeated violations? As such, the test of the validity of these decisions is whether the predictions are accurate—for example, in the absence of custody, would the suspect appear for trial? Would the victimization stop without physically removing the suspect?

In practice, of course, much custody is taken without regard to its necessity (in a predictive sense). In most jurisdictions, the police use arrest as the way in which the process is invoked.[76] And there are critical differences between making custody decisions at the scene of the offense, where errors in prediction can have critical implications, and making these decisions dispassionately at a later time (see Chapter 4).[77] Still, it is informative to ask the question, What criteria are used, in practice, to determine whether there is a need for custody?[78]

Little systematic study has been done to determine either the factors police use when making a custody assessment or, even more critically, the factors that are actually related to the need for custody. On the basis of observations of arrest decisions in three jurisdictions, LaFave was able to identify criteria that seemed to be used when determining that need.[79] Among the factors thought prominent were the seriousness of the offense (those facing graver punishments were thought to be more likely to flee prior to trial), the nature of the offense (numbers writers were thought to be good risks), residence in the community, prior criminal history, and likelihood of conviction. Absent a systematic study of how such factors are in fact related to the concerns of custody, however, they must be considered at best as plausible hypotheses that do not constitute information upon which to make such decisions.

A concern that for many arrests there is no legitimate need for custody has stimulated the growth of alternative mechanisms for initiating the criminal justice process, the most widely discussed of which is the use of citations in lieu of arrest. The call for expanded use of citations is, of course, not new (it was made, for example, by the Wickersham Commission nearly fifty years ago). What is relatively new, however, are studies of the innovative use of citation programs that permit the empirical study of the need for custody and some of the correlates of such need.[80]

One such study concerning the use of police citations has been presented by Berger.[81] The New Haven program described by Berger was an extension of nonmoney bail release programs, in which a suspect facing criminal charges was informed of his rights and then given a citation at the scene of the arrest. The citation included a written promise to appear in court. Data then were collected to ascertain how effective the citation program was as an alternative to arrest, with respect to later appearances in court.[82]

As described by Berger, the aims of the program (which was restricted to misdemeanors) were to reduce the number of arrests in which custody was not required, to reduce police costs by reducing the time and effort inherent in custody decisions (for example, transportation to the station), and to do so without an increase in the proportion of persons arrested (that is, without the citation program being used in addition to the normal arrest procedures rather than instead of them).[83]

The twelve month evaluation data cited by Berger are informative. There was considerable variability among offense types with respect to citation use by the police, but there was no major variability with respect to defendant characteristics (that is, deviations from expectations based on arrest data). But of most interest were the relatively low rates of cited persons failing to appear in court. For criminal offenses the proportion appearing was 86 percent; of those not appearing at the proper time a follow-up letter induced over half to appear the next week.[84] The project thus appeared to demonstrate that a sizeable number of persons need not be taken into custody in order to effectively initiate criminal prosecution against them. To the extent that such persons ordinarily would be taken into custody because of predictions that they would not appear if custody were not taken, these errors of prediction are avoided.[85]

There is an obvious need for detailed study of the factors that influence custody decisions and the factors that are actually predictive of custody need.[86] To be most informative, studies of the latter issue should be conducted to the extent feasible as experiments, with observations made of both experimental (released) and control (custody) groups randomly assigned, and should include follow-up data. With careful planning and monitoring, such studies could assess the custody need not only with respect to appearance at later proceedings, but with respect to the incapacitative aims of many custody decisions as well. The validity of restricting alternatives to misdemeanors also is in need of study. Properly designed, the results of such studies could add critical information to aid police in this difficult decision if the results of such research were incorporated into policy guidelines designed to enhance the rationality of arrest decisions. We will return to a detailed discussion of the development of systems specifically for such purposes in the final chapter.

ALTERNATIVES TO ARREST—ASSESSING THE NEED TO INITIATE THE CRIMINAL JUSTICE PROCESS

The second common feature of arrest decisions (the component of initiating the criminal justice process) is also of fundamental importance. Thus, we may ask what is known about alternatives to arrest that have as their aim the avoidance of the criminal justice process. Such an inquiry involves a discussion of the police "diversion" literature.

The rationales for diversion from further criminal justice processing are as diverse as the aims of the criminal justice system. Many programs have an explicit crime reduction aim: the implicit theory underlying many diversion programs is that processing through the system is itself criminogenic. Thus, recidivism will be less if this process is avoided. Many juvenile diversion programs adopt this rationale.

For other programs, there is a desire to avoid the costs involved in traditional criminal justice processing: the implicit theory underlying many diversion programs is that an economy of resources may be served if minor cases are not processed by the criminal justice system, leaving the system to deal more efficiently with the most serious cases.

For still other diversion programs, the criminal justice process is thought to be an inappropriate response to the behavior: the implicit theory underlying many of these programs is that a medical or social welfare response is more suited to alleviate the behavioral problem than is the criminal justice response. Many diversion programs aimed at alcoholic or other drug-dependent persons adopt this rationale.

The number of police diversion projects, many of which cannot be sorted neatly into the foregoing classification, is rapidly increasing. Although a detailed review of this literature is beyond the scope of this chapter,[87] some common results from this literature may be noted. First, most diversion programs are designed for juveniles, a situation that perhaps demonstrates the dominance of the first rationale for diversion. Second, and unfortunately, the number of diversion projects that provide clear and measurable definitions of purpose, adequate research designs for an assessment of the achievement of purpose, and sufficient data for an evaluation of both intended and unintended consequences of the program are very few. As a consequence, the information that most diversion projects supply the decisionmaker is meager.[88]

Third, there is some evidence to suggest that many diversion programs become, in practice, extensions of the criminal justice system rather than an alternative to arrest. Klein and associates found, for example, a tendency for those youth in police-citizen encounters who would not be arrested normally (for example, the young, the minor offenders, and those without prior records) were the persons most likely to be selected for diversion:

> while there is clearly a desire in some police departments to divert juveniles from the system, the more common feeling is that referral should be used as an alternative to simple release. In short, the meaning of diversion has been shifted from "diversion from" to "referral to". Ironically, one of the ramifications of this is that in contrast to such earlier cited rationales for diversion as reducing costs, caseload, and the purview of the justice system, diversion may in fact be extending the costs, caseload and system purview even further than had previously been the case.[89]

Not all the police diversion programs are equally susceptible to these criticisms. Serious efforts to operationalize the purpose and method of diversion programs and to assess their impact have been made. A notable example is the area of family crises counseling.[90] The findings from some of these studies encourage the belief that arrest alternatives can be effective, for some purposes. Furthermore, some of this research has provided the groundwork for the improvement of these alternatives.

One persistent point involving the issue of decision alternatives pertains to the extent to which the decisionmaker will use them. In addition to the perceived appropriateness of the alternatives to the goals the decisionmaker wishes to maximize, there may be important structural advantages that inhere in normal processing that impede the use of alternatives in specific cases. On the basis of their review of the police diversion literature, Neithercutt and Moseley identified several features of "successful" diversion programs (in the sense that they were actually used by the decision-makers).[91] They discovered that to be successful the alternative must be: (1) physically easily accessible (near where the police are); (2) without paper work; (3) the least time consuming of the alternatives; (4) open at the times the police need them; (5) physically attractive to visit; (6) obviously available; (7) within the scope of police power to use; (8) in a known location; and (9) in communication with referral services. Many of these points may appear obvious, but they often are curiously lacking in the operation of diversion alternatives.

If rationality is desired, the development and availability of alternatives to arrest will not suffice. The simple availability of a choice does not ensure a relation between individual decisions to use the alternative and the goal that is sought. Each of the classifications of common diversion aims described above implies a perceived optimization of some decision goal. The logic underlying the diversion program may seem sound, but the test of soundness that rationality requires is an empirical demonstration that the alternative better serves the purpose of the decision. Thus, whether or not diversion decisions result in less recidivism, fewer costs, or more effective treatment are questions that only data—and not mere implicit theory, plausible hypothesis, or hunch—may answer. And the most convincing data derive from the experimental programs, including a random assignment component and follow-up treatment on both diverted and nondiverted cases. The questions require the empirical identification of factors associated with success in both groups. Quality studies of diversion that permit the assessment of how well these decision alternatives serve common aims of the arrest decision are almost wholly lacking.

It should be noted also that formal diversion programs are only a small part of the diversion that is used routinely by the police every day. Many of these alternatives have never been studied systematically to ascertain their utility. Such studies will not be easily designed nor implemented. They require, at a minimum, the systematic collection of data on arrest opportunities, both when the decision is to use an alternative (do nothing, warn, refer, etc.) and when the decision is to arrest, as well as follow-up data on both. As Goldstein has noted:

> If the police are to fulfill their responsibilities in a fair and effective manner, they must be provided with a set of alternatives, in the form of authority and resources, sufficient in number and variety to enable them to deal appropriately with the situations they commonly confront. This means that informal alternatives now in use must be evaluated-legitimated and refined when necessary, or discarded.[92]

THE ENHANCEMENT OF RATIONALITY IN ARREST DECISIONS

The research reviewed in this chapter suggests that a considerable amount is known about arrest decisions generally. The empirical evidence implies that arrest practices vary by jurisdiction; that the gravity of the infraction against legal norms is a strong correlate of individual arrest decisions; that citizens influence arrest decisions both by calling the police in the first instance and by expressing their preference concerning arrest; that among the less serious offenses, who the suspect is and how he or she reacts to the police may influence arrest decisions; that officer characteristics may not strongly influence individual arrest decisions but that some officers are much more likely than others to produce arrests that result in conviction; that the victim-offender relationship is an important factor in arrests and in subsequent dismissals; that for a large proportion of arrestees the custody need is minimal; and that the quality of evidence gathered at the scene of an arrest has important implications for later decisions. Other common findings could be identified.

The police officer does indeed have a decision problem with respect to arrest. Discretion exists and is a proper component to just and effective arrest decisions. Decision goals may be identified, for particular circumstances, as including desert, as well as predictive concerns such as incapacitation, treatment, and deterrence. The alternatives available are many (although their availability varies considerably by jurisdiction). What is lacking with respect to arrest decisions is mainly the third component to rationality—information. A consideration of rationality requires that we ask how the data related to arrest decision outcomes are related to the goals of that decision.

At the aggregate level, plausible arguments could be advanced that the common correlates uncovered in the studies of arrest serve the purposes of desert and the utilitarian aims of the criminal law. We advance some of these arguments in the final chapter. But the requirements of rationality, as we have defined and used that term, focus our attention on specific cases or "types" of specific cases, on the goal(s) of arrest for that particular case and on the information available to the police in making a decision for that case. Research that can help to answer such questions is only beginning to be done. It involves the systematic tracking of cases beyond the arrest decision (whether or not the decision involves arrest) to see whether or not goals were accomplished. Was the suspect convicted? Why or why not? Did arrest result in higher than expected recidivism? Was the domestic disturbance resolved by referral to a social agency? Answers to such questions are essential if rationality is to be enhanced. And, quite critically, that enhancement can be accomplished only by feeding back the results of that research to the police officers responsible for arrest decisions.

The value of feedback of this sort cannot be overemphasized. Consider the results of the Forst research and the gains in rationality that policies structured on such research might bring. Improvements in rationality are not the only benefits that a research-feedback cycle afford. Such data have the potential of reducing the apparent conflict among components of the criminal justice system and of diminishing the number of decisions based on faulty assumptions about the decisions of other agencies.[93] For example, evidence cited in subsequent chapters documents considerable consistency in the factors used by various criminal justice decision-makers. There is a successive "tightening" along the same criteria as cases move through the system. Police impressions about what prosecutors and judges do might be altered significantly were data feedback systems in place routinely.

Consider the oft-aired complaint by police that much of their work is to no avail because the prosecutor or judiciary dismisses so many arrests. The study by Forst, Lucianovic, and Cox did indeed document this: "What happens after arrest, most often, is that the prosecutor drops the case"[94] But then consider their findings further: "the facts suggest that in most of the cases that were dropped it was appropriate both for the police to make an arrest and for the prosecutor to either refuse it at the initial court appearance or dismiss it after initially accepting it."[95] Differences in standards of proof, relative seriousness, and resources may converge to produce apparent conflict where none exists.

Such interagency tracking and feedback systems are essential also for the identification of circumstances where decision alternatives are necessary. The Forst study and the Vera Institute study, both of which employed a case-tracking method, identified the critical role played by nonstranger crimes and the problems associated with processing such cases. Such findings highlight the need for the discovery of decision alternatives (and then their evaluation) at the arrest stage for disputes between nonstrangers.[96]

The mere existence of discretion in such a critical exercise of state power as arrest raises the problem of abuse. When the common alternatives in a decision are not known publicly when taken, there is the added difficulty of controlling discretion in ways that can minimize abuse. This difficulty has plagued police scholars and has led some to conclude that because of inherent difficulties in control, arrest discretion should be wholly eliminated.

In a sense many problems in discretion control for arrest are analogous to problems at subsequent stages of processing. The identification of rules for decisionmaking that structure choices but do not eliminate the individualization of decisions based on unique circumstances of the case transcends the problem of arrest. But in other respects police discretion to arrest is unique. There are no systematically collected written records that permit the study of decisions not to proceed with full processing (such as exist at all subsequent decisions). And there are profound difficulties even in operationalizing the pool of potential arrestees about whom such decisions are made. Thus, it is nearly impossible to ascertain whether in decisions not to arrest, the decision process operates fairly.

There are, of course, extant mechanisms of control on abuses of arrest discretion. Civil actions brought by the offended citizen against the police, civilian review boards, criminal actions brought against officers who fail to arrest, departmental supervision, and judicial review are all methods that to some extent seek to structure and control arrest discretion. None serves, however, to adequately encompass the range of problems that may arise or to offer specific and public guidance concerning routine arrest decisions. Judicial review by means of the exclusionary rule, for example, serves to constrain only specific behaviors and only for those cases in which prosecution is sought. Civil and criminal actions are costly, make demands on complainants that may be unrealistic, and provide only for *ad hoc* rulemaking. Civilian review boards undoubtedly are useful for some problems (for example, the use of force) but cannot be expected to provide routine arrest policy.[97]

We outline a general model for the control of discretion in Chapter 10 that we believe has considerable potential if applied to arrest decisions. Here we may briefly describe one major difference between our approach and the approach commonly proffered in the literature.

Many scholars recognize that it is the patrol officer who, by default, is the real policymaker within police departments with respect to when to arrest and where to choose an alternative. The absence of clearly articulated policies for the exercise of arrest discretion that can be monitored, however, raises serious issues of accountability, both with respect to abuses of discretion and concerning the achievement of common decision goals.[98] Many proposals designed to increase the visibility of the factors influencing arrest practices and to enhance evenhandedness in arrest decisions have centered on administrative rulemaking by top officers within police departments.[99] The absence of administrative guidelines that structure their discretion turns what for the patrol officer is already a difficult task into a virtual no-win situation. In Goldstein's words:

> the police really suffer the worst of all worlds: they must exercise broad discretion behind a facade of performing in a ministerial fashion; and they are expected to realize a high level of equality and justice in their discretionary determinations though they have not been provided with the means most commonly relied upon in government to achieve these ends.[100]

Our own proposal for the enhancement of rationality in these decisions also focuses on the development of administrative guidelines. But it recognizes that it is the patrol officer who is the principal policymaker now. Our model seeks first to discover the implicit policy that these decisionmakers follow; to make that policy more widely known; and then to debate its propriety and effectiveness, to systematically modify it, and to study the effects of modification as a continuous process of development. The day-to-day decisionmakers in the criminal justice system are the best sources to begin such a process of evolutionary policy development. Decision guidelines built in this fashion, when actually used, can both enhance equity and preserve individualization of justice. Thus we propose a method of rulemaking; our method begins with observation of the behavior of the lower level decisionmakers rather than the "top officers." To be effective, administrative rulemaking needs to be predicated on the policies that currently exist, albeit implicitly.

And that requires empirical studies (of the types reviewed in this chapter) of how arrest decisions are made, of the available alternatives, of the effectiveness of these alternatives, of the specific goals of the various decisions and, most critically, of the relation between case data and the achievement of these goals. We present these ideas more systematically in the last chapter.

NOTES

1. One recent bibliography of works only about police decisions listed 138 entries. See M. Neithercutt and W. Moseley, *Arrest Decisions as Preludes to?: An Evaluation of Policy Related Research*, vol. III (Davis, California: National Council on Crime and Delinquency Research Center, 1974).

2. Of the many scholarly discussions of police work, the three that should be consulted first are: H. Goldstein, *Policing A Free Society* (Cambridge, Massachusetts: Ballinger, 1977); E. Bittner, *The Functions of the Police in Modern Society* (New York: Aronson, 1975); and W. LaFave, *Arrest: The Decision to Take A Suspect Into Custody* (Boston: Little, Brown, and Co., 1965).

3. Bittner, *supra* note 2.

4. The law of arrest is complex and varies, to a limited extent, by jurisdiction. For a discussion of the legal requisites for arrest and the problems inherent in defining arrest for research or analytical purposes, see LaFave, *supra* note 2 at ch. 1. Our definition here is purposefully restrictive (e.g., excluding citizen arrests and arrests of witnesses).

5. *Id.*

6. E. Bittner, "Florence Nightingale in Pursuit of Willie Sutton: A Theory of the Police" in H. Jacob, ed., *The Potential for Reform in Criminal Justice* (Beverly Hills: Sage, 1974), p. 23.

7. A. Reiss, *The Police and the Public* (New Haven: Yale University Press, 1971).

8. See, e.g., E. Cumming, I. Cumming, and L. Edell, "Policeman as Philosopher, Guide, and Friend," *Social Problems* 12:276 (1965); T. Bercal, "Calls for Police Assistance: Consumer Demands for Governmental Service," *American Behavioral Scientist* 13:681 (1970); Reiss, *supra* note 7; and J. Wilson, *Varieties of Police Behavior* (Cambridge, Massachusetts: Harvard University Press, 1965).

9. It clearly would be easy to minimize the impact of the criminal law function of police work on the daily activities and roles of the police. Such an impression, even if generated on the basis of the studies cited above, would be profoundly erroneous. Even though the amount of time police actually spend engaged in criminal law matters such as arrest is small, the impact of this activity on the role of the police is pervasive. See Goldstein, *supra* note 2.

10. Reiss, *supra* note 7.

11. *Id.*

12. Because of these relations, Reiss, *id.*, characterizes citizens as "enforcers of the law."

13. Quite obviously this is something of an overstatement. It applies most convincingly to the crimes of common theft and assault and much less so to the so-called victimless crimes—e.g., prostitution and drug offenses—although some evidence indicates that citizen complaints are equally important in bringing drunkenness offenses to the attention of the police. See, R. Lundman, "Routine Police Arrest Practices: A Commonweal Perspective," *Social Problems* 22:127 (1974). There are other types of criminal behavior for which the police role is extremely limited—e.g., corporate fraud. Here, as in the rest of this book, our discussion pertains principally to the routine common law crimes.

14. See Wilson, *supra* note 8.

15. *Id.*

16. Bittner, *supra* note 6 at 18.

17. *Id.* at 30.

18. The significant exception of course is the use of deadly force. The decision to use deadly force is beyond the intended scope of this chapter. We believe that this decision could, however, be analyzed according to the requirements of rationality employed in this book, particularly with respect to agency policy about the use of deadly force. For extended commentary about deadly force policies and their consequences, see L. Sherman, "Execution Without Trial: Police Homicide and the Constitution," *Vanderbilt Law Review* 33:71 (1980).

19. Bittner, *supra* note 2 at 113.

20. J. Goldstein, "Police Discretion Not to Invoke the Criminal Process: Low Visibility Decisions in the Administration of Justice," *Yale Law Journal* 69:562 (1969).

21. This position has striking analogues to other decisions we discuss in this book. At the sentencing decision, for example (see Chapter 6), recent reform proposals that seek more determinacy and greater consistency would have the legislature define explicitly the penalty that must be given for a certain offense. The motive for determinant sentencing is the same as discussed here for arrests—eliminate discretion by legislation in order to control its abuses. We see the same problems in both solutions. The immense variability inherent in criminal acts, persons, and circumstances precludes the elimination of discretion at both decisions. The inequities that such "discretionless" systems would foster would compel resolution by decisionmakers somewhere in the system. And the problems of low visibility, reviewability, and control would again surface. As we describe in detail in the final chapter, we believe it possible to design systems of decisionmaking that at once both acknowledge the legitimate role of individualized decisionmaking (discretion) and adequately control it.

22. Some may argue that individualized decisionmaking is indeed a value to be pursued by criminal law, but that others (prosecutors or judges) who are elected representatives should be empowered to exercise such discretion or that visibility (and hence reviewability) is enhanced by requiring these latter decisionmakers to exercise such judgments. Such a position has merit, but must be balanced against the impact that arrest decisions per se can involve. Thus, if an arrest would aggravate the situation, unfairly stigmatize the suspect, or otherwise be detrimental to important values, the police may be in the best position to employ discretion.

Police discretion involves a good many activities other than deciding, in a given case, whether to arrest. Whether to enforce a law at all, whether to use force, where to patrol, how to patrol, and so forth are all areas of considerable discretion. Although our focus is exclusively on arrest decisions (as defined earlier), these aspects of police discretion are critically in need of study. See, Goldstein, *supra* note 2 at ch. 5.

23. Decision problems such as these are far from uncommon. See the examples and analysis in R. Parnas, "The Police Response to Domestic Disturbance," *Wisconsin Law Review* 1967:914 (1967); and R. Parnas, "Police Discretion and Diversion of Incidents of Intra-Family Violence," *Law and Contemporary Problems* 36:539 (1971).

24. Goldstein, *supra* note 2 at 94. Similar positions are advanced by others. Wilson, *supra* note 8, argues, for example, "Discretion exists both because many of the relevant laws are necessarily ambiguous and because, under the laws of many states governing arrests for certain forms of disorder, the 'victim' must cooperate with the patrolman if the law is to be invoked at all" (at 21). See also LaFave, *supra* note 2 at ch. 3.

Most contemporary standard-setting bodies argue for the acknowledgement of arrest discretion. See, American Bar Association, *Standards Relating to the Urban Police Function*, Approved Draft (Chicago, 1973); National Advisory Commission on Criminal Justice Standards and Goals, *Police* (Washington, D.C.: Government Printing Office, 1973); and President's Commission on Law Enforcement and Administration of Justice, *Task Force Report: The Police* (Washington, D.C.: Government Printing Office, 1967).

25. President's Commission on Law Enforcement and Administration of Justice, *The Challenge of Crime in a Free Society* (Washington, D.C.: Government Printing Office, 1967), p. 106.

26. K. Davis, *Police Discretion* (St. Paul: West Publishing Co., 1975), p. 52. Davis has argued convincingly that discretion in arrests (selective enforcement) is legal.

27. We describe these aims fully in Chapter 6, where sentencing decisions are discussed. Most of the contemporary discussion about the goals of the criminal law has taken place in the context of sentencing. One theme of this book is that these goals transcend a narrow focus on sentencing; they are critically important to the evaluation of victim, police, bail, correction, and parole decisions as well. As we argue in the final chapter, however, any one of these aims is best pursued within the context of specific decision points.

28. Wilson, *supra* note 8 at 84.

29. The general prevention function of police work has received some evaluation attention recently (see, e.g., G. Kelling, T. Pate, D. Dieckman, and G. Brown, *The Kansas City Preventive Patrol Experiment*, Summary Report, [Washington, D.C.: The Police Foundation, 1974]). Although a review of this growing literature is beyond the scope of our inquiry here, it is a critical contribution to the information requirements (as we use that term) for rational police decisions. For a review of this and similar issues, see Goldstein, *supra* note 2 at 44-68.

30. For a discussion of these standards, see LaFave, *supra* note 2 at ch. 1.

31. An extensive discussion of reasons for "noninvocation" in arrest decisions is found in LaFave, *supra* note 2. On the basis of observations in three states, LaFave discovered that some common reasons were: the legislature may not desire full enforcement; there are limited enforcement resources; the victim refuses to prosecute; the victim is involved in the misconduct; to benefit other aspects of law enforcement (e.g., protect the informant system); the harm caused to the offender or to the victim would outweigh the risk of inaction.

32. It may strike some as strange to consider "doing nothing" a major alternative in arrest decisions. But, we agree with Goldstein, *supra* note 2, that "in trying to develop a rational scheme for handling police business, the option of doing nothing should be recognized as an appropriate alternative in some situations" (at 40).

33. *Id.* at 21.

34. *Id.* at 74.

35. Recently, Sherman has provided a classification of research studies concerning police behavior and has reviewed many of their results. L. Sherman, "Causes of Police Behavior: The Current State of Quantitative Research," *Journal of Research in Crime and Delinquency* 17:69 (1980).

36. See Wilson, *supra* note 8, for a study using this analytical approach. For a study that compares the relative influence of community characteristics and type of police organization, see C. Swanson, "A Comparison Of Organizational and Environmental Influences in Arrest Policies," in F. Meyer and R. Baker, eds., *Determinants of Law-Enforcement Policies* (Lexington, Massachusetts: Lexington Books, 1979); and S. Talarico and C. Swanson, "Styles of Policing: An Exploration of Compatibility and Conflict," in *id.* For an interesting approach that considers individual rather than organizational policy styles to be influential, see W. Muir, *Police: Streetcorner Politicians* (Chicago: University of Chicago Press, 1977).

There are considerable difficulties involved in interagency studies of policy correlates of arrest rates, not the least of which involves the definition and subsequent control of extraneous variance. For a review of many of these studies, and discussion of potential limitations, see Sherman, *supra* note 35.

37. Unfortunately for the present purposes, most of the empirical studies of arrest decisions have focused on the arrest of juveniles. We will summarize much of that literature, although it must be stressed that factors operating in adult decisions may differ from those pertinent to juvenile arrests. It seems reasonable to hypothesize that age itself is a major factor influencing the arrest decision. Alternatives to arrest may not only be sought more vigorously for juveniles, but more alternatives probably are available (e.g., referral to parents, to schools, and to social agencies).

38. I. Piliavin and S. Briar, "Police Encounters With Juveniles," *American Journal of Sociology* 70:206 (1964).

39. The proportion of cases falling into these categories is not given. It should be noted, however, that these data indicate that the juvenile officers in this study may not be characteristic of police on patrol, given the widely reported finding that calls to the police, rather than direct observation, is by far the principal way that police become involved in such encounters.

40. Piliavin and Briar, *supra* note 38 at n. 17, do not present tabulations of arrest by specific offense type, and therefore the extent of the relation between offense behavior and the arrest decision cannot be determined. They do report that the importance of demeanor appeared to be much less significant for offenders with known prior records.

41. D. Black and A. Reiss, "Patterns of Behavior In Police and Citizen Transactions," in *Studies of Crime and Law Enforcement in Major Metropolitan Areas* (Washington, D.C.: Government Printing Office, 1967), § 1; D. Black and A. Reiss, "Police Control of Juveniles," *American Sociological Review* 35:63 (1970); D. Black, "The Social Organization of Arrest," *Stanford Law Review* 23:1087 (1971).

Their data have been analyzed also by R. Friedrich, "The Impact of Organizational, Individual, and Situational Factors on Police Behavior" (Ph.D. dissertation, University of Michigan, 1977).

42. As discussed heretofore, Black and Reiss found that the vast majority of police-citizen encounters were initiated by citizens. For juveniles, for example, 72 percent of the encounters were initiated by citizens and 28 percent by policemen on patrol. They comment that "The mobilization of police control of juveniles is then overwhelmingly a reactive rather than a proactive process. Hence it would seem that the moral standards of the citizenry have more to do with the definition of juvenile deviance than do the standards of policemen on patrol." Black and Reiss, "Police Control of Juveniles," *supra* note 41 at 67.

43. *Id.* at 68.

44. The Black and Reiss data show that, within types of crime, black youth were more likely than white youth to be arrested. They attribute this differential not to discriminatory arrest practices by the police, but to differences in arrest preferences by complainants; black complainants tended to prefer arrest more so than white complainants. Black and Reiss commented: "In not one instance did the police arrest a juvenile when the complainant lobbied for leniency. When a complainant explicitly expresses a preference for an arrest, however, the tendency of the police to comply is also quite strong." *Id.* at 71.

45. Black, *supra* note 41. There were only forty-five citizen-initiated felonies and thirty-nine citizen-initiated misdemeanors in this analysis. Thus the findings should be regarded as suggestive only, particularly when more variables than one are examined simultaneously.

46. Most of the misdemeanors in this sample were police witnessed. Since there are no evidence difficulties in police-witnessed events (at least from the police's point of view), they are more likely to result in arrest. Because these events so disproportionately influence the probability of arrest for misdemeanors in this sample, the effect of the "seriousness variable" can be determined only by making comparisons within similar categories (i.e., between citizen-initiated felonies and citizen-initiated misdemeanors).

47. The numbers of cases upon which this comparison was based were eleven and twenty-three, respectively.

48. Friedrich, *supra* note 41.

49. The probability of arrest varied from 57 percent for felonies, to 35 percent for misdemeanors, to 13 percent for traffic offenses, to 3 percent for "disturbances and disputes." *Id.* at 361, Table 7.1.

50. For misdemeanors the respective percentages of arrest were 5, 24, 25, and 41; for felonies they were 4, 58, 83, and 72.

51. *Id.* at 386. Friedrich also examined how well the characteristics of the officers in the study (e.g., race, length of service, and job satisfaction) predicted their arrest decisions in multiple regression analysis. Virtually none of the variance in arrest ($R = 0.014$) was explained by these factors.

52. A number of papers have been generated by these data: R. Sykes, J. Fox, and J. Clarke, "A Socio-Legal Theory of Police Discretion," in A. Niederhoffer and A. Blumberg, eds., *The Ambivalent Force*, 2nd ed. (Hinsdale: Dryden Press, 1976) pp. 171-83; R. Sykes and J. Clarke, "A Theory of Deference Exchange in Police-Citizen Encounters," *American Journal of Sociology* 81:58 (1975); R. Lundman, R. Sykes, and J. Clarke, "Police Control of Juveniles: A Replication," *Journal of Research in Crime and Delinquency* 15:74 (1978); and R. Lundman, "Routine Police Arrest Practices: A Commonweal Perspective," *Social Problems* 22:127 (1974).

53. Sykes, Fox, and Clarke, *supra* note 52, classify two citizen arrests and one "escape" as not involving arrests. If these are considered to be arrests, then arrests always were made in felony encounters.

54. Lundman, *supra* note 52. A similar study of drunkenness offenders that reached similar conclusions is D. Petersen, "Police Disposition of the Petty Offender," *Sociology and Social Research* 56:320 (1972).

55. Lundman, Sykes, and Clarke, *supra* note 52.

56. At least one body of sociological theory, however, posits no relation between decisions made in the criminal justice system and behavioral differences among the clients of the system. For a data-oriented critique of these theories, see M.R. Gottfredson and M.J. Hindelang, "Theory and Research in the Sociology of Law," *American Sociological Review* 44:27 (1979); and M. Gottfredson and M. Hindelang, "Trite But True," *American Sociological Review* (April 1980).

57. A now common practice in the sociological literature is to classify variables into "legal" and "extralegal" categories and to assess their relative contributions to explaining processing decisions. Some such variables are more easily sorted into these classifications than are others (e.g., "amount of evidence" is "legal" and suspect's race is "extralegal"). Others are considerably more difficult to classify. The preference of the complainant certainly has evidence implications, although it is often considered to be an "extralegal" variable. The demeanor of the suspect (e.g., antagonistic) may be perceived (either rightly or wrongly) by the police to be indicative of the need for custody pending adjudication. It also may be a proxy for racial prejudice and, hence, an "extralegal" consideration.

58. G. Nettler, *Explaining Crime*, 2nd ed., (New York: McGraw-Hill, 1978), p. 70. Bittner has made a similar point: For major crimes, whenever the rule is transgressed, there will be an arrest for that reason alone. For less serious events,

however, an arrest might be made but is not determined by the law—these arrests are made within the law but for other reasons. See E. Bittner, "The Police on Skid-Row: A Study of Peacekeeping," *American Sociological Review* 32:699 (1967).

59. D. Sullivan and L. Siegal, "How Police Use Information to Make Decisions," *Crime and Delinquency* 18:253 (1972).

60. A related study is J. Finckenauer, "Some Factors in Police Discretion and Decisionmaking," *Journal of Criminal Justice* 4:29 (1976). Finckenauer studied the data important to 209 police recruits in arrest decisions involving "grey areas" of behavior through simulation techniques.

61. We argue in the final chapter that data systems permitting such studies should be in place and studied routinely by police departments as one step toward the enhancement of rationality.

62. Several excellent reviews of the police referral decision for juveniles are available. See, L. Cohen and J. Kluegel, "Selecting Delinquents for Adjudication," *Journal of Research in Crime and Delinquency* 16:143 (1979); T. Hirschi, "Labelling Theory and Juvenile Delinquency: An Assessment of the Evidence," in W. Gove, ed., *The Labelling of Deviance* (New York: Halsted Press, 1975) pp. 181-203; G. Nettler, *supra* note 58 at 64-70. The general findings from this research are compatible with the correlates discussed in the text. In deciding whether to refer arrested juveniles to court, the police seem to rely principally on the seriousness of the alleged behavior and any record of prior illegal conduct. When offense seriousness is controlled, suspect characteristics (e.g., race and social class) appear to play a role in some places at some times, but not as significant a role as does offense. See Chapter 10 for some implications of these findings, along with the correlates of the other major decisions discussed in this book, for conceptualization about the criminal justice process. Although most police referral studies deal with youth, Pope recently studied police referral decisions for a group of adult burglary arrestees in California. The criterion variable was the postarrest decision (by police) to release suspects or to detain them prior to trial. Although the results are restricted to one type of crime (and hence do not permit inferences about whether the crime itself is related to the decision) the results are informative. The single strongest correlate, among those Pope studied, of the release decision was whether or not the suspect had a prior record—those without such priors were more likely to be released. Among those with prior records, the young (under eighteen) and those without a history of drug use were less likely to be released. For those without priors, blacks were more likely to be detained than were whites. See, C. Pope, "Postarrest Release Decisions: An Empirical Examination of Social and Legal Criteria," *Journal of Research in Crime and Delinquency* 15:35 (1978).

63. B. Forst, J. Lucianovic, and S. Cox, *What Happens After Arrest?*, Institute of Law and Social Research (Washington, D.C.: Government Printing Office, 1977). For a description of PROMIS data, see Chapter 5.

64. Forst, Lucianovic, and Cox, *supra* note 63 at 93.

65. Although we discuss it at length in Chapter 10, it can be noted here that the victim-offender relationship seems to play a critical and persistent

role in decisions across the system. When the victim and offender are strangers, the victim seems more likely to report the offense (Chapter 2), the police to arrest, and the arrest to end in conviction.

66. There are, of course, numerous confounding factors—such as type of assignment—that could condition these results. These are acknowledged, and, within the limits of the data, explored by Forst, Lucianovic, and Cox, *supra* note 63.

67. We put quotations around goal here because we are using the term in a different context than we do usually in this book. Conviction may be better thought of as an objective—that is, as one method of achieving the aims of desert, deterrence, and the like that are associated typically with decision goals in this book.

68. Many of these are suggested by Forst, Lucianovic, and Cox, *supra* note 63.

69. Vera Institute of Justice, *Felony Arrests: Their Prosecution and Disposition in New York City's Courts* (New York, 1977).

70. Compare with the findings from the referral studies cited in note 62, *supra*.

71. *Supra* note 69 at xv.

72. Certainly not every arrest is made with the objective of further criminal justice processing in mind. For a sizeable number of arrests there is no intention of prosecution, but rather the arrest is made to serve some immediate incapacitation objective (e.g., in domestic assaults) or a treatment objective (e.g., the chronic inebriate). Thus, the distinction is a crude one. Note, however, that in these exceptions, the concept of custody may be involved critically (as discussed in the text subsequently). For a thorough discussion of arrests with no prosecutorial intent, see LaFave, *supra* note 2 at pt. V. See also F. Feeney, "Citation in Lieu of Arrest: The New California Law," *Vanderbilt Law Review* 25:367 (1972).

73. LaFave, *supra* note 2.

74. Asher and Orleans, "Criminal Citation as a Post-Arrest Alternative to Custody for Certain Offenses," unpublished paper cited in M. Berger, "Police Field Citations in New Haven," *Wisconsin Law Review* 2:382 (1972). See also, LaFave *supra* note 2.

75. A somewhat separate, yet nevertheless important issue is the question of how much detention is necessary to serve the objective at hand. For a good discussion of the ways in which the need for custody interacts with legal requirements about investigative functions, see LaFave, *supra* note 2.

76. *Id.*

77. *Id.* A consideration of errors in predictive judgments is important here, as with most criminal justice decisions. We take up this topic in detail in Chapter 4, where pretrial detention decisions are discussed. Much of what we say there is indeed applicable to predictive custody decisions at the arrest stage. And the omnipresence of predictive judgments throughout the system weighs heavily in our model designed to enhance rationality, presented in Chapter 10.

78. At one level, it may be argued that the custody dimension influences the type of cases in which arrests are even contemplated by the police. That is,

some offenses, such as landlord-tenant disputes or shoppers defrauded by a business, are always dealt with by referral of the complainant to the prosecutor. Bittner, *supra* note 6, for example, argues: "I believe the police tend to avoid involvement with offenses in which it is assumed that the accused or suspected culprits will not try to evade the criminal process by flight" (at 24). Even granted the validity of this perspective, the predictive aspect of custody decisions at arrest is still present among those for whom arrest is the method of invoking the law. Thus, the validity of these predictive judgments is an issue. Historically, the distinction Bittner draws may have emerged from the common law practice of arresting (detaining) all felons because they were largely capital crimes. As penalties changed over time, and as new felonies were added that had less severe penalties, detention in fear of flight became less of an issue. At one time arrest was even the normal method by which defendants were brought before the court in civil cases. See, Berger, *supra* note 74, esp. n. 21.

79. LaFave, *supra* note 2.

80. In addition to the Wickersham Commission—National Commission on Law Observance and Enforcement, *Report on Criminal Procedure* (Washington, D.C.: Government Printing Office, 1931)—others who have considered the custody question have called for increased use of citations. See, President's Commission on Law Enforcement and Administration of Justice, *Task Force Report: The Courts* (Washington, D.C.: Government Printing Office, 1967).

81. Berger, *supra* note 74.

82. The citation program described by Berger is a procedure for police-initiated field release; although discussed as an alternative in the text, technically, an arrest is made (i.e., there is detention of the accused) but release is by the police in the field. This procedure should be distinguished, technically, from citations prior to arrest, in which no custody is taken. This latter approach may involve questions pertaining to the legality of searches. See *id* at 382. An important distinction between the use of summons to appear and citations should be drawn also. As described by Berger:

> The criminal summons . . . is one means to secure on the scene release of a criminal suspect. The process involves judicial or prosecutorial issuance of a summons to appear in lieu of an arrest warrant. The summons is served upon the suspect, directing him to appear in court on a specified date. There is no formal arrest, nor any detention of the suspect . . . . Although the summons is a useful tool, its applicability is severely limited, primarily because it cannot be employed without prior judicial or prosecutorial approval. Thus the summons process offers merely an alternative to the arrest warrant procedure and is useless in handling on site violations where arrests can be made without warrants.

Id. at 389.

83. Certain classes of offenses were excluded from the program. *Id.* at 399–401.

84. *Id.* at 407.

85. Although not usually discussed in this context, these errors are "false positive" errors. One importance of false positive errors is that they are hidden errors—in the absence of an experiment, there is no way of knowing for sure how many exist. Because predictive judgments are made throughout the criminal justice system, these errors are an issue at every major decision. Predictive judgments are discussed more fully in our consideration of bail decisionmaking (Chapter 4) where they have received more scholarly attention.

86. To some extent the correlates of arrest decisions, identified in the previous section, are indicative of the presumed need for custody. For example, it may be thought that the more serious the offense and the greater the penalties attendant upon conviction, the greater is the custody need at the arrest decision. Such presumptions are in need of empirical testing.

87. Several recent comprehensive reviews are available: see, Neithercutt and Moseley, *supra* note 1; F. Dunford, "Police Diversion: An Illustration?" *Criminology* 15:335 (1977); M. Klein, K. Teilman, J. Styles, S. Lincoln, and S. Labin-Rosensweig, "The Explosion in Police Diversion Programs: Evaluating the Structural Dimensions of a Social Fad," in M. Klein, ed., *The Juvenile Justice System* (Beverly Hills: Sage, 1976); Goldstein, *supra* note 2 at 77–81; and R. Carter and M. Klein, *Back On The Street—The Diversion of Juvenile Offenders* (Englewood Cliffs, New Jersey: Prentice-Hall, 1976).

88. One review of this literature concludes: "While there seems to be widespread agreement about the desirability of diverting youth from the juvenile justice system and a sizeable mobilization of federal, state and local resources for the development of community diversion projects, little has been done to examine how diversion programs have been operationalized or how effectively they function." Dunford, *supra* note 87 at 336.

89. Klein et al., *supra* note 87 at 10.

90. See M. Bard, *Training Police as Specialists in Family Crisis Intervention* (Washington, D.C.: Government Printing Office, 1970); M. Bard, *Family Crisis Intervention: From Concept to Implementation* (Washington, D.C.: Government Printing Office, 1974).

91. *Supra* note 87.

92. Goldstein, *supra* note 2 at 71.

93. See generally, Davis, *supra* note 26.

94. Forst, Lucianovic, and Cox *supra* note 63 at 71.

95. *Id.*, page 88.

96. As Forst, Lucianovic, and Cox put it: "An especially challenging research issue consists of determining effective ways for the police to deal with criminal episodes among nonstrangers, without resorting to arrest. These episodes have been found to consume a substantial amount of prosecution and court resources with little apparent benefit" (*id.* at 91).

97. For excellent discussions of the problems with and prospects for these various methods of discretion control, see H. Goldstein, "Administrative Problems in Controlling the Exercise of Police Authority", *Journal of Criminal Law, Criminology and Police Science* 58:160 (1967); Goldstein, *supra* note 2 at ch. 5; LaFave, *supra* note 2 at 157–64; and Davis, *supra* note 93.

98. Certainly inhibitions about acknowledging the legitimate role of discretion in arrest detracts from the development of meaningful arrest guidelines. As Davis, *supra* note 26 at iii–iv, has noted:

> The false pretense prevents *open* selective enforcement, prevents top officers from making and announcing enforcement policy, prevents special studies of enforcement policy, prevents the use of professional staffs for making enforcement policy, prevents enlistment of public participation in policymaking, and discourages efforts of the police to coordinate their enforcement policy with the policy of prosecutors and judges.

99. See, for example, American Bar Association, *supra* note 24; Wilson, *supra* note 8; Goldstein, *supra* note 2; Davis, *supra* note 26.

100. Goldstein, *supra* note 2 at 110.

※ *Chapter 4*

Pretrial Release Decisions

Once an alleged offender has been taken into custody
by arrest, it then must be decided whether he or she
will remain in custody pending trial or will be released
(and if so, under what conditions). Traditionally, this decision has
been a responsibility of the magistrate at the initial appearance.
Pretrial release decisions illustrate many of the most important
issues of concern in this book. They must be made in the face of
potentially conflicting goals. At the heart of every pretrial release
decision, the goal of preserving the defendant's liberty before conviction (when he or she is presumed to be innocent) must be
balanced against the goals of community protection and orderly
justice. This difficult juxtaposition of the defendant's interest
in liberty with the community's interest in safety was aptly described by the President's Commission on Law Enforcement and
Administration of Justice:

The importance of this decision to any defendant is obvious. A released
defendant is one who can live with and support his family, maintain his
ties to his community, and busy himself with his own defense by searching
for witnesses and evidence and by keeping close touch with his lawyer.
An imprisoned defendant is subjected to the squalor, idleness, and possible criminalizing effect of jail. He may be confined while presumed
innocent only to be freed when found guilty; many jailed defendants,
after they have been convicted, are placed on probation rather than
imprisoned. The community also relies on the magistrate for protection
when he makes his decision about releasing a defendant. If a released
defendant fails to appear for trial, the law is flouted. If a released defendant commits crimes, the community is endangered.[1]

The difficult issues that arise about the goals of the pretrial release decision are similar to the problems that plague other critical decisions in the criminal justice system. As Goldstein noted:

> Place this problem within the same context as so many of the other critical issues in the criminal justice system; the need for striking a delicate balance between the concern for the protection of society and the desire to guarantee maximum freedom for the individual; the desire to prevent future crimes vs. the desire to allow the suspect to be free prior to trial.[2]

The problem of adequacy of information is clearly in evidence at the pretrial release decision. What data are known to be relevant to the achievement of the goals of pretrial release decisions? Is the information useful for achieving the goal of community protection also useful for attaining the goal of maximum pretrial liberty for the accused? What information about the consequences of pretrial release decisions is available to the decisionmaker?

Pretrial release decisionmaking also serves to illustrate the importance of decision alternatives. For many years, in most American jurisdictions, the principal issue confronting the magistrate at initial appearance was, for those eligible for bail, how much money should be required from the defendant in order that the defendant be released.[3] But the last two decades have witnessed a substantial increase in the decision alternatives available to the magistrate, such that in many areas the judge now may have the option of deciding among outright release on a simple promise to appear in court at the proper time and place (typically referred to as "release on own recognizance" or ROR); release to private third party custody; supervised release; release to some treatment program; release upon deposit of some portion of the bail amount (for example, 10 percent); release upon receipt by the court of the full bail amount; or preventive detention. Each of these decision alternatives may have its own information requirements. And each may embody quite different goals and procedural issues; consider, for example, the likely differences in objectives between fixing the amount of bail and issuing an order for preventive detention.

The variety of decision alternatives that are manifested at the pretrial release decision serve to illustrate also the nature of varied decision consequences. Some of the research examined in this chapter indicates how criminal justice decisions may have consequences (both to the defendant and to the decisionmaker) that go far beyond the immediate outcome of the decision. Apart from the choice of detention and the attendant consequences of that confinement, the decision alternatives available to the magistrate at pretrial release may have quite different consequences with respect to later decisions; thus the decision itself may provide information necessarily considered in rational decisionmaking at a later stage. A concern of researchers in this field has been the ways in which the pretrial decision may influence other important decisions made about defendants, such as the determinations of guilt or innocence and punishment. Indeed, studies of collateral consequences of bail decisions were among the earliest investigations of the interplay among components of the criminal justice system.

Perhaps in no other criminal justice decision is the issue of prediction so centrally involved, so hotly debated, or so difficult to circumvent. Although there is disagreement about the proper goals of the pretrial decision, it generally is agreed that at a minimum the magistrate's task involves a consideration of what conditions (if any) are necessary to assure the defendant's appearance at trial. Many argue that the protection of the community (including witnesses) from additional crimes during the pretrial period is equally important. Because they involve future events, these considerations involve predictions of behavior. As such, they raise all of the issues of reliability, validity, propriety, and consequences that necessarily surface whenever an individual's liberty is conditional on perceptions or measures of what he or she may do in the future.

In this chapter all of these issues will be explored in light of contemporary research findings. Although pretrial release decisions have emerged as a significant area of research activity, it will be shown that much more needs to be known before these decisions can meet the requirements of rationality. There is, indeed, little reason to challenge the assertion made by the National Advisory Commission in 1973 that "among the problems plaguing the criminal justice process, few match the irrationality of decisionmaking, the waste of resources, and the unsystematic efforts at reform that characterize the pretrial period."[4]

SIGNIFICANCE TO THE DEFENDANT

The most obvious potential outcome of moment from pretrial release decisions is the detention or liberty of accused persons prior to trial.[5] The numbers of persons thus affected by such decisions in the United States are extremely large. It has been estimated that pretrial custody accounts for a greater proportion of those incarcerated each year than does imprisonment following sentencing.[6] The 1970 National Jail Census showed that half of the adults and two-thirds of the youth confined in jails on March 15, 1970, were pretrial detainees or other persons not convicted.[7] In an analysis of data from the 1972 "Survey of Inmates of Local Jails" conducted by the U.S. Bureau of the Census, Goldkamp discovered that on a given day, nearly 50,000 persons were detained prior to trial in American jails.[8] Landes estimated that about one in six adults in confinement are persons whose guilt has not been formally established.[9]

These figures take on added significance when read in light of the deplorable conditions found in many American jails. Numerous surveys have characterized jails as the worst aspect of the correctional system, lacking in space, programs, privacy, security, and even cleanliness.[10] Pretrial detainees routinely are housed with convicted persons serving their sentences. It has been found that the incidence of self-destructive behavior among jail inmates is disturbingly high—higher than that found in prisons.[11] A recent survey of pretrial detention issues concluded that "there is no question that the conditions of pretrial detention are typically far worse than prison: more security oriented; less programmed; no job training or education; more restricted access to visitors; less recreation and medical or psychiatric care; more overcrowding."[12]

An unfortunate irony also exists for many pretrial detainees: they are incarcerated prior to trial, when they are presumed to be innocent, but are freed once convicted. The sentence for many jailed defendants does not include imprisonment. Goldkamp found, for example, that 72 percent of the convicted persons in a sample of defendants from Philadelphia were detained prior to trial but were not imprisoned after conviction.[13] Landes, in a study of 858 indigent defendants in New York City, discovered that 34 percent of the detained defendants did not receive additional detention as part of their sentences.[14]

An even greater irony concerns those persons who are detained prior to trial but who are not then convicted. The evidence suggests that a disquietingly large number of persons—as much as half of those confined before trial—fall into this category. In his study of Philadelphia detainees, Goldkamp found that of those defendants detained more than twenty-four hours after arrest, 55 percent were not convicted of anything. And of those defendants detained until their final disposition, 45 percent were not convicted.[15]

THE CONSEQUENCES OF DETENTION

Apart from the fact of imprisonment itself, it has long been argued that detention before trial has numerous adverse consequences to the defendant.[16] Pretrial detention may unduly induce some defendants to plead guilty in order to get freed from confinement. This may be particularly true for defendants charged with minor crimes for which the penalty may not include jail. Also, it is frequently argued that relative to freed defendants, detained defendants are more likely to be convicted and, once convicted, are more likely to be given more onerous punishments (for example, more likely to be imprisoned and more likely to be given longer sentences). There are several hypotheses as to why detention prior to trial may have adverse consequences for the defendant at later stages of the criminal justice process. Detained persons may be less able to prepare adequately for their defense against the charges, because they are less free to consult with counsel, to gather witnesses in their behalf, and to muster the evidence required. There may be, furthermore, psychological consequences of detention affecting decision-makers adversely to the defendant—persons confined may be less "presentable" to the court at trial. The critical legal importance of the pretrial period for persons accused of crimes has been summarized by Wald:

> During this period, defense counsel is retained or assigned, negotiations for dismissal or reduction of charges are carried on, indictments are handed down, motions to sever, to dismiss, to remove, to change venue, and to discover are argued, pleas are settled upon, witnesses are interviewed, evidence is sought, strategy is planned, and presentence reports may be written.[17]

Several empirical studies have been undertaken that shed some light on the question of the adverse effects of pretrial detention on subsequent judicial decisions (such as conviction and sentence). These studies may be categorized into two groups for purposes of discussion: (1) studies that compared the conviction rate and/or typical sentence length for groups of defendants detained prior to trial or not; and (2) studies that compared detention rates and typical sentence lengths for detained and released groups while statistically controlling for factors believed to be relevant to both decisions (that is, both bail and conviction).

The first type of study, perhaps first performed by Morse and Beattie in 1932,[18] is exemplified by research undertaken by Foote, Markle, and Woolley in Philadelphia in 1954.[19] They studied the dispositions of 946 cases, which were all dispositions of the court during a two month period for selected offenses (rape, robbery, arson, burglary, assault, auto theft, property crimes, sex offenses, and narcotics). In comparisons between jailed and bailed defendants for similar offenses, they found that a much higher percentage of jailed defendants were convicted than were bailed defendants (72 versus 52 percent). Furthermore, they discovered that, once convicted, jailed defendants were much more likely than were bailed defendants to be given sentences that included imprisonment (59 versus 22 percent).

Foote and his coworkers cautiously suggested a number of factors that could have influenced the obtained results. They pointed out that such unmeasured variables as judges imposing high bail (with resulting detention) on defendants who were more likely to be guilty or setting high bail where there were substantial factors in aggravation could have a bearing on the interpretation of the results. Nevertheless, they concluded that "[D]espite these unmeasurable variables . . . the contrast in comparative dispositions was so striking that it is reasonable to conclude that jail status had a good deal to do with it."[20]

There is much consistency among studies of this type concerning the influence of pretrial detention on the probability of conviction and the type of sentence.[21] The procedure of simply comparing the dispositions for jailed and bailed defendants, however, leaves substantial room for competing hypotheses. That is, these studies leave us unsure as to whether detention itself is prejudicial or whether the factors that are influential in setting high bail (and hence, detention) are the same factors that lead to conviction or more punitive sentences. Examples of the latter could include factors that increase convictability (and perhaps lead a magistrate to believe there is greater flight risk) or that aggravate the offense (and lead the magistrate to believe the defendant is dangerous).

Unfortunately, in the absence of an experimental design with random allocation to "released" and "detained" groups, there can be no entirely satisfactory resolution of these competing hypotheses. Such a study has not been undertaken; but studies that attempt to approximate such procedures through the use of statistical controls do exist and are informative.

Four studies have looked at the question of the prejudicial effects of detention with the aid of some form of statistical control. Rankin[22] studied a sample of defendants with bail set by a Manhattan felony court. Prior to establishing statistical controls, Rankin found substantial differences in disposition between those defendants who made bail and were set free pending trial and those who spent the pretrial period in jail. The freed defendants were less likely than those jailed to be given prison terms (17 versus

64 percent) and were also less likely to be convicted (27 versus 47 percent).

Rankin then studied the question of whether these findings of prejudice held up once she controlled statistically for factors believed to influence both bail setting and conviction and sentencing. Thus, she studied the relations cited above within categories of prior record, bail amount, type of representation, family organization, and employment history. In each case (family organization and employment history were unrelated to the decisions), the original relation consistent with a prejudicial effect remained. Furthermore, she found that simultaneous controls did not remove the finding of prejudice, leading her to conclude that "[t]hese findings provide strong support for the notion that a causal relationship exists between detention and unfavorable disposition."[23]

A similar study, which reached similar conclusions, was reported by Single.[24] The study was undertaken in conjunction with a suit against the judges of New York City that claimed prejudicial effects of pretrial detention. The study sample consisted of 857 cases drawn from the closed files of the city's Legal Aid Society. Single studied the differences in conviction and sentences between released defendants and those held because of inability to afford bail. In viewing these differences, Single controlled, sequentially, for offense, prior record, weight of evidence, family ties, and employment. Large differences supporting the claim of a prejudicial effect for detention were found consistently.

The results of these two studies, although supportive of the notion of prejudicial effects of pretrial detention, must be interpreted in light of their shortcomings. First, both employ statistical rather than experimental controls, a limitation that subsequent studies have been unable to overcome. Second, both rely on relatively small samples, a problem that is compounded when statistical controls are used. Third, neither sample can be expected to be representative of the population of pretrial defendants; Rankin's study sample excluded persons released on their own recognizance and those denied bail, whereas Single's study sample was comprised only of cases defended by the Legal Aid Society of New York. Fourth, it has been suggested that the procedures used in the Rankin study for simultaneous control of variables was inefficient; Single did not introduce simultaneous controls.[25]

Confidence in the overall findings of these studies, however, is increased by later studies that improved the basic methods but that corroborate, at least to some extent, the finding of a prejudicial effect of pretrial detention on later judicial decisions. Landes studied the same data used by Single (and, hence, his study is subject to the same limitation of the unrepresentativeness of the sample and its small size) using multivariate procedures.[26] Landes' results are partially supportive of a claim of a prejudicial effect of detention. In a series of analyses, Landes regressed the length of defendants' sentences on a number of variables designed to control for sentence determinants, as well as variables measuring pretrial detention. When the dichotomous variable "detained or not detained prior to trial" was studied in a regression analysis in which the length of sentence was the dependent variable and the amount of bond (Landes' proxy for the judge's prediction of sentence length), the seriousness of the offense, and the defendant's prior record were additional independent variables, there was no effect for the detention variable. When, however, the amount of bond was excluded from the analysis (but the offense severity and prior record were left in), detention was correlated with more severe sentences.

Further support for the claim that detention prejudices later decisions came from analyses in which the length of time spent in pretrial detention rather than "detained versus not detained" was the variable used to measure pretrial detention. Landes reasoned that "[i]f pretrial detention has an adverse effect on the outcome [sentence], one might expect that the greater the amount of detention, as measured by days detained, the greater the defendant's sentence."[27] His results supported this reasoning, leading him to conclude that "[p]retrial detention, therefore, has an independent and adverse effect on the defendant's sentence . . . ."[28] An examination of the relative contributions of the variables affecting the defendant's sentence in his study led Landes to conclude, however, that the effect of detention on sentences was not large.

Perhaps the most thorough study of the question of prejudicial effects of pretrial detention on subsequent judicial decisions was undertaken by Goldkamp.[29] In his study based on an estimated 8300 defendants in the Philadelphia Municipal Court, he investigated how pretrial status was related to several possible outcomes of the cases—dismissal, acquittal, pretrial diversion, conviction, and sentence. For each of these outcomes, Goldkamp studied the relation to pretrial custody for the group of defendants facing each decision, while statistically controlling for factors other than detention thought relevant to each decision. Thus, he studied a much more exhaustive array of decision outcomes than had earlier studies. And his sample was drawn to be representative of the Philadelphia pretrial population, thus overcoming, to a degree, the limitations of the Single and Landes studies. Also, the number of cases studied was far larger.

When pretrial status was dichotomized to classify those who were released within twenty-four hours of arrest (by ROR, bail, etc.) versus those who were detained longer than twenty-four hours after arrest[30] he discovered that the persons in the detained group were equally likely to have the charges dropped as were the freed group (33 percent each). The detainees, however, were less likely to be acquitted (8 versus 12 percent) and were less likely to be diverted (7 versus 39 percent), but they were more likely (either as a result of a plea or trial) to be found guilty (46 versus 20 percent).[31]

Goldkamp then used multiple linear regression to see whether these differences were maintained when statistical controls were applied to factors thought to be relevant to both pretrial custody and these later judicial decisions. As controls he entered variables measuring the seriousness of the charge, whether detainers were present, the number of prior arrests, whether the defendant was currently on parole or probation, the number of open cases, and the number of offenses charged. Both the number and complexity of these statistical controls were greater than those used in earlier studies.

The results may be summarized briefly. Pretrial custody appeared to be unrelated to the dismissal decision, unrelated to the diversion decision, and unrelated to adjudication (acquitted versus convicted) once these statistical controls were exercised. Goldkamp concluded that, for this group of defendants, pretrial custody was not influential in these later judicial decisions. Rather, the observed relations between custody status and these outcomes at the bivariate level were thought to be the result of the common association between custody status and the control variables on the one hand and the control variables and judicial decisions on the other.

The final judicial decision studied by Goldkamp was sentencing. Here he studied the range of sanctions given to the defendants in his sample, from fines and suspended sentences to incarceration for several years. Again, at the bivariate level of analysis, marked differences in dispositions were observed between the freed and detained groups. In general, the freed group was more likely to be given probation whereas the detained group was more likely to be incarcerated.

He then undertook two multivariate analyses of the sentencing decision; one considered the decision whether or not to incarcerate, and the other, for those incarcerated, considered how long a sentence was given. He found that whether or not a convicted defendant received a sentence of incarceration was related to pretrial custody, even after the statistical controls were exercised. Those persons detained prior to trial were more likely to be given sentences to prison, although only a weak relation between pretrial custody and sentence length was uncovered.

Goldkamp's study serves to illustrate the complexity of the question of whether pretrial custody affects later judicial decisions. The complexity of pretrial conditions, the variability in judicial alternatives, and the need to construct statistical controls because of the absence of experimental conditions all serve to complicate the answer to this critical question. The latter problem, requiring that inferences be made only from nonexperimental designs, is especially troublesome and inhibits all but the most cautious conclusions.

Nevertheless, some conclusions may be reached on the basis of these studies. First, none have been able to reject the hypothesis that pretrial custody influences sentencing decisions to the detriment of those detained. Despite the best statistical controls possible and with the aid of sophisticated statistical models, each of these studies found, in some form, an effect of detention on sentence. Second, the magnitude of this effect is, from a purely statistical perspective, small. Other factors—principally the offense of conviction and prior record—appear to be much more influential in determining sentence. Third, Goldkamp's study casts some doubt on the existence of a major effect of pretrial custody on whether or not a defendant is convicted; whether Rankin's and Single's data would continue to show such an effect once similar statistical controls were exercised is unknown. It may be, however, that in their data, as in Goldkamp's, judges set bail or other release conditions in part on the basis of factors that also are predictive of conviction.

That none of the available studies shows an absence of prejudicial effects for defendants on subsequent judicial decisions weighs heavily in discussions of pretrial release decisions. In addition to the issues already discussed—the detention of presumably innocent persons, the detention of persons who will not be detained past conviction, and the deplorable conditions found in many places of pretrial detention—the consequences of the pretrial release decision to defendants also appear to include some negative effect on decisions taken later in the criminal justice decision process.

SIGNIFICANCE TO SOCIETY

Particular importance must be ascribed to these decisions, from the standpoint of the community, in view of the conflicting purposes so clearly posed in this decision. On the one hand, freedom from confinement before an impartial adjudication of guilt in which the accused has the opportunity of presenting a defense symbolically and practically embodies the cherished concept of due process of law. As Dill has observed, pretrial freedom is important to society because it "reinforces the adversary nature of the criminal process and underlies other basic procedural guarantees—rights of notice, specific charge, fair hearing, counsel—theoretically granted to all persons accused of crime."[32]

On the other hand, the pretrial release decision may have an impact on the security of the community and the ability of the justice system to operate in an orderly fashion. When a pretrial releasee commits a crime while on release, members of the community are apt to feel that the justice system somehow is not working adequately to ensure their safety. When an accused fails to appear for trial, the justice system is flouted.

Data on the magnitude of these two problems are scarce and of unknown reliability. They are subject to all the problems associated with crime statistics, including undercounting due to unreported crimes, overcounting due to fallaciously charged persons, and variability in definitions. Several surveys, however, have provided some evidence of the scope of these problems.

In a survey of failure to appear rates in seventy-two cities, Wice discovered officially reported rates ranging from 4 to 24 percent, with nearly 90 percent reporting rates of less than 10 percent.[33] Thomas surveyed twenty cities for the years 1962 to 1971, finding that the failure to appear rates for felony defendants ranged from 1 to 15 percent in 1962 and from 3 to 17 percent in 1971.[34] The medians were about 6 percent for 1962 and 11 percent for 1971. The variability among the cities surveyed in definitions of "failure to appear" and in the proportions of people released prohibit all but the most cautious interpretations, but overall, these rates do not appear to be disquieting.

Estimates of the amount of crime committed by pretrial releasees are quite variable. A study of pretrial releasees in Washington, D.C., conducted by the National Bureau of Standards, showed that 17 percent were rearrested.[35] In his Los Angeles study, Gottfredson found a rearrest rate of 5 percent for crimes against the person.[36]

More recently, in a study of the pretrial releasees in the District of Columbia, it was found that of all those released prior to trial in 1975, 20 percent were brought before the court again in 1975.[37]

GOALS OF THE PRETRIAL RELEASE DECISION

With the possible exception of the sentencing decision, perhaps no decision in the criminal justice system has been the object of more recent commentary concerning legitimate aims than has the decision to release or detain defendants prior to trial. The interests at stake in the decision are profound, complex, sometimes contradictory, and hotly debated. Unfortunately, all too often the resulting debates are shrouded by speculation. In most urban courtrooms, the magistrate, sometimes with the aid of probation staff, police, prosecutors, public defenders, and pretrial service agency staff, must weigh these concerns and balance these interests extremely rapidly. The magistrate may receive bail recommendations from the police, the prosecutor, or the public defender, each of whom may be responding to different goals.[38] Data about the defendant, the alleged offense, prior record, income, residence, family life, and the like may be supplied by probation staff. The magistrate may have extensive experience in setting bail or may be a novice. Most typically, he or she will be unsure of how the wealth of data presented relates to the task at hand (much data, little information). Almost never will the magistrate be informed systematically how other judges in the same court—or perhaps even how he or she—decided similar cases in the past. And almost never will the magistrate be informed of how well the goals sought to be accomplished were met: Was the defendant able to make the amount of bail set? Did he or she show up for trial? Was a new offense committed during the period of release? Thus, these important decisions are made rapidly, in large numbers, with little information, and generally without feedback on the consequences.

A discussion of the goals of the pretrial release decision must attend to the confluence of law and social science. The debates about the proper functions of bail are, on the one hand, constitutional in origin and take place as well in the context of state statutes that outline the criteria to be considered by judges in making release decisions. On the other hand, these debates necessarily concern social scientific knowledge about the ability of decisionmakers to make predictive judgements and estimates of the costs involved in errors. As with most decisions in the criminal justice system, symbolic goals and system constraints also enter into discussions of the proper aims of the pretrial decision.[39] Moreover, important latent functions may be served by bail decisions—for example, it has been suggested that bail setting often serves to diffuse the responsibility for the defendant's release.[40] Public criticism of a release decision may be muted by the "excuse" that the defendant was released because he made bail—a latent function perhaps seen as more important in jurisdictions in which judges are elected. Similarly, bail may appear to diffuse responsibility for detention. A magistrate may claim that detention was not intended but rather was a consequence of the defendant's inability to post the amount of bail required to assure appearance for trial.

Most of the controversy about the goals of pretrial release decisions centers on the issues of appearance at trial and preventing new crimes in the interim between arrest and adjudication. The legal arguments address the constitutionality of "preventive detention" and inquire into whether the Eighth Amendment imparts a right to bail.

The most extensive historical and constitutional analysis of the permissible concerns of the bail decision has been undertaken by Foote.[41] He traced the origins of the Eighth Amendment clause that "Excessive bail shall not be required . . ." through English common law to the framers of the Constitution in order to discover the parameters of the "right to bail" and the constitutionally permissible purposes of bail. His analyses lead him to conclude that a right to bail was intended by the framers to be construed broadly, despite certain offenses (capital) that were seen as nonbailable. That the specific language of the Eighth Amendment does not convey this more precisely was the result of an historical accident: "the excessive bail clause was meant to provide a constitutional right to bail and the inadequacy of the form adopted for this purpose was the result of inadvertance."[42] Foote concluded:

> What the precise scope and substance of this right should be under modern conditions neither can nor should be deduced from history. But however such detail may be resolved, the only end which seems consistent with these historical antecedents is that the clause was intended to afford protection against pretrial imprisonment in a broad category of cases.[43]

Furthermore, on Eighth Amendment grounds, on grounds that prediction of dangerousness is inherently impossible without unacceptable error rates, on grounds that it is pretrial punishment, and on grounds that it impairs fair trial, Foote's analyses lead him to reject preventive detention.[44]

Foote's legal analysis of the purposes of pretrial release decisions serves well to frame the contemporary debate about pretrial release. First, he raised the question of whether the excessive bail clause imparts a "right to bail." He argued that the origins of the clause strongly implies this right. The English precedents for the bail clause did allow denial of bail for capital offenses, but procedures were available to provide remedies for unlawful detention. The purpose of bail, in English law, was to assure the appearance of defendants at trial. Refusal of bail was permitted for some defendants—those accused of capital crimes—because of their great flight risk, not because of their "danger to the community."

Second, Foote raised the question of whether a right to bail implies a right to pretrial release—a right that may be sacrificed only by a showing by the government of great danger.[45] That is, does the excessive bail clause of the Eighth Amendment strongly favor the release of defendants before trial? Foote and many others have argued forcefully that it does.[46]

Third, Foote raised the question of the constitutionality of setting money bail for the poor—regardless of the legitimate aims of the pretrial release decision. Because many defendants cannot afford any bail (hence bail for them is tantamount to pretrial detention), there is the question of whether bail for indigents is unconstitutional because it violates equal protection of the laws.[47] As Justice Douglas wrote in *Bandy v. United States*

> to continue to demand a substantial bond which the defendant is unable to secure raises considerable problems for the equal administration of the law. We have held that an indigent defendant is denied equal protection of the law if he is denied an appeal on equal terms with other defendants, solely because of his indigence . . . . Can an indigent be denied freedom, where a wealthy man would not, because he does not happen to have enough property to pledge for his freedom?[48]

Fourth, Foote's analysis raised numerous issues about mechanisms other than money bail that might achieve the goal of assuring appearance at trial but that would avoid pretrial detention and the discrimination against the poor inherent in money bail. These suggestions, not wholly adopted today, gave rise to two decades of active bail reform.

Foote's analysis has not gone unchallenged. Although there appears to be a consensus that assuring the appearance of accused persons is a legitimate goal of the pretrial release decision,[49] the issues of a right to bail and whether other goals of the decision (such as protecting the community from dangerous crimes) are constitutionally permissible continue to be debated.[50]

Among those who find no right to bail in the Eighth Amendment and who see the prevention of dangerous crimes by defendants as a legitimate decision goal are former United States Attorney General John Mitchell and Senator Roman Hruska.[51] These authors also rely on historical interpretations of the excessive bail clause in inferring no right to bail and the legitimacy of preventive detention on the grounds of dangerousness. The arguments advanced by proponents of preventive detention have been summarized succinctly by Wald in a critique of these views:

> There is no Eighth Amendment right to absolute bail. The mere fact that such an absolute right is not specifically granted in the Judiciary Act of 1789 speaks for itself. There is a long tradition of pretrial detention in England and Europe, and in fact judges have since 1789 used high bail as a way to keep dangerous offenders confined before trial. Capital crimes have always been detainable and many of the crimes for which detention is now sought were in fact capital crimes in 1789 . . . . Pretrial defendants can already be jailed not only for want of bail but if the court finds it necessary to protect witnesses. Forty-nine states have excessive bail clauses in their Constitutions and 37 of these also have an absolute right to bail, thereby showing that they are not coextensive.[52]

Thus some, most notably Mitchell, argue that the Eighth Amendment was adopted to permit pretrial detention because of concerns about danger to the community.[53] Whereas Foote argues that bail was denied historically in capital cases because the flight risk of those facing the death penalty if convicted was so great, Mitchell argues that those accused of capital crimes were considered to be dangerous. Thus, according to Mitchell, because many offenses have been removed from the list of capital crimes since the time the Constitution was written, preventive detention should be permitted for those offenses for which the danger to the community is still great. He argued that "because the [Eighth] Amendment does not specifically grant the right to bail, it can be construed to mean only that bail shall not be excessive to those cases in which it is proper and that the setting of no bail in certain cases is not excessive."[54]

For others, the controversy about the constitutionally legitimate goals of pretrial release decisions simply cannot be resolved by historical analyses. For example, Dershowitz notes:

> I do not believe that the framers clearly intended to authorize or clearly intended to prohibit denial of bail on grounds of dangerousness . . . .

because all dangerous crimes were also capital crimes in 1790 the framers simply never had to confront the issue of whether a dangerous offender not facing the death penalty and therefore not likely to flee could be detained solely because of his alleged dangerousness. I suspect the framers simply never thought of the problem.[55]

The constitutionally legitimate purposes of bail and the question of whether the Eighth Amendment necessarily imparts a right to bail have not been resolved by the Supreme Court of the United States. Consequently, there is no authoritative judicial resolution of these questions.[56] Twice in the same term, the Supreme Court discussed the legitimate purposes of bail with a result that leaves the issue unresolved. The first case, *Stack v. Boyle*, which did not consider specifically whether there is a right to bail but only the question of excessiveness, suggests strongly that the sole purpose of bail that is constitutional under the Eighth Amendment is to ensure the appearance of the defendant at trial:

From the passage of the Judiciary Act of 1789 . . . federal law has un-equivocally provided that a person arrested for a non-capital offense *shall* be admitted to bail . . . . Unless this right to bail before trial is pre-served, the presumption of innocence, secured only after centuries of struggle, would lose its meaning.

The right to release before trial is conditioned upon the accused's giving adequate assurance that he will stand trial and submit to sentence if found guilty . . . . Like the ancient practice of securing the oaths of responsible persons to stand as sureties for the accused, the modern practice of requiring a bail bond or the deposit of money subject to forfeiture serves as an additional assurance of the presence of an accused. Bail set at a figure higher than an amount reasonably calculated to fulfill this purpose is "excessive" under the Eighth Amendment.[57]

The other case, *Carlson v. Landon*, concerned alien communists accused of Smith Act violations. The aliens claimed that they were entitled to bail. The Supreme Court disagreed, and in so doing wrote:

The bail clause was lifted with slight changes from the English Bill of Rights Act. In England that clause has never been thought to accord to a right to bail in all cases, but merely to provide that bail shall not be excessive in those cases where it is proper to grant bail. When this clause was carried over into our Bill of Rights, nothing was said that indicated any different concept . . . . Thus in criminal cases bail is not compulsory where the punishment may be death. Indeed, the very language of the Amendment fails to say all arrests must be bailable.[58]

These apparently contradictory discussions have the effect of leaving open the questions of the constitutionally legitimate purposes of bail and whether there exists a constitutional right to bail. Recent Supreme Court opinions only enhance this ambiguity.[59] Most state constitutions do grant a right to bail in noncapital cases,[60] and some do not permit goals of bail other than assuring appearance at trial.[61] Thus, the fundamental issue of the constitutionally legitimate purpose of bail is unresolved.

Apart from the debates surrounding the aims of assuring appearance of defendants at trial and preventing crimes in the interim between arrest and trial, several other goals of pretrial release decisions have been suggested. It has been argued that one function of detention before trial may be to protect the integrity of the trial process by inhibiting a defendant's opportunity to tamper with witnesses or other evidence. There can be little doubt that in some situations such protection is necessary, although there may be options short of detention that would be suitable substitutes. Police protection for witnesses or restrictive release conditions might be examples.

It has been suggested also that bail or pretrial detention sometimes is used explicitly for punishment.[62] That is, it may be alleged that some magistrates give certain defendants high bail or otherwise detain them in order to inflict suffering for the unproved offense. There is some evidence that suggests such practices are not uncommon. Landes, for example, interprets the results of his study of bail setting in New York as indicating that pretrial punishment may be a major rationale for these decisions. He argues that his results suggest

> the possible adaptations of a criminal justice system to a situation where disappearance rates are extremely high and resources for reapprehension are severely limited. In these circumstances the determination of bond becomes the vehicle for effecting punishment because if the accused is released at this time, punishment becomes a remote possibility. This interpretation is clearly consistent with our empirical evidence.[63]

His interpretation is plausible; it is undoubtedly true that sometimes, in some areas, bail-setting magistrates believe that a "taste of the bars" would be a good thing for some defendants who will not face incarceration if convicted. Unlike the constitutional ambiguity regarding protection of the community as a goal for the pretrial release decision, however, there is no doubt that using the bail decision to inflict preadjudicatory punishment is repugnant to the Fifth Amendment.

BAIL REFORM—A STEP
TOWARD RATIONALITY

In 1927, after studying the bail system in Chicago, Arthur Beeley wrote that a large proportion of the defendants in the Cook County Jail were being detained needlessly. He theorized that using data relating to a defendant's background, family ties, and reputation in the community, it would be possible to rate defendants as "dependable" or "undependable" regarding the probabilities of their appearing in court when required.[64] More than three decades later the idea that defendants could be evaluated for appearance on the basis of their "community ties" became a major bail reform innovation through the pioneering efforts of staff of the Vera Institute of Justice.[65]

The Vera strategy was based on a thorough prebail interview with defendants in order to obtain reliable data on their employment, residence, and family ties in the area. According to a weighting scheme devised by Vera, defendants were scored on their ties to the community and either recommended or not for outright release on their own recognizance (ROR) on the basis of their scores. By providing judges with more reliable data on defendants' backgrounds at a very early stage, it was thought that it would be possible to facilitate the release of far greater proportions of defendants than had been the practice previously. Court bail reform projects modeled after the Vera prototype in Manhattan were implemented in many jurisdictions in the United States in the mid-1960s.

Apart from the large numbers of defendants needlessly detained, another stimulus for the reform that launched the "community ties" movement was the growing awareness of problems associated with bail bondsmen. Historically, and in many jurisdictions today, the bail bondsman rather than the magistrate holds the keys to the jail cell and uses them to pursue the ends of personal economy rather than those of justice.[66] The problems associated with the bondsman system are well documented. First, the bondsman system lacks credibility. The theory underlying bail is that the defendant will be deterred from absconding because if he absconds he will forfeit the bond. But when the defendant secures his release by payment of a nonrefundable 10 percent of the bond to a bondsman, this theory breaks down. As Judge Bazelon has explained:

> Under present practice the bondsman ordinarily makes the decision whether or not to require collateral for the bond. If he does, then appellant's stake may be related to the amount of the bond. If he does not,

then appellant has no real financial stake in complying with the conditions of the bond, regardless of the amount, since the fee paid for the bond is not refundable under any circumstances. Hence the court does not decide—or even know—whether a higher bond for a particular applicant means that he has a greater stake.[67]

Thomas outlines numerous other problems with the bondsman system, including widespread failure to pay off on forfeited bonds, the influence of organized crime, and corruption of police and other officials. Furthermore, it has been found that bail jumpers are most frequently caught by the police, rather than by bondsmen,[68] thus negating the notion that bondsmen serve a meaningful apprehension function.

Thus stimulated by the inadequacies and unfairness of the bail bondsman system, by the concern over the number of defendants needlessly detained prior to trial, by the lack of a demonstrated relation between money bail and appearance at trial, and by the discriminatory effect that the bail system has on the poor, many bail projects have developed in recent years. Many of these projects attempt to bring rationality to the pretrial release decision by providing magistrates with verified background information on defendants that is thought to be related to the likelihood of appearance at trial.

The pioneer was Vera Foundation's Manhattan Bail Project, initiated in the fall of 1961, which provided a model for program development in other jurisdictions. As reported by Freed and Wald,[69] a staff of New York University law students, supervised by a Vera Foundation director, interviewed approximately thirty newly arrested felony defendants each morning before arraignment. The accused persons were for the most part indigents to be represented by assigned counsel. Initially, persons accused of a variety of serious offenses were excluded, but later exclusions were restricted to homicide, some narcotics offense charges, and sex charges.

The evaluation of flight risk was based upon information in four areas of concern—residential stability, employment history, family contacts in New York City, and prior criminal record. A point system was used in order to weight the various factors considered, and if the defendant scored a sufficient number of points (and if he could provide an address at which he could be reached), then verification of the information was attempted. This investigation was confined to references cited in the defendant's signed statement of consent. The project staff then reviewed the case and decided whether to recommend release on recognizance (ROR).

In 1964 Freed and Wald reported:

the Manhattan Bail Project and its progeny have demonstrated that a defendant with roots in the community is not likely to flee irrespective of his lack of prominence or ability to pay a bondsman. To date, these projects have produced remarkable results, with vast numbers of releases, few defaulters, and scarcely any commissions of crime by parolees, in the interim between release and trial.[70]

These authors point out that projects such as these serve two purposes:

1. They free numerous defendants who would otherwise be jailed for the entire period between arraignment and trial; and
2. They provide comprehensive statistical data never before obtainable on such vital questions as what criteria are meaningful in deciding to release the defendant, how many defendants paroled on particular criteria will show up for trial, and how much better are a defendant's chances for acquittal or a suspended sentence if he is paroled.[71]

The impact of the Vera program was widespread. In 1967, the President's Commission on Law Enforcement and Administration of Justice reported that

The first step [in bail] reform is to introduce fact-finding procedures which will furnish immediately after arrest verified information about the accused and his community ties. With this information a rational assessment of the risks can be made, and where there is no significant risk, the defendant can be released without bail.[72]

The most recent national commission, the National Advisory Commission on Criminal Justice Standards and Goals, reasoned that "In many instances, the personal promise of the accused to appear should be sufficient. This is particularly true where the accused has substantial ties with the community."[73] In offering standards concerning the type of information that magistrates should consider in making the pretrial release decision (and hence assuming a relation with appearance at trial), this commission included Vera type information regarding employment, residence, family relationships, and prior record, as well as the defendant's reputation, the charged offense, and the likelihood of guilt.

In setting forth its standards regarding pretrial release practices, the American Bar Association expressed a preference for "own recognizance" release, suggesting that items similar to those used by the Vera Institute are relevant in determing risk of flight prior to trial.[74] The Federal Bail Reform Act of 1966 provided that an accused will be released on own recognizance or unsecured bond unless the magistrate determines, on the basis of specific items of information, that he or she does not have reasonable assurance that the accused will appear. The information deemed relevant in the Bail Reform Act includes items relating to the defendant's community ties (for example, family relationships) as well as the nature of the offense charged and the weight of the evidence against the accused.[75]

The recently issued *Performance Standards and Goals for Pretrial Release and Diversion* of the National Association of Pretrial Service Agencies demonstrate the strong influence of the Vera project in arguing that in deciding whether to release a defendant on personal recognizance, the length of residence, family ties, employment status, and relationships in the community should be taken into account.[76] In few areas of criminal justice has a reform effort had such widespread and rapid impact as did the Vera program of increasing pretrial release by providing verified information about a defendant's "community ties." It has been estimated that the bail reform movement stimulated by the Vera Institute and these standard setting bodies has reached over 200 cities.[77] Discussing the results of this decade and a half of bail reform activity, Thomas concluded:

> Clearly, the bail reform movement has accomplished much . . . . The obvious correlation which [this] study showed between the development of pretrial release programs and the substantial increase both in the overall percentage of defendants released and the proportions released on own recognizance and other forms of nonfinancial release clearly bespeaks the success these programs have collectively enjoyed in reforming American bail practices.[78]

THE PROBLEM OF PREDICTION

It was noted at the beginning of this chapter that pretrial release decisions are bound inextricably to the concept of prediction. Whether the concern is with appearance at trial, the prevention of crimes in the interim between arrest and trial, or the protection of witnesses, the magistrate is faced with the task of forecasting the behavior of defendants. The ability to make such judgments accurately and the consequences of errors are topics that have attracted much social scientific attention in recent years. The results of these studies cast serious doubt on current abilities to predict with great accuracy the statistically rare events of failure to appear at trial and pretrial crime. These studies serve to emphasize again the importance of the concept of rationality in criminal justice decisionmaking. As we have seen, much attention has been given to the legal issues surrounding the legitimate goals of the pretrial release decison, but there is a fundamental difference between the propriety of a decision goal and its feasibility. Regardless of its propriety, if the decision aim cannot be achieved with current knowledge within tolerable costs (both social and economic) then it is difficult to see how the decision may be regarded as rationally made in respect to that goal.

The Vera Foundation criteria developed in the Manhattan Bail Project work in one restricted sense. That is, experience reported thus far supports the view that persons released as a result of recommendations based upon the interview schedule rarely fail to appear for trial. There has been, however, no demonstration that the items used actually are predictive. In order to be useful as predictors, it must be demonstrated that the items help to discriminate between the groups of persons who appear for trial and those who do not. A logical case may be made easily for the relevance of items presumably reflecting roots in the community or employment stability. That is, it is reasonable to hypothesize that these items have some predictive relation to appearance for trial or other outcomes of interest in the decision process. Until these items are shown to be related to the various consequences of the decision, however, we must assume that actually they may be unrelated to these consequences. That is, these hypotheses need to be tested. What is the degree of validity of the individual items, for example, in terms of correlation with appearance or nonappearance for trial? Are the items equally valid with respect to conviction for new offenses during the period of release? How are the items correlated with one another, and how should they be weighted in order to provide, in some specific sense, an optimal predictive guide to the court?

A recent study by Michael Gottfredson demonstrated clearly the needs for such investigations.[79] It had two objectives: The first was to assess the predictive validity of the Vera Institute's instrument and of its individual items. The second was to improve prediction from a variety of background characteristics of defendants. The design of the study, through a special arrangement with the courts, allowed comparisons of subjectively chosen good and bad risks. That is, not only were persons recommended by the ROR project staff and approved by a judge released on their own recognizance, but also 328 defendants not deemed eligible by usual procedures were released. The latter group was compared with a randomly selected 201 defendants released normally. Although there were differences in the rates of failure to appear for trial for the two groups, a striking result was that about 85 percent of the ROR sample and about 73 percent of the experimental sample either appeared for trial or returned voluntarily. Similarly, about three-fourths of the ROR sample and slightly more than half of the experimental sample had no arrests during the ninety days just after release. None of the individual items that made up the Vera instrument was substantially related to the criteria studied (appearance or arrests), and the total score accounted for only 2 or 3 percent of the variance in these criteria. (Although a variety of additional items was studied, the resulting prediction equations, when applied to a validation sample, failed to achieve substantially better prediction than the Vera instrument.)

Thus, although the items included in the Vera instrument seemed plausibly to be related to the goals of the decision, such relations when investigated empirically were found to be slight. This evidence provides a strong argument for the need to test the hypotheses involved in developing screening procedures to determine whether the expected relations indeed are found in practice. Otherwise, decisions may be based on mere data, plausibly related to the decision aims, but in actuality providing little or no information.

A recent project in Des Moines, Iowa, sought the safe pretrial release of defendants jailed as a result of inability either to post money bail or to meet Vera type criteria for release on recognizance.[80] During the project's first eight months of operation, 81 of 141 defendants interviewed were released to a community treatment program. The cases of 61 defendants reached the court disposition stage, and all appeared for trial. The program was reported as "showing that defendants, who have been considered poor risks for pretrial release, can be released with no greater danger to the community than that presented by persons on money bail."[81] The released defendants, compared to members of a nonreleased control group, were less likely to be incarcerated after conviction, a finding adding further credence to the view that pretrial release decisions may have an impact on later sentencing decision outcomes.

Other studies of pretrial release decisions confirm the inability to predict either failure to appear or pretrial crime with great efficiency. Feeley and McNaughton analyzed data on 1642 cases occuring in a three month period in New Haven, about which pretrial status decisions were made. The vast majority (86 percent) of the cases in their sample received some form of pretrial release. It should be noted that while some restriction of the range occurred, this was less a constraint than in other, similar studies; therefore, considerable confidence can be placed in the results obtained for the sample.[82] Measuring failure to appear by whether or not a warrant was issued, they tried to predict appearance from data on a number of background factors. These included the seriousness of the charge, prior record, marital status, number of dependents, residency, length of time in the area, and employment status. Thus, the authors incorporated items that measured "community ties" and the alleged offense. None of the items studied, however, were found to be related substantially, either at the bivariate or multivariate levels of analysis, to failure to appear for trial or to rearrest while on pretrial release.[83]

In a carefully conducted study in Charlotte, North Carolina, Clarke selected a random sample of about one-third of all criminal defendants arrested (excluding drunkenness, traffic, and fish and game offenses) during the first quarters of 1971, 1972, and 1973.[84] As in the Feeley and McNaughton study, an extremely high proportion of defendants secured some form of release—over 90 percent in each of the three years. (The program selected defendants according to a point scheme based on the defendant's community ties and gave supervision after release.)

Among all defendants, the factors found most highly associated with failure to appear for trial were the court disposition time, the form of release, and the defendant's criminal history. Data items found not to be strongly related to failure to appear were income, employment, seriousness of the charge, and race. Those items found most highly associated with rearrest while on release were the length of time from arrest to disposition, prior record, and the type of release. Consistent with the usually found results, prediction of either pretrial crime or failure to appear at trial, although improved somewhat over the "base rate,"[85] were not made with a good deal of accuracy. The single variable best able to account for pretrial success was found to be supervision while on release.

Others have examined the ability to predict "dangerousness" while on pretrial release, with generally poor results. The National Bureau of Standards studied the issue in 1970 with a sample of misdemeanor and felony defendants.[86] It was found that of those defendants originally charged with "crimes of violence," 17 percent were rearrested during the pretrial period, but only 5 percent of those originally charged with a violent offense were rearrested for a violent offense. They reported, moreover, little ability to discriminate between the two groups on the basis of background factors. Similar results were reported by Angel and coworkers in a study of the predictive validity of the criteria in the preventive detention code of the District of Columbia.[87] Reinforcing these results, a recently conducted study in Washington, D.C., confirmed the generally low degree of predictive validity in the area of pretrial misconduct.[88] In this study of a large sample of persons released at the pretrial stage, neither the seriousness of the charge nor community ties were found related to failure to appear at trial. Those who were unemployed and those who were drug users were, however, significantly less likely to appear for trial. This study discovered also that those charged with felonies (especially property crimes), those with lengthy prior records, those unemployed, blacks, and younger defendants were more likely to be rearrested. The general ability to predict pretrial crime accurately again proved to be poor.

It would be inaccurate to claim on the basis of these studies that it is impossible to predict failure to appear at trial or pretrial crime. Most studies that have examined the issue have found that such predictions could be made, based on background factors, that improve on chance. Predictive validity is, after all, a matter of degree. At issue when such fundamental issues as liberty and safety are at stake, however, is the accuracy of those predictions and whether the costs of the errors associated with them can be tolerated.

The prediction problem posed by pretrial release decisions is made difficult by the relative rarity of the undesired behavior of concern. For example, in the Clarke study, the overall failure to appear rate was only 10 percent in 1973 (the highest of all the years studied). The rearrest rate was the same. In the Feeley and McNaughton study only 7 percent were rearrested while on release. In the Gottfredson sample, only 5 percent were rearrested for crimes against persons while on release. On statistical grounds, with such a small number of failures, it is extremely difficult to find predictors that can discriminate adequately between successes and failures. As has been discussed repeatedly in the literature, the unfortunate consequence of predictions resulting from low failure rates is the extremely high number of "false positives"— cases in which the prediction is made that the individual will fail when, in fact, he will succeed. In the Gottfredson study, 73 percent of the sample of defendants not normally released were false positives according to the major classification of failure to appear at trial. When it is recalled that some empirical evidence suggests there are negative consequences that failure to secure release from confinement pending trial can have to defendants (in addition to the consequences of incarceration *per se*), the false positive issue takes on paramount importance. An additional consequence of the difficulty in these predictive aspects of pretrial release involves the issue of requiring conditions on the release of defendants. It follows that if it is difficult to establish predictors of either failure to appear or future criminality—that is, to find factors associated with these behaviors—then it is virtually impossible to know which defendants can be released only with specified conditions.

After an elaborate statistical analysis of failure to appear and pretrial crime in the District of Columbia, including study of a wide variety of factors, Roth and Wice were led to conclude:

> the power of our model to predict the outcomes of individual cases is extremely limited. Low values of R^2 (. . . 0.05 in the nonappearance equation, and 0.10 in the rearrest equation) indicate a high degree of randomness in individual equations . . . . Based on an analysis of our sample, the model was "wrong" in predicting misconduct only about half as often as random guesses made with appropriate frequencies; however, it was "wrong" about as often as a guess that every defendant would appear when required and that no released defendant would be arrested before disposition of his original case.[89]

One finding that emerges consistently in these prediction studies is that the length of time elapsing between arrest and trial is associated substantially with pretrial misconduct. Gottfredson reported a correlation of 0.53 between length of pretrial release and arrest while in that status.[90] Clarke reported a similar relation.[91] The research thus suggests strongly that the most adequate way to diminish the rates of failure to appear and of pretrial crime may be to shorten considerably the time between arrest and trial. Roth and Wice dispute this, arguing instead that speedier trials might simply mean earlier failures to appear.[92] Absent an experimental design, such competing hypotheses are difficult to dismiss. It may be plausible to assume that a defendant who will abscond may do so sooner the earlier the trial, but it is less plausible that the relation of time of trial to pretrial crime may be similarly explained. In the case of pretrial crime, the operational meanings of "time between arrest and trial" and "exposure to the risk of committing new offenses" are identical; extending the period of risk should not occasion surprise that the proportions with new offenses increase.

In any event, the available studies demonstrate the difficulty of achievement of either of the predominantly expressed goals of the pretrial release decision, both of which require predictions—failure to appear for trial and pretrial crime. It should be emphasized that this does not imply that such predictions cannot be made more accurately than chance; reliable correlates of both failure to appear and pretrial crime have been shown to exist. What it does imply is that the errors involved in such predictions are very large: both failure to appear and pretrial crime may be expected to be substantially overpredicted from the information now available.[93]

Related studies have sought to answer the question of whether supervision during pretrial release reduces the rates of absconding and pretrial crime. Clarke presented data bearing on these issues.[94] Of all defendants arrested in the year before the pretrial release project was undertaken (a limited supervision program), 28 percent were released on an unsecured bond, whereas in the year that the project began this figure dropped to 10 percent. These data indicated to Clarke that most of the defendants released to supervision would have been released by magistrates on unsecured bond without supervision had the program not existed. Accepting this premise, and noting that the major difference between the two types of release is supervision of the project releasees, Clarke argued that supervision is an effective method of decreasing rates of failure to appear by showing that the rate for the supervised release cohort was statistically lower than the rate for the unsecured bond group (5.8 versus 1.4 percent). Such a comparison is certainly not definitive. It is possible that the project selected only the best risks and left the worst risks to be released by other means. Furthermore, the difference is not large. These figures nevertheless give some support to the supervision theory; but it must be noted that the same comparison indicated that supervision did not decrease rearrest rates over the level achieved by outright release.

Taylor evaluated a supervised pretrial release program in Santa Clara County, California,[95] designed to secure the release of defendants who were not released on their own recognizance and who could not afford bail by affording them supervision. The supervised releasees were reported no more likely than the group released on recognizance to fail to appear at trial, and they were only slightly more likely to be rearrested. After conviction, more than a third were not sentenced to any jail time. That is, without the supervision program, the only incarceration for these defendants would have been prior to an adjudication of guilt. Finally, Taylor found (as did Clarke) some indication that the supervised sample may have been drawn from the group that normally would have received release on their own recognizance. Given the alternatives of ROR or release with supervision, magistrates may choose supervision for cases they might otherwise release on their word.

Such an inference is supported also by Thomas' study of the effects of the implementation by the District of Columbia Bail Agency of supervised conditional release.[96] The standard conditions included (1) supervisory custody, (2) reporting weekly to the D.C. Bail Agency, (3) living at a certain address, (4) curfew, (5) obtaining or maintaining a job, (6) staying away from witnesses, (7) staying within the D.C. area, and (8) reporting for narcotics testing.[97] Thomas found that this program did achieve the goal of securing the release of greater numbers of defendants on nonfinancial conditions over a four year period. He showed also, however, that the use of conditions greatly reduced the number of straight own recognizance releases. He stated:

> where previously over 40 percent of the defendants in the District were released on O.R. without conditions, by 1972 less than 5 percent were so released. Thus, a large segment of defendants who had established their reliability on straight O.R. release were burdened with conditions.[98]

The results of these studies are clearly relevant to the prediction problem faced by the pretrial release decisionmaker. The problem in the context of this book is one of information. What conditions, if any, are known to be necessary to ensure the appearance of the defendant? What conditions, if any, help to protect the community? Both the studies of supervision and those of predictive ability suggest that this problem will not be solved easily.

Some data are known to provide information, but much remains to be learned if rationality is to be enhanced. We know, for example, that for many, perhaps most, defendants, financial conditions are not necessary to ensure their appearance at trial. We know that many more defendants can be released safely before trial than was thought prior to the bail reform movement of the 1960s and early 1970s. We know that it is possible to discriminate statistically between defendants who will appear for trial and those who will not. Similarly, those who will be rearrested and those who will not can be distinguished at better than chance levels. We know also, however, that our ability to make such predictions currently is weak—that is, predictions are of low validity. When such predictions are used to define decision rules, they therefore involve substantial "overpredictions" that would result in the erroneous detention of very large numbers of defendants. Significantly, these "false positives" or errors in predictions would be hidden errors. That is, they would be hidden in the sense that it never would be known to the decisionmaker that persons confined on the bases of predictions about their conduct would, if set free, not engage in the expected misconduct. The person kept in jail cannot demonstrate the invalidity of the prediction for him or her.

The legal debates over the legitimate goals of pretrial release must be read in the light of this social scientific research. Propriety and feasibility are not necessarily synonymous in the realm of criminal justice decisionmaking. Propriety (as for example of detention for dangerousness) may have to be conditioned substantially by feasibility.

CORRELATES OF THE DECISION
TO RELEASE

As with all discretionary decisions in the criminal justice system, it is possible to infer, from the avowed goals of pretrial release decisions, too much about how these decisions are made. Such an assessment must rely as well on research that examines the bail-setting behavior of judges as it takes place in the courtroom.[99]

Many have suggested that, whatever the legal or social scientific problems associated with the goal of community protection, that goal might be given priority by magistrates in practice. Furthermore, it has been suggested often that judges seek to accomplish this aim by attending especially to the gravity of the charges facing the defendant. For example, Vorenberg has argued:

> what is usually on the minds of magistrates and prosecutors [on whose recommendation magistrates often rely] is whether the defendant will commit another crime while awaiting trial. . . . almost always the issue for the magistrate is not how much bail will make the released defendant reappear, but how high it must be set in order to prevent release.[100]

Similarly, Wald wrote that, "[The] fear of repetition of crimes has probably been the major factor in the nonrelease of accuseds."[101] Thomas explained the connection between the gravity of the charge and setting bail as follows:

> Reasoning that the likelihood of a defendant failing to appear increases with the severity of the charge and the consequent sentence which can be imposed upon conviction, judges generally increase the amount of

bail in relation to the seriousness of the alleged charges. The single most important factor in the setting of bail is therefore the alleged present offense.[102]

The disjunction between setting bail principally on the basis of charge seriousness and the aims of the bail reform movement, which sought to encourage magistrates to set bail according to the defendant's community ties, is large. Several researchers have studied the factors that seem to influence bail setting in practice and have confirmed the preeminence of the charge criterion.

Bock and Frazier studied the criteria used in bail decisions in one Florida judicial district.[103] The amount of bail given (including none or own recognizance release) was analyzed in relation to the defendant's community ties, prior record, seriousness of the charge, and demeanor at the bail hearing (respectful versus disrespectful). They found that the seriousness of the charge was the factor most highly correlated with bond; demographic characteristics, community ties, employment, and family ties were not found to be significantly related to bond. (The "disrespectful," however, were given higher bonds, all other factors in the study held constant.)

Bynum studied the influence of community ties, demographic characteristics, prior record, and charge on whether defendants in three release programs were released on their own recognizance.[104] The study sample included only those eligible for release in the three programs. Of all the variables studied, only prior record was consistently related to the probability of a defendant being granted release; both demographic characteristics and community ties were found to have little impact.

Roth and Wice, in their study of 11,000 pretrial releasees in Washington, D.C.,[105] found, at the bivariate level of analysis, considerable evidence that the seriousness of the charge had an impact on the pretrial release decisions of the judges in their study. So also did the extent of the defendant's prior record. Race, sex, age, employment status, and residence were unrelated at the bivariate level.

In multivariate analyses of these same data, they found that when the criterion of interest was release on nonfinancial conditions versus financial conditions, the type of charge, prior record, judge, and the capacity of the D.C. jail were consistently related to the decision.

Of interest to the question of rationality in pretrial release decisionmaking was their comparative analysis of the factors found influential in setting bond with those they found to be related to failure to appear at trial and pretrial rearrest. Table 4-1, from their report, shows these comparisons. As summarized by Roth and Wice:

> The exhibit illustrates that, with few exceptions, variables that seem to predict misconduct do not influence the financial-nonfinancial decision; moreover, variables that seem to affect the decision do not predict misconduct. For one example, holding other variables constant, a history of drug use is associated with greater risks of both nonappearance and rearrest, yet known drug users were found no more likely than others

Table 4-1. Comparison of Variables Explaining Financial Conditions, Failure to Appear, and Pretrial Rearrest, Felony Cases.

Explanatory Attribute	Use of Financial Bond	Failure to Appear	Pretrial Rearrest
Current charge			
Homicide	+	0	0
Assault	−	−	0
Drug violation	−	0	0
Bail violation	+	0	0
Sexual assault	0	−	0
Weapon violation	0	−	0
Robbery	0	0	+
Burglary	0	0	+
Larceny	0	0	+
Arson-property destruction	0	0	+
Crime severity			
No weapon used	−	0	+
Defendant history			
Nonappearance in pending case	+	0	0
Parole-probation when arrested	+	0	0
Number pending cases	+	0	+
Number prior arrests, all crimes	+	0	0
Number prior arrests, crimes against persons	0	0	+
Arrested last five years?	+	0	0
Number arrests in preceding twelve months	0	0	+
Defendant descriptors			
Local residence	−	0	0
Employed	−	−	−
Low income	−	0	0
Drug user	0	+	+
Caucasian	+	0	−
Older	0	0	−

Source: J. Roth and P. Wice, "Pretrial Release and Misconduct in the District of Columbia," PROMIS Research Project Publication 16 (Washington, D.C.: INSLAW, 1978).

to receive financial conditions, and accused drug violators were actually less likely to receive such conditions. For another, defendants not accused of using a weapon in the alleged offense were less likely to receive financial conditions, yet more likely to be rearrested while on release. In contrast, controlling for other variables, defendants having a local residence faced financial requirements less often than others, yet a local residence was not found to affect the likelihood of either failure to appear or rearrest. Finally, none of the four crime types—robbery, burglary, larceny, and arson-property destruction—that seem to predict rearrest influences the financial-nonfinancial decision. Of the three crime types—assault, sexual assault, and weapons violations—associated with nonappearance, only the first seems to affect the release decision.

Three exceptions to this inconsistency should be noted. As expected, employed defendants, who present less risk of nonappearance and rearrest, are less likely to receive financial conditions. Assault defendants, who present less nonappearance risk, receive financial conditions less often. And defendants with more pending cases, who present a greater rearrest risk, are more likely to receive financial conditions. But the other 21 variables present a striking picture of inconsistency.[106]

Finally, Goldkamp examined the bail-setting process for a large sample of defendants in Philadelphia.[107] At the bivariate level of analysis, he found that bail decisions were related to age, race, sex, employment, income, prior record, and criminal charge. Older persons, whites, females, employed persons, those without prior convictions, and those with the least serious charges alleged were more likely to be given release on their own recognizance than were their counterparts. After exercising statistical controls by means of multiple regression, however, the single variable that remained substantially correlated with the own recognizance release decision was charge seriousness. Goldkamp concluded:

Perhaps the most interesting of these results is the finding that bail decisionmaking, in its various facets, seems to operate almost exclusively on the basis of the seriousness of the charge. That is, the ROR decision option appears to screen "out" defendants who are not charged with serious crimes. . . . community-ties indicators, such as family ties and residence in the community, appear in the face of charge and prior-record concerns to have had almost no impact at all on the granting of ROR or on the setting of cash bail. This finding may suggest that Philadelphia bail judges do not deem community ties reliable indexes for assessing defendants' propensities toward flight. But, it may also demonstrate a lesser concern for the evaluation of flight-risk, pointing instead to the dominance of other bail decision concerns that may be intuitively linked to charge seriousness and past criminal history criteria—such as a concern for potential defendant dangerousness or a tendency to pre-judge or even prepunish defendants at their first appearance.[108]

EQUITY IN BAIL DECISIONMAKING

Just as equitable decisions are sought at the sentencing stage of the criminal justice process, fairness in bail decisionmaking dictates that similarly situated defendants be treated similarly. The much discussed problem of disparity in sentencing (see Chapter 6) is relevant as well to the problem of pretrial release decisions. Just as there are various sentencing options for convicted persons, there are a number of possible decision outcomes at bail, ranging from release on recognizance to cash bail to outright detention. Because these decision options can be viewed as less or more drastic in terms of the hardships they impose on defendants, equity requires that persons in similar circumstances receive similar treatment.

There are, however, two principal obstacles to the achievement of equity in bail decisionmaking. The first is basic: There is little agreement concerning the meaning of the concept "similarly situated" as applied to bail. Should "similarly situated" in bail decisionmaking be understood in terms of offense seriousness, for example? Should it include measures of the defendant's community ties or even financial resources? It is difficult to respond to these questions principally because the purposes of the bail decision are not articulated clearly and authoritatively.

The second major obstacle to effecting equity in bail decisionmaking is the lack of feedback of data to decisionmakers about their decisions. Decisionmakers may, for various categories of defendants, vary in their decisions over time. Groups of magistrates may differ from one another in their decisions. Both kinds of variation may contribute to inequity in bail decisionmaking. Without some mechanism that systematically can provide feedback about bail dispositions in previous cases to the decisionmakers responsible for them (both as individuals and as a group), consistency will be difficult to attain, and equity may be expected to be reduced.

Several studies indicate that equity, in the sense of similar treatment for similar persons, is problematic in the realm of the pretrial release decision. In one Chicago court, Sperlak found a great deal of variability among judges in the proportion of cases given release on personal recognizance.[109] In the Roth and Wice study already discussed, it was discovered that the judge deciding the case strongly affected the release conditions. Variability in release conditions was associated with judges preferring release on recognizance versus those with a preference for supervised release.

A recent study by the comptroller general's office concluded that marked disparities exist in bail practices in the federal courts. Inconsistent use of money bail, widely varying detention rates, and differential weighting of the criteria of the Bail Reform Act were found to characterize federal bail practices. The principal recommendation of the report to reduce these inequities squares precisely with the major theme of this book. A system should be established

> to provide judicial officers feedback on the results of their bail decisions in relation to the decisions of other judicial officers and to monitor and evaluate the bail process. Such a system is needed to enable judicial officers and the judiciary to identify and correct problem areas and promote more consistent bail decisions.[110]

The research reviewed in this chapter suggests strongly that information as to the outcome of the bail decision should be added to such a system. When such systems are routinely in place in criminal justice agencies, we will have moved a long way toward enhanced rationality.

IMPLICATIONS FOR RATIONALITY

The research reviewed in this chapter thus might be viewed as the first step that needs to be taken on the road toward increased rationality in pretrial release decisionmaking. Much has been learned about the ways that magistrates make pretrial release decisions, about the consequences of these decisions to defendants and to society, about the goals of these decisions and current abilities to meet those goals, and about the effectiveness of various decision alternatives. The implications of these studies for subsequent steps that must be taken if pretrial release discretion can fairly be said to be exercised rationally should be discussed next.

Pretrial release decisions, in which an accused person either is set free pending trial or held in custody, are a direct consequence of two features of our system of justice. First, recall that the principal way in which the law is invoked is by arrest—that is, the taking of a suspect into physical custody. Second, note that there is a period of time between arrest and adjudication that permits the accused some time to prepare a defense. The latter feature is central to the American notion of due process of law. The state may not make decisions affecting liberty without the accused having a fair chance to rebut the charges with the aid of counsel. In the absence of summary adjudication, which would be repugnant to the concept of fairness, there always will be a period of time between custody decisions (made on the basis of suspicion) and adjudication (made on the basis of an impartial hearing). The first ingredient of pretrial release decisions, however—that of arrest as the principal method of invoking the law—is a matter that merits reflection. We know, from the studies reviewed in this chapter, that the vast majority of defendants pose no risk of failing to appear for trial or of committing crimes before trial. We know also that we have very little information—in the sense that we use that term in this book—about defendants to aid in distinguishing those who will appear and those who will not. It might be, therefore, that the most profitable enhancement of rationality in these decisions rests not with the magistrate, but with the police. This unusual claim merits more discussion.

As Thomas has stressed, most arrestees are jailed "not because someone has decided that there is a need for their incarceration, but because the traditional method of beginning criminal cases is by arrest, the taking of the person into physical custody."[111] As discussed in Chapter 3, in deciding whether or not to arrest a person suspected of committing a crime, the police officer may operate primarily on the basis of perceived guilt. Certainly this is an oversimplification of that complex decision; however, in the routine case, the decision may not include an assessment of whether there is a need for custody. The rationality of taking persons into physical custody on the basis of guilt certainly is questionable. Surely the evidence available about flight risk does not support the contention that absconding is significantly related to convictability.[112]

It may be then, as LaFave,[113] Foote,[114] Thomas, and others[115] have suggested, that the most significant inroads into the problems posed by pretrial release decisions may be made by reforming the decision immediately prior—that is, the more critical decision to be addressed may be that of arrest. Projects modeled after the Vera Institute's point system, designed to increase the use of summons instead of arrest, have been found to be effective in increasing the use of summons for misdemeanants.[116] Research designed to assess the custody need for arrest decisions and to study the information needs of such decision goals is clearly indicated. It should be noted, however, that current evidence suggests that custody taken because of perceived flight risk probably is taken too routinely and that large numbers of detainees could be freed by the police pending trial.

The evidence concerning both ROR and bail release encourages the belief that requiring money bail generally is illogical, unnecessary, and discriminatory. There still is no valid empirical demonstration that money bail serves any purpose of deterring flight. Thus, the requirement of rationality suggests that the use of bail should continue to decline in prominence as a principal mechanism justifying pretrial release decisions.

From a comprehensive review of the bail reform movement, Thomas offered a model pretrial release system that provides an integration of the various experimental projects. His model, reproduced as Figure 4-1, was designed to serve these objectives: "first, to ensure that each defendant receives the quickest and least restrictive form of release compatible with the smooth administration of criminal justice and the public safety, and second, that the system be one that is reasonably cost effective."[117] He calls also for continued experimentation with release conditions to gather information about failure rates under different conditions.[118]

Despite the inroads that decision alternatives such as ROR and citation in lieu of arrest should make in the bail system, the difficult problem of prediction will continue to haunt the pretrial release decisionmaker. If it has no other purpose, money bail undoubtedly will continue to serve a preventive detention function.

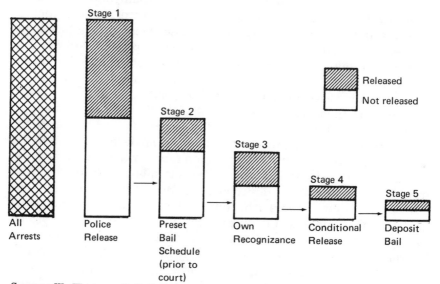

Source: W. Thomas, *Bail Reform in America* (Berkeley: University of California Press, 1976), p. 257.

Figure 4-1. A model pretrial release system.

There are people that magistrates will refuse to set free prior to trial because, perhaps subjectively, they are perceived as posing a danger to the community or seem very likely to flee. To ensure their detention, magistrates will fix very high bail. The central question that faces further reform with respect to rationality in bail practices is whether such preventive detention should continue to be accomplished *sub rosa* through money bail or whether it should be openly acknowledged, guided by explicit criteria, and regulated by due process guarantees. At least one standard-setting body has selected the latter choice.[119] Certainly, it does not seem too much to ask of a justice system that the goals of such a significant decision be stated openly, explicitly, and honestly.

Both roads, in any case, are fraught with hazards. Ignoring the significant constitutional questions that surround preventive detention, it may be asked what criteria are thought to serve the required predictive purpose. The evidence reviewed in this chapter suggests that none now perform that function adequately. Given the apparent negative influence of detention on later decisions, how should that information be used? Would an explicit provision for pretrial detention result in needless increases in detention simply because it would be a practical expedient for magistrates?

On the other hand, it hardly can be denied, from the studies reviewed here, that much preventive detention currently takes place. It might be, as Vorenberg has suggested, that at least as much overprediction of dangerousness goes on under the guise of setting bail to "ensure appearance" as would take place under a system of explicit criteria and procedural safeguards.[120] Explicit criteria and an evidentiary hearing would have at least the merits of visibility. The prediction problem, of course, remains.

Improved rationality of the pretrial release decision need not rest entirely on the outcome of this debate, which is dependent eventually upon more definitive guidance from the Supreme Court of the United States. Much has been learned about the value of decision alternatives and about information that can enhance rationality.

Perhaps the most important future requirement is the design and implementation of systems of feedback to the magistrates about the consequences of their decisions. Such feedback systems, as discussed in Chapters 6 and 9, have been implemented already in the areas of sentencing and parole decisions. Besides routinely providing magistrates with information about the proportions of defendants eventually released who fail to appear for trial and about pretrial crime, such systems should also include information about how similar cases have been decided by other judges within the same jurisdiction. Such a data feedback system then should be studied routinely by the decisionmakers themselves to ascertain how well their goals—including equity—are being accomplished.[121]

The days in jail are long for the innocent as well as for the guilty. If the traditional presumption of innocence is valued and if every citizen is entitled to liberty unless deprived of it by due process of law, then the goals, information needs, and alternatives consistent with ensuring those values are deserving of much more attention than thus far has been given. Today, magistrates make pretrial release decisions in virtual ignorance of their consequences. Only through feedback can such ignorance be reduced. Only with a reduction of present ignorance can rational decisionmaking in pretrial release decisions be claimed with any assurance.

NOTES

1. President's Commission on Law Enforcement and Administration of Justice, *The Challenge of Crime in a Free Society* (Washington, D.C.: Government Printing Office, 1967), p. 131.

2. H. Goldstein, "Setting High Bail to Prevent Pretrial Release," in *Proceedings* (National Conference on Bail and Criminal Justice, Washington, D.C., 1964), pp. 151-60.

3. Certainly this is a simplification of the operation of bail in the past. For discussions of the history and purposes of bail, see C. Foote, "The Coming Constitutional Crisis in Bail," *University of Pennsylvania Law Review* 113:959, 1125 (1965); F. Dill, "Bail and Bail Reform: A Sociological Study" (PhD. dissertation, University of California at Berkeley, 1972); J. Goldkamp, "Bail Decision-Making and the Role of Pretrial Detention in American Justice" (PhD. dissertation, State University of New York at Albany, 1976); and W. Thomas, *Bail Reform in America* (Berkeley: University of California Press, 1976).

4. National Advisory Commission on Criminal Justice Standards and Goals, *Corrections* (Washington, D.C.: Government Printing Office, 1973), p. 98.

5. In some cases, somewhat analogous issues are raised by considerations of detention or liberty after conviction by a trial court during the course of appeals from conviction.

6. National Advisory Commission, *supra* note 4 at 102.

7. *Id.*

8. Goldkamp, *supra* note 3.

9. W. Landes, "The Bail System: An Economic Approach," *Journal of Legal Studies* 2:79 (1973).

10. For a review see H. Mattick, "The Contemporary Jails of the United States: An Unknown and Neglected Area of Justice," in D. Glaser, ed., *Handbook of Criminology* (Chicago: Rand McNally, 1974).

11. J. J. Gibbs, "Psychological and Behavior Pathology in Jails: A Review of the Literature" (paper prepared for the Special National Workshop on Mental Health Services in Local Jails, Baltimore, Maryland, September 1978).

12. P. Wald, "The Right to Bail Revisited: A Decade of Promise Without Fulfillment," in S. Nagel, ed., *Rights of the Accused in Law and Action* (Beverly Hills: Sage, 1972), pp. 177-205.

13. Goldkamp, *supra* note 3.

14. W. Landes, "Legality and Reality: Some Evidence on Criminal Procedure," *Journal of Legal Studies* 3:287 (1974).

Note that if it were not for the period of detention prior to trial, some of these persons released after conviction may have been required to serve some time in prison—that is, the judge, in passing sentence, may consider the pretrial detention period in setting the penalty.

There is some reason to believe this. See Landes, *supra*; Goldkamp, *supra* note 3; and D. McCarthy and J. Wohl, "The District of Columbia Bail Project: An Illustration of Experimentation and a Brief for Change," *Georgetown Law Journal* 55:218 (1965).

Freed referred to this problem as the "imbalance ratio," defined as the number of people detained prior to trial minus the number detained subsequent to trial divided by all persons detained prior to trial. See D. Freed, "The Imbalance Ratio," *Beyond Time* 11:25 (1973).

15. Goldkamp, *supra* note 3.

16. For early discussions, see A. Beeley, *The Bail System in Chicago* (Chicago: University of Chicago Press, 1927); and C. Foote, *supra* note 3. The literature on the detrimental consequences to defendants is substantial. An excellent review of the legal and empirical work is provided by Goldkamp, *supra* note 3.

17. P. Wald, "Pretrial Detention and Ultimate Freedom: A Statistical Study," *New York University Law Review* 39:631 (1964).

18. W. Morse and R. Beattie, *Survey of the Administration of Criminal Justice in Oregon* (New York: Arno Press, 1974).

19. C. Foote, J. Markle, and E. Woolley, "Compelling Appearance in Court: Administration of Bail in Philadelphia," *University of Pennsylvania Law Review* 102:1031 (1954). Several studies using similar methods report essentially the same results; see G. Alexander, M. Glass, P. King, J. Palermo, J. Roberts, and A. Schury, "A Study of the Administration of Bail in New York City," *University of Pennsylvania Law Review* 106:685 (1958); C. Ares, A. Rankin, and H. Sturz, "The Manhattan Bail Project: An Interim Report on the Use of Pre-Trial Parole," *New York University Law Review* 38:67 (1963); and A. Angel, E. Green, H. Kaufman, and E. Van Loon, "Preventive Detention: An Empirical Analysis," *Harvard Civil Rights - Civil Liberties Law Review* 6:301 (1971).

20. Foote, Markle, and Woolley, *supra* note 19 at 1054.

21. See sources in note 19, *supra*.

22. A. Rankin, "The Effect of Pretrial Detention," *New York University Law Review* 39:641 (1964).

23. *Id.* at 655.

24. E. Single, "The Unconstitutional Administration of Bail: *Bellamy v. the Judges of New York City,*" *Criminal Law Bulletin* 8:459 (1972).

25. For critiques of the methods of these studies see M. J. Hindelang, "On The Methodological Rigor of the Bellamy Memorandum," *Criminal Law Bulletin* 8:507 (1972); and Goldkamp, *supra* note 3 at ch. 6.

26. Landes, *supra* note 14.

27. *Id.* at 334.

28. *Id.* at 335.

29. Goldkamp *supra* note 3 at ch. 8.

30. Goldkamp used several measures of pretrial custody in his analyses, but for simplicity only this measure is discussed here. Generally, his results maintained regardless of the measure used.

31. *Id.* at 542.

32. Dill, *supra* note 3.

33. P. Wice, *Freedom for Sale* (Lexington, Massachusetts: Lexington Books, 1974).

34. Thomas *supra* note 3 at 89.

35. J. Locke, R. Penn, R. Rick, E. Bunten, and G. Hare, *Compilation and Use of Criminal Court Data in Relation to Pretrial Release of Defendants: Pilot Study* (Washington, D.C.: Government Printing Office, 1970).

36. M. R. Gottfredson, "An Empirical Analysis of Pre-Trial Release Decisions," *Journal of Criminal Justice* 2:287 (1974).

37. J. Welsh and D. Viets, *The Pretrial Offender in the District of Columbia* (Washington, D.C.: District of Columbia Bail Agency, n.d.).

38. For example, in a study in which police, prosecutors, public defenders, and judges were asked about the most important concerns of the bail decision, the police were much more likely to express concern about danger to the community than the others, whose main expressed concerns were assuring appearance at trial and equity. See, National Center for State Courts, *Policymakers' Views Regarding Issues in the Operation and Evaluation of Pretrial Release and Diversion Programs: Findings from a Questionnaire Survey* (Denver, 1975).

39. An example of a "symbolic" goal might be a case in which a magistrate set very high bail for a notorious white collar crime defendant, even though the risk of flight and the potential danger to the community were perceived to be low. An example of a system constraint may be an impetus to set low bail or ROR for a time because the detention facilities are full. To the extent that detention induces guilty pleas, it may have "system advantages."

40. See F. Suffet, "Bail Setting: A Study of Courtroom Interaction," *Crime and Delinquency* 12:318 (1966).

41. Foote, *supra* note 3. See also Goldkamp, *supra* note 3.

42. Foote, *supra* note 987.

43. *Id.* at 989.

44. *Id.* at 1182.

45. See Goldkamp, *supra* note 3 at ch. 2, for a discussion of these legal issues.

46. Foote, *supra* note 3. See also N. Fabricant, "Bail as a Preferred Freedom and the Failures of New York's Revision," *Buffalo Law Review* 18:303 (1969);

and Note, "Preventive Detention Before Trial" *Harvard Law Review* 79:1489 (1966).

47. For discussion, see Foote, *supra* note 3; and Wald, *supra* note 12.

48. Bandy v. United States, 81 Sup. Ct. 197 (Douglas, Circuit Justice, 1969).

49. Whether the requisite knowledge exists to meet this goal adequately is another matter, discussed later in this chapter.

50. The question of the existence of valid empirical knowledge that would be required to meet these other goals also will be addressed later in this chapter.

51. J. Mitchell, "Bail Reform and the Constitutionality of Pretrial Detention," *Virginia Law Review* 56:1223 (1969); R. Hruska, "Preventive Detention: The Constitution and Congress," *Creighton Law Review* 3:36 (1969).

52. Wald, *supra* note 12 at 192.

53. Mitchell, *supra* note 51.

54. *Id.* at 1224. For a critique of this view, see L. Tribe, "An Ounce of Detention: Preventive Justice in the World of John Mitchell," *Virginia Law Review* 56:371 (1970).

55. A. Dershowitz, "Imprisonment by Judicial Hunch: The Case Against Pretrial Prevention Detention," *Prison Journal* L:12, 13 (1970).

56. For a discussion, see the testimony of Caleb Foote before the Subcommittee on Governmental Efficiency and the District of Columbia of the Committee on Governmental Affairs, United States Senate, 95th Congress, Second Session, February 6, 1978.

57. Stack v. Boyle, 342 U.S. 1 4-5 (1951).

58. Carlson v. Landon, 342 U.S. 524 545-46 (1952).

59. For example, in Bell v. Wolfish, 99 S. Ct. 1861 (1979), a case that involved the conditions of pretrial detainees, Rhenquist, writing for a majority of the court, wrote in a footnote that "[t]he only justification for pretrial detention asserted by the Government is to ensure the detainee's presence at trial. [Citations omitted.] Respondents do not question the legitimacy of this goal. [Citations omitted.] We, therefore, have no occasion to consider whether any other governmental objectives may constitutionally justify pretrial detention" (at 1871, n. 15).

For a critique of the view that Carlson v. Landon is in any way a dispositive holding that the Eighth Amendment does not impart a right to bail, see Foote, *supra* note 56 at 134.

60. Wald, *supra* note 47.

61. For example, the California Supreme Court has ruled (*In re* Underwood, 9 Cal. 3d 345, 348): "The purpose of bail is to assure the defendant's attendance in court when his presence is required, whether before or after conviction. [Citations omitted.] Bail is not a means for punishing defendants [citations omitted] nor for protecting public safety."

62. Foote, *supra* note 3 at 1145.

63. Landes, *supra* note 14 at 333.

64. Beeley, *supra* note 16. Portions of this discussion draw upon J. Goldkamp and M. Gottfredson, "Bail Decisionmaking and Pretrial Release: Surfacing Judicial Policy," *Law and Human Behavior* (1980).

65. Ares, Rankin, and Sturz, *supra* note 19.

66. For thorough discussion and critiques of the bail bond system see R. Goldfarb, *Ransom* (New York: Harper and Row, 1965); and Thomas, *supra* note 3.

67. Pannell v. United States, 320 F. 2d 698, 701-702, (D.C. Cir., 1963), concurring opinion of Bazelon, Chief Judge.

68. F. Feeney, "Forward," to Thomas, *supra* note 3. One study looked at the effectiveness of bondsmen in preventing defaults in comparison to an alternative of having defendants post 5 percent of the bail with the court and sign a bond to pay the rest upon default. The 5 percent was returned to the defendant when he or she showed up for trial. A before and after design was used that indicated that the default rates for all defendants released on bail were about the same under the professional bondsmen system and under the deposit system. See, J. Conklin and D. Meagher, "The Percentage Deposit Bail System: An Alternative to the Professional Bondsman," *Journal of Criminal Justice* 1:299 (1973).

69. D. Freed and P. Wald, *Bail in the United States: 1964* (Washington, D.C.: U.S. Department of Justice and the Vera Foundation, 1964).

70. *Id.* at 62.

71. *Id.*

72. President's Commission on Law Enforcement and Administration of Justice, *Task Force Report: The Courts* (Washington, D.C.: Government Printing Office, 1967), p. 38.

73. National Advisory Commission, *supra* note 4 at 102.

74. American Bar Association, *Standards Relating to Pretrial Release* (New York: Institute of Judicial Administration, 1968).

75. Bail Reform Act of 1966, 18 U.S.C. § 3146 *et seq.*

76. National Association of Pretrial Services Agencies, *Performance Standards and Goals for Pretrial Release and Diversion, Pretrial Release* (Washington, D.C., 1978).

77. J. Roth and P. Wice, "Pretrial Release and Misconduct in the District of Columbia," PROMIS Research Project Publication 16 (Washington, D.C.: INSLAW, 1978).

78. Thomas, *supra* note 3 at 251-52. The Vera-based release schemes have not been without their critics, however. Apart from concerns of the requirements of rationality discussed in the text below, critics have charged that the Vera point scales are fundamentally discriminatory because the factors comprising them are biased against the poor. See Foote, *supra* note 3.

79. Gottfredson, *supra* note 36.

80. P. S. Venezia, "Delinquency Prediction: A Critique and A Suggestion," *Journal of Research in Crime and Delinquency* 8:108 (1971). See also P. Venezia, "Pretrial Release With Supportive Services for 'High Risk' Defendants: Evaluation Report Number 3" (Davis, California: NCCD, 1973).

81. Venezia, "Delinquency Prediction," *supra* note 80 at viii.

82. M. Feeley and J. McNaughton, "The Pre-Trial Process in the Sixth Circuit (New Haven, 1974). Mimeograph.

83. The pretrial rearrest rate was only 7 percent.

84. S. Clarke, *The Bail System in Charlotte: 1971-1973*, Charlotte-Mecklenburg Criminal Justice Pilot Project (Chapel Hill, North Carolina: Institute of Government, 1974).

85. The "base rate" refers to the accuracy in prediction achieved by assuming that everyone in the sample will be a success or that everyone will be a failure.

86. Locke et al., *supra* note 35.

87. Angel et al., *supra* note 20.

88. Roth and Wice, *supra* note 77.

89. *Id.* at IV-6.

90. Gottfredson, *supra* note 36 at 293.

91. Clarke, *supra* note 84 at 43.

92. Roth and Wice, *supra* note 77 at IV-28.

93. For general discussions of the prediction problem posed by pretrial release decisions and related issues see, A. Dershowitz, "The Law of Dangerousness: Some Fictions About Prediction," *Journal of Legal Studies* 23:24 (1970); N. Morris, *The Future of Imprisonment* (Chicago: University of Chicago Press, 1974); A. von Hirsch, "Prediction of Criminal Conduct and Preventive Confinement of Convicted Persons," *Buffalo Law Review*, 21:717 (1972); and Foote, *supra* note 3. One aspect of the difficult prediction problem found by magistrates that has not received adequate attention is the differential consequences of decision errors. That is, not all decision errors have the same costs. A decision error that permits release of a child molester who repeats his offense has gravely different consequences than a similar release error involving a check forger. Similarly, the release of certain defendants, regardless of their risk of failure to appear, might be impractical from the point of view of the bail judge—for example, if it were clear that they would threaten victims or witnesses or if the feeling in the community against a defendant were strong.

94. Clarke, *supra* note 84.

95. G. Taylor, "An Evaluation of the Supervised Pretrial Release Program" (Sacramento: American Justice Institute, 1975). Manuscript.

96. Thomas, *supra* note 3 at ch. 15.

97. *Id.* at 173.

98. *Id.*

99. The criteria that are intended to influence the bail decision have been surveyed widely in recent years. In addition to the several standard-setting bodies (see notes 72, 73, 74, and 76, *supra*), many states and specific courts outline the criteria to be relied on, in theory. In all, the major influence of the Vera Institute's "community ties" criteria is obvious. For reviews, see Goldkamp, *supra* note 3; Thomas, *supra* note 3; and P. Wice, *Bail and Its Reform: A National Survey* (Washington, D.C.: Government Printing Office, 1973).

100. J. Vorenberg, "Narrowing the Discretion of Criminal Justice Officials," *Duke Law Journal* 4:651 (1976).

101. Wald, *supra* note 12 at 189.

102. Thomas, *supra* note 3 at 12.

103. E. Bock and C. Frazier, "Official Standards versus Actual Criteria in Bond Dispositions," *Journal of Criminal Justice* 5:321 (1977).

104. T. Bynum, "An Empirical Exploration of the Factors Influencing Release on Recognizance" (Ph.D. dissertation, Florida State University, 1976). The programs studied were in Duluth, Minnesota; Salt Lake City, Utah; and San Mateo, California.

105. Roth and Wice, *supra* note 77.

106. *Id.* at IV-4, IV-5.

107. Goldkamp, *supra* note 3. Other researchers who have studied bail-setting behavior include Landes, *supra* note 14; and E. Ebbesen and V. Konecni, "Decisionmaking and Information Integration in the Courts: The Setting of Bail," *Journal of Personality and Social Psychology* 32:805 (1975). The Landes sample, however, was restricted to only those cases handled by the Legal Aid Society of New York, and thus generalization of his results to bail-setting behavior in general is hazardous. Ebbesen and Konecni undertook a simulation study with eighteen judges and found that community ties, prior record, and the D.A. recommendation were related to bail.

108. Goldkamp, *supra* note 3 at 157-58.

109. D. Sperlak, "Bail: A Legal Analysis of the Bond-Setting Behavior of Holiday Court Judges in Chicago," *Chicago-Kent Law Review* 51:757 (1974).

110. Comptroller General of the United States, *The Federal Bail Process Fosters Inequities*, Report to the Congress, (Washington, D.C.: GGD-78-105, October 17, 1978).

111. Thomas, *supra* note 3 at 200.

112. See Roth and Wice, *supra* note 77.

113. W. LaFave, "Alternatives to the Present Bail System," Conference on Bail and Indigency, (1965).

114. Foote, *supra* note 3.

115. Thomas, *supra* note 3. See also American Bar Association, *supra* note 74; and National Association of Pretrial Service Agencies, *supra* note 76, both of which argue for the increased use of summons in lieu of arrest.

116. For a discussion, see Thomas, *supra* note 3 at ch. 17. See also, F. Feeney, "Citation in Lieu of Arrest: The New California Law," *Vanderbilt Law Review* 25:367 (1972).

117. Thomas, *supra* note 3 at 257.

118. A rather novel reform idea has been offered by Landes, who suggests that persons detained prior to trial and later found not guilty should be compensated financially for the violation of their presumption of innocence. Those found guilty would have their time served credited toward their sentence. His argument is that paying defendants who are not released shifts the burden of the bail system from the defendant to the state. That is, because the state would have to pay for persons detained who are innocent, there would be less detention. Landes, *supra* note 9.

119. See National Association of Pretrial Service Agencies, *supra* note 76. Preventive detention statutes that coexist with the money bail system have been found to be little used, in part because the procedural requirements and

the time involved in invoking preventive detention may be circumvented simply by setting high bail. See Roth and Wice, *supra* note 77.

120. Vorenberg, *supra* note 100 at 672.

121. For general discussions of such systems, see D. M. Gottfredson, L. T. Wilkins, and P. B. Hoffman, *Guidelines for Parole and Sentencing* (Lexington, Massachusetts: Lexington Books, 1978); for their application to bail, see Goldkamp and Gottfredson, *supra* note 64.

✳ *Chapter 5*

The Decision to Charge

After a suspect has been arrested, and in the absence of
a dismissal by the police or a magistrate at first appearance,
it must be decided whether to initiate prosecution and,
if so, for what crime or crimes. In most American jurisdictions this
decision rests with the district attorney.[1] In this chapter we will
review selected empirical studies bearing on this important decision;
investigate the goals, information, and alternatives pertaining to this
decision; and assess how what is learned bears on the requirements
of rationality.

The discretionary power to initiate formal criminal charges against
a suspect places the prosecutor in a position of influence perhaps
unparalleled in the entire system of criminal justice. This power and
control has long been recognized by students of prosecutorial discretion. In 1940 Jackson wrote: 'The prosecutor has more control
over life, liberty and reputations than any other person in America.'[2] Similarly, Mills argued:

> A State's attorney potentially has more control over the liberty and future
> of an individual than any other public official or public body. His dis-
> cretion and authority are vast and vest him with powers which are un-
> paralleled by those of any other single person.[3]

Prosecutorial influence on the system of justice has many aspects.
It includes, in addition to the charging decision, negotiating guilty
pleas, trying contested cases, and investigating proactively to discover
crimes. The focus of this chapter on the decision to charge is based
on the belief that such decisions, perhaps more than any others

made by the prosecutor, affect critically the lives of suspects and victims and the flow of cases through the criminal justice system. Moreover, the decision to charge embodies all of the significant issues of goals, information, and alternatives that also characterize other prosecutorial decisions.[4] As Abrams says, "The most significant decision that a prosecutor makes is the initiation of criminal action against a suspect."[5]

The discretion granted the prosecutor in making charging decisions is indeed vast. The principal decision alternatives, of course, are to charge a suspect with a crime or not. In addition, the prosecutor, in some jurisdictions, may decide to refer the suspect elsewhere; diversion programs, mental hospitals, community agencies, and misdemeanor courts are examples. Also, the prosecutor may charge a suspect initially and decide later to drop the charges. The power of *nolle prosequi* enables a prosecutor to decide not to pursue a case despite enough evidence to do so.[6]

The breadth of this discretion is not matched, however, with extensive formal controls over its exercise. Certainly, subsequent review by the courts, in the nature of the potential for adjudication of guilt, is a major control on overextensive prosecution. But the decision whether or not to charge is the single most unreviewed exercise of the power of the criminal law available to an individual in the American system of justice. Wide discretion both to abstain from prosecution and to prosecute selectively generally is recognized in case law.[7] Although, as will be seen in this chapter, the charging decision is influenced by other decisionmakers in the criminal justice system (such as victims, police, and judges), it generally does not involve the suspect or the suspect's counsel in an adversarial way.

The necessity and the propriety of prosecutorial discretion in pressing charges is accepted by most commentators. That not all arrests do or should result in prosecution is clear. Some victims may not be interested in prosecution. There may be insufficient evidence to convict "beyond a reasonable doubt."[8] The suspect may be innocent of any wrongdoing. Appropriate noncriminal alternatives may exist; and full charging may be unrealistic given available resources. According to the President's Commission on Law Enforcement and Administration of Justice:

Among the types of cases in which thoughtful prosecutors commonly appear disinclined to seek criminal penalties are domestic disturbances; assaults and petty thefts in which victim and offender are in a family or social relationship; statutory rape when both boy and girl are young; first offense car thefts that involve teenagers taking a car for a short joyride; checks that are drawn upon insufficient funds; shoplifting by first offenders, particularly when restitution is made; and criminal acts that involve offenders suffering from emotional disorders short of legal insanity.[9]

Despite agreement on the existence and propriety of prosecutorial charging discretion per se, the form that its exercise should take and the purposes that it is thought to serve are unclear. Typically, virtually no guidance is available from penal statutes, and charging decisions are almost never supervised judicially. At this stage in the process the prosecutor has few facts about the suspect, the offense, or the alternatives available. As a result, the prosecutor may rely on intuition, beliefs about the value of various sanctions, or personal assessment of the purposes of the criminal law.[10] Rarely does he or she have systematic knowledge of past decisions in similar cases. Almost never is information about the consequences of his or her decisions routinely conveyed back to the prosecutor. Seldom are the goals articulated clearly in a way that facilitates individual case decisions. The absence of these requirements of rationality produce low visibility, and assessments of fairness and justice are thereby made especially difficult.

The importance of studying the ways in which prosecutors decide whether to charge a suspect with a crime is conveyed vividly in Figure 5-1. This graphic, taken from a study by Forst and his colleagues[11] of felony processing in Washington, D.C., portrays the major influence of the charging decision. In fully half of the felony arrests brought by the police, the prosecutor decided not to charge, either at initial screening or later (by *nolle prosequi*). Obviously, the procedures by which such dramatic selection occurs can influence greatly the rationality of the entire process.

The central significance of the decision to charge is that it radically changes the status of the alleged offender. It transforms the accused from a suspect to a defendant. The decision to charge is the consequence of the prosecutor's belief that the accused should either bear the economic and social costs of a defense or plead guilty and suffer the attendant legal and social consequences. The charging decision itself may irreparably damage the defendant's reputation. It requires that the defendant provide money bail (or other surety) or remain incarcerated pending further action by the court. Charged defendants who are subsequently acquitted suffer these consequences needlessly. Guilty persons who are not charged cannot be subject to the penalties of the criminal law.

Apart from the profound consequences for the defendant, charging decisions by prosecutors can influence greatly other significant actors in the criminal justice process. Repeated refusals

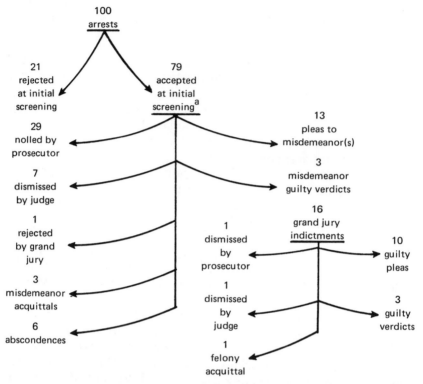

Source: Based on the actual flow of 17,534 arrests recorded in the Prosecutor's Management Information System (PROMIS). B. Forst, J. Lucianovic, and S. Cox, *What Happens After Arrest?*, Institute for Law and Social Research, Publication Number 4 (Washington, D.C.: Government Printing Office, 1977). p. 17.
[a]Total does not agree due to rounding error.

Figure 5-1. Outcomes of 100 "typical" arrests brought to the Superior Court of Washington, D.C. in 1974.

to prosecute certain types of arrests may lead to a decline in such arrests. Evidence standards adhered to by prosecutors may lead to changes in evidence-gathering practices by the police. The charging decision largely circumscribes the adjudicatory and disposition functions of trial judges. Use of such extended penalty provisions as prior record or weapon possession aggravations or of habitual criminal statutes influences the parole board's release decisions.

The critical function served by the charging decisions of the prosecutor in the American system of justice is quite clearly difficult to overestimate. We begin our assessment of rationality by an examination of the goals of this complex decision.

GOALS OF THE CHARGING DECISION

The purposes to be served by charging a suspect with a crime may, without some reflection, seem straightforward and noncontroversial: Those persons against whom sufficient evidence exists to sustain a finding of guilt by a court should be charged, whereas cases lacking the requisite evidence should not. Charging only the guilty, and all of the guilty, serves to maximize the proportion of charged persons who are eventually convicted. Some argue that conviction is itself the primary goal of the charging decision. As Forst, Lucianovic, and Cox suggest: "[T]hat the principal objective of the prosecutor is to convict offenders is well beyond dispute.[12]

Consideration of the prosecutor's place in the system of justice, however, indicates strongly that aims other than the maximization of conviction rates play a prominent role in this complex decision. Mr. Justice Sutherland suggested in *Berger v. United States* what some of these other aims might be:

> The United States Attorney is the representative not of an ordinary party to a controversy, but of a sovereignty whose obligation to govern impartially is as compelling as its obligation to govern at all; and whose interest, therefore, in a criminal prosecution is not that it shall win a case, but that Justice shall be done. As such, he is in a peculiar and very definite sense the servant of the law, the twofold aim of which is that guilt shall not escape or innocence suffer. He may prosecute with earnestness and vigor—indeed, he should do so. But, while he may strike hard blows, he is not at liberty to strike foul ones. It is as much his duty to refrain from improper methods calculated to produce a wrongful conviction as it is to use every legitimate means to bring about a just one.[13]

Thus, in addition to assessing the odds of conviction in deciding whether or not to bring charges, the prosecutor is rightly concerned as well with determining the desirability of charging.[14] The idea that the prosecutor should assess impartially the justice of prosecution is consistent with the historical antecedents of the office. Miller suggests that the prosecutorial role developed as a distinctively American institution, to prevent overzealous charging by partisan victims of crime. The theory was that a person in a position of public trust could make more impartial decisions than could victims.[15]

Apart from notions of convictability and justice (both of which present obviously difficult operational problems for prosecutors), it is commonly asserted that charging decisions should attend also to crime reduction. Such a concern is expressed in numerous ways. It might find expression in an emphasis, in terms of resources, on repeat offenders[16] or in the invocation of habitual offender statutes. In both cases, the thought is that a greater reduction in future crime will attend the incarceration of those who have committed the most offenses. Thus, the issue of prediction again surfaces as an important component of criminal justice decisionmaking. As we will see later in this chapter, the consequent issues of validity and of prediction errors must also then arise.[17]

Other major goals of charging decisions might be identified similarly. Certainly, the best utilization of scarce resources is an important pragmatic aim with significant implications. In many jurisdictions there simply are not enough resources to permit prosecution of every case desired.[18] The rehabilitative needs of the suspect also might be a frequent goal of the decision to charge, as recommended by the President's Commission on Law Enforcement and Administration of Justice.[19] Although seldom acknowledged, there may be political and personal goals. Satisfaction of the political aims of publicly elected prosecutors doubtless also directs the charging decision, perhaps principally shown in the desire to maintain a "winning record." Finally (although not exhaustively), certain system constraints impinge on the goals of the charging decision. Thus, the decision not to charge a chargeable suspect may stem from the desire to support the police informant network or to accommodate the prosecution of more significant "higher ups" in a criminal conspiracy.[20]

Besides the problem of articulating goals associated with selective prosecution, there is a problem of specifying those classes of cases that the prosecutor decides not to prosecute at all. That is, there may be a "policy of nonprosecution."[21] In such situations, rarely studied by social scientists, prosecutors decide not to enforce a particular statute. Several commentators have outlined criteria that might properly influence the prosecutor to refuse to prosecute a specific class of offenders. Abrams suggests four criteria—opposition by the community, difficulties in enforcing a statute in a legal manner, existence of an effective alternative, and the ability to prosecute for another offense.[22] The requirements of rationality, however, mandate the articulation of the aim of nonprosecution decisions, just as for selective prosecutions, so that the degree of their achievement can be assessed.

Crime reduction, efficiency, equity, just desert, politics, and both inter- and intra-agency relations are all to some extent identifiable aims of the decision to charge. Several may be present in any one charging decision; often they will conflict quite obviously.

The complexity of the goals of charging decisions is reflected in the criteria urged upon prosecutors by such standard-setting bodies as the American Bar Association. In addition to "the weight of evidence," the ABA suggests that in deciding whether or not to bring charges, the following criteria be considered: the prosecutor's assessment of guilt; the extent of harm caused by the offense; the disproportion of the punishment to the offense; possible improper motives for a complaint; prolonged nonenforcement of a statute, with community acquiescence; reluctance of the victim to testify; cooperation of the accused in the apprehension or conviction of others; and the availability and likelihood of prosecution by another jurisdiction.[23]

Criteria such as these are important starting points for the development of a rational charging policy, but they do not go far enough. Application of such criteria requires that they be ranked in priority and weighted in some fashion. Most are broad and only loosely defined (for example, "the extent of the harm caused by the offense"). As written, such criteria could be construed very differently by different prosecutors in relation to identical cases. Thus, they are not likely to enhance consistency (and thus, equity) in charging decisions.

The complexity of concerns that may legitimately influence the decision to charge, and the innumerable vagaries of individual cases, may lead some to argue that explicit criteria for the achievement of rationality or even equity are unattainable.[24] Such an assessment should, perhaps, await at least a survey of what the research literature implies about the principal influences on the decision to charge.

SOME CORRELATES OF THE DECISION TO CHARGE

Studies of charging decisions are not extensive. The widely acknowledged importance of this topic has not yet begun to be matched by systematic study. The research that has been done,[25] however, tells a good deal about how prosecutors make charging decisions.

One early report about how prosecutors decide to charge is Kaplan's discussion of personal experiences as an assistant United States attorney.[26] According to Kaplan, the first and most important factor influencing the decision to charge was the assistant's view of the guilt of the accused. Even if there was more than enough evidence to sustain a charge, Kaplan reports that the assistant U.S. attorneys themselves needed to be convinced of guilt before they would file charges. Second, the question of whether the case could result in conviction was considered. Both resource pressure and the attorney's conviction record were important factors in this assessment, according to Kaplan. He also reports that there were lower conviction standards for serious cases, which was an attempt to give some weight in the charging decision to the likelihood of future crimes by the accused. Kaplan notes that some defendants were seen to be more valuable as witnesses than as defendants and thus were not prosecuted in order to "preserve" their testimony against others. Finally, Kaplan stressed that a major factor in charging decisions was the assistant U.S. attorney's assessment of proportionality: Was the sanction associated with the charge considered as too severe given the nature and circumstances of the offense?

The significant influence of many of these factors was reaffirmed by the single most important observational study of the charging decision. This was Miller's 1970 multijurisdictional study for the American Bar Foundation.[27] Studying charging decisions in Kansas, Michigan, and Wisconsin, he amply demonstrated the complexity of this important decision and documented the many influences upon it. The detail of his study makes difficult its adequate summary, but the major correlates he identified may be discussed briefly.

Besides the minimum requirement that the prosecutor believe in the guilt of the accused, Miller suggested several factors important in determining that a person would not be charged—the attitude of the victim, the cost to the system, attendant undue harm to the suspect, the availability of alternative procedures, and the suspect's willingness to cooperate in the achievement of other enforcement goals. Thus, for example, if the victim refuses to testify, if extradition is possible, if the penalty is too severe, if revocation of parole or an insanity commitment is preferable, or if the suspect agrees to be a witness against more significant defendants, the prosecutor may decide not to charge even though there is enough evidence to do so.

Similarly, Miller enumerated and illustrated some factors that influence the decision to charge when otherwise the prosecutor would not. In the jurisdictions studied, pressure from the public or the press, the perceived ability to perform a social service for the suspect, the facilitation of other investigations, the anticipation of new developments in the case (for example, more evidence), and the desire to be rid of a particular suspect all could induce a prosecutor to charge an accused when regular enforcement procedures would indicate nonprosecution.[28]

McIntyre stresses that public acquiescence to, or toleration of, certain crimes also may play an important role in the decision to charge:

> The public does not demand rigid enforcement of certain laws, and this is an important consideration in the decision not to prosecute. When the prosecutor feels that the community no longer considers criminal a pattern of behavior prohibited by statute, he either refuses to prosecute or strives to convince the complainant to drop charges.[29]

Such observational studies are valuable. They can identify the multitude of factors bearing on the decision to charge and underscore its complexity. If systems are to be designed to enhance rationality, however, it is important also to know what factors are the primary influences in most cases. This requires systematic empirical study based upon representative samples and quantifiable data. Recently, several such important studies have been done.

Bernstein, Kelly, and Doyle studied all males arraigned for felonies in New York City during a five month period in 1975.[30] Their aim was to determine the factors most influential in the decision to prosecute fully (rather than terminate by dismissal). Of the 1213 cases in their study, 40 percent were dismissed. The independent variables studied included the suspect's race, age, education, marital status, prior record, cooperation during the arrest, and type of offense, as well as a measure of the seriousness of the charge. Their analysis indicated that the likelihood of any given suspect being dismissed increased if the most serious charge was a burglary or an assault, if the number of charges was fewer, and if the suspect was not subjected to pretrial detention. They interpreted these major correlates as indicating the primary influence of the weight of the evidence on the decision. Burglaries rarely involve witnesses and thus lack this important type of evidence, and a large number of charges may be an early indication that a strong case can be made. The demographic variables studied had little apparent impact on charging decisions.

In a separate study, Bernstein and her colleagues studied the issue of charge reduction.[31] Again, the aim was to assess the major influences of this aspect of the charging decision. They studied 1435 persons convicted of burglary, robbery, assault, and larceny charges in a New York court. Independent variables were similar to those of the previous study. Charge reduction was defined in terms of the magnitude of reduction relative to the absolute reduction possible. They discovered that the higher the original charge, the greater the reduction. No race or sex effects were found, but older defendants received larger reductions. The greater the defendant's prior record, the greater was the reduction in charges, suggesting to Bernstein and her coworkers that more experienced defendants fare better in this aspect of the criminal process.

Forst, Lucianovic, and Cox used data from the Prosecutor's Management Information System (PROMIS)[32] in Washington, D.C., to study the interaction between the police and prosecutors and to assess influences in the charging decision.[33] The PROMIS system permitted Forst and his colleagues to "track" cases from arrest through charge, discovering where and why cases fell out along the way. Besides defendant criminal history and case data, the PROMIS system included data on the reasons given by prosecutors for their charging decisions.

As we saw in Chapter 3, the study confirmed the significant role that the evidence-gathering ability of arresting officers can play in subsequent prosecutorial decisions. Table 5-1 shows the reasons given by the prosecutor for refusing prosecution at initial screening. In 21 percent of the arrests the prosecutor decided at initial screening not to charge. Witness and evidence problems were the reasons given by the prosecutors for not charging in more than half the

Table 5-1. Arrest Rejections at Initial Screening, Reasons Given by Prosecutor, by Major Offense Group, 1974 (percent).

	Crime Group					
Rejection Reason	*Robbery*	*Other violent*	*Nonviolent property*	*Victimless*	*Other*	*All Crimes*
Witness problem	43	51	25	2	5	25
Insufficiency of evidence	35	18	37	40	41	34
Due process problem	0	0	2	20	3	5
No reason given	0	0	1	0	1	1
Other	22	30	36	38	50	36
Total rejections	100	100	100	100	100	100
Number of rejections	242	876	1,257	654	621	3,650
Number of arrests	1,955	3,176	6,562	3,659	2,182	17,354
Rejection rate	12%	28%	19%	18%	29%	21%

Source: B. Forst, J. Lucianovic, and S. Cox, *What Happens After Arrest?*, Institute for Law and Social Research, Publication November 4 (Washington, D.C.: Government Printing Office, 1977), p. 67.

cases. Witness problems include failure to appear, refusal to testify, and lack of credibility, while evidence problems include the availability of physical evidence. Witness problems seem especially important in violent offenses, and tangible evidence appears to be similarly important in property crimes. Arrest problems associated with police violations of due process rights of suspects appear to be a major problem only with victimless crimes, a factor probably associated with the lack of complaining witnesses for these events.

Forst and associates also studied the reasons given by prosecutors for dismissing cases accepted initially for prosecution. Of the 8766 arrests made in 1974 which the prosecutor decided not to charge, 58 percent were dismissed (*nolle prosequi*) after having been accepted initially.[34] A substantial portion of these later dismissals (28 percent) were the result of the successful completion of diversion programs. Again, witness problems accounted for a sizeable share of the dismissals (13 percent), but evidence and due process problems were cited very infrequently at this stage.

The ways that victim characteristics may influence the prosecutor's decision to charge a suspect were studied by Williams (also using Washington, D.C., PROMIS data). Examining homicide, assault, sexual assault, and robbery arrests, she discovered that attributes of the victim did indeed play a significant role in such decisions.[35] Cases in which victim provocation seemed to be a factor and cases involving victims with known histories of alcohol abuse were refused prosecution twice as often as cases lacking these factors. She found no effect on the charging decision of the victim's arrest record or age, but cases with female victims were rejected more frequently. The victim-accused relationship was found to vary in its effect on the charging decision depending on the type of crime. In aggravated assault, cases involving spouses or friends were more likely to be dropped than others, as were cases involving friends in sexual assault cases. When the victim and accused were ex-spouses, cohabiting, or in a girlfriend-boyfriend relationship, cases of simple assault tended not to be prosecuted.

A third study using the same data set examined whether prosecutors gave priority to cases involving recidivists.[36] Examining data for the years 1971 through 1975, Forst and Brosi discovered that of the 37,840 persons prosecuted, persons who were prosecuted twice accounted for 28 percent of all, and persons who were prosecuted three times accounted for 12 percent. Of all prosecutions, persons prosecuted two times accounted for 53 percent, and persons prosecuted three times accounted for 32 percent. "The apparent conclusion is that a small number of individuals represent a signifi-

cant proportion of the prosecutor's and court's work load . . . ."[37]
They argued that goals of both crime reduction and minimization
of workload might be better served if these cases received special
prosecutorial attention:

> Given the disproportionately large share of crime commited by repeat
> offenders, prosecutors seem more than justified in structuring their dis-
> cretion so that an appropriate percentage of time and staff is focused
> on recidivists, even though this might mean that other cases with as
> much or more evidence and involving less frequent or less serious of-
> fenders would have to be rejected or pursued with less-than-normal
> intensity . . . .
>
> A greater reduction in future crime rates and future workloads . . .
> is likely to follow the incarceration of those whose criminal histories
> reflect their relatively high potential for future criminality.[38]

The relative importance that the prosecutor attached to the
seriousness of the current case, the defendant's criminal history,
and the probability of conviction was assessed by Forst and Brosi
by a multivariate analysis of 6000 felony cases. The probability
of winning (that is, of conviction) was measured by empirical relations of various factors to conviction. These factors included
assessments of witnesses, of tangible evidence, of the number of
days between the offense and arrest, and of the victim-offender
relationship. Their aim was to discover the extent to which the
prosecutors employed the strategy of priority to repeat offenders.
Prosecutorial effort was measured by the number of days the prosecutor carried the case.

They discovered that, *certeris paribus*, prosecutors attached the
most importance to the strength of the evidence and, to a lesser
degree, to the seriousness of the case. Their findings were thus
consistent with both the observational and systematic empirical
studies already discussed. They discovered also, however, that
virtually none of the prosecutorial effort could be accounted for
by the criminal history of the defendant. They conclude that their
data "provide no empirical support to the hypothesis that the
prosecutor attempts to give more attention to cases involving
defendants with extensive arrest records."[39]

This study by Forst and Brosi illustrates the predictive element
of many prosecutorial charging decisions. To the extent that prosecutors select out some defendants from a larger group of otherwise chargeable defendants for a crime control purpose (for example,
to incapacitate them so that their future crimes will be delayed
if not avoided), their selection decisions are predictive ones. (Simi-

larly, if prosecutors select cases with a view to the probability of conviction, this selection too involves prediction.) It is appropriate, though, to assess the predictive validity of the basis for such selections. Forst and Brosi cite the large number of persons who are prosecuted for the second and third time as evidence of the need for a crime reduction aim for charging decisions, and they suggest that prior record be given a priority in the charging process. Such a rationale undergirds the many career criminal programs that have sprung up in prosecutors' offices throughout the country.

It should be realized, however, that the large number of recidivists who are subject to new prosecution is not convincing evidence of the predictive utility of prior record in such a crime reduction program. The questions that need to be asked are, What proportion of those prosecuted once are again prosecuted for a new offense? And, What proportion of those prosecuted a second time are again prosecuted for a new offense? Although prior record is found consistently to be a predictor of subsequent offending, the association typically is a very modest one. Considering prior criminal history only, a very substantial number of errors are likely to be made in predicting future offending. It is likely that less attention will be generated by these "false positives" than by those that attend predictive decisions at the bail, sentencing, and parole decisions, since all of the cases from which the selections are made are theoretically chargeable. Assigning priorities in charging decisions on the basis of unverified predictive criteria may nonetheless be questioned.[40] To the extent that crime reduction is regarded as a proper prosecutorial charging aim, there is a clear need for empirically demonstrated predictive criteria.

Besides these studies of the decision to charge in a single jurisdiction, there have been some informative systematic-empirical studies of comparative practices. Greenwood and his colleagues examined charging practices among various counties in California and within offices in Los Angeles County.[41] They discovered substantial variation in the charging practices among counties in the proportions of felony arrests that actually resulted in the district attorney filing felony charges. Much of this variation seemed attributable to the proportion of arrests that initially were classified by the police as felonies. Within Los Angeles County (where 78,000 felony complaints were studied), they also discovered substantial interoffice variability in charging. Overall, the district attorney refused to file felony charges against over half of the defendants arrested by the police, although there was considerable variation in felony charging according to the type of offense. The highest rates of prosecution rejection were associated with wife and child beating (85 percent rejected), assault with a deadly weapon (87 percent), and rape (63 percent). The lowest rejection rates were found for bookmaking (7 percent rejected), attempted robbery (10 percent), and the sale of dangerous drugs (7 percent). Most of the rejected felony arrests were based on a lack of evidence and the district attorney's belief that the case was not serious enough to warrant felony processing.[42]

Greenwood and his colleagues interpreted these results (particularly those pertaining to interoffice variability) as demonstrating a lack of equity in the charging decision. Their evidence suggests that many defendants may be overcharged by the police (that is, charged with an offense more serious than is warranted) and, thus, that "Many citizens who are subsequently found not guilty of behavior deserving felony punishment are subjected to the anxiety, costs and loss of freedom associated with a felony arrest, as opposed to the much more limited costs and inconveniences associated with a misdemeanor arrest."[43] Such findings emphasize the need for clear, specific, and carefully articulated criteria upon which to base charging decisions. They suggest also an important need for routine feedback to the decisionmakers so that they may determine the decision patterns of their colleagues. Without knowledge of how similar decisions are made by other decisionmakers within the same jurisdiction, inequity must continue to be expected.

In another recent interjurisdictional analysis of felony-charging decisions, Brosi studied the attrition of felony cases in several large cities (using PROMIS data).[44] Although overall about half of the cases dropped out of the system after arrest and prior to disposition, there was considerable variability in the ways these arrests fell out. Figure 5-2 demonstrates these interjurisdiction differences in the proportions of arrests rejected at screening (that is, with no charge by the prosecutor), *nolle prosequi*, referred, and adjudicated. These comparisons must be judged in light of the procedural differences among these jurisdictions. In Washington, D.C., for example, almost all arrests are taken to the prosecutor. In others (for example, Los Angeles), the police screen cases first. In most jurisdictions the police book suspects with a charge and suggest the charge to the prosecutor, who can accept, modify, or drop the charge.[45] Regardless of the jurisdictional variation in how cases are brought to the prosecutor, however, Brosi found considerable rates of rejection at intake (that is, decisions by prosecutors not to charge); these ranged from 18 percent in Cobb County, Georgia, to 40 percent in New Orleans.

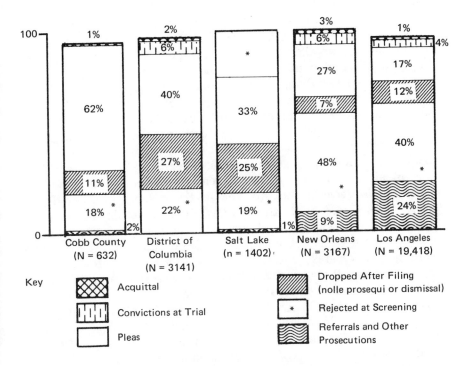

Key

Acquittal	
Convictions at Trial	
Pleas	

Dropped After Filing (nolle prosequi or dismissal)

* Rejected at Screening

Referrals and Other Prosecutions

Note: Totals do not always add to 100; open cases and administrative and "other" dispositions are not included.

*Data not available.

Source: K. Brosi, *A Cross-City Comparison of Felony Case Processing* (Washington, D.C.: Institute for Law and Social Research, 1979), p. 7.

Figure 5-2. Dispositions of criminal cases from arrest (PROMIS data, January to June 1977, felonies).

Different types of crimes were found to have different rates of rejection. Accusations of assault and of rape consistently were more often rejected at screening by the prosecutor than were other felony allegations. Those involving property (for example, robbery) were less often rejected. Brosi suggests that the victim-offender relationship is critical in this initial charging decision. Some victims who desire prosecution initially later reconcile with the defendant. Also suggested as a major factor in some of these decisions not to prosecute is the quality of the arrest; in others, the initial arrest was intended principally as a technique to stop an ongoing victimization.

In many arrests in each jurisdiction studied, the prosecutor filed charges initially but latter dropped them (*nolle prosequi* or dismissal). Seven percent of the arrests in New Orleans and 27 percent in the District of Columbia were dropped in this fashion. Thus, the total proportion of cases in which the prosecutor decided not to prosecute (including those rejected at screening, referred elsewhere, and dropped after filing) ranged from about a third in Cobb County to about half in the District of Columbia to about three-fourths in Los Angeles. These data demonstrate quite clearly that the prosecutor's decision whether or not to charge plays a major role in the criminal justice process.

Brosi also studied the reasons given by prosecutors in these jurisdictions for deciding not to charge the suspect in these felony arrests. Consistent with the studies cited earlier in this chapter, both evidence problems and witness problems accounted for the greatest share of rejections (among those cases in which reasons were given). Overall, these two reasons accounted for over half of the arrests that were rejected.[46] Witnesses appear to present special problems in accusations of felonious assault. She reported data showing that about a fourth of the "noncooperative" witnesses were people who could not be located because their names, addresses, or phone numbers were recorded incorrectly at the crime scene. Half of the rest of the "noncooperative" witnesses did not receive adequate information about court appearances.[47] The majority of the arrests rejected at screening because of evidence problems involved insufficient testimonial evidence to corroborate the offense or to establish a necessary element of it. Such problems were most prevalent in burglary and larceny arrests.

Again consistent with previous studies, Brosi discovered that due process problems played only a minor role in decisions not to charge at screening. From 1 to 9 percent of the rejected arrests were rejected for this reason. She concludes that "While it may be that the police do not arrest some suspects because of search and seizure limitations, these percentages seem to counter the conventional wisdom that Supreme Court decisions cause many arrests to fail because of technicalities."[48] Most of the due-process-related decisions not to charge occurred with drug arrests.

The complexity of goals in prosecutorial charging decisions perhaps is evidenced by Brosi's finding that a sizeable proportion (from 3 to 22 percent) of the rejections at screening were due to the reason that the case "lacks prosecutive merit." Although interpretation of this reason is difficult because of its ambiguous phrasing, she inferred that this category is the "fairness valve" in the exercise of prosecutorial discretion—used for cases that violate the letter but not the spirit of the law.[49]

TOWARD RATIONALITY

The results of these studies are at once encouraging and discouraging. They are encouraging because they show that the charging decision is not beyond the province of social science methods. Many of the goals and influences pertaining to this complex decision are capable of measurement and systematic study. These studies indicate, as is found throughout the criminal justice system, that relatively few factors have a good deal of salience in the decision. In this case, evidence sufficiency, witness problems, the victim-offender relationship, and the seriousness of the alleged behavior have critical influences on the charging decision. They are discouraging because they report such variability—not only among prosecutors' offices but within them as well—in the goals, information, and alternatives used in the charging process.

We noted at the beginning of this chapter the very large grant of discretion given to prosecutors in making charging decisions. In a sense, the studies reviewed provide some indications of the consequences of this discretion. In pursuit of individualizing case decisions, and in the absence of well-defined criteria and goals, similar cases often are not treated similarly; and this, of course, raises fundamental issues of fairness. The need for discretion in this decision is clear. In order to accommodate the variety of offenses, offenders, and alternatives with the many goals of prosecution, rigid and mechanical policy standards insufficient to deal with this complexity are inappropriate. No doubt, they simply would be circumvented if they existed.

The existence of discretion, however, need not mean that inconsistency must exist as well. The problem, as with the other decisions discussed in this book, is the creation of standards that structure the discretion in such a way as to enhance equity of treatment simultaneously with maximizing the achievement of the other important goals. The creation of such flexible standards requires, however, an undergirding. The base needed is relevant knowledge upon which the prosecutor can draw that relates empirically the data available to the alternative goals sought, and a systematic process is essential to permit judging the consistency with which these standards are applied. It also requires that the goals be given a clear priority ordering, with some degree of consensus.

As Abrams has indicated:

> There is a competing tension between the need in prosecutorial decision-making for certainty, consistency, and an absence of arbitrariness on the one hand, and the need for flexibility, sensitivity, and adaptability on the other. The problem is to design the system so as to reach an acceptable balance between the two sets of values.[50]

In later chapters we discuss what we believe to be such a system in some detail. Here, we can describe the significant advances toward such methods that have been made in the area of charging decisions.

One such important advance has been the development, testing, and implementation of computerized case evaluation systems in many prosecutors' offices.[51] The aim of the system (known as PROMIS—Prosecutor's Management Information System) is to indicate priorities for prosecution from the cases available for prosecution. Priorities are assigned to cases on the basis of computer-generated scores that evaluate the gravity of the alleged crime and the criminal history of the suspect. The scores are tallied on the basis of two scales. The first, developed by Sellin and Wolfgang,[52] evaluates the seriousness of the alleged criminal behavior by assigning weights to various elements of the offense and summing these values. The factors used typically pertain to physical injury, property loss or damage, and intimidation. Thus, for example, if a particular crime involves the loss of property worth less than $10 and no injury or intimidation, it might receive a value of 1, whereas a crime involving death to the victim might receive a value of 26. The assumption underlying the use of this scale is that the greater the seriousness of the offense, the higher should be the prosecutorial priority. This assumption, then, seems consistent with some commonly stated prosecution goals reviewed earlier in this chapter and with some of the empirical data on charging decisions. The second scale attempts to measure the gravity of the criminal history of the defendant. Developed originally by one of us as a parole prediction device,[53] this scale weights, inter alia, the extent of the defendant's prior record and its characteristics. The assumption underlying the use of this scale is that defendants with more serious prior records should be prosecuted with priority; or because the scale was developed to measure the probability of recidivism on parole, its use perhaps reflects a crime control purpose.

Each case entering the system is scored according to these dimensions. In some jurisdictions another dimension is added—the evidentiary strength of the case.[54] Figure 5-3, from Jacoby's discussion

COPY 1 - mail to evaluator as soon as possible COPY 2-3 - your files
COPY 4 - if case accepted, send to evaluator upon final disposition

Pre-Trial Screening Evaluation		000-00-000
(Office Name) _____	Evaluation Received Date _____	(Serial Number preprinted)
(Address) _____	Coder _____	_____
_____ (phone) _____	Verifier _____	
Name of Defendant	Sex Race DOB	Complaint Number
		Defendent I.D. No.
Address:	Date Offense Date Arrest	Court Case Number
Prosecutor Action: Accepted Refused Other		Coding only
Reason (if not accepted)		
Police Arrest Charge(s)		
Prosecutors Charge(s)		Coding only
Charging Assistant Name: _____ Date: _____		

A. NATURE OF CASE	check if applicable	pts	B. NATURE OF DEFENDANT		
Victim			Felony Convictions		
one or more persons	☐ ☐	2.0	one	☐	9.7
			more than one	☐	18.7
Victim Injury					
received minor injury	☐	2.4	Misdemeanor Convictions		
treated and released	☐	3.0	one	☐	3.6
hospitalized	☐	4.2	more than one	☐	8.3
Intimidation			Prior Arrests—Same Charge		
one or more persons	☐	1.3	one	☐	4.5
Weapon			more than	☐	7.2
defendant armed	☐	7.4	Prior Arrests		
defendant fired shot or			one	☐	2.2
carried gun, or			more than one	☐	4.2
carried explosives	☐	15.7			
			Prior Arrest—Weapons Top Charge		
Stolen Property			more than one	☐	6.4
any value	☐	7.5			
			Status When Arrested		
Prior Relationship			state parole	☐	7.1
victim and defendant—			wanted	☐	4.2
same family	☐	-2.8			
Arrest					
at scene	☐	4.6			
within 24 hours	☐	2.9	DISTRICT ATTORNEY'S EVALUATION _____		
Evidence					
admission or statement	☐	1.4			
additional witnesses	☐	3.1	TOTAL SCORE _____		
Identification					
line up	☐	3.3	RANKING CLERK _____		

FOR EACH CHARGE, RECORD: (1) Disposition, (2) Reason, (3) Process Step, (4) Date _____

Source: J. Jacoby, *The Prosecutor's Charging Decision: A Policy Perspective* (Washington, D.C.: Government Printing Office, 1977), p. 42.

Figure 5-3. Model form for evaluation of an individual local pretrial screening project.

of the case evaluation system instituted in the Bronx District Attorney's Office, indicates how these scores are derived. (The "Nature of Defendant" score here is based on prior record items and legal status.) The sum of the weighted items determines the priority score for the case. There could be several uses of such a scoring procedure: cases with the highest scores might be subject to special prosecutorial effort; score values might be useful in determining whether or not to charge in the first instance; and so forth.

Some of the potential advantages of such systems have been proposed. For example, Jacoby notes that "since each case presented for prosecution review is scored on the basis of the *same* factors, the evaluation is uniform and consistent. Objectivity is achieved also because the factors used for the evaluation are statistically derived (quantifiable) and require only minimal subjective interpretation."[55] In addition, visibility is enhanced when such systems are used routinely, since the policy (for example, crime seriousness and offender record deserve emphasis) is explicit, as are the criteria to be used (for example, the Sellin-Wolfgang weights). This then permits informed debate about the propriety of both. (For example, should a measure of recidivism determine who is to be prosecuted?).

Additional advantages of the PROMIS method of prosecutorial priorities have been suggested.[56] Legal nomenclature may mask underlying differences among cases—for example, not all aggravated assaults are alike—whereas this system permits the assessment of cases on the basis of specific elements of the offense. Also, once the similarities of cases are taken into consideration on the basis of consistent criteria, then major differences that require different handling may be more readily apparent. By emphasizing the major differences among defendants, moreover, such systems may increase the motivation to seek alternatives suitable to the individual case.

Perhaps the most important advantage to a computerized evaluation system, however, is that it facilitates the acquisition of information, as the term is used in this book. Thus, the development and application of explicit criteria permit the study of how those criteria relate to the goals of the charging decision. In the absence of a relation they may be modified. Perhaps the most salient example would relate to factors predictive of future offending.

Such systems permit the acquisition of another type of information—how consistently cases are handled by the prosecutors making charging decisions. That is, cases with similar scores may be followed to see whether or not they receive similar treatment at each of the major charging decisions (that is, charge–no charge, plea bargaining, etc.). Relevant to the equity goal, information about inconsistent treatment may be reported back to the decisionmakers with the aim of enhancing uniformity of treatment. Only when explicit criteria exist that identify what is meant by "similar offenders," such as those that exist with the PROMIS system, may such information be available. The point to be made is simply that in order to have consistency, each prosecutor in a jurisdiction must know what the others are doing. In order to know this well, systematic, reliable procedures keeping track of representative cases are essential.

If the systems implemented are truly evolutionary ones, in the sense that they are judged repeatedly against the data and, where they do not fit, are adapted accordingly, it should be possible to "fine tune" the case evaluations.[57] Some of the apparent disparity in case processing, for example, may be the result of application of criteria in individual cases that, although they may be both proper and rational, are not included among the case evaluation criteria. A significant challenge at all of the decision points discussed in this book is to identify, articulate, and structure the influence of nonapparent, difficult to weigh, and uncommon criteria.[58] If prosecutors were required to give specific reasons for their belief that a particular case should deviate from "consistent" treatment, then, if appropriate, these reasons could serve as the fuel for adapting future case evaluation procedures. Equity should be sought in charging decisions, but not at the cost of treating unequal cases alike. The development of explicit standards with uniform application should facilitate the identification of significant differences among cases that permit alternative decisions within a rational, flexible decision policy.

The development of decision aids such as PROMIS go a long way down the road toward increased rationality. Research of the type reviewed in this chapter permits additional steps to be taken. Some of the fundamental correlates of the decision to charge are becoming known. What needs now to be known is how these correlates of the decision relate or fail to relate to the goals that also have been identified and to the various decision alternatives. As we repeatedly stress, only when confidence can be held that these correlates of the decision are adequately informative about the goals of the decision can charging decisions claim to be made rationally.

NOTES

1. For discussion of comparative practices in different jurisdictions, see F. Miller, *Prosecution: The Decision to Charge a Suspect With a Crime* (Boston:

Little, Brown and Co., 1970); D. McIntyre, ed., *Law Enforcement in the Metropolis* (Chicago: American Bar Foundation, 1967); and President's Commission on Law Enforcement and Administration of Justice, *Task Force Report: The Courts* (Washington, D.C.: Government Printing Office, 1967). In some jurisdictions the police may file charges directly with the court without prior screening by a prosecutor.

2. R. Jackson, "The Federal Prosecutor," *Journal of American Judicature Society* 24:18 (1940).

3. R. Mills, "The Prosecutor: Charging and 'Bargaining'," *Illinois Crim. Proc.* 1966:511 (1966).

4. In some respects the distinction between the decision to charge and decisions made about guilty plea negotiations is artificial. The charging decision, with respect to what to charge and how many counts, can be greatly influenced by negotiation strategies. See, D. Newman, *Conviction: The Determination of Guilt or Innocence Without Trial* (Boston: Little, Brown and Co., 1966). The complex interplay among decisions throughout the system need always be kept clearly in mind in discussions presented in this book. Plea bargaining is a large and important topic in its own right. See Newman, *id.*; and A. Rosett and D. Cressey, *Justice By Consent* (Philadelphia: Lippincott, 1976).

5. N. Abrams, "Prosecutorial Charge Decisions Systems," *University of California Law Review* 21:1 (1975). As Newman pointed out, and as will be demonstrated in this chapter, the decision to charge consists of two components—one qualitative and one quantitative.

Qualitatively, the question is whether, in the judgement of the district attorney, the accused ought to be charged with a crime at all, or if in the interest of equity, individualization of justice, or mitigating circumstance, it would be fairer, more just, or sufficient for the purposes of law and the objectives of his office to refrain from prosecuting at all. The quantitative facet relates to the *vigor* of prosecution once it is determined to be possible and desirable. In some cases the prosecutor may charge a crime as serious as the evidence permits, may multiply charges to their fullest, or may even level "extra-Maximum" charges by invoking habitual-criminal statutes or similar provisions.

D. Newman, "Role and Process in the Criminal Court," in D. Glaser, ed., *Handbook of Criminology* (Chicago: Rand McNally, 1974), p. 608.

6. Although sometimes provided by statute, this power originates in common law. See Newman, *supra* note 5 at ch. 15. For discussions of informal charging alternatives, see F. Remington, et al., *Criminal Justice Administration* (New York: Bobbs-Merrill, 1969), esp. pp. 417-19; and President's Commission, *supra* note 1.

7. For citations and discussions, see W. LaFave, "The Prosecutor's Discretion in the United States," *The American Journal of Comparative Law* 18:532 (1970); and Comment, "Prosecutorial Discretion in the Initiation of Criminal Complaints," *Southern California Law Review* 42:518 (1969).

8. Although the formal evidence standard to charge is the same as to arrest— "probable cause"—for the prosecutor this standard must be forward looking

to the conviction standard of "beyond a reasonable doubt." See, D. Newman, *supra* note 5. Miller's observations of prosecutorial charging lead him to conclude: "it is not inaccurate to assert that an affirmative initial charging decision usually requires a belief on the part of the prosecutor that the suspect is guilty beyond a reasonable doubt." Both limitations on resources and the belief that it is unfair to charge a suspect who cannot be convicted result in this standard. Miller, *supra* note 1 at 22. Miller found no evidence in his study to indicate that prosecutors charge suspects who would be unconvictable so as to coerce a guilty plea. *Id.* at 23. On the other hand, McIntyre reports that unconvictables are sometimes charged—for example, when the police promise that additional evidence will be forthcoming. McIntyre, *supra* note 1.

9. President's Commission, *supra* note 1 at 5.

10. See, generally, Abrams, *supra* note 5.

11. B. Forst, J. Lucianovic, and S. Cox, *What Happens After Arrest?*, Institute for Law and Social Research, Publication Number 4 (Washington, D.C.: Government Printing Office, 1977).

12. *Id.* at 65.

13. Berger v. United States, 294 U.S. 78, 88. Cited in Mills, *supra* note 3.

14. See also Newman, *supra* note 5.

15. Miller, *supra* note 1 at 295.

16. For example, Forst, Lucianovic, and Cox, *supra* note 11, argue: "the prosecutor might reject or dismiss a convictable arrest in favor of another somewhat less highly convictable one when the latter case involves an arrestee who has revealed a high propensity for the repeated commission of serious criminal acts" (at 63).

17. The charging decision is fundamentally predictive in another important sense—the forecast of convictability by the court.

18. Forst, Lucianovic, and Cox, *supra* note 11.

19. President's Commission, *supra* note 1.

20. See Newman, *supra* note 5; and Miller, *supra* note 1.

21. See Abrams, *supra* note 5.

22. *Id.*

23. American Bar Association, Project on Standards for Criminal Justice, *Standards Relating to the Prosecution and the Defense Function*, Approved Draft (New York: Institute for Judicial Administration, 1971), p. 34.

24. See, for example, D. McIntyre and D. Lippman, "Prosecutors and Early Disposition of Felony Cases," *American Bar Association Journal* 56:1154, 1155 (1970).

25. Given the secrecy that surrounds most prosecutor's offices and their politically inspired reluctance to engage in outsider research, any empirical research on the topic must be considered an accomplishment.

26. J. Kaplan, "The Prosecutorial Discretion—A Comment," *Northwestern University Law Review* 60:174 (1965).

27. Miller, *supra* note 1.

28. The influence of outside agencies in the decision to charge is documented amply by Miller, *supra* note 1. He shows that to some extent the police may control the charging decision by their decisions not to arrest. That is, if the

police decide that prosecution is not warranted, they do not arrest the suspect, effectively negating the prosecutor's influence. Judicial dismissals serve an analogous function at the other end.

Other observational studies report similar interagency influences on charging decisions. G. Cole, "The Decision to Prosecute," *Law and Society Review* 4:313 (1970), reports that in Seattle the decision whether or not to charge often is made with other criminal justice agencies in mind, particularly the police.

29. McIntyre, *supra* note 1 at 111.

30. I. Bernstein, W. Kelly, and P. Doyle, "Societal Reaction to Deviants: The Case of Criminal Defendants," *American Sociological Review* 42:743 (1977).

31. I. Bernstein, E. Kick, J. Leung, and B. Schulz, "Charge Reduction: An Intermediary Stage in the Process of Labelling Criminal Defendants," *Social Forces* 56:363 (1977).

32. The PROMIS system will be discussed more fully in a subsequent section.

33. Forst, Lucianovic, and Cox, *supra* note 11.

34. *Id.* at 68.

35. K. Williams, *The Role of the Victim in the Prosecution of Violent Offenses*, Institute for Law and Social Research, Publication Number 12 (Washington, D.C.: Government Printing Office, 1978).

36. B. Forst and K. Brosi, "A Theoretical and Empirical Analysis of the Prosecutor," *Journal of Legal Studies* 6:177 (1977); also *Curbing the Repeat Offender: A Strategy for Prosecutors*, Institute for Law and Social Research, Publication Number 3 (Washington, D.C.: Government Printing Office, 1977).

37. *Curbing the Repeat Offender, supra* note 36 at 4.

38. *Id.* at 12.

39. Forst and Brosi, "A Theoretical and Empirical Analysis," *supra* note 36 at 191. Of interest is the apparent correspondence between the major factors that were found to influence convictability and those that seem to influence prosecutorial priority. This, of course, is consistent with the notion that the individual prosecutor's goal is to win cases. Both witnesses and tangible evidence play significant roles.

40. Because the vast majority of persons charged with an offense who subsequently are found guilty are found guilty by virtue of a plea to the charge, and because in most jurisdictions the charge largely circumscribes the available sanctions, the charging decision also can be considered (for some purposes) as a sentencing decision. So conceived, the predictive aim of charging to reduce crime may give many contemporary sentencing theorists considerable pause. See the discussions in Chapter 6.

41. P. Greenwood, S. Wildhorn, E. Poggin, M. Strumwasser, and P. DeLeon, *Prosecution of Adult Felony Defendants in Los Angeles County: A Policy Perspective* (Washington, D.C.: U.S. Department of Justice, 1973).

42. *Id.* at 16.

43. *Id.* at vii.

44. K. Brosi, *A Cross-City Comparison of Felony Case Processing* (Washington, D.C.: Institute for Law and Social Research, 1979). Brosi notes that

a study of charging decisions in Cleveland in the early 1920s, based on analysis of 5000 arrests, found that the most common dispositions of arrests were refusal to prosecute and dismissals before trial (F. Frankfurter and R. Pound, *Criminal Justice in Cleveland* [1922; rpt. ed., Montclair, New Jersey: Patterson Smith, 1968]). Brosi reported comparable findings in several cities in 1977.

45. Brosi, *supra* note 44 at 11.

46. *Id.* at 16.

47. *Id.* at 17.

48. *Id.* at 19.

49. As with rejections at screening, Brosi found that the major reasons for postfiling dismissals and *nolles* were evidence and witness related. Plea bargaining was an important factor in some of these later decisions not to charge, while again due process problems rarely occurred.

50. N. Abrams, "Internal Policy: Guiding the Exercise of Prosecutorial Discretion," *U.C.L.A. Law Review* 19:1 pp. 3-4 (1971).

51. For discussions of these systems and their purposes, see W. Hamilton and C. Work, "The Prosecutor's Role in the Urban Court System: The Case for Management Consciousness," *Journal of Criminology and Criminal Law* 64:183 (1973); J. Jacoby, *The Prosecutor's Charging Decision: A Policy Perspective* (Washington, D.C.: Government Printing Office, 1977); and Institute for Law and Social Research, *Uniform Case Evaluation and Rating*, INSLAW Briefing Paper Number 3 (Washington, D.C.: INSLAW, 1976).

52. T. Sellin and M. Wolfgang, *The Measurement of Delinquency* (New York: John Wiley, 1964).

53. D.M. Gottfredson and J.A. Bonds, "A Manual for Intake Base Expectancy Scoring," Form CDC-BE61A (Sacramento: California Department of Corrections, 1961). Mimeograph.

54. See, e.g., Jacoby, *supra* note 51.

55. *Id.* at 47.

56. These arguments are taken from Institute for Law and Social Research, *supra* note 51.

57. The concept of evolutionary policy models is discussed in more detail in later chapters.

58. Abrams, *supra* note 50 at 8, makes this point well.

✳ *Chapter 6*

Sentencing Decisions

Once convicted, the offender must be sentenced. This human decision lies at the hub of current controversies about the basic purposes of the whole criminal justice system. Indeed, recent trends in the philosophy of sentencing address issues so fundamental to criminal justice that they must be expected to have a profound impact on the entire system in the next few years.[1] These tendencies toward changed conceptions of the purposes of sentencing also involve debates about the extent of discretion that ought to be allowed judges in choosing alternative sentences. In this chapter we seek to summarize these trends, to speculate about their potential implications for rationality in decisionmaking, and to identify some of the research challenges that they present.

In contrast with the European model of criminal procedure, which emphasizes a unity of proceedings, the American criminal trial consists of two distinct phases to determine (1) criminal liability and (2) the appropriate sentence. In the first phase the court deals with "a finding on those limited facts which match the form and model of the elementary statutory requirements of the penal code section allegedly violated."[2] In the second, perhaps more complicated phase, the court must deal with "four complicated, extensive, and variegated complexes" of correctional-penological aims—information on the background and personality of the offender, data from social science, and the availability of sanctioning methods and institutions.[3] The sentencing decision thus has the three familiar parts of any decision—goals, information, and alternatives, and all are extremely complex.

171

In fixing the sentence, the judge occupies a central role capable of markedly influencing all other parts of the system. Sentencing decisions can and do have an impact on the roles and behaviors of police, prosecutors, and correctional authorities. Thus, changes in sentencing law or practice may have very important implications for the entire law enforcement, court, and correctional enterprise.[4]

The purposes of sentencing, however, are by no means agreed upon. There is disagreement not only about the proper goals of the sentencing decision but also much current debate about appropriate alternatives. It is in the context of these arguments that the trends to be discussed in this chapter have emerged. Before discussing these trends, however, it may be useful to define the disputes by outlining briefly the most commonly held theories of sentencing and their philosophical underpinnings.

SENTENCING GOALS

The bifurcation of American criminal trials (between determinations of criminal liability and of the sentence) is such that one important sanction already has been imposed before sentencing. This is the conviction itself, which, as described by Weiler, publicly, authoritatively, decisively, and enduringly certifies that the defendant is guilty of blameworthy conduct causing harm to an innocent victim. Although, as Weiler notes, it often is overlooked in discussions of sentencing, this stigmatization of a person as an offender inflicts "not only a damaging, but also one of the most enduring, sanctions which the state can mete out."[5]

Rarely, however, is the conviction alone considered to be a sufficient sanction, and a variety of justifications for additional ones have been argued. The controversies have endured for thousands of years, and the disputes of today continue to be lively.

Weiler points out that two basic moral conflicts lie at the root of this complex of theories of sentencing. The first distinction is found between utilitarian and desert perspectives.[6] The former is committed to maximizing the general good; the latter is addressed to principles of justice, fairness, and equity. A second, related distinction poses the conflict between reductionism and retributionism. This fundamental difference has profound implications not only for the basis of sentencing in the criminal law but also for the judge as sentencing decisionmaker. It is a critical distinction as well in respect to debates about the justifiable role of prediction in sentencing decisions. As summarized by Weiler:

The one view holds that criminal penalties can be justified if, but only if, they will reduce the level of crime within the community. The other responds that sanctions are justified if, but only if, the defendant has done something for which he merits their infliction. It is clear then that the arguments within the first perspective are focused forward in time, toward the future beneficial consequences of punishment; within the second the arguments look backward, to events which have already occurred, as the source of moral support.[7]

The literature on sentencing goals is vast, but the major currently debated perspectives may be identified in order to examine the implications for rationality in sentencing.[8] Accordingly, we shall discuss four sentencing aims widely advocated and argued about— deterrence, incapacitation, treatment, and desert.[9] Each has a long history in philosophy, in literature, and in criminology.

Deterrence

The concept of deterrence "refers to the prevention of criminal acts in the population at large by means of the imposition of punishment on persons convicted of crime."[10] This concept often is called "general deterrence" in order to distinguish it from "special" or "specific" deterrence—"the latter referring to the inhibition of criminal activity of the person being punished as a result of the imposition of that punishment."[11] (The term, "deterrence" is used here to refer only to general deterrence, since "special deterrence" may be subsumed under the general term "treatment.")

In this theory, the punishment given to an individual or class of individuals is explicitly designed to decrease the probability that others will engage in unlawful behavior. Hence, the validity of deterrence as a sentencing goal is determined by the effect that a given punishment applied to a particular offender has on the future criminality of those not punished.[12]

Thus, the deterrent aim is future oriented, and its objective is "to persuade or warn others not to commit criminal acts."[13] The goal is clearly the prevention of crime; the term "general prevention" is sometimes used for the same concept (especially in Europe).

The aim of reducing the probability of crime in the population at large has long been held to provide a justification for punishment. Publilius Syrus wrote: *"qui culpae ignoscit uni, suadet pluribus"* ("pardon one offense and you encourage many").[14] Herbert Spencer claimed that "failure of justice tempts men to injustices" and that "every unpunished delinquency has a family of delinquencies."[15]

And Daniel Webster, in a similar vein, argued that "Every unpunished murder takes away something from the security of every man's life."[16] Not merely crime but by implication, sinful behavior is to be controlled by punishment in Shakespeare's words: "Nothing emboldens sin so much as mercy."[17] The concept of prediction is fundamental to this perspective, since it is expected that the punishment of offenders will decrease the likelihood of crime by others.

Incapacitation

Incapacitation (sometimes called "neutralization" or "isolation") refers to the sentencing aim of restraining the person being punished from committing further criminal acts. To the extent that the intent of the sentence is purely incapacitative, "attention is not focused on the reduction of the offender's *propensity* for future criminal acts; rather, the offender is controlled so as to preclude his *opportunity* for such behavior, at least while under the authority of the state."[18] Clearly, this aim, too, is future oriented:

> An essential component of the incapacitative purpose is prediction—that is, an assessment is made of the probability of future criminal conduct by the offender and the imposition of penalties for the offense reflects that assessment. Thus, incapacitative dispositions are meant to be preventive. . . .[19]

The incapacitative perspective is similar in this way to that of deterrence; but while the latter focuses on prevention of crime by others, the incapacitative frame of reference seeks prevention of crime by the convicted offender. Its justification must be that restraints are necessary for what the offender may do, rather for what he or she has done. Again, the frame of reference is clearly predictive.

Treatment

Treatment aims in sentencing are future oriented, preventive in design, and focused on the individual offender. The goal "is to lessen the propensity of those convicted of crime to commit further crimes."[20] The term "treatment" is used here in its broadest sense to include anything done to, with, or for the offender for the purpose of reducing the probability of new criminal acts. Thus, potential vehicles for achieving this aim include all programs designed for rehabilitation, restoration, or reintegration of the offender into the community, the punishment of the offender with the aim of "specific" deterrence, and variations in place of confinement or length of sentence when designed to change the offender's behavior. In short, it includes all means intended to reduce the offender's proclivity toward future criminal acts. (It must be recognized that the term treatment is widely used with other meanings—for example, to refer to procedures intended to modify some state of the person in ways not necessarily related to crime reduction.) As with the other utilitarian purposes of deterrence and incapacitation, "the prediction of future events. . . is inextricably involved with a treatment purpose."[21]

Plato combined a treatment aim (special deterrence) with that of general deterrence; he explained the purpose of punishment as at once a means of correction and a warning to others: "not that he is punished because he did wrong, for that which is done can never be undone, but in order that in future times, he, and those who see him corrected, may utterly hate injustice, or at any rate abate much of their evil-doing."[22] Hobbes would limit the use of punishment to these same two aims: "In revenges or punishments men ought not to look at the greatness of evil past, but at the greatness of the good to follow, whereby we are forbidden to inflict punishment with any other design than for the correction of the offender and the admonition of others."[23]

Beccaria in 1764 named various criteria for the justification of punishment that continue to provide bases for current debates. In addition to his widely cited arguments for general deterrence, to be acceptable for Beccaria, punishment had to be public and prompt, it had to be "necessary," and moreover (besides being lawful), it had to be proportional in severity to the seriousness of the offense. At the same time, it had to be the least severe sanction possible under the circumstances.[24]

The goals of deterrence, incapacitation, and treatment thus each have a probabilistic nature. Although the element of prediction is perhaps most obviously necessary for the incapacitative and rehabilitative rationales, it is inherent equally in the concept of deterrence. That concept requires the assumption that there is an expected relation (prediction) between the punishment of individuals or classes of individuals and the future behavior of other individuals and groups.[25] All three of these major goals are aimed at reducing the probability of crime.

Desert

In the desert theory of sentencing, the only question to be answered is, What sanction is deserved in this case? The desert rationale has no explicit crime control aim; its purpose is to express disapprobation or to exact retribution.[26] Desert thus differs from the other three major purposes "in that it focuses exclusively on the *past* criminal behavior of the offender and punishment is given solely to express condemnation of that behavior."[27]

The concept of desert may be, of course, a component of various other perspectives on the purposes of punishment. It may be used with a utilitarian aim, for example, for the prevention of anomie. Or it may refer to retribution, to an affirmation of moral values, or to reprobation.[28] But the hallmark of this position is that as a result of his or her offense, the offender deserves a certain amount of punishment, and the severity of punishment ought to be in proportion to the gravity of the criminal conduct—taking into account the culpability of the offender. Thus, the concept contains neither utilitarian nor predictive components, distinguishing it in principle from deterrence, incapacitation, and treatment purposes.

Like the utilitarian aims of deterrence, incapacitation, and treatment, the concept of desert as a purpose of the sentence is as old as philosophy and is found repeatedly in literature. Thus Aristotle used the term: "Justice is that virtue of the soul that is distributive according to desert."[29] Similarly, Justician defined justice: "*Justitia est constans et perpetua voluntas jus suum cuique tribuendi*" ("justice is the firm and continuous desire to render to everyone that which is his due").[30] The principle of proportionality (to the gravity of harm done) is implicit in a psalm of David, who prayed "Give them according to their deeds, and according to the wickedness of their endeavors: give them after the work of their hands; render to them their desert."[31] If Shakespeare was a utilitarian, believing in general deterrence as implied by the aforementioned quotation, he must be regarded also as recognizing the principle of just desert: "Where the offense is, let the great axe fall."[32] The term "justice" often is equated with "desert," as in Fielding's Tom Jones: "Thwackum was for doing justice, and leaving mercy to Heaven."[33]

The concept of desert alone providing a legitimate basis for punishment was quite acceptable to Kant, as illustrated by this famous example:

> Even if a civil society resolved to dissolve itself with the consent of all its members—as might be supposed in the case of a people inhabiting an island resolving to separate and scatter themselves throughout the whole world—the last murderer lying in prison ought to be executed before the resolution was carried out. This ought to be done in order that everyone may realize the desert of his deeds. . . .[34]

Indeed, Kant spoke of the penal law as a categorical imperative[35] and cautioned "woe to him who creeps through the serpent-windings of utilitarianism. . . ."[36] The categorical imperative is contrasted with the hypothetical in that the former is unqualified and absolute.[37]

It is clear that the principle of desert has nothing whatever to do with the utilitarian purposes of crime control, with prevention, with deterrence, with the ideas of incapacitation or rehabilitation, or with any other aim of crime reduction. This is not to say that the application of the concept of commensurate desert may not have such effects; that is a different question. The aim is satisfaction of a moral imperative. Rewards and punishments provide means to the end of desert.

INDIVIDUALIZATION OF PURPOSE IN
SENTENCING—A LOOK AT SOME DATA

If purposes conflict, the possibility exists that the individual judge, in selecting among sentencing alternatives, may also select among purposes. That is, in the individual case the judge may emphasize one or another purpose in the process of decisionmaking, and this emphasis may vary among cases. Some evidence that this is so is derived from a study by Gottfredson and Stecker of sentencing in one court in a large eastern metropolitan county.[38]

In this study, eighteen judges completed forms documenting their judgments on various factors at the time of sentencing, including (for 982 cases) identification of the sentencing purposes that they defined as appropriate to each case. Purposes listed were retribution, incapacitation, special deterrence, rehabilitation, and "other" (including general deterrence). (The list was devised in collaboration with the judges at the start of the study.) The judges were asked to distribute 100 points among these items or to assign this value to any one item, provided only that sums would be 100 points.

The judges usually did not select any one aim as the single purpose of the sentence. Rather, it was more typical to distribute the 100 points among the alternative purposes listed. (Of course, the nature of the question may have suggested such distribution.) When the purpose given the highest weighting was classified as the "principal purpose," the most commonly identified main purpose was that of rehabilitation. That is, rehabilitation most often was given the most weight. That was the case in 36 percent of the sentences. When, as suggested in the previous section of this chapter, special deterrence was regarded as a variety of rehabilitation (that is, treatment), then 45 percent of the sentences were classified as having a treatment aim according to the judge who imposed the sentence.

When all utilitarian aims were combined (forward-looking goals with a predictive element), then 83 percent of these sentences were included. The aim of retribution was cited relatively infrequently as the main reason for the sentence, although it was selected 17 percent of the time. (Note that the term "desert" was not used in the question, since it was not suggested by any judge when the item was formulated.) Incapacitation was cited as the aim given the greatest weight in only 4 percent of the cases. The proportions of sentences for which these aims were given the largest weightings by these judges are shown in Figure 6-1.[39]

A further analysis of differences between offenders sentenced with a primary retributive purpose and those sentenced mainly with a rehabilitative intent was done (using the discriminant function). The results suggested that:

Generally, these judges were more inclined to sentence offenders retributively when the conviction offense was more serious, when the offender had a record of prior prison incarceration, when the judge expected recidivism (and particularly when a new offense against persons was predicted) and when social stability was questioned. When the converse was true, the judges tended to see rehabilitation as an appropriate sentencing aim.[40]

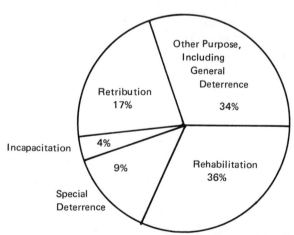

Source: Adapted from D. Gottfredson and B. Stecker, "Sentencing Policy Models" (Newark, New Jersey: School of Criminal Justice, Rutgers University, 1979). Manuscript.

Figure 6-1. Main purposes cited by 18 judges in sentencing 982 adult offenders.

The one item that appeared from the discriminate analysis to have the strongest association with the choice of primary aim (in the context of all the items included) was the judge's prediction of recidivism by an offense against persons. This suggests that the relatively infrequent selection of incapacitation as a principal goal may be misleading and that judges may employ this concept without necessarily labeling it as such. Alternatively, it may suggest that, for those judges, utilitarian purposes may provide a partial justification for retributive aims.

In any case, these data support the contention that all the main purposes of sentencing play a role in the choice of alternative sanctions. The specific purposes related to judgments are rarely specified explicitly, however, and such identification is required if it is desired to learn how the rationality of such decisions can be improved.

SENTENCING DISPOSITIONS

Sir Francis Galton noted a peculiarity of the distributions of punishments when he studied the sentences of all males imprisoned in England in 1893 without the option of a fine.[41] The frequencies of sentences of years (rounded up to the nearest tenth) are shown in Figure 6-2, adapted from a presentation of his work by Banks, who cited Galton as follows:

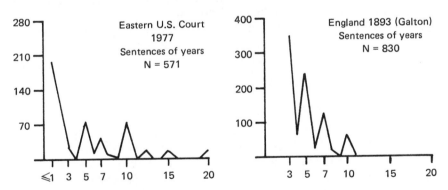

Source: Adapted from E. Banks, "Reconviction of Young Offenders," *Current Legal Problems* 17:74 (1964). Banks compares 1893 sentencing data taken from F. Galton, *Nature* (June 1895) with sentences (of months and years) in 1959. The peaks found for quarter years seemed even more pronounced than Galton's.

Figure 6-2. Number chosen in sentencing to years, Eastern U.S. County Court (1977) and England (1893).

It would be expected that the various terms of imprisonment . . . should fall in a continuous series. Such, however, is not the case. . . . The extreme irregularity of the frequency of the different terms of imprisonment forces itself on the attention . . . [and] it is impossible to believe that a judicial system is fair which allots only 20 sentences to 6 years, allots as many as 240 to 5 years, as few as 60 to 4 years and as many as 360 to 3 years.[42]

As may be seen in the figure, sentences of three, five, seven, and ten years seem preferred to the values between, resulting in an irregular polygram with a series of spikes.

Galton noted a similar phenomenon when sentences to months were plotted. Thus, although there were some 300 sentences to eighteen months there were none to seventeen and only 20 to nineteen. Moreover, he noted a rhythmical series of three, six, nine, fifteen, and eighteen or greater years, "a round figure which must commend itself to the judges by its simplicity." Besides this rhythm, however, Galton accounted for his results "by the undoubted fact that almost all persons have a disposition to dwell on certain numbers, and an indisposition to use others . . ."; and he remarked that "These trifles determine the choice of such widely different sentences as imprisonment for 3 or 5 years, 5 or 7, and of 7 or 10 for crimes whose penal deserts would otherwise be rated at 4, 6 and 8 or 9 years respectively."[43]

The sentences of the court in the eastern United States discussed in the previous section of this chapter are also shown in Figure 6-2. Sentences of six, twelve, and eighteen months were common, so the figure is not comparable with that derived from Galton at the lower range, but the tendency to use sentences of five, seven, ten (twelve, fifteen, twenty) is apparent.

CORRELATES OF SENTENCING DECISIONS

Before we begin a discussion of recent trends in sentencing, we should pause to examine how sentencing decisions appear to be made in practice. As with the other decisions discussed in this book, we think it imperative that the correlates of actual practice be understood as far as existing research permits.

Galton apparently was among the earliest to suggest comparison of different courts or judges who might, for the same kind of person, assign very different penalties.[44] There since have been many studies that show, or at least suggest strongly, that variation among courts and among individual judges even in the same court contributes substantially to sentence variations. In an early study, Gaudet and others found, for example, that from a study of more than 7000 persons sentenced in a New Jersey court by six judges, a percent variation in imprisonment ranging among judges from 34 to 58 percent.[45] Although cases were assigned on a rotational basis, so that it is plausible that types of cases were distributed evenly, this was not demonstrated, and the variation in sentences might have been due to differences in that distribution. Recently Sutton studied variability in sentences imposed in federal district courts, using multiple regression procedures. He discovered that the factors that appeared to influence whether or not an offender was sentenced to prison, as well as the factors that appeared to influence the length of imprisonment, varied considerably among the district courts.[46]

A sizeable body of research literature exists that focuses on the issue of what factors are most determinative of sentencing dispositions. A major theme of much of this research, apart from the variability issues discussed above, is whether "legal" or "extralegal" factors are more influential in sentencing. Unfortunately, much of the existing research is quite limited in the extent to which inferences about the relative importance of these factors can be determined. Problems in design and analytical methods have been numerous.[47] Common problems include the failure to control statistically for "legal" variables when assessing the relevance of "extralegal" variables, failure to compute measures of association for the factors with significant effects, and the use of very crude proxy measures.

Some recent research on sentencing of adult offenders has attempted to overcome some of the problems of earlier studies. Tiffany, Avichai, and Peters studied sentencing practices in the federal district courts for the four crimes of bank robbery, auto theft, interstate transportation of forged securities, and forgery for the years 1967 and 1968.[48] The dependent variable in their multiple regression analyses was a scale of possible sentences that ranged from zero (suspended sentence) to fifty (over 120 months imprisonment). Their independent variables included the type of crime committed, prior record, age, type of counsel, race, and the type of trial (bench versus jury). They discovered that the seriousness of the crime committed had the greatest impact on sentencing and that prior record and type of conviction were also significantly related to disposition, although less strongly. Prior record seemed to have its greatest effect on the least serious crimes, and type of conviction appeared to be more influential than did prior record. Persons convicted by jury trials tended to get more severe dispositions than did persons convicted by judge trials. Overall, age, race, and type of counsel did not appear to be related to disposition.

Sutton used multivariate methods to analyze incarceration and sentence length decisions in the federal district courts.[49] His analyses are complicated; separate analyses were undertaken for different types of offenses, and the results depend, to a degree, upon the offense under consideration. A variety of factors were used to try to predict sentencing dispositions, including offense, prior record, method of conviction, sex, race, and so forth. Overall, the best predictors of both the decision to incarcerate and the decision about the length of sentence were the "legal" variables in the study. Demographic characteristics of the offenders seemed to play a relatively small role in these decisions.

Sutton also found differences in the factors that seemed to be used in the decision to incarcerate compared to the factors used in the decision about sentence length. In determining the length of prison term, the conviction offense and whether the conviction was by a jury trial or not were the strongest correlates in multivariate analyses. On the other hand, the strongest correlate of the decision to incarcerate was the offender's prior criminal record, with method of conviction and type of offense less strongly related.

In a recent series of papers, Pope has analyzed sentencing correlates in several California counties using offender-based transaction statistics.[50] A considerable variety of independent variables was included, and the data permitted study of sentencing differences according to lower and superior courts and according to whether the court was in an urban or a rural area. As with Sutton's study, Pope's research is complicated and difficult to summarize without violating the intricacies of the results. The factors correlated with sentencing dispositions did vary between urban and rural courts and between lower and superior courts. Overall, Pope discovered that two "legal" variables were relatively strong predictors of sentencing for burglary and assault offenders—the seriousness of the prior record and whether the offender was on some form of supervised release at the time of arrest. Pope summarizes the results of his multivariate analyses as follows:

> The legal variables of status and record were consistently associated with high incarceration rates in that those who had a record or were under criminal commitment were most likely to be incarcerated. Similarly, male offenders fared worse than their female counterparts. Race proved

not to be as strongly associated with sentence outcome as might have been expected, although in those instances where it did appear . . . blacks were generally more likely to be incarcerated than whites.[51]

Pope's study is valuable, not just for the substantive results it produced, but also for its demonstration of the value of transaction data—data that have as their base the individual offender (or suspect) and that trace the individual through various steps in the criminal justice process. As we have seen, many criminal justice decisions are predicated upon decisions made earlier in the process, and prior decisions may greatly influence subsequent decisions. Transaction data can play a major role in the evaluation of these decisions because, if a lengthy enough follow-up on the individuals is made, they can reveal to decisionmakers some of the consequences of their decisions (in addition to permitting evaluations of fairness, such as those undertaken by Pope). We argue in the last chapter that such data systems are a requisite for the enhancement of rationality in criminal justice decisionmaking.

Studies of sentencing correlates using transaction data are rare. One additional study of the sentences received by a cohort of felony arrestees in New York City has been reported by the Vera Institute.[52] The Vera researchers tracked these arrestees through to disposition, and although the number of independent variables studied was not large and multivariate statistical methods were not used, their results generally confirm what prior research had found:

> the more serious the offense charged at arrest . . . , the stiffer is the sentence likely to be following conviction, whether the conviction was for the felony originally charged, a lesser felony, or a misdemeanor. . . . Defendants with heavier criminal histories were more likely to be convicted and, if convicted, more likely to receive heavier sentences than those with lighter or clean records. Seventy-seven percent of the convicted defendants with no prior record avoided jail or prison; only 16 percent of convicted defendants who had previously been sentenced to prison were as fortunate.[53]

These results also clearly indicate the value of transaction data in the study of decisions in the criminal process—subsequent decisions may "accommodate" earlier decisions in ways that heavily influence the final outcome. In Chapter 9 we report similar results with respect to the ways in which parole decisions may "supersede" earlier decisions by prosecutors and judges.

Some research attention has also been devoted to the ways in which judicial attitudes may influence sentencing decisions. Green, in a study of 1437 cases sentenced in Philadelphia in 1956-1957 by eighteen judges, concluded that legal factors such as the type of crime, the number of indictments, prior criminal record, and recommendations to the court accounted for most of the disparity apparent from a simple comparison.[54] Using a prediction measure combining these factors to classify the convicted as to expected sentences, Green concluded, however, that "as cases move from the extreme of gravity or mildness toward indeterminacy [of seriousness] judicial standards tend to become less stable and sentencing increasingly reflects the individuality of the judge."[55] Related studies of sentencing variation among courts or among judges tend to emphasize, as contributing to it, either differences in the sentencing policies of courts (as between smaller, rural courts or larger, urban ones) or a rather vague reference to the attitudes, habits, or individuality of judges.

Hood and Sparks, in a review of some of these studies, discussed various possible meanings of the variation among courts or judges in a way that shows both the complexity of the issue and the need for careful assessment of a variety of possibilities. Thus, such variation does not necessarily show that judges do not follow any single consistent policy or policies, with completely arbitrary sentencing. Neither does it demonstrate that judges are influenced, consciously or unconsciously, by invidious or biasing factors. Without ruling out these possibilities, they suggested three others:

1. Individual judges may be following substantially different sentencing policies, which make different sentences appropriate for the same type of case; alternatively or additionally,
2. Different judges may be receiving different kinds of information about the offenders whom they sentence; or
3. They may be *classifying* offenders and/or offenses in different ways, even though they receive the same kinds of information about them and have the same general aims in sentencing.[56]

Hood and Sparks pointed out that any of these may result in disparities in sentencing, even though each judge may consistently be following a policy of rational decisionmaking.

In his study of sentencing by seventy-one judges in Ontario, Canada, Hogarth found substantial correlations between various attitudinal measures and a variety of sentencing behaviors.[57] Although he was appropriately cautious in interpretations concerning the impact of judicial attitudes on sentencing behavior, his results are persuasive that such attitudes can indeed be quite influential.

In the study by D. Gottfredson and B. Stecker of sentencing discussed in the preceding section, data items from case files and various ratings made by the judges at the time of sentencing were analyzed to determine their association with various sentencing alternatives. Since the judge makes not one but a variety of decisions in sentencing, this is a complex matter; but the results may be illustrated by summarizing the findings mainly with respect to one aspect—namely, the decision whether or not to require the offender's incarceration.[58] These analyses were based on 976 of the sentences by seventeen judges. (The data on one judge's sentences were excluded since he experienced a number of lengthy trials and had sentenced few persons while the study was being done.)

Besides the sentence imposed, data concerning the offender and the present offense were collected for each person sentenced. Included were the offense charged and convicted; the number of counts charged and convicted; the number of prior probations, probation revocations, and jail and prison terms; the prosecutor and probation department recommendations as to sentence; and data on prior sentences still being served. Also available were judges' assessments of the seriousness of the offense, of the propensity of the offender toward future crimes (of any type, for a violent person-to-person offense, and for a property offense), of the length of the prior arrest and conviction record, of the seriousness of prior convictions, and of the social stability of the offender.

In order to provide a summary description of the decision as to whether or not to incarcerate the offender, the discriminant function was used (Table 6-1). That is, the aim was to describe those offenders who did and did not receive sentences to any incarceration. A sentence to any confinement (in county or state facilities) was counted, regardless of length of confinement, given only that it was not wholly suspended. Fifty-eight percent of the sample of offenders were incarcerated.

The offenders sentenced to confinement tended to be those with more serious offenses, by two measures of that concept. The average scores for the legal offense class were higher (more serious) for those sentenced to incarceration, and the judges' ratings of seriousness were on the average higher as well. On other variables there were significant differences between the groups in the variability of the scores on the items. Generally, it appeared from the univariate analyses that judges tended to incarcerate the offenders who were convicted of crimes with greater legislatively set sanctions and perceived as having committed more serious offenses. Lower

Table 6-1. Discriminant Analysis of the Incarceration Decision, Eastern Court.

Variable	Discriminant Weights		Wilks' Lambda	Classification Weights	
	Standardized	Unstandardized		Noncustodial sentence	Custodial sentence
Judges' prognoses for recidivism, any offense	−0.437	−0.151	0.644	1.126	1.522
Judges' ratings of seriousness of the offense	−0.344	−0.142	0.570	0.277	0.649
Legal class of offense	−0.234	−0.209	0.544	2.180	2.728
Judges' ratings of social stability	0.133	0.126	0.537	4.543	4.213
Number of probation revocations	−0.083	−0.103	0.534	0.656	0.927
Number of counts of conviction	−0.080	−0.080	0.531	0.633	0.842
Judges' prognoses for recidivism, property offense	−0.083	−0.028	0.529	−0.111	−0.037
Number of prison terms	−0.038	−0.048	0.529	0.774	0.900
Centroids	0.805 −0.584				
Constant		1.997		−11.489	−16.440

scores on other items might also tend to indicate a noncustodial sentence, but there was considerable variability on these items among the incarcerated group. The multivariate analysis (that is, the discriminate analysis) is the better guide, since the overlap among items is taken into account.

The strength of the association of each item with the decision to incarcerate when all other items are taken into account at the same time may be judged from the first column of Table 6-1, which lists the standardized coefficients for the discriminant function. It can be seen that in the context of all the items included, the judges' prognoses for any recidivism, his or her ratings of the seriousness of the offense, and the legal class of the offense are the best indicants of the outcome. Indeed, the fourth column (Wilks' lambda) shows that these three items do most of the work of discriminating the two groups. The remaining items add very little if anything to the discrimination. The item "number of prior prison terms" does not help discriminate the groups after the other items have been taken into account. The classification coefficients listed enabled the correct classification of offenders into incarcerated and non-incarcerated groups (in the same sample) in 83 percent of the cases (whether or not an adjustment was made for group size).

If the judge's assessment of risk (prognosis for recidivism) and offense seriousness, together with the legal class, are interpreted to be major determinants of the decision (which is plausible though not proved by this analysis), it may be asked how this relates to the sentencing purposes discussed above. The latter two items both may be interpreted as indicants of seriousness—one reflecting the judges' assessments, the other that of the legislature in establishing the legal offense classes. Thus, the use of these factors may be regarded as attuned to the desert aim. At the same time, however, they may reflect concern for general deterrence or treatment, including special deterrence. From this analysis it is not possible to tell. The situation is similar when one considers the factor of recidivism probability. At first glance, it may appear that this item is deemed relevant in respect to incapacitative aims. It is possible, though, that this may imply to the judge a greater need for treatment, in order to reduce the perceived probability of repeated offending.

Similar multivariate analyses were completed in respect to other decision outcomes. The place of confinement (county facility, reformatory, or state prison system) was described by two discriminant functions. The first included items related to the legal class of the offense, the length of the arrest record, the judges' judgments of seriousness of the conviction record, the judges' prognoses for recidivism by an offense against persons, and the rating of the seriousness of the offense. The second function included the judges' ratings of seriousness of the conviction record, the prognosis for recidivism by a property offense, and the number of counts at conviction. A multiple regression equation with length of sentence, if incarcerated, as the dependent variable (i.e., maximum sentence) included these variables—the legal class of the offense, offense seriousness, number of counts at conviction, and prognosis for recidivism of a violent person offense ($R = 0.62$). A similar analysis with respect to length of probation, resulting in a more modest $R = 0.47$, led to including in the equation the items legal class of the offense, number of counts charged, length of conviction record, fines imposed, offense seriousness, prognosis of recidivism by a property offense, and seriousness of prior conviction record.

Overall these studies of sentencing decisions yield some important and consistent findings. It appears that a major correlate of these decisions, whether the decision relates to the question of incarceration versus nonincarceration or to the question of maximum sentence to imprisonment, is that some measure of the offense seriousness plays a central role. Studies have operationalized the concept differently, but the type of behavior for which the offender has been convicted (or, in some cases, the behavior charged) exerts a powerful, and not unexpected, influence on sentencing decisions.

So too does the nature and gravity of the offender's prior record. Again, different measures have been studied, and not all of the research reports an effect. But in the aggregate these studies support the claim that the prior criminal history of the offender is influential, although not as influential as offense seriousness, in determining sentence. There is also evidence that a critical concern in sentencing is the judge's prognosis for the recidivism of the offender.

Most of the existing research also indicates that there is considerable unexplained sentencing variation, both between and within courts. There is some evidence that some of this variation is due to individual differences among judges—that is, to variations in particular attitudes or beliefs about the purposes of sentencing. And there is some evidence that suggests that a portion of the unexplained variation may be due to "extralegal" decisionmaking criteria, although the "legal" factors appear to be, in the recent past anyway, considerably more predictive of sentencing.

JUDICIAL CONTROL OF
SENTENCING CONSEQUENCES

One aspect of sentencing decisions often overlooked in assessments of them is that the extent of control by the judge over later consequences of the disposition may vary markedly with different sentences. With sanctions usually thought of as least severe, such as the imposition of fines or of alternative service, the judge may remain quite in control. When more severe sanctions are imposed but suspended with placement of the convicted offender on probation, a considerable degree of control still is maintained, since the probation service usually is considered to be an arm of the court and since the court maintains a power of revocation and imposition of the original sentence. Some degree of control is lost if the person is sent to jail, usually managed by county administrations; and perhaps more control is given up when the offender is sentenced to prison, usually operated by the states. Although in some jurisdictions the judge may specify the particular prison of confinement, it is more usual that this is decided by the prison administration. When the time comes for parole decisions, the judge has but limited impact, which in any case usually may be ignored if the paroling authority chooses to do so.

With the data now available, one may only speculate about the consequences of these differences for the decisionmaking behavior of the judge, but they may have some impact on choices of sentencing alternatives. The nature of such impact may depend in part upon the judge's sentencing objectives for the particular case. If, for example, a principal aim is rehabilitation, the judge may maintain a greater degree of control over the specifics of a treatment program he or she would prescribe if the offender is placed on probation rather than sentenced to prison. These conjectures, recast as hypotheses, warrant considerable study.

Sentencing Trends

Until the last few years, sentencing and correctional structures in the United States have been guided mainly by utilitarian principles. Consistent with the treatment ideal, the indeterminate sentence has been the general rule, adopted increasingly since the early 1900s. Usually, the actual determination of the specific sentence has been deferred (when incarceration was used) until late in the term of confinement, when it has been decided by a parole board. The premise at the origin of this common model was that the offender could be diagnosed and treated and should be released when ready to assume a law-abiding life. Thus, the treatment goal of sentencing—future oriented, preventive in design, and focused on the individual offender—was paramount.

Now this is being changed. One reason, but perhaps not the most important, is a widespread disenchantment with the effectiveness of the design. Increasingly it has been argued that we do not have enough knowledge of diagnosis and treatment to implement this model—in short, it is argued that it does not work.[59] (Thus, this utilitarian regime is criticized on utilitarian grounds, often by those arguing from a desert perspective. Such criticism may be in order from the utilitarian orientation, if justified, but it is hardly consistent with a position that already has rejected pragmatism.) The more fundamental challenge, however, rests on moral arguments about justice and fairness, and its basis is in the desert perspective. The shift, which is readily apparent and pronounced, is to determinate sentencing,[60] to an emphasis on desert,[61] and to an assertion of the right not to be treated (or of the "right to be different"[62]). At the same time there may be an emergence of the concept of a right to treatment.[63]

Determinate Sentencing

Arguments against the indeterminate sentence have been many and varied. Besides the criticism of ineffectiveness, they have addressed two areas of perceived basic weaknesses. First, there has been a set of criticisms of procedures on grounds of unfairness. Both sentencing and paroling decisions have been widely faulted as arbitrary, capricious, and leading to unwarranted disparity.[64] Second, the uncertainty felt by the convicted offender has been said to be unfair. (Alternatively, the utilitarian argument that such uncertainty is counterproductive to rehabilitative aims also has been made.)[65] These assertions, combined with the decline of support for the rehabilitative model, have been persuasive to many, and recent legislation in a number of states (and proposed federal legislation) has moved generally in the direction of greater determinacy.

Desert Trend

Combined with this trend toward more determinate sentences has been an increased acceptance of desert as the fundamental purpose of sentencing and justification of punishment. That is, there has been increased support for the view that the sentence should not only be specified more precisely, at the time of sentencing or soon after, but that it should provide penalties commensurate with the gravity of the offense of conviction—that is, with the harm done by the conduct, considering the culpability of the offender. These assertions have been made on ethical rather than scientific grounds, but the present lack of firm empirical support for treatment effectiveness often has been cited for good measure. The central argument has been that it is a fundamental requirement of justice, including fairness, that offenders with similar crimes be punished similarly and that the severity of the penalty be related to the seriousness of the offense. The basic concepts of the theory therefore are closely related to the idea of equity, and hence they are intertwined with issues of sentence disparity—about which there also has been widespread concern.

Discretion and Disparity

Criticisms of sentencing and parole structures in the United States have focused on the problem of disparity, or unwarranted variation, in penalties imposed on offenders convicted of similar crimes. Three types of structural changes have been proposed as remedies, and each has been adopted in various jurisdictions. First, there are advocates of mandatory sentencing—with specific, unvarying penalties for specific crimes.[66] Second, there are proposals for "presumptive sentencing," according to which punishments would be set for the "normal" case within much narrower bounds than has been customary under the previously prevailing philosophy of indeterminacy.[67] (Some deviation ordinarily would be allowed for unusual cases involving aggravating or mitigating circumstances.) Third, systems of "guidelines" have been developed, with sentences determined according to an explicit policy intended to structure and control, but not eliminate, the exercise of discretion.[68] Specific ranges of penalties are provided for combinations of offense and offender characteristics, with some discretion permitted within the prescribed range and also with provision for further deviation for specified reasons. Each of these models (including the latter, although to a lesser extent) reduces the discretion of the sentencing judge.

The sentencing trends now in progress thus may be summarized as tending toward more definite sentences, according to desert principles, with markedly reduced discretion by the relevant authorities. The word "discretion" has interesting ambiguities. It may mean either being discrete (making distinctions) or being discreet (being prudent or careful). It may also mean the "liberty or power of deciding or acting without other control than one's own judgment."[69] Current debates focus, of course, on issues of the judge's discretion in the latter meaning of the word. Although the making of careful distinctions seems desirable in a judge, the proper degree or amount of uncontrolled freedom in judicial decisionmaking is a subject of considerable controversy.

But discretion in sentencing, in the sense of freedom to exercise judgment, may be justified on the grounds that it allows for individual handling of each offender. Thus, if each person is unique (as must be agreed) or if each criminal act is in some way different from all others (as must certainly be the case), then it may be expected that sentences will be disparate (that is, variable). The word "disparity" in sentencing, however, has acquired a surplus meaning. It has come to be a pejorative referring to variation in sentences that is perceived as inequitable and, hence, unfair and unjust. (It may also be used to refer to sentences that are claimed to be irrational in the sense that they lack an appropriate proportionality or severity of sanction commensurate with the offense seriousness, as when two offenders' crimes seem obviously different in seriousness but the same sanction is imposed.[70]) If some discretion is justified on grounds of individual differences and it is not assumed that all variation in sentencing outcomes for ostensibly similar "cases" (offenders and criminal events) is based on invidious factors, then some disparity (that is, variation) may be warranted. (Therefore, it is undoubtedly preferable to refer not to the problem of "disparity" but to that of "unwarranted" disparity.)

Proposals for dealing with the problems of sentencing discretion, and particularly of unwarranted variation, have emphasized the need for consistent policy. At the same time, the appropriate range or license for discretion has been noted widely as a significant problem at each decision point in the processing of offenders.[71] Remington et al. have summarized the principal object for research about discretionary decisions as follows: "For every government decision there is an optimal point on the scale between the rule-of-law at one end and total discretion at the other end. The task of research is to find that optimum point and to confine discretion to the degree which is feasible."[72] Thus, although most of the current discussions about sentencing focus on the problems associated with too much discretion, there is also the danger in overly rigid decision rules that do not permit the taking into consideration of legitimate individual differences. It should be noted that the latter also involves a sacrifice of justice: rigid, discretionless systems may produce "equity" only at the expense of treating unequal cases alike. It was sensitivity to both of these concerns that resulted in the notion of "sentencing guidelines."

SENTENCING GUIDELINES

The feasibility of developing the policy models that include guidelines to assist the judiciary in structuring and controlling the exercise of their discretion was demonstrated in a recent study.[73] The concept of such policy control methods was generally that of a prior study of parole decisionmaking.[74] (The parole guidelines concept and method are reviewed in some detail in Chapter 9.)

The current shift toward greater determinacy in sentencing would, if carried to its logical extreme, mean that a fixed penalty would be required for every offender-offense combination. The penalty would be specified in advance, and no room for variation in the discretion of the judge would be allowed. Thus, discretion in sentencing would be entirely removed. At the other extreme, a completely indeterminate system of sentencing would allow complete freedom in selecting the appropriate penalty (or treatment). Actually, few persons argue that the judge should have no discretion in sentencing, and similarly, few now argue that it should be unlimited. The concept of establishing an explicit sentencing policy in which the idea of guidelines plays a critical part has been proposed as a practical solution that begins by rejecting both extremes of determinacy and indeterminacy.

An example of sentencing guidelines as developed through collaboration with judges of the Denver, Colorado, court (Figure 6-3) shows that the method devised there requires the classification of convicted offenders on dimensions found to be relevant to the sentencing decision. After study of a large number of items of data on 200 randomly selected sentencing decisions of two participating courts (the second was that of the state of Vermont) it was concluded that "the two most influential groupings of information items were those measuring the seriousness of the current offense and the extent of the offender's criminal record."[75] From this analysis, various guideline models were designed for consideration by the judges involved. The example of Figure 6-3 is a portion of one such model, addressing one specific "level"of felony offenses. An analogous grid or matrix was provided for each offense level.

Prior studies suggest that although decisionmakers may desire a very large number of data items before making a decision, a relatively small number of items may be most important or at least highly correlated with many others. Thus, the study of paroling that resulted in the invention of this type of guideline model was based in part upon the finding that the board apparently emphasized, in arriving at decisions, three dimensions of focal concern—offense

Offender Score

	−1 −7	0 2	3 8	9 12	13+
10-12	Indeterminate minimum 4-5 year maximum	Indeterminate minimum 8-10 year maximum	Indeterminate minimum 8-10 year maximum	Indeterminate minimum 8-10 year maximum	Indeterminate minimum 8-10 year maximum
8-9	Out	3-5 month work project	Indeterminate minimum 3-4 year maximum	Indeterminate minimum 8-10 year maximum	Indeterminate minimum 8-10 year maximum
6-7	Out	Out	Indeterminate minimum 3-4 year maximum	Indeterminate minimum 6-8 year maximum	Indeterminate minimum 8-10 year maximum
3-5	Out	Out	Out	Indeterminate minimum 4-5 year maximum	Indeterminate minimum 4-5 year maximum
1-2	Out	Out	Out	Out	Indeterminate minimum 3-4 year maximum

(Offense Score)

The Colorado Penal Code contains five levels of felonies (Felony 1 is the most serious) and three levels of misdemeanors. This Felony 4 category includes crimes such as manslaughter, robbery, and second degree burglary.

The legislated maximum sentence for a Felony 4 offense is ten years. No minimum period of confinement is to be set by the court.

"Out" indicates a nonincarcerative sentence such as probation, deferred prosecution, or deferred judgement.

Source: J. Kress, L. Wilkins, and D. Gottfredson, "Is The End of Judicial Sentencing in Sight?" *Judicature* 60:221 (1976). Reprinted by permission.

Figure 6-3. Suggested sentencing guidelines for Denver, Colorado.

seriousness, parole prognosis, and institutional discipline. In a yet earlier study by Carter,[76] who used a decision game devised by Wilkins,[77] federal probation officers were found generally to formulate and maintain sentencing recommendations after considering relatively few items.

In the Denver court guidelines the offender is classified on the two dimensions of "offense" and "offender." That is, scores are assigned first to the seriousness of the offense and second to the offender (on the basis of prior record and other items). Thus, a grid is provided such that the intersection of the offense seriousness and offender scores provides the location of the guideline sentence. The guidelines provide, in this fashion, a part of an explicit statement of sentencing policy. There are other features of such a policy, however, that the developers of the model consider to be critical to an appropriately flexible system that is perceived as an instrument for policy development as well as discretion control.

First, it is not required, nor is it expected, that all sentences must be set according to the guidelines prescription. The judge retains the discretion to set the sentence "outside the guidelines," allowing the consideration of unusual circumstances (such as aggravating or mitigating factors not already included or other concerns). In doing so, however, the judge must specify the reasons for the deviation.

Second, the consideration of general sentencing policy by the court (that is, by the judges collectively) can be informed by a monitoring system to provide them with feedback on the use of the guidelines. At periodic policy meetings, judges can be informed of both the rates of decisions for various categories consistent (within) the guidelines and of the deviations therefrom (and reasons therefore). Thus, a system may be provided for the repeated modification of policy along with legal and social change as well as gains in knowledge.

A major objective of the development of judicial policy through devising guidelines has been the articulation of the basis for decisions in more explicit terms in order that sentencing may be more open, more public, and hence more subject to review and criticism. If this can be achieved, then sentencing rationales may be more open to debate in more specific terms. Similarly, the empirical issues may more readily be tested, and the moral issues may be examined with a sharper focus.

The guidelines–policy model perspective may be criticized on the ground that the development and implementation of such models will merely legitimate past practice and militate against needed revisions of sentencing practices. The implicit policy may be defined from the analyses of prior decisions, but that may provide no guidance as to what an explicit policy ought to be. The proponents of the guidelines orientation have argued that the guidelines initially developed are descriptive, not prescriptive. If an implicit model (or various models) can be defined or invented that fits reasonably well with past sentencing practices, then it can be examined more readily and revised but the ball is then properly in the judges' court. Although it is agreed that "what is" is not necessarily "what ought to be," it may be pointed out (as by Wilkins) that every "what is" was once one judge's "what ought."[78]

The guidelines models have also been proposed as a potential aid to increased equity in sentencing. If equity in sentencing is taken to mean that similar offenders are dealt with similarly, guidelines such as those described may help to achieve it. The test would be a decreased variance in sentences for persons assigned to the various cells of the grid. This general hypothesis should be tested wherever guidelines are implemented.[79] But such tests cannot wholly answer the issues of equity that may be expected to arise— for many issues may be hidden by the easy phrases "similar offenders" and "similar sanctions." A complexity of moral, legal, and scientific concerns may be expected to be raised. What are the relevant and morally and socially justifiable bases for the classifications of offender/offenses as "similar?" And what are the appropriate scale values of the sanctions? It seems clear that many evaluation issues will stem from the implementation, in any jurisdiction, of the sentencing guidelines concept.

In a general sense, this is precisely what the guidelines concept has been supposed to provide—a more open system for evolution of sentencing policy. If sentencing can be rehabilitated, the concept of sentencing guidelines may help.

SENTENCING POLICY DEVELOPMENT

Setting the equity issue aside, however, the fundamental issues of sentencing remain to be addressed if the ideal of rationality is not to be abandoned. A first question must be answered—namely, What is sentencing for?

If desert is concluded to be primary, or even just important, many empirical questions remain along with moral issues. How is the "seriousness of the offense" to be measured? What scale values are to be assigned to discrete offense seriousness categories? Is the concept of "offense seriousness" a unidimensional one? Can rape be assigned a seriousness value of x times shoplifting, in additive, linear fashion? Or are the social harms of these behaviors perceived by most people as of a fundamentally different kind? What degree of consensus among various groups or "publics" on such judgments will be found? How are sanctions to be measured or assessed for severity? Is a year in prison (say at the minimum custody institution at Chino, California) an equivalent penalty to a year in the Los Angeles County Jail or to a year in San Quentin? How much restitution, in dollars, is equal to a month in jail; and what is the equivalence in months under probation supervision? Is "severity of punishment" a unidimensional concept, or is confinement in the Trenton, New Jersey, State Prison fundamentally different from a "split sentence" with weekend jail confinement, probation supervision, and a fine?[80]

Whether or not desert is accepted as the primary aim of sentencing or as an important one, the utilitarian goals of treatment, incapacitation, and deterrence will remain—perhaps constrained by the principle that no more than the sanction deserved may be imposed in their pursuit (see Chapter 10). Concerning these aims, which are pragmatic, there is the potential and the challenge of providing empirical evidence to guide sentencing policy developments.

If desert principles, argued on moral grounds, are increasingly accepted, the assumptions underlying the change in emphasis do not justify any lessening of the need to examine the consequences of such a shift.

Concerning each sentencing aim, more specific questions need to be asked and answered than heretofore. Thus, we may ask, What classification of offender (or potential offender) is effectively incapacitated, deterred, or treated by what sanctions (or treatment placements) in respect to what specific objectives of the criminal justice system? Concerning the treatment aims of sentencing particularly, the study of "cohorts" of offenders sentenced, to determine the comparative consequences of alternative sentences for later careers of the persons sentenced, is critically needed (analogously to the studies of arrests reported in Chapter 3). The results of these investigations at least can inform the courts from a systematic assessment of the evidence rather than from merely plausible argument, and this is a requisite to more rational sentencing policy and practice.

This requires keeping track of sentenced offenders and keeping score on the criteria relevant to criminal justice system aims, including new offense behavior. Judges, when sentencing, do not do experiments with random assignment to various sentence alternatives. As a result, the interpretation of the differences in consequences is complicated by the circumstance that the groups assigned different "treatments" are not apt to be comparable. If records are also kept on characteristics of offenders known to be related to these consequences, however, statistical (or "quasi-experimental") designs may be used to aid in the unraveling of the long-range results of sentencing choices. Such investigations could provide a much more solid base for increased rationality than the pure conjecture that presently provides the weak undergirding of current sentencing practice.

The first stage of evaluation of a proposed sentencing model may be limited to an assessment of how well the model describes decisions currently made without the use of the model. If the model has been revised after a first such assessment, then a second study may help determine whether the degree of fit (of the model to practice) has been improved. Thus, the process of the development of a sentencing model may itself include the assessment and reassessment that can begin to form a policy control method as a gradual evolutionary process.[81]

The development of the model may then move from a descriptive to a more prescriptive phase.

> A second stage of evaluation should address the question as to whether or not the model, now demonstrably fitting decisions with the desired degree of accuracy (say, eighty percent) is a model the [judiciary] wishes to adopt. If the model, as a description of heretofore implicit policy, is found inadequate for meeting the objectives of the judges, they themselves may wish to modify the model to define the decision process as they perceive to be necessary. It must be remembered that the guidelines were developed principally as a means for making the policy of the judiciary more explicit—partly for the purpose of enabling just such modifications.[82]

The systematic follow-up study of offenders in order to permit the assessment of relations of offense and offender attributes (information), dispositions (alternatives), and consequences (outcomes) in terms of sentencing objectives can provide one direct route to improving sentencing decisions—especially in regard to utilitarian, crime reduction aims. Another avenue, which can be quite congruent with the first, is the development of sentencing policy models as evolutionary systems for modification and control.

ALTERNATIVES

Throughout history, doctrines concerning the aims of sentencing (or of punishment) have been intertwined with theories of crime and criminal responsibility, and the alternative means invented for dealing with convicted offenders have been related closely to such purposes and conceptions. Thus, a great variety of alternatives has been used—death, exile, payment of compensation; flogging, clubbing, mutilation; running the gauntlet, public ridicule; exact, *lex talionis*; restitution, fines, and transportation; flogging, branding, the stocks and pillory, and the yoke; confinement in irons, the galley, and the chain gang; the ducking stool. Within various kinds of punishments, a similar ingenuity has been shown: it is possible to apply the death penalty by beheading, hanging, shooting, electrocution, or lethal gas; flaying, impaling, exposure to insects or serpents, drowning, stoning, poisoning, burning, and crushing the head by an elephant have been used as well.[83] A more recent invention, which presented a reform of the barbarous treatments just noted, is the present system of jails and prisons; the first

American penitentiary, the Walnut Street Jail, was made a state prison (in Pennsylvania) in 1790.

Currently, the most common sentencing alternatives available to the judiciary are imprisonment, jail, fines, probation, and suspension. There is debate, however, on both the humanity and utility of incarceration and the extent to which other forms of sentencing (available in some jurisdictions) might be used more widely as alternatives—for example, a greater use of restitution and/or of community service sentences instead of confinement.[84] Thus, it is to be expected that sentencing alternatives available to the court will continue to be changed and that new ones will be invented; and an evolutionary model of policy development should be capable of incorporating such new alternatives as well as improved information. The general nature of sentencing guidelines, as outlined above in the brief discussion of the Denver study, does not necessarily suggest what may be the most important utility of such policy development and control methods—that is, the role such methods may play in repeated assessments and revision of policy. Once a policy model has been developed, the stage is set for a sequence of evaluations that may lead to both research and management activities that can combine to provide a more rational control of the system.

Thus, the development of guideline models may begin as a research operation but may be converted into management operations in order to continue as management tools for policy control. There may be, however, a continuing liaison between policy modification (evolution) through feedback to the judiciary and the research operation of developing new or different guidelines models.

A combination of guidelines models conceived as an evolutionary process of policy development and cohort studies to test questions of effectiveness of existing and new alternative sentences could together provide a powerful tool for lessening confusion and increasing effectiveness in the critical arena of sentencing decision-making. We propose such an evolutionary model in our last chapter.

NOTES

1. Portions of this chapter are adapted from D.M. Gottfredson, "Sentencing Trends in the United States: Implications for Clinical Criminology" (paper presented at the VIth International Seminar on Clinical Criminology, Santa Margharita, Italy, May 1975).

The literature on sentencing is vast and is growing rapidly. Perhaps the best account of the many issues and complexities of sentencing is R. Dawson, *Sentencing: The Decision as to Type, Length, and Conditions of Sentence*

(Chicago: Little, Brown and Company, 1969). A good annotated bibliography of current sentencing controversies is J. Ferry and M. Kravitz, *Issues in Sentencing: A Selected Bibliography* (Washington, D.C.: National Institute on Law Enforcement and Criminal Justice, 1978).

2. G.O.W. Mueller, *Sentencing: Process and Purpose* (Springfield, Illinois: Charles E. Thomas, 1977), p. 304.

3. *Id.* at 9-10.

4. See L. Ohlin and F. Remington, "Sentencing Structure: Its Effects Upon Systems for the Administration of Criminal Justice," *Law and Contemporary Problems* 23:495 (1958).

5. P.C. Weiler, "The Reform of Punishment," in Law Reform Commission of Canada, *Studies on Sentencing* (Ottawa: Information Canada, 1974), p. 107.

6. This is an oversimplified distinction. Mueller, *supra* note 2 at 38-58, distinguishes between "utilitarian" and "nonutilitarian" aims. By the latter he means "those aims or methods for achieving crime prevention of which it is usually said that they are not designed at all to achieve prevention—in fact, that it would amount to a perversion of high ideals to use them in a utilitarian manner" (at 38). As nonutilitarian aims he includes vindication, retribution, and penitence.

Some, however, would use the concepts of desert or of punishment in a clearly utilitarian sense—for example, to prevent anomie or to affirm moral values. Weiler, *supra* note 5, divides sentencing perspectives as utilitarian versus "neo-Kantian," including in the latter category "he who locates morality in adherence to principles of right, justice or fairness" (at 122).

7. Weiler, *supra* note 5 at 121.

8. See, for example, H.L.A. Hart, *Punishment and Responsibility: Essays in the Philosophy of Law* (New York: Oxford University Press, 1968); Weiler, *supra* note 5; J. Rawls, *A Theory of Justice* (Cambridge, Massachusetts: Belknap Press of Harvard University Press, 1971); J. Feinberg, *Doing and Deserving: Essays on the Theory of Responsibility* (Princeton, New Jersey: Princeton University Press, (1970).

9. This section summarizing common sentencing aims draws heavily on V. O'Leary, M. Gottfredson, and A. Gelman, "Contemporary Sentencing Proposals," *Criminal Law Bulletin* 11:555 (1975). As these authors point out, various other sentencing goals not easily classified into these categories could be cited, such as penitence or control of vigilantes or personal vendettas.

10. *Id.* at 558.

11. *Id.*

12. *Id.*

13. *Id.*

14. Publilius Syrus *Sentential*, No. 578, as cited in B. Stevenson, *Handbook of Quotations* (New York: Dodd, 1967), p. 1031.

15. H. Spencer, *The Study of Sociology* (New York: D. Appleton and Co., 1924), p. 385.

16. D. Webster, *Argument*, Salem, Mass., Aug. 3, 1830, The Murder of Capt. Joseph White. Cited in Stevenson, *supra* note 14 at 1036.

17. W. Shakespeare, *Timon of Athens*, act III, sc. 5, line 3.

18. O'Leary, Gottfredson, and Gelman, *supra* note 9.

19. *Id.* at 558-59.

20. *Id.* at 559.

21. *Id.*

22. Plato, *Laws II*, 934, as cited in G. Newman, *The Punishment Response* (New York: J.B. Lippincott Co., 1978), p. 201.

23. *Id.*

24. C. Beccaria, *On Crimes and Punishments* (1764; rpt. Indianapolis: Bobbs-Merrill, 1963).

25. O'Leary, Gottfredson, and Gelman, *supra* note 9 at 559.

26. *Id.*

27. *Id.* at 559-60; see also A. von Hirsch, *Doing Justice: The Choice of Punishments* (New York: Hill and Wang, 1976).

28. O'Leary, Gottfredson, and Gelman, *supra* note 9 at 560.

29. Aristotle, *Metaphysics: On the Virtues and Vices—Justice*, as cited in B. Stevenson, *Handbook of Quotations* (New York: Dodd, 1967), p. 1027.

30. Justician, *Institutions*, book I, sec. 1, as cited in Stevenson, *supra* note 29 at 1027.

31. Psalms 28:4.

32. Shakespeare, *Hamlet*, act IV, sc. 5, line 218.

33. H. Fielding, *The History of Tom Jones*, book III, ch. X (Garden City, New York: International Collector's Library), p. 76, n.d.

34. I. Kant, *The Philosophy of Law*, trans. W. Hastic (Edinburgh: T.T. Clar, 1887), as cited by Weiler, *supra* note 5 at 140.

35. I. Kant, *Rechslekre* (1797), as cited in H. Gross, *A Theory of Criminal Justice* (New York: Oxford University Press, 1979), p. 489.

36. Kant, cited by Weiler, *supra* note 34 at 140.

37. A. Messer, *Immanuel Kants Leben and Philosophie* (Stuttgart: Streaker and Schroder, 1924), p. 89.

38. D.M. Gottfredson and B. Stecker, "Sentencing Policy Models" (Newark, New Jersey: School of Criminal Justice, Rutgers University, 1979). Manuscript.

39. *Id.* In a major study of sentencing in Canada, Hogarth did a factor analysis of 107 attitude item scores. A result was that the first factor found, accounting for more than 70 percent of the explained variance (42 percent of total variance), seemed to the author easy to interpret as measuring "the degree to which an individual wishes to see offenders punished severely" (at 126). High loadings were found on items agreeing with capital and corporal punishment, that prisons should be places of punishment, and "the most important single consideration in determining the sentence to impose should be the nature and gravity of the offense" (at 126). Hogarth labeled this factor "justice" and related it to the concept of just deserts. After rotation, he found factors labeled "punishment corrects," "intolerance," "social defense" (apparently related to general deterrence), and "modernism" (" 'new world' puritanism") (at 128-129). J. Hogarth, *Sentencing as a Human Process* (Toronto: University of Toronto Press, 1971), pp. 103-29.

40. Gottfredson and Stecker, *supra* note 38.

41. E. Banks, "Reconviction of Young Offenders," *Current Legal Problems* 17:74 (1964), citing F. Galton, *Nature* (June 1895).

42. *Id.* at 75.

43. *Id.* at 75-76.

44. *Id.* at 77.

45. F. Gaudet, G. Harris, and C. St. John, "Individual Differences in the Sentencing Tendencies of Judges," *Journal of Criminal Law and Criminology* 23:811 (1933), as cited in H. Barnes and N. Teeters, *New Horizons in Criminology* (New York: Prentice-Hall, 1950), p. 334.

46. L. Sutton, *Federal Sentencing Patterns: A Study of Geographical Variations* (Washington, D.C.: National Criminal Justice Information and Statistics Service, 1978).

47. Because several comprehensive reviews of this literature exist, including methodological critiques, a thorough review of the early research will not be undertaken here. See, *id.;* J. Hagan, "Extra-Legal Attributes and Criminal Sentencing: An Assessment of a Sociological Viewpoint," *Law and Society Review* 8:357 (1974). Hagan reviewed twenty studies of sentencing to assess the contribution of socioeconomic status, race, age, and sex in disposition. He concluded: "Review of the data indicates that, while there may be evidence of differential sentencing, knowledge of extra-legal offender characteristics contributes relatively little to our ability to predict judicial dispositions" (at 379).

Our focus in this book is on the adult criminal justice system, but it should be noted that a substantial body of research on the correlates of sentencing for juveniles also exists. For a review and an interesting empirical study, see L. Cohen and J. Kluegel, "Determinants of Juvenile Court Dispositions: Ascriptive and Achieved Factors in Two Metropolitan Courts," *American Sociological Review* 43:162 (1978). A recent general review of this research indicates that the "legal" factors (seriousness of the offense and prior record) are the most powerful predictors of disposition. See T. Hirschi, "Labelling Theory and Juvenile Delinquency: An Assessment of the Evidence," in W. Gove, ed., *The Labelling of Deviance* (New York: Halsted Press, 1975).

48. L. Tiffany, Y. Avichai, and G. Peters, "A Statistical Analysis of Sentencing in Federal Courts: Defendants Convicted After Trial, 1967-68," *Journal of Legal Studies* 4:369 (1975).

49. L. Sutton, *Variations in Federal Criminal Sentences: A Statistical Assessment at the National Level* (Washington, D.C.: National Criminal Justice Information and Statistics Service, 1978).

50. C. Pope, *Offender-Based Transaction Statistics: New Directions in Data Collection and Reporting* (Washington, D.C.: National Criminal Justice Information and Statistics Service, 1975); C. Pope, "The Influence of Social and Legal Factors on Sentence Dispositions: A Preliminary Analysis of Offender-Based Transaction Statistics," *Journal of Criminal Justice* 4:203 (1976); C. Pope, "Sentence Dispositions Accorded Assault and Burglary Offenders: An Exploratory Study in Twelve California Counties," *Journal of Criminal Justice* 6:151 (1978).

51. Pope, "Sentence Dispositions Accorded Assault and Burglary Offenders," *supra* note 50 at 161. A recent study of sentencing practices in some southern

states has also found that "legal" variables account for a greater proportion of the variation in sentencing than do "extralegal" variables (in particular, socioeconomic status); see T. Chiricos and G. Waldo, "Socioeconomic Status and Criminal Sentencing: An Empirical Assessment of a Conflict Proposition," *American Sociological Review* 40:753 (1975).

52. Vera Institute of Justice, *Felony Arrests: Their Prosecution and Disposition in New York City's Courts* (New York, 1977).

53. *Id.* at 13, 20.

54. E. Green, *Judicial Attitudes in Sentencing* (London: Macmillan, 1961), pp. 16–19, as cited in R. Hood and R. Sparks, *Key Issues in Criminology* (New York: McGraw-Hill, 1970), pp. 146–51.

55. Green, *supra* note 54 at 147.

56. Hood and Sparks, *supra* note 54 at 154.

57. Hogarth, *supra* note 39 at 147–65.

58. Adapted from D.M. Gottfredson and B. Stecker, *supra* note 38.

59. See, for example, R. Martinson, "What Works? Questions and Answers About Prison Reform," *The Public Interest* 35:22 (1974); W.C. Bailey, "Correctional Outcome: An Evaluation of 100 Reports," *Journal of Criminal Law, Criminology, and Police Science* 57:153 (1966); G. Kassebaum, D.A. Ward, and D.M. Wilner, *Prison Treatment and Parole Survival* (New York: Wiley, 1971); J. Robison and G. Smith, "The Effectiveness of Correctional Programs," *Crime and Delinquency* 17:67 (1971). *Contra,* see T. Palmer, "The Youth Authority's Community Treatment Project," *Federal Probation* 38:3 (1974); and T. Palmer, "Martinson Revisited," *Journal of Research in Crime and Delinquency* 12: 133 (1975). For a more recent analysis, see L. Sechrest, S. White, and E. Brown, eds., *The Rehabilitation of Criminal Offenders: Problems and Prospects* (Washington, D.C.: National Academy of Sciences, 1979).

60. For a review and discussion of this trend in the United States, see "Determinate Sentencing: Making the Punishment Fit the Crime," *Corrections Magazine* 3:3 (1977). Recently, legislation in the direction of greater determinacy has been passed in the states of Maine, California, and Indiana. Similar legislation was passed in Colorado but vetoed by the governor of the state. Related proposals, at the time of the *Corrections Magazine* report, were being debated in sixteen other states across the country and in the District of Columbia. Similarly, a proposed new federal criminal code, incorporating features of greater determinacy, in 1978 passed in the United States Senate (though not in the United States House of Representatives).

61. von Hirsch, *supra* note 27. See also, M.K. Harris, "Disquisition on the Need for a New Model for Criminal Sanctioning Systems," *West Virginia Law Review* 77:263 (1975).

62. N. Kittrie, *The Right to be Different: Deviance and Enforced Therapy* (Baltimore: The Johns Hopkins Press, 1971).

63. See, for example, the standards (*re* civil commitments) ascribed to Judge David Bazelon in Rouse vs. Cameron, 373 F 2d. 451, (1966), *in* Mueller, *supra* note 2 at 100.

64. See M.K. Harris, *supra* note 61. But see the discussion concerning disparity reduction by parole boards in Chapter 9.

65. *Id.*

66. See, for example, D. Fogel, *We are the Living Proof: The Justice Model for Corrections* (Cincinnati: Anderson, 1975).

67. A. Dershowitz, *Fair and Certain Punishment: Report of the Twentieth Century Fund Task Force on Criminal Sentencing* (New York: McGraw-Hill, 1976).

68. D.M. Gottfredson, L.T. Wilkins, and P.B. Hoffman, *Guidelines for Parole and Sentencing* (Lexington, Massachusetts: Lexington Books, 1978); L.T. Wilkins, J. Kress, D.M. Gottfredson, J. Calpin, and A. Gelman, *Sentencing Guidelines: Structuring Judicial Discretion* (Washington, D.C.: Government Printing Office, 1978).

69. J. McKechnie, ed., *Webster's New Twentieth Century Dictionary of the English Language*, 2nd ed. (Collins-World, 1975).

70. See, M. Zalman, "A Commission Model of Sentencing," *Notre Dame Lawyer* 53:266 (1977), for a general discussion of perceived problems of sentencing in terms of the concepts "irrationality, disparity, ineffectiveness, and diffusion." He apparently would consider the problem cited as an example of perceived irrationality rather than disparity, reserving the latter for differences in sentencing that are associated with insidious criteria.

71. K. Davis, *Discretionary Justice* (Baton Rouge: Louisiana State University Press, 1969).

72. F. Remington et al., *Criminal Justice Administration* (Indianapolis: Bobbs-Merrill Co., Inc., 1969), p. 889.

73. Wilkins, Kress, Gottfredson, Calpin, and Gelman, *supra* note 68. See also J. Kress, L. Wilkins, and D. Gottfredson, "Is the End of Judicial Sentencing in Sight?" *Judicature* 60:216 (1976).

74. D. Gottfredson, Wilkins, and Hoffman, *supra* note 68.

75. Kress, Wilkins, and Gottfredson, *supra* note 73.

76. R. Carter, "The Pre-Sentence Report and the Decision-Making Process," *Journal of Research in Crime and Delinquency* 4:203 (1967).

77. L.T. Wilkins, *Social Deviance* (Englewood Cliffs, New Jersey: Prentice-Hall, 1964), pp. 294-304.

78. L.T. Wilkins, personal communication.

79. An alternative mechanism that has been offered as a means by which sentencing disparity may be reduced is the sentencing council. For a documentation of the types of disparity that can exist and a study of the limited effect of reducing disparity by this means, see S. Diamond and H. Zeisel, "Sentencing Councils: A Study of Sentencing Disparity and Its Reduction," *University of Chicago Law Review* 43:1 (1975). For a study using different methods but with comparable results, see, Sutton, *supra* note 46.

80. For an exploratory study of some of the issues, see L. Sebba, "Some Explorations in the Scaling of Penalties," *Journal of Research in Crime and Delinquency* 15:247 (1978).

81. Gottfredson, Wilkins, and Hoffman, *supra* note 68.

82. D.M. Gottfredson, C.A. Cosgrove, L.T. Wilkins, J. Wallerstein, and C. Rauh, *Classification for Parole Decision Policy* (Washington, D.C.: Government Printing Office, 1978), p. 280.

83. See H. Barnes, and N. Teeters, *supra* note 45 at 391–454.

84. M.K. Harris, and F. Dunbaugh, "Premise for a Sensible Sentencing Debate: Giving Up Imprisonment," *Hofstra Law Review* 7:417 (1979); M.K. Harris, "Community Service by Offenders" (submission draft prepared for the American Bar Association's Basics Program, January 1979).

❋ *Chapter 7*

Correctional Decisions in the Community

Decisions about convicted offenders do not end with the sentence of the judge. Indeed, a new series of decisions is only beginning—whether the offender is placed on probation (usually with suspension of a more severe sanction), whether he or she is sent to jail (or these sanctions are used in combination), whether another alternative is selected, or whether the person is sent to prison. All these decisions that are now required may be called "correctional," not because they necessarily are corrective of the person's behavior, but because the term "corrections" has come into common usage to designate the complex of activities, programs, and systems such as probation, jail, prison, and parole that have been designed to deal with adjudicated persons in state custody. Setting aside issues of paroling decisions for Chapter 9, we seek in this chapter and the next to outline the general nature of some common decision problems in areas of corrections.

The term corrections suggests the dominance, during the last half century, of utilitarian aims—particularly treatment—rather than of retribution or desert as a principal raison d'etre for these systems. (As discussed in Chapter 6, desert recently has been more widely argued and debated as placed more properly in this role.) In any case, even a cursory review of the kinds of decisions made daily by corrections staff will show that rehabilitation is not now, and never has been, a sole concern.

Immediately upon arrival in jail or prison, for example, some screening ordinarily is seen as necessary, whether done informally and haphazardly or systematically. The concerns addressed require decisions aimed at preventing low probability but high risk events.

Especially notable are three classes of events that appropriate screening (classification) might help avoid—suicide (or self-injury), escape, and victimization (for example, homosexual rape).

In large correctional systems, the first weeks after institutional commitment or placement in programs of community supervision will see a great variety of procedures aimed at assessment of the offender for the purpose of program assignment. Much data concerning the individual's personal and social history, present offense of conviction, prior record, and aspirations often will be collected. Educational and psychological tests may be administered, and vocational counseling may be provided. Following this assessment, when the offender has been incarcerated, decisions such as these must be made:

What level of custody must be assigned initially?

In what geographical region should the offender be housed?

In what institution should the offender be placed initially?

Should the offender be placed in an academic program? At what level? A vocational program?

Should the person be assigned to any program of counseling or psychotherapy? Group or individual? Therapeutic community program? Behavior modification program?

What work assignments should be recommended?

If the convicted offender is not sent to prison but, alternatively, placed in a community program such as probation, a similar variety of decisions may be required:

Should the person be placed in a "regular" case load or is more "intensive" (or more "minimal") supervision called for?

Should the person be placed in a "specialized" case load?

Are referrals to treatment or other social service agencies to be made?

For these and other decisions, the correctional agency staff will have much data but little information. Large sums of money and a great deal of concerned, even dedicated, effort will have been made collecting data on individual offenders. Much effort and more financial resources often will have been expended to record these data in individual folders, to prepare detailed personal and social histories, and to record recommendations of the clinical and custodial staff or of probation officers. Further large expenditures of time, energy, and funds will be made later in efforts to restudy the person, to reassign him or her, or to implement those recommendations already made. Little will have been spent in assessing the relevance of these data to the goals the agency wishes to achieve—either for the individual offender or for the agency's general mission. In short, there may be much data, but there is little information, and relatively meager resources are expended to improve the quality of information on which the decisions rely.

The term "corrections" has, as already noted, come to include a wide range of criminal justice programs. These include probation services (usually, but not always, provided as "an arm of the court," usually within county but sometimes state structures), jail programs (usually operated by counties through sheriff's departments, sometimes called prisons or correctional centers, usually confining sentenced persons for a year or less plus persons awaiting trial), prison programs (usually operated by state corrections departments and handling persons whose maximum sentence is more than a year), and parole programs (usually operated by state departments of corrections or parole boards). In view of this complexity, programs of probation and parole will be discussed in this chapter, since they are the most common forms of "community corrections." Then, in Chapter 8, institutional corrections programs will be examined.

It must be noted that distinctions between "community" and "institutional" corrections programs are somewhat arbitrary and have become so increasingly in recent years. That is, distinctions between programs of confinement and of community supervision have become increasingly blurred. A brief look at the history of corrections in the United States, in terms of predominant emphases on differing correctional goals, will show why this is so.

In a useful discussion of "model correctional policies," O'Leary identifies four differing orientations as reflecting emphasis on reform, on rehabilitation, on reintegration, and on restraint.[1] Early in the development of correctional systems in the United States, when imprisonments began to replace punishments used previously such as mutilation, whipping, or public humiliation, stress began to be placed on the reformation of the convicted person. Whether reform was to be achieved through isolation, deprivation, and penitence (in the "penitentiary") or through work (and development of "good work habits") was debated; but that the reform of the person who had behaved badly was a principal aim seems clear.

With the advent of social science development and its increased impact on social thought, and particularly with psychoanalysis and its offspring in psychiatry and in social work, this stance tended to change. Less often was the offender perceived as "bad" and in need of reform through penitence or work; more often he or she was regarded as sick, disturbed, or disordered. Hence, the goals of confinement tended to shift toward increased emphasis on treatment that would be rehabilitative. In recent decades, the term "reintegration" has been used increasingly to denote a concept that includes rehabilitative aims but gives stress to the role of the community environment (and to interactions of person and community) in achieving the status of productive, or at least law-abiding, citizen behavior on the part of the convicted offender. If lesser emphasis in correctional programs were to be given to reform, or rehabilitation, or reintegration, and more to the incapacitation of the offender (to prevent further crimes), then what O'Leary called the "restraint" perspective would dominate. Emphasis in this model is not given to changing the offender, or to preparing him or her for release, but to institutional control, survival, and maintenance of the system. O'Leary provides convincing illustrations of how these particular emphases may have profound effects on a prison system, including the location of the institution, the selection and training of personnel, the activities and opportunities provided for inmates, and the selection of parole board members. These emphases may be thought of as changing over time but also as being reflected, in varying degrees, among correctional systems and within them. These shifting orientations have consequences also for the now frequently blurred distinctions between "community" and "institutional" corrections.

One commonly held conception among correctional workers is that if the offender is imprisoned, the degree of custodial control required may perhaps be reduced gradually, as depicted in Figure 7-1. Thus, there may be incremental decreases in custody classification within the institution (for example, from maximum, through close, medium, and minimum, with increasing freedom for the convicted person). There could be similar decreases periodically in the level of parole supervision assigned (such as high or intensive supervision, medium or average level supervision, and low or minimal supervison).[2] It should be noted that within correctional structures characterized by a degree of indeterminacy in sentencing, both institutional confinement and parole supervision traditionally have been regarded as part of the sentence—one portion to be served in the institution and the other on parole.

In practice, various placement decisions (made by institutional or parole staff as well as the critical parole decision) may be made that affect whether the convicted offender is housed in the institution or in the community. Thus, in various jurisdictions there are programs of work or study release, various community corrections programs such as "halfway houses," or programs allowing for short-

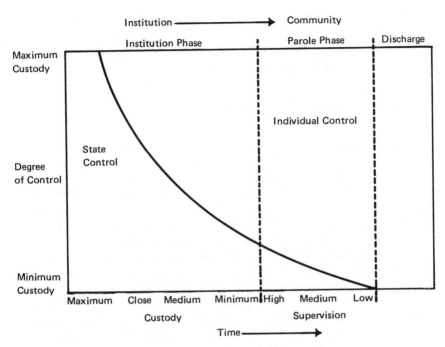

Figure 7-1. Degree of control as a function of time served.

term return to confinement for rules violations by a parolee. There may be programs of weekend or overnight jail confinement or use of probation conditions requiring such short-term periodic institutionalization. All these provide examples of the blurred, often arbitrary distinction between institutional and community correctional programs.

Even the distinction between probation and parole may be more a matter of the location of responsibility for supervision, within government structures, than of substantive difference in underlying concepts. The term "probation" usually implies community supervision in lieu of incarceration (such sentences usually having been imposed but suspended conditional upon following orders of the court regarding the conditions of probation), while parole usually refers to community supervision after a period of confinement. "Split" sentences often are used, however, negating even that distinction. This refers to the circumstance that the convicted offender is required by the sentence to serve a portion, first, in jail, then a further term on probation. Thus, Figure 7-1 could, for split sentences, refer as well to a notion of decreasing control by levels of custody in jail, followed by increasing freedom during probation supervision. Despite these ambiguities, it is convenient to divide the discussion of correctional decisions between concerns of traditional community corrections (probation and parole) and institutional corrections (jails and prisons).

GOALS AND ALTERNATIVES IN COMMUNITY CORRECTIONS DECISIONS

Both probation and parole are subjects of considerable controversy at present, widely heralded by some as the best hope of effective, humane, and efficient corrections and marked by others as systems that should be abolished.[3] The 1973 report on corrections of a national commission asserted "probation is viewed as the brightest hope of corrections . . . ."[4] Some leading scholars are more skeptical, suggesting that probation be "virtually abolished"[5] or severely limited.[6] Another offers an exquisite ambivalence when he remarks that an important latent function of probation is "to allow a judge to give the appearance of doing something while in fact doing nothing."[7] There is similar debate about parole. In the National Advisory Commission report, one proposed standard would require legislation in each state "authorizing parole for all committed offenders,"[8] while von Hirsch and Hanrahan suggest that "instead of routinely imposing supervision on ex-prisoners, supervision should be eliminated entirely, or if retained, should be reduced substantially in scope . . ." (and that other substantial changes are needed).[9] The objective of this chapter, however, is not to enter these debates except insofar as an examination of goals, alternatives, and information for decisionmaking in community corrections may be found relevant to them.

The aims sought in community corrections programs are, like those of sentencing discussed in Chapter 6, diverse and often apparently in conflict. The placement of the convicted offender on probation (by the judge) may reflect any of the broad goals of sentencing (general deterrence, incapacitation, treatment, or desert). Once those actions have been taken, however, a somewhat different question may be raised: What are the goals of probation or parole supervision? Generally, it may be assumed that three main goals are paramount—treatment, control, and organizational maintenance.

The treatment aim—that is, the rehabilitative-reintegrative goal—has been reflected in writings on both probation and parole since their invention. Probation, as is widely cited, began in concept with the volunteer efforts of a Boston shoemaker, John Augustus, who in 1841 apparently persuaded the court to release some offenders to him. This led to the first formal establishment, by legislation, of probation in 1878 in Massachusetts.[10] (Some brief history of parole is discussed in Chapter 9.) This was, of course, a crime reduction aim: the objective was to decrease the likelihood that the convicted person will engage in further criminal behavior. The system of treatment or supervision, however, was not to be trusted completely: there is also a control function of supervision.

This control function may be perceived in the attention given not only to remedial, rehabilitative, or reintegrative efforts of assistance but also to surveillance. Thus, if rules violations can be demonstrated, the suspended sentence may be imposed (by the court), usually meaning the incarceration of the violator. The purpose generally is held to be the prevention of further crime (rather than desert). This function, too, is thus aimed at crime reduction. As with other social agencies, it is reasonable to assume as well that probation decisions include objectives of continuing or enhancing the organization or making it more efficient and effective.

The two principal purposes of probation and parole are thus apparently utilitarian, reductionist goals (see Chapter 6 for a discussion in the context of sentencing; compare with Chapter 9 concerning paroling decision purposes). Given the crime reduction, prevention, or control aims of these two types of community corrections systems, a principal question to be answered empirically is how well these aims are achieved.[11] In relation to sentencing goals, the treatment aim is paramount: incapacitation may be a perceived goal when the control function is exercised and culminates in confinement of the offender; the aims of general deterrence and desert appear to be much less emphasized.

Given the broad array of differences in administrative structure, government subdivision, geography, economics, and legal frameworks that characterize probation and parole supervision programs, it must be expected that the resources available to administrators of these programs will be highly varied. Nevertheless, there are certain program issues concerning the classification of probationers or parolees and their assignment (that is, with program placement decisions) that have been of wide interest. A topic closely related to issues of differential classification and assignment is that of case load size. These concerns have to do both with the question of "optimal" case load size for probation or parole supervision programs generally and with the question of whether differing "levels of intensity" of supervision are appropriate with differing classifications of probationer or parolee populations. This issue, which involves the hypothesis that differential assignment to levels according to "risk" will be more effective than random assignment, involves also the problem of classification of offenders according to predicted "success" or "failure" on probation or parole.[12] Thus, an examination of alternatives available to probation or parole administrators should include a brief overview of the current status of research on probation and parole prediction, on the case load size question, on relevant differential treatment hypotheses, and on certain troublesome problems related to criteria for judging "success" as required by the crime reduction and control aims of these services. Each of these issues is complex. For each, there is substantial literature.

PROBATION AND PAROLE PREDICTION

Most studies of probation and parole prediction have been done in the areas of parole, beginning more than a half century ago,[13] although probation studies date at least to 1932.[14] Since thorough reviews of the large literature on parole and probation prediction are available,[15] our focus here will be on certain methodological and management issues thought to be most pertinent to the decision problems related to program placement of the offender.[16] These issues, of course, are interrelated.

In any discussion of prediction methods in criminology (or other areas of human affairs), the issue of the relative efficiency and effectiveness of "clinical" (that is, global judgmental) predictions and "statistical" (numerical or "objective" classification) predictions soon arises. The continuing debate may be due, as suggested by Mannheim and Wilkins, to the circumstance that "People seem . . . to be more inclined to accept the judgment of other people than to trust numerical procedures which appear abstract and impersonal," a conjecture that led them to assume that "if this prejudice is to be overcome we require the experience table procedures to be *more accurate* than other systems of making assessments." And they reported that in their study it seemed that "the statistical procedures were at least three times as efficient as the subjective judgments of Governors of the Institutions, and far more accurate than a psychologist's prognosis."[17]

The classic work on the topic is that by Meehl, who found, after reviewing studies that compared clinical and actuarial (that is, statistical, methods), that in all but one study the predictions made actuarially were either approximately equal or superior to those made by a clinician.[18] A further review, with a generally similar result, was done by Gough.[19] Thus, when empirically derived statistical prediction devices are pitted against clinical judgment and the accuracy of prediction compared, the statistical prediction instrument generally has fared better in the comparison.

One study that pitted clinical prediction against statistical prediction for parole success can serve as an example of the general finding. D. Gottfredson compared, for the same 283 parolees, the validity of prediction scores obtained by subjective ratings made by a prison associate superintendent (after prerelease interviews) and ratings of clinical staff (psychiatric) reports with ratings based on a statistical device. The two subjective prediction ratings and the statistical prediction method all were related to parole outcomes, in the expected direction. (Correlation coefficients between scores and parole outcome as a dichotomous variable were 0.20 for the administrator's ratings, 0.21 for the clinical team ratings, and 0.48 for the statistical prediction method scores. Multiple correlation of all combinations of the three measures failed to increase the value of R beyond 0.48). The clerks using the prediction method were much better predictors than were the administrators or the clinical team. Furthermore, the clinical ratings did not improve the prediction beyond that demonstrable using the prediction device alone.[20] This, of course, is only one case, but it is consistent with the generally found result.

That the subjective judgments made in this small study did not improve the efficiency of prediction does not, of course, imply that such improvement may not result if other persons make them or if other methods are used. But the methods used in this study, seeking to determine whether subjective ratings add to predictive validity, provide a way to test for such utility. If helpful predictive factors can thereby be identified, then the newly discovered information can be added to the prediction device. The important point, very often overlooked by proponents of the clinical method, is that whether a statistical or clinical method is used, the proof of its worth should be the same—empirically demonstrated validity.

When a statistical prediction device is available to the decisionmaker, the decision policy may include the provision for discretion as to relying on it or revising the "prognosis" on the basis of specified reasons for the decisionmaker's judgment. One current example of the use of such individualized decisionmaking is given by the use of a "salient factor" prediction device as one dimension in the guidelines policy of the United States Parole Commission (see Chapter 9). Given the "advice" of the statistical prediction method, the decisionmaker may "override" it, giving specific reasons that, in his or her judgment, the prediction may be in error—a case of clinical via statistical prediction. If these instances of subjective impressions supplementing the statistical prediction device are recorded and later tested for their potential contribution to prediction, those items that are helpful may be added to the prediction device, while those found useless may be discarded.

The practical application of both statistical and clinical predictions thus may involve both, preferably as cooperative rather than competitive functions in the process of decisionmaking.[21] The use of statistical tools need not imply a rigidity or mechanical attitude in decisionmaking, as seems often to be supposed.

> What statistical tools provide is a clearer picture of the odds against or for a particular move, so it can be made or not made with eyes open to what is involved in the form both of rewards and of consequences. And, if the decision is to go ahead and make the move, then it can be done with more intelligent attention to what is needed to bring it off successfully. That is quite a different thing from letting the statistics dictate the decision.[22]

A variety of methodological problems that arise frequently in prediction studies tend to affect the usefulness of the resulting devices for probation or parole decision problems. Issues of representativeness of the samples studied,[23] of sample size,[24] of improvement over the "base rate,"[25] and of the methods used to combine predictor items[26] provide examples. Some of these are discussed in a later section of this chapter. The point to be made now, however, is that such devices, when appropriate attention is given to these concerns (all related to the validity of the instrument), may have direct utilities for probation and parole decisionmaking in several ways. These potential uses include applications in program evaluation studies, in program planning, in classification for program assignment, and in other decision problems. Thus, prediction methods may be useful tools for both institutional policy decisions and individual case decisions.

In program evaluation studies, probation or parole prediction measures can provide a measure of control for demonstrable selection bias when comparisons are desired to be made in the absence of experimental designs (for example, with "control" groups randomly assigned). Various writers have discussed this use or offered examples.[27] Such measures have been called "expectancy tables" by early research workers[28] or "experience tables"[29] or "prediction tables"[30] or "base expectancies."[31] All these designations are apt: on the basis of experience, they provide a base for further research by quantifying expectations (in terms of probabilities of "success" or "failure") before the intervention of interest.

Although experimental designs provide more rigorous means to test hypotheses about treatment or supervision effects, such designs are difficult to implement in practice. In addition, it is rare that the opportunity obtains for a comparison of a treatment with the absence of any treatment.[32] Furthermore, even with prediction methods based on information known only before treatment, the circumstances of derivation of the method ordinarily are such that it must be considered to reflect an average expectancy from a variety of treatments (rather than a "treatment-free" expectancy).[33] Nonetheless, a search for treatment or supervision contingencies that invalidate previously validated expectations may be useful in eliminating some plausible but incorrect hypotheses and in directing research toward fruitful areas.[34]

In program planning, prediction methods may be found useful in classifying offenders as an aid to administrative policy decisions that in turn affect individual case decisions. An example is given by an application in California that sought to alleviate problems of prison overcrowding and increased confinement costs. The prison administration, through its research division, screened the entire confined population of California's prisons (more than 20,000 persons), first by base expectancy (parole prediction) scores, then by further clinical criteria.[35] The result, with both male and female prisoners, was that some persons were referred for parole consideration at a date earlier than originally scheduled. Some of these were then released on parole by decisions of the parole board.

In an application of a base expectancy measure more directly relevant to assignment to supervision, minimal supervision case loads of male and female parolees were established (also in California). Persons assigned to classifications having a high probability of successful parole completion received minimal supervision. Experience demonstrated that these cases may be given less supervision with no increase in the parole violation rate.[36] This enabled parole workers to deploy their forces from areas where help was demonstrably less needed to concentrate efforts to where it was perceived as likely to be more helpful.

These efforts resulted in reported substantial monetary savings with no increase in parole violations. It was claimed that by the female offender classification program, the institutional population was reduced; and it was the opinion of correctional administrators that this program had accomplished avoidance of the necessity to build a new women's prison.

In 1961, the California legislature approved a program based on screening of inmates by base expectancy scores combined with programs for more intensive institution and parole services. The goal was reduction of institutional costs for nonviolent cases by release slightly ahead of the expected time. By 1963 the Department of Corrections reported to the legislature that this program had reduced the institution population by more than 840 men and women, that support savings were at least $840,000, and that $8.5 million in capital outlay was deferred. These savings were attributed to the new program and to initial efforts by the paroling authorities to base decisions partly on base expectancy measures.[37]

By 1969, the California Department of Corrections reported an assignment system for parolees with three classes of supervision. The program objectives were to increase community protection, improve performance by parolees, and save institutional costs. The base expectancy measure provided a basis for the assignment procedures. The agency reported to the legislature that total prison returns for new crimes and violation of parole rules were reduced by 25 percent since the 1965 start of the program. They concluded (from analysis of base expectancy scores and actual outcomes, incidentally illustrating a research use of these measures) that 1543 additional men had succeded on parole who, on the basis of past experience, would have been expected to fail. The saving from men kept in the community rather than in prison was estimated as the equivalent of the entire population of an average-sized major prison. Savings in operating expenses were estimated at $4.5 million yearly and in construction savings at $20 million.[38]

Subsequent to these explorations of differential supervision for various risk classifications in California, a number of authors have proposed using prediction scales as an aid in supervision assignment. The suggestions for use have been varied—for example, as an administrative tool to equalize high-risk offenders among various caseloads[39] or to focus services and attention on the probationers who need the most help,[40] or to assist case managers in making decisions about how much time and effort to devote to working with certain groups of persons.[41] Nicholson in 1968 reported a modified version of a scale developed from study of California parolees (by D. Gottfredson) useful in classifying "high, medium, and low" case loads of federal offenders.[42]

CASE LOAD SIZE

A large body of correctional literature addresses the general question of how the size of case loads of probation or parole officers affects the subsequent "success" or "failure" of the offenders who are supervised. Various reviews are available, including a number that provide detailed discussions of the methodological issues involved in evaluations of programs manipulating case load size.[43] These issues are much more complex than may seem at first glance; the results of the studies are mixed, and the methods used are critized frequently as flawed. It may be said with assurance, however, that (1) no "optimal" case load size has been demonstrated and (2) no clear evidence of reduced recidivism, simply by reduced case load size, has been found.[44] The importance of this general negative result to the concerns of this chapter may be seen by a brief examination of the history of public policy on a "proper" case load size—policy that has been unrelated to any empirical evidence whatever.

The earliest assurance on proper case load size known to the authors is that of Chute, who asserted in 1922 that no probation officer should have more than fifty cases.[45] By twelve years later, Sutherland stated that fifty probationers was generally regarded as the maximum number for one officer.[46] By 1946, the American Prison Association described "sound practice" as no more than fifty cases under continuous supervision, and the 1954 Manual of Correctional Standards also included this standard.[47]

Similarly, the National Council on Crime and Delinquency has argued that fifty cases seemed an appropriate maximum.[48] The President's Commission on Law Enforcement and Administration of Justice reduced this value to an average of thirty-five.[49]

Such pronouncements, devoid as they are of empirical support, may serve political purposes or humanitarian ones—for example, by assisting managers to obtain resources for what seem to be more reasonable case load levels than those with which they may currently struggle. They cannot, however, be justified as demonstrably rational—leading to more efficient or effective practice toward correctional objectives. What is needed for more rational planning and program development is the assessment, through experimentation or, at least, quasi-experimental systematic study, of this and related issues. Such repeated assessments should be a part of a general program of study and evolutionary development of the agency. We will return to this proposed method for solution of such complex issues in later sections of this book, including our final chapter.

DIFFERENTIAL TREATMENT

Offenders are not all alike; and, indeed, the belief that each is unique has been posed often as an argument against the idea that they can be classified usefully for the prediction purposes just described.[50] Predictive classifications, however, are based more on similarities than on differences. Thus, Wilkins has asked whether the decisionmaker has, if each case is unique, any experience to guide decisions.

> If experience of the past is of any value at all, then it can be applied only by observation of similarities not differences. It is not the uniqueness that concerns the clinician but the similarities between the particular case and prior cases in his or other people's experience.[51]

Thus it does not seem reasonable to argue at once that the past provides no guide (each case is unique) and that it is experience (with similar cases) that counts. Rather, it seems reasonable to agree with Kluckhohn and Murray that

Every man is, in some respects,
Like all other men,
Like some other men,
Like no other man.[52]

Since people are in some ways all alike, we seek general behavioral laws, for example, of learning. Since each person is in some ways unique, we know that he or she may be best understood when we identify not only what that individual has in common with others but also what is distinctive about the person. And, because "every man is, in some respects, . . . like some other men," there is a role to be played also by classification methods.

The prediction methods discussed previously are classification methods, but the classifications are defined for a specific purpose (of defining expected probation or parole outcomes according to specific criteria of "success"). There is no particular reason to expect that such classifications of offenders would be relevant to "treatment" when that term is used to refer to procedures intended to rehabilitate or specifically deter new offenses.

There is also a wealth of literature on the topic of interaction of type of offender and type of treatment. The question to be asked from this perspective is not, What type of treatment works best? but, What type of treatment works best for what type of offender? (to which may also be added, In respect to what specific purposes?). The construction may, of course, be further elaborated, since we may have, for example, the question of effectiveness of

Kinds of offenders with
Kinds of treatments in
Kinds of treatment settings by
Kinds of treaters and
Kinds of posttreatment environments, in respect to
Kinds of objectives.

As described in Chapter 1, methods of classification for purposes of choice of treatment are diverse but may be regarded generally as reflecting either empirical or theoretical orientations. An example of the former may be given by the "risk-screening–differential level of supervision" programs discussed previously, since the classifications, empirically derived, are now to be tested for relevance to a treatment modification. Examples of theoretical classifications abound; some well-known ones, on which there is a wealth of research literature, are derived from psychological,[53] sociological,[54] or psychiatric[55] theories.

In a critical review of the small number of studies related to the general hypothesis of differential treatment up to 1970, Hood and Sparks noted that these invariably had focused on recidivism reduction, to the neglect of the study of other aims:

> In its most general form, the presupposition which underlies research on this problem can be stated as follows: for any type of offender, there is one type of treatment which is (in some sense) the most appropriate. In fact, researchers in this field to date have neglected general prevention and other possible aims of sentencing, and have concentrated on the objective of reducing recidivism.[56]

As they imply, there seems to be no reason that the interaction hypotheses might not be applied to general deterrence as well as to specific deterrence, incapacitation, or other utilitarian aims of sentencing and corrections. This is an avenue of possibly fruitful research that has not been followed—perhaps because the research workers interested in differential treatment hypotheses were themselves most inclined to the rehabilitation orientation.

By 1970 Hood and Sparks, finding the results to that time not very encouraging, nevertheless found the perspective important and promising. They called for more "basic typological research" —research on the relations between types of offenders and alternative types of sentences (as distinct from alternatives within, say, sentences to imprisonment) and typologies of treatment. Finally, they asserted that "In the case of research on the comparative effectiveness of different sentences, a typological approach should surely become a standard part of research procedure. . . ."[57] It is argued in later sections of this book that such research should, furthermore, become a usual part of a standard, continuing, systematic research procedure in correctional systems.

THE CRITERION PROBLEM

> For so it is, O Lord, my God,
> I measure it.
> But what it is I measure
> I do not know.

This statement, attributed to St. Augustine,[58] may refer aptly to uncritical pronouncements about "recidivism" or recidivism rates that are too common in discussions of correctional effectiveness. There is little agreement on any preferred operational definition of the term; and this clearly makes comparisons of outcome studies in probation and parole exceedingly difficult and complex. Some relevant issues concerning parole are discussed in Chapter 9; to illustrate the variance in probation recidivism definitions that are used, we cite as examples (from a recent review by Powell[59]) several studies of adult probation conducted since 1951. In order to analyze various criteria used in these studies, she noted that it is useful to distinguish between "on probation" and "postprobation" periods. For example, in an "on probation" study, such as that by Frease,[60] a "failure" rate may refer to the ratio of the number of failures while on probation to the total number on probation. (He defined failure as service of an active letter or a bench warrant or revocation of probation.) A "probation termination" study may, on the other hand, define failure as the ratio of failures upon termination to the total number terminated—as, for example, by Landis, Mercer, and Wolff or by Kusuda.[61] (Landis, and colleagues used, as criteria of failure, revocation or new offense conviction; Kusuda defined failure as revocation for new offense, rules violations, or absconding.) Or in a "postprobation" study, where interest is focused on postprobation outcome, a failure rate may be defined as the ratio of failures of probationers who have been terminated to all those terminated. Combinations of these also have been used.[62] And adding to the complexity, cohort studies provide yet another (perhaps for many purposes better) means of defining rates of success and failure. An example is given by Davis's "cohort/probation-termination" study.[63]

Problems in comparisons of studies using such varied definitions of probation success or failure are well known. These are similar when, rather than single project studies, annual reports by probation systems are examined. Thus, Rector, in a comment still apt although written twenty years ago, after reviewing 146 such reports received in one year, stated: "any thought of compiling recidivism data from annual reports for comparative purposes had to be abandoned early because of wide differences in definitions, in methods of computing, and in factors of measurement."[64]

Problems of comparison, of course, are compounded also by differing follow-up periods and samples of offenders. These vary widely on factors known from many studies to be related to outcomes, such as offense, age, and prior record of criminal offenses.

Is this diversity of "recidivism" definitions a problem? In a sense, of course, it is; it certainly provides a source of frustration for those who seek comparisons while rendering useless the heretofore mentioned uncritical claims or allegations concerning probation recidivism rates without further definition. Seeking a standardization, the recent National Advisory Commission on Criminal Justice Standards and Goals provided (for system reviews) their recommended definition:

Recidivism is measured by (1) criminal acts that resulted in conviction by a court, when committed by individuals who are under correctional supervision or who have been released from correctional supervision within the previous three years, and by (2) technical violations of probation or parole in which a sentencing or paroling authority took action that resulted in an adverse change in the offender's legal status.[65]

In another sense, however, the variability in definition is not a problem. Each investigator may have his or her reasons for preferring a different definition, and it is the same with program administrators. Notably, the National Advisory Commission, in enunciating the definition just quoted, listed differing criteria for "program reviews." And it may be noted that the comptroller general, soon after the National Advisory Commission report, used a different definition. The utility of various definitions of outcome, for differing purposes, has been discussed well by Glaser. After considering the multiple manifest and latent goals characteristic of corrections and hierarchies of goals and types of success, he discussed criteria under the headings "most objective," "most attainable," "most continuous," and "most support-relevant." Arguing that more rational choices in fund allocation (for programs) requires cost-benefit analyses, he also provided a helpful discussion of criteria in relation to these.[66]

It is also of considerable interest to note that despite the tremendous variation in recidivism rates used by various probation studies there is a remarkable consistency in findings with respect to factors associated with "failure." One study that compared the correlates of failure in ten studies published since 1951 found considerable stability in correlates despite widely differing failure criteria.[67]

INFORMATION

Any discussion of data available for probation or parole decision-making, whether individual or program decisions are at issue, must, it seems, begin with some discussion of the presentence report. For most probation services, this is a basic document intended not only to serve the court (in the disposition of the case) but also to guide the initiation of supervision. If the offender is jailed, it may provide nearly the only resource for classification and assignment purposes, including the issue of custody (that is, security) assignment. It would provide, in most instances, the only basis for allocation to counseling, training, education, or work assignment. If the offender is imprisoned, this document provides the basis from which any study of the offender and written reports therefrom are derived. Thus, it may have impact on the institutional program placements of the prison inmate as well, and data from the presentence investigation find their way also into the materials on which paroling decisions may be based. Given this importance (and noting that decisions are not made about persons but about information about persons[68]), it is perhaps surprising that so little attention has yet been given to assessing the relevance of the data of presentence reports to the objectives of the myriad decisions made on its basis. If that is surprising, it must be said to be astounding that for great numbers of cases, the report is not prepared at all. This is true notably in the misdemeanor courts: a survey conducted for the 1967 President's Crime Commission found that presentence investigations were made in less than 20 percent of nearly 300,000 misdemeanor cases in a sample of seventy-five counties.[69]

A first need of many if not most probation and parole systems, if more effective decisions are to be made and if a learning from experience is to occur in a more systematic manner, must be to improve the quality of data collected on each offender at the time of the presentence investigation. Extensively discursive social histories with opinions and judgments of the writer will not serve, no matter how excellent in literary style. A core set of the same data for each person, collected with attention to reliability concerns, is needed. Such data then can be examined to determine the relevance of individual items, or combinations of them, to a wide array of significant decision problems. These include, it must be stressed, not only the sentencing decision, but decisions such as those at issue earlier in this chapter. Without such careful, systematic data collection, the probation or parole administrator is in the familiar correctional situation—much data, collected unsystematically, variably, and subjectively for individual case studies; no information demonstrably relevant to either program or individual decisions.

The needs for information are similar when jails are considered; and although it is a digression in this chapter, the relevance of the presentence reports to management in jails must be stressed. If the offender is jailed, whether by sentence of the court or while awaiting trial, a first concern is for security. That is a broad term, however, and the jailor must be concerned with the security of the institution, while maintaining custody of the person, and with the offender's personal safety. Usually he or she has not much more than the presentence report—and often not even that.

The essentially predictive purpose of these decisions—and the requirements that such a purpose raises—need be stressed. Maintaining the security of the institution, for example, may imply a need for identifying assault-prone persons. Keeping the person in custody may imply that predictions are made about the likelihood of attempted escape. Ensuring the offender's personal safety may require identification of persons with a high risk of suicide attempts, those with a high probability of becoming a target of abuse by other inmates, or those in need of emergency physical or psychiatric care. (It may be noted that each of these prediction problems is especially difficult due partly to the relatively low prevalence of the undesired event.)

The data collected for preparation of the presentence investigation report, traditionally intended primarily as an aid to the court in choosing among sentencing alternatives, do not serve well the additionally needed functions of analyses aimed at improving these correctional decisions. (The same shortcomings militate also against useful analyses for improving the court's selections among available alternatives.) The inadequacies of presentence reports for these analytical functions (that is, variability in content, lack of attention to definitions, absence of reliability assessments, and a high degree of subjective judgment) stem understandably from the individualized case analysis perspective that was central to the historical development of these documents.

This history has been well described by Carter.[70] The emphasis in preparation of the report traditionally has been that of diagnosis. Carter traces the development to Healy, who in 1910 argued for the "individual study of the young criminal [and for] the importance of a thorough-going study of the individual case at the period of life when something, if ever, can be done in the way of individual modification." Healy further noted: "The case consequently must require careful, individual diagnosis before the rational treatment can be instituted which is really adapted to its needs."[71]

In Chapter 1 of this book the concepts of diagnosis and classification were distinguished, and it was asserted that diagnoses (as descriptions of the state of the person) may or may not be useful toward establishing classifications for various specific purposes. In order to establish the latter, careful uniform record keeping in which the same data are collected reliably on all offenders is necessary. And it should be remembered that not only judicial decisions but many decisions occurring later in the correctional process are served, if at all, by whatever information content is found in the presentence report. The President's Commission Task Force on Corrections commented in 1967:

> In order to evaluate the information needed in a presentence report, it is important first to take account of the variety of decisions that depend upon it. Besides helping the judge to decide between probation and prison, it also assists him to fix the length and conditions of probation or the term of imprisonment. Beyond these functions, the report is usually the major information source in all significant decisions that follow—in probation programming or institutional handling, in eventual parole decision and supervision, and in any probation and parole revocation.[72]

The Task Force also noted that the reports contain much data of doubtful relevance to dispositions, that terminology used varies widely, and that some information "is of marginal relevance" to correctional treatment placement decisions.[73]

The diversity of data included typically in presentence investigation reports is well illustrated by some results of a 1976 survey by Carter; they serve also to depict the types of data collected. The survey addressed 735 probation agencies, of which 147 responded (from forty-two states, the District of Columbia, and Guam).[74] Concerning the "cover sheet," Carter identified 118 data elements (tabulated from 105 cover sheets analyzed). (He noted, incidentally, that "it was the exceptional report which indicated whether data on the cover sheet or in the report itself had been verified.")[75] His analysis of the content of these reports, by frequency of occurrence, is summarized in Table 7-1. He noted, perhaps with understatement, that "it appears that individual officers have considerable discretion as to the details of pre-sentence report narrative content," and "[t]he general practice seems to be that the content of the pre-sentence report is the concern almost solely of the probation organization and its officers."[76]

Our purpose here is not to argue against diversity. As Carter asserts, there may be a need for both standardization and localization—for example, for adapting a common model, with some constant set of standards, in individual jurisdictions. But if ever a consistent set of data elements suitable for the classification studies needed (and for an assessment of the relevance of information to decisions) is to be available for analyses, these obvious shortcomings cannot be ignored.

Table 7-1. Presentence Report Content (arranged by frequency of occurrence of section headings: N = 123).

Section Heading	Number of Occurrences	Percent
Offense: official version	113	91.9
Social and family history	111	90.2
Prior record	106	86.2
Evaluative summary	106	86.2
Employment	105	85.4
Education	103	83.7
Offense: defendant's version	97	78.9
Health: physical	97	78.9
Marital history	91	74.0
Military service	89	72.4
Financial assets and obligations	84	68.3
Health: mental and emotional	83	67.5
Recommendation	79	64.2
Religion	60	48.8
Substance use or abuse	52	42.3
Home and neighborhood	49	39.8
Interest and leisure time activities	48	39.0
Collateral contact or references	42	34.2
Treatment plan	21	17.1
Available resources	19	15.5
Offense: statement of arresting officer or complainant	17	13.8
Offense: statement of victim(s)	16	13.0
Character traits, behavioral adjustment, socialization	16	13.0
Offense: statement of co-defendants	10	8.1
Present attitude toward offense	10	8.1
Offense: statement of witnesses	4	3.3

Source: R. Carter, *Presentence Report Handbook* (Washington, D.C.: Government Printing Office, 1978), p. 12.

The argument that there is a need to improve the consistency and reliability of data collected about offenders in presentence investigations may seem rather far afield from the central thesis of this book that rational decisionmaking requires the selection among alternatives in the light of information demonstrably relevant to specified objectives. But it is information in this sense—not merely data—that is required. Thus, an analysis of the available data, to determine its information content, is needed; and this in turn requires a consistently and systematically acquired data set. Stated another way, it is necessary to have information about the information if its utility is to be assessed.[77]

There is little evidence from systematic study of how the data now included typically in presentence investigation reports is used in decisionmaking, either by the courts or by probation or parole administrators. There is some evidence that (1) only a small number of data elements tend to be used in decisionmaking in individual cases[78] and that (2) the recommendation of the probation officer as to granting probation, when made,[79] tends to be consistent with that made later by the judge.[80]

Data items used by probation officers in arriving at presentence recommendations were investigated in a small study by Wilkins and Chandler.[81] Using an "information board," they asked probation officers to select items in order of their importance. Items were arranged on cards, with a heading at the top and content below extracted from a case file; only the heading was visible until an item was selected. After choosing four items and examining the content of each in turn, a decision was requested (as well as ratings of confidence and difficulty in the decision) after each subsequent selection. Wilkins found no persistent pattern used by the seventeen officers studied (in this one case) and considered that the way information was sought and used was perhaps more characteristic of the officers than of the information.

In a study by Carter, using a similar method, fourteen United States Probation Officers in California with five hypothetical cases were used and twenty-four data items were studied.[82] Of these, an average of only seven or eight per case were used. Carter reported a considerable consistency, or "style," in selection by the individual officers, but noted that the final recommendations made by these officers were considerably divergent. (Gottfredson, Wilkins, and Hoffman, in a related study of parole decisions, reported similarly that different decisions may be reached on the basis of the same information.[83]) Of the twenty-four data items available to the probation officers, only eight were selected more than half the time.

Offense and prior record were examined invariably. Eighty percent of the time the psychological-psychiatric data were examined, and 70 percent of the time the defendant's statement was selected. The statements of the defendant's attitude (62 percent), employment history (61 percent), age (54 percent), and family history (52 percent) were fairly popular items for examination.

Carter and Wilkins also studied the relation between probation officer recommendations and judges' decisions as to probation.[84] They found that when probation was recommended, it was granted in most of the cases studied. Of course, it may be that the probation officer and judge are arriving at a similar decision on the basis of the same or similar information; there was, however, a considerable variation in the proportions of persons granted probation by different courts, and this seemed to be associated with variation among the probation officers.

INFORMATION ON PROGRAM ASSIGNMENT—THE CASE OF PROBATION[85]

As already noted, probation programs currently are heralded both as the best hope of corrections and regarded as relatively useless. Positions on community corrections may be derived from a review of the state of the art in this field; they may reflect mere opinion, wish, or hope; or they may be based upon a careful analysis of systematic empirical knowledge about the success or failure of efforts to rehabilitate offenders in the community. There is, however, little conclusive evidence from the latter source. An often cited study, that of Lipton, Martinson, and Wilks, analyzed and summarized 231 studies of correctional rehabilitation.[86] But what can be learned from that review about adult probation services in the United States is quite limited. Only five pertinent adult probation studies were included in that review. Four of them assessed probation in respect to recidivism, and one evaluated also the effect of probation on vocational adjustment. One study assessed personality and attitude changes associated with intensive probation services and supervision.

Recently, Gottfredson and colleagues sought to define and discuss some critical issues about adult probation in the United States and to seek out and review the evidence since 1950 bearing on these issues.[87] About 130 available studies concerning probation client case load characteristics, probation prediction, probation revocation and recidivism, and probation treatment modalities were reviewed.

An attempt was made to find and obtain reports from all relevant studies conducted since 1950.[88]

This is a substantial set of research reports, with conclusions reached. But there are questions of "information about the information" that must be considered in seeking to determine what is known with confidence. To what extent do faults in research designs, difficulties in research implementation, errors of methods, or flaws in logic require that research conclusions must be accepted only cautiously or even discounted? How much reliable information is left?

In correctional research there are many opportunities along the path from the research design to a conclusion for a study to veer off course, a deviation that can limit the confidence that may be placed in the findings. Some of these pitfalls, noted in the Gottfredson, Finckenauer, and Rauh review, may be examined briefly to illustrate these problems. Research done in action settings is criticized easily after the fact, in the manner of the traditional "Monday morning quarterback." This is not our purpose, and we are aware that many of the faults identified may have been a function of the circumstances of time and place that precluded the use of what we (and perhaps the research workers involved) perceive as better methods. The problems we wish to cite, however, set limits to the conclusions that can be drawn.

It should not be assumed that all the studies reviewed suffered from the problems described nor that examples of useful research procedures were not found. Rather, it is hoped that it is understood that we wish to highlight some frequently encountered problems that seriously limit what can be learned from the entire set of studies to provide information useful in decisionmaking.

An obvious essential first element is the careful formulation of the research design prior to implementation of a study. A carefully planned research design is important to keep the study on course. A lack of careful, detailed planning was apparent in many of the studies reviewed.

The selection of an appropriate sample (or samples) for study is, of course, another critical element. It is a fundamental point that if a sample is selected for study that is not representative of the population of interest, the findings may not be generalized appropriately to that population. There are techniques available, such as probability sampling, that can ensure that a sample may be considered representative. Unfortunately, this requirement is sometimes not understood. "Random" is equated with "haphazard," or samples are drawn on some basis of convenience, with a consequent introduction of possible bias.

The use of a classical research design generally provides a useful procedure in evaluation of program effectiveness, but numerous difficulties often are encountered in attempts to use such designs. This type of plan requires the selection of samples such that an experimental group (treated) and control group (untreated) are created. Subjects are randomly allocated to both. Typically, "before" measures are made of each group to determine a base line against which change can be measured. The experimental group is then exposed to treatment, controlling or restricting the interference of unwanted outside factors. After treatment, an "after" measure is taken in both groups to determine the changes that have occurred. Because of difficulties in implementing and adhering to this type of research design in probation work, compromises frequently are made in order to conduct the evaluations. Gottfredson and his associates found that a commonly used compromise design in probation studies is the "after-only" design. In such a study, a group receives treatment and then a measurement is made, ostensibly to determine what changes have occurred. No control group is used for comparison, and there is no measurement of the prior state of affairs and no basis for estimating expected outcomes. It is thus not possible to determine the extent to which treatment may be considered responsible for any change.

Another compromise design frequently encountered in the probation literature is the "before-after" design. It may provide some evidence, although a control group still is lacking. A measure of the dependent variable is taken both before and after treatment. Various potential sources of error are inherent in this design, particularly the possibility of selection bias, such that attributing any observed change to treatment is hazardous at best.

If one asks about the effectiveness of probation or of specialized probation services, one must ask, Compared with what? The importance of comparisons in probation evaluation research is apparent; yet many of the studies reviewed by Gottfredson and colleagues lacked this vital element. Various studies are reported that lack either a control group in the sense of a classic experimental design, comparison groups considered to serve this purpose, or any statistical correction for known bias entering into the comparison.

A frequent problem encountered in the review of those probation studies was a lack of clear definition of critical terms. Thus, the operational meanings of critical variables or concepts often was unclear. An important variable not defined in any of the studies reviewed, for example, was the concept of "individual counseling."

Despite the wide variety of behaviors that may reasonably be considered to fall within this general concept, studies were found that purported to study "individual counseling" without specifying what such treatment entailed.

Although it often is recognized that the sampling of probationers is important to generalizations about persons on probation, little if any attention is given to the problem of sampling of treatments of a given type. Since, for example, "individual counseling" is not all alike, and indeed may proceed from a wide variety of theoretical frames of reference, the simple, unelaborated characterization of the treatment variable as "individual counseling" clearly will give little if any information about individual counseling in general, no matter how the study comes out. Problems of representative sampling of treatments of a given type are extremely complex; but in any treatment study there at least should be a careful description of the treatment used.

Thus, inadequate operational definitions of the treatment provided, and inadequate descriptions of the treatment afforded comparison groups, were commonly encountered in this review. From the study reports, it often appeared that each staff member was left to interpret individually the treatment to be delivered. Lack of consistency in the delivery of treatment may affect the results, and certainly it would preclude the rigorous examination of consistent application of the treatment technique. Minimally, three dimensions of concern must be clear from the description of "treatments." The first is that of intent, or of the theory underlying the treatment. The second is some measure of intensity, or, to choose a medical analogy, of the dosage administered (not in the plan only but also in the practice); and the third is some evidence of the consistency with which the treatment actually was administered.

It is well known that the quality of information obtained is a critical element in all correctional research and that the most sophisticated analytical techniques cannot compensate for poor quality data. It is well known too that care must be taken during data collection to ensure its reliability. Thus, it is surprising that the reliability of data used in evaluations is so rarely assessed and reported. In one exception, a study of probation prediction models and recidivism, Ford and Johnson reported that "[a] survey of the reliability of offender self-report information about work history revealed that, on the average, offenders overestimated their most recent wage by 51 cents per hour and their length of employment by 13 weeks. . . ."[89] Left undiscovered, such differences could have led to inaccurate conclusions, and the example illustrates the need for systematic assessment of the accuracy and reliability of the data used.

The issue of reliability should be, but often is not, considered when subjective ratings about probationers (for example, by probation officers) form the data base for determining risk levels or the need for treatment and services. Since the use of such subjective ratings results in different interpretations by different raters, leaves room for personal bias, and is notoriously unreliable, the need for reliability measurement is apparent.

Thus, there are many opportunities at each step of a research plan for a study to go astray, and some of the probation studies reviewed did so to a greater or lesser degree. Each detour from the prescribed path can have serious consequences for appropriate and warranted conclusions and generalizations.

Methods are available for the careful formulation of research designs, for ensuring careful and adequate sample selections, for statistical control of the "nuisance variables" of selection factors biasing comparisons, for measurement of reliability, and for statistical tests of significance appropriate to the level of measurement possible with the data obtainable. The issues involved in improving the quality of information about probation and its results are critical to the general problem of increased rationality in probation program placement decisionmaking.

It is a tenet of faith in corrections that persons on probation are less likely to recidivate than those in prison. There is some evidence that this is true. The comparison may be biased, of course, because judges have deliberately placed the best risks on probation in the first place. There is evidence that this also is true. As a result, comparisons of probation versus prison outcomes typically have been akin to comparisons of apples and oranges. Probationers have different characteristics than prisoners—and these differences are related to success or failure, however defined.

The Gottfredson, Finckenauer, and Rauh review of adult probation studies unfortunately disclosed very little that will add to the little already known about the profiles of the types of offenders who receive probation and the types who are incarcerated. Some evidence is provided by a Missouri Division of Probation and Parole study covering the fiscal years 1968 to 1970 which compared individuals committed to the Missouri Department of Corrections (3197) to those placed on probation (5083).[90] The probationers were mostly young first offenders without significant alcohol or drug problems. The prison commitments were older than the probationers (averaging twenty-six years versus twenty-one), and the prison commitments were more likely to be divorced (15 percent versus 6). There were significant differences in educational level, and there were no differences in ethnic classifications of the two groups. The authors found some differences in the types of offenses committed by probationers and prisoners. Offenders against the person—particularly persons convicted of robbery—constituted a greater proportion of the prison population than the probation population. On the other hand, those convicted of auto theft and drug offenses more frequently were placed on probation.

A study by Babst and Mannering compared male offenders who were imprisoned with similar types of offenders who were placed on probation.[91] The population sampled included all adult males released from a state correctional institution or placed on probation from 1954 through 1959. Three items were found to be most predictive of violation rates for both probationers and parolees— number of prior felony convictions, type of offense, and marital status at the time of commitment. (These three items were found also to have been related to the initial judicial decision as to placement.)

Certain personal characteristics repeatedly have been found to be positively correlated with successful probation outcomes. Kusuda found that 97 percent of the probationers who were employed at least 75 percent of the time, lived with their spouse, and had "nondisreputable" associates successfully completed probation.[92] Hopkinson and Adams, in their study of a specialized alcoholic case load project, found prior arrest history, mandatory attendance at Alcoholics Anonymous, and marital status (married) to be associated with a "favorable response" to probation.[93] Irish found that an offender's adjustment on probation was related to type of crime committed—that is, probationers convicted of crimes against persons, drug offenses, or other offenses were more likely to make a successful adjustment on probation than those convicted of property offenses.[94] Kavanaugh examined the effects of employment on probation adjustment and found that unemployment resulted in lower "relative adjustment" scores and a greater likelihood to engage in criminal activity.[95]

Some studies relevant to the issue of program placement decisions for probationers report positive results, while others report no difference. It should be noted that both types of results, if the quality of the analysis can be accepted, provide information useful in decisionmaking. A drug unit case load evaluation found that nearly five contacts (half in person) per month did seem to have an effect on probation outcomes ("recidivism," welfare, and educational program involvement).[96] Similarly, Clarkson reported that reducing case load size improved the probability of successful probation completion.[97] Sheppard's evaluation of an intensive supervision project reported lower one year rearrest and reconviction rates for intensive samples compared with "regular" case loads.[98]

Other studies report different results. In a preliminary evaluation of the San Francisco project the authors concluded:

> The findings in our preliminary evaluation of intensive, ideal, and minimum supervision caseloads raise some serious questions about the nature and efficiency of the prevailing models of supervision. We have observed that the probationers, parolees, and mandatory releases routinely assigned to these various caseloads, despite substantial differences in the supervision effort, exhibit violation rates which are not significantly different from one another.

Furthermore, they observed that "in the intensive caseloads, despite fourteen times as much attention as provided the minimum supervision cases, the violation rate not only failed to decline significantly, but increased with respect to technical violations."[99]

Even when rigorous experimental designs have been utilized in studies of client and case load characteristics (and that has been unusual), the time perspective has been generally no longer than the project duration. Without more detailed research, including more extensive follow-up study, it is impossible to know what it is about intensive supervision or reduced case loads that is or is not working. It is reasonable to agree with Vetter and Adams that

> The concept of fifty or any other number unit caseload is likely to be meaningless without systematic classification based upon empirically demonstrated criteria and a corresponding organization of caseloads according to variations in treatment, offender, and officer.[100]

SOME INFERENCES FROM THE DATA ON PROBATION

The probation studies we have discussed in this chapter and elsewhere[101] do permit some limited inferences that are useful starting points for rational decisions in this arena. For example, these studies collectively provide some evidence as to which probationers succeed. Probationers who have no previous record of arrests and who are convicted of property crimes have the greatest probability of successfully completing their probation terms. These same offenders, having been released from probation as "improved," have also the greatest probability of postprobation success. On the other hand, variables most often significantly associated with failure are measures of previous criminal history, youthfulness, unemployment, and the classification "not married."

But the inferences possible from the research in probation are not limited to statements about classifications of probationers who are probable "successes." We believe that several questions are addressed by these studies collectively; some questions remain unanswered, and yet other questions are raised.

If we ask who is placed on probation, some observed differences with selected imprisoned offenders may be cited, but a detailed profile of such differences, generalizable to probationers and prisoners in general, cannot be given. The necessary research has not been done.

If we ask whether probation is more effective as a rehabilitative treatment than is imprisonment, we must respond again that the necessary research has not been done.[102]

If we ask whether the personal characteristics of offenders are more important than the form of treatment in determining future recidivism, we must answer that evidence tends to support this conjecture, but that critical tests of the hypothesis have not been performed.

If we ask whether the size of the case load makes any difference to results in terms of recidivism, we must answer that the evidence is mixed. From limited evidence, it appears that intensive supervision may result in more technical violations known and acted upon and also to fewer new offense convictions.

If we ask who succeeds and who fails on probation supervision, we may reply that a useful technology for development and validation of prediction instruments is available, that there is some information on the question (for some jurisdictions), that attempts to develop such instruments for probationers have been rare, and that these attempts have been put to relatively little use.

If we ask "what works," out of interest in discovering what forms of treatment and supervision provide more effective results when applied to probationers generally or to any particular classification of offenders, we must reply that there is limited evidence and that it is mixed.

If these issues are indeed critical to adult probation decisions, pointing as they do to inadequacies of the information on which placement decisions currently are based, then the most obvious conclusion to be reached is that too few resources have thus far been applied to providing adequate evidence on the questions raised. Trite as it may be to plead that further research is needed, this is inescapable.

This is not to say that nothing has been learned, but rather that there have been too few studies of these probationer issues, many of which—because of the nature of the studies or because of faulty research designs or implementations—cannot give the definitive, general answers that are sought. And although space prohibits an analogous review of relevant parole studies here, we are familiar enough with that literature to draw a similar conclusion. As a result, these studies cannot give planners, judges, or parole or probation managers the guidance that could provide a systematic program for increased rationality in probation decisionmaking. In the final chapter we outline in some detail a general model that we believe is applicable for probation and parole decisionmaking. However, some brief notes in that direction can be given here in the context of probation decisions.

In any probation or parole agency, a management information system is needed. Smaller agencies might have to collaborate or join larger agencies in order to develop and use this system. The management information system must be designed to provide feedback on such critical issues as are discussed in this book. This requires the reliable collection of standardized and comprehensive information on the characteristics of probationers or parolees at the time of sentence. Also needed is a system of follow-up, with carefully defined and agreed upon measures of outcomes. Prediction measures, based upon relevant information about offenders, must be developed and tested to assure their validity. Such measures can provide, for any classification of probationers or parolees, the expected outcomes (such as recidivism rates) through the follow-up system. Differences between the expected and observed outcomes can then be assessed, to provide some information on the programs that appear to be useful and those that do not—for what kinds of offenders, with respect to various definitions of "success" and "failure." Those treatment programs identified as apparently effective can then be investigated by the use of more rigorous research designs. Such a system can provide a continuous assessment of probation or parole programs, making use of presently available technology and guiding the development of programs much more rationally than the hit or miss basis that has thus far characterized program development in this field.

If probation and parole are on trial, the evidence is not yet in. Much of the presentation of both the "prosecution" and the "defense" must be regarded as scientifically inadmissible. Methods are available to provide the needed evidence in a systematic management information program. Those who judge probation and parole can then be better informed, and more rational decisions in the administration of community corrections may be expected.

NOTES

1. V. O'Leary, *Correctional Policy Inventory* (Hackensack, New Jersey: National Council on Crime and Delinquency, n.d.). The correctional policy models discussed are due to O'Leary, but he cannot be held responsible for the historical interpretations we have superimposed on his conception. Also, it should be noted that O'Leary recognizes, while describing the four correctional policies as independent of each other, that "many systems have all four policies operating in a greater or lesser degree, at the same time." He adds,

> probably it is just as well that correctional practitioners are able to employ each of the policies at different times and under different circumstances. Some restraint concern is likely necessary for the operation of a correctional system. Some offenders may respond best for a time to a reformist stance and others may require a rehabilitative response. Ultimately, however, all offenders must face the task of living in the community and reintegration is the policy which most directly faces this issue.

2. If, according to the desert perspective outlined in Chapter 6, "deserved punishment" is to be measured by the extent of deprivation of liberty, the question must be raised as to how the degrees of state control suggested in Figure 7-1 are to be scaled. For example, placement in maximum custody may be agreed to be a more severe deprivation than placement in minimum—but how much more is a question not yet answered.

3. Portions of this section are adapted from D.M. Gottfredson, J.O. Finckenauer, and C. Rauh, *Probation on Trial* (Newark, New Jersey: School of Criminal Justice, Rutgers University, 1977).

4. National Advisory Commission on Criminal Justice Standards and Goals, *Corrections* (Washington, D.C.: Government Printing Office, 1973), p. 311.

5. J.Q. Wilson, *Thinking About Crime* (New York: Basic Books, 1975), p. 202.

6. E. van den Haag, *Punishing Criminals: Concerning A Very Old and Painful Question* (New York: Basic Books, 1975), p. 177.

7. N. Morris, *The Future of Imprisonment* (Chicago: University of Chicago Press, 1974), p. 48.

8. National Advisory Commission, *supra* note 4 at 587.

9. A. von Hirsch and K.S. Hanrahan, *Abolish Parole?* (Washington, D.C.: Government Printing Office, September 1978), p. iii. For full discussion, see A. von Hirsch and K.S. Hanrahan, *The Question of Parole* (Cambridge, Massachusetts: Ballinger, 1979).

10. National Advisory Commission, *supra* note 4 at 312.

11. Not all criticism of these systems is based on negative or questionable evidence of effectiveness in reducing crime. See, for example, von Hirsch and Hanrahan's arguments, concerning parole supervision, that lower standards of proof and differing standards of disposition (from those affecting other offenders) lead to undesirable consequences to fairness or the imposition of justice. Von Hirsch and Hanrahan, *Abolish Parole?*, *supra* note 9 at 17-19.

12. See Chapter 1 for a general discussion of prediction in relation to classification.

13. A.A. Bruce, E.W. Burgess, and A.J. Harno, *The Working of the Indeterminate Sentence Law and the Parole System in Illinois* (Springfield, Illinois: Illinois Parole Board, 1928), ch. 28-30; A.A. Bruce, A.J. Harno, E.W. Burgess, and J. Landesco, *Parole and the Indeterminate Sentence* (Springfield: Illinois Parole Board, 1928), pp. 205-49.

14. E.D. Monachesi, *Prediction Factors in Probation* (Minneapolis: The Sociological Press, 1932).

15. For reviews, see the following sources: H. Mannheim and L.T. Wilkins, *Prediction Methods in Relation to Borstal Training* (London: Her Majesty's Stationery Office, 1955) (Chapter I provides a historical survey of American and European prediction studies in criminology. The book also provides a review of pertinent methodological issues up to the time of its publication and, so far as we know, the first use in criminological research of prediction as a control tool in quasi-experimental designs [see, e.g., Chapter IX, "A Note on the Future of Criminological Research," pp. 211-24, especially p. 211]); F.H. Simon, *Prediction Methods in Criminology* (London: Her Majesty's Stationery Office, 1971) (Chapter 3 is titled by the author "A Review of Some Selected Prediction Studies" but she seems conservative; the review provides a quite thorough analysis of many important studies.); D.M. Gottfredson, "Assessment and Prediction Methods in Crime and Delinquency," in President's Commission on Law Enforcement and Administration of Justice, *Task Force Report: Juvenile Delinquency and Youth Crime* (Washington, D.C.: U.S. Government Printing Office, 1967), pp. 171-87; J.S. Albanese, "Predicting Probation Outcomes: An Assessment of Critical Issues," in D.M. Gottfredson, J.O. Finckenauer, and C. Rauh, *supra* note 3 at ch. IV, pp. 129-78; D.M. Gottfredson, L.T. Wilkins, and P.B. Hoffman, *Guidelines for Parole and Sentencing: A Policy Control Method* (Lexington, Massachusetts: Lexington Books, 1978), ch. 3, pp. 41-67.

16. This discussion has been informed by that of Albanese, *supra* note 15.

17. Mannheim and Wilkins, *supra* note 15 at 140-41.

18. P.E. Meehl, *Clinical Versus Statistical Prediction* (Minneapolis: University of Minnesota Press, 1954).

19. H.G. Gough, "Clinical Versus Statistical Prediction in Psychology," in L. Postman, ed., *Psychology in the Making* (New York: Alfred A. Knopf, 1962), ch. 9, pp. 526-84.

20. D.M. Gottfredson, "Comparing and Combining Subjective and Objective Parole Predictions," *Research Newsletter* 3 (Vacaville: California Medical Facility, California Department of Corrections, September-December 1961).

21. See D.M. Gottfredson, J.A. Bonds, and J.D. Grant, "La Combinazione Della Previsione Clinica e di Quella Statistica Nelle Decisione Penitenziare," *Quaderni di Criminologia Clinica* (Roma: Tipografia della Mantellate, Gennaio-Marzo 1962).

22. "The New Techniques of Decision Making," *Acme Reporter* (New York: Association of Consulting Management Engineers, Inc., January 1955).

23. See, e.g., Simon, *supra* note 15 at 6-7; Gottfredson, *supra* note 15 at 174 and 178.

24. See e.g., Simon, *supra* note 15 at 6-7; D. Geason and F. Hangren, "Predicting the Adjustment of Federal Probationers," *National Probation and Parole Association Journal* 4:265 (1958); R.C. Ford and S.R. Johnson, "Probation Prediction Models and Recidivism" (Geneva, Illinois: Kane Country Diagnostic Center, 1976), p. 12. Mimeograph.

25. See P.E. Meehl and A. Rosen, "Antecedent Probability and the Efficiencies of Psychometric Signs, Patterns, or Cutting Scores," *Psychological Bulletin* 52:215 (1955); E.E. Cureton, "Recipe for a Cookbook," *Psychological Bulletin* 54:494 (1957). For illustrations in the field of delinquency, see: Gough, *supra* note 19; C. Hanley, "The Gauging of Criminal Predispositions" in H. Toch, *Legal and Criminal Psychology* (New York: Holt, Rinehart and Winston, 1961), pp. 213-42; A.A. Walters, "A Note on Statistical Methods of Predicting Delinquency," *British Journal of Deliinquency* 6:297 (1956); Gottfredson, *supra* note 15 at 176.

26. A summary of most commonly used methods is given in Gottfredson, *supra* note 15 at 176-78. See also Simon, *supra* note 15, especially pp. 80-167. A recent study is D. van Alstyne and M. Gottfredson, "A Multidimensional Contingency Table Analysis of Parole Outcome," *Journal of Research in Crime and Delinquency* 15:172 (1978).

27. See especially Mannheim and Wilkins, *supra* note 15; L.T. Wilkins, "What is Prediction and Is It Necessary in Evaluating Treatment?" in Citizens' Committee for Children of New York, *Research and Potential Application of Research in Probation, Parole, and Delinquency Prediction* (New York: Research Center, New York School of Social Work, Columbia University, July 1961); D.M. Gottfredson, "The Role of Base Expectancies in the Study of Treatments" (paper presented as part of the *Symposium on Methods for the Study of Effectiveness of Treatment*, Western Psychological Association meeting, April 1959, San Diego, California); D.M. Gottfredson, "The Practical Application of Research," *Canadian Journal of Corrections* 5:212 (1963); R. Hood, "Research on the Effectiveness of Punishments and Treatments," in *Collected Studies in Criminological Research* I (Strasbourg: Council of Europe, 1967); L.T. Wilkins, *Evaluation of Penal Measures* (New York: Random House, 1969); R.F. Sparks, "Types of Treatment for Types of Offenders," in *Collected Studies in Criminological Research* III (Strasbourg: Council of Europe, 1968).

28. This term was used by Burgess, *supra* note 13.

29. This term was preferred by L.E. Ohlin, *Selection for Parole: A Manual of Parole Prediction* (New York: Russell Sage Foundation, 1951).

30. Mannheim and Wilkins, for example, used this term, or "experience tables"; see Mannheim and Wilkins, *supra* note 15.

31. For example, D.M. Gottfredson, "The Role of Base Expectancies in the Study of Treatments," *supra* note 27.

32. See, for example, D.M. Gottfredson, "One Approach to Social Agency Self-Study," *Canadian Journal of Corrections* 5:271 (1965).

33. F. Simon, *supra* note 15 at 8.

34. In a related discussion, Mannheim and Wilkins, *supra* note 15 wrote: "The processes of efficient research may be seen as analogous in many ways with fishing. First a net is made and lowered to see what comes up; then the contents are examined and much is found to be useless; the mesh is changed and the depth of the drop is modified so that the amount of fish required is maximized and the amount of other material and other fish is minimized" (at 215). They thus proposed research and administrative record keeping "as a continuing 'winnowing' and consolidating process" (at 216). This concept is reflected in our proposals toward more rational decisionmaking in Chapter 10.

35. W. Dunbar, "Provision of Base Expectancy Information to the Adult Authority," *California Department of Corrections Administrative Bulletin* 61/115 (Sacramento: Department of Correction, December 1961). The parole prediction measure used was devised for the specific purpose discussed and is described in D.M. Gottfredson, *A Shorthand Formula for Base Expectancies*, Research Report No. 5 (Sacramento: California Department of Correction, December 1961).

36. J. Havel, *Special Intensive Parole Unit, Phase IV: A High Base Expectancy Study* (Sacramento: California Department of Correction, June 1963).

37. M. Burdman, "Increased Correctional Effectiveness Progress Statement," memorandum from the California Department of Correction to the California Senate Finance Subcommittee and the California Assembly Ways and Means Subcommittee, January 1, 1963. Unpublished.

38. Parole and Community Services Division, *The Work Unit Parole Program: 1969* (Sacramento: California Department of Correction, December 5, 1969).

39. D. Frease, "Probation Prediction for Adult Offenders in Washington" (Olympia, Washington: Department of Institutions, 1965), p. 36. Mimeograph.

40. "Probation Prediction Models: Tools for Decision-Makers," in *State and County Probation: Systems in Crisis*, Report to the Congress by the Comptroller General of the United States (Washington, D.C.: Government Printing Office, 1976), p. 52.

41. W.E. Hemple, W.H. Webb, Jr., and S.W. Reynolds, "Researching Prediction Scales for Probation," *Federal Probation* 40:34 (1976).

42. R.C. Nicholson, "Use of Prediction in Caseload Management," *Federal Probation* 32:54 (1968).

43. See, for example, M.G. Neithercutt and D.M. Gottfredson, *Caseload Size Variation and Difference in Probation/Parole Performance* (Pittsburgh: National Center for Juvenile Justice, 1973); S. Adams, "Some Findings From Correctional Caseload Research," *Federal Probation* 31:48 (1967); H.J. Vetter and R. Adams, "Effectiveness of Probation Caseload Sizes: A Review of the Empirical Literature," *Criminology* 8:33 (1971); B.A. Fiore, "Clients and Caseloads: An Assessment of Critical Issues," in Gottfredson, Finckenauer, and Rauh, *supra* note 3 at ch. 3, pp. 75-122.

44. This is not to say that no positive results have been reported, but that differences generalizable to other jurisdictions or otherwise having sufficient generalizability for formulating of general public policy are not available. Perhaps this is, however, too much to expect from single project evaluations, and the questions have not been asked in the right way. The development of information systems for individual corrections agencies, as outlined later in this chapter, can guide policy decisions in that particular agency without the requirement of such jurisdictionwide generalizability.

45. C.L. Chute, "Probation and Suspended Sentence," *Journal of the American Institute of Criminal Law and Criminology* 12:558 (1922).

46. H. Sutherland, *Principles of Criminology* (Philadelphia: J.B. Lippincott Co., 1934).

47. Cited in Neithercutt and Gottfredson, *supra* note 43 at 23.

48. H.P. Reed, "Caseloads," *National Probation and Parole Association Journal*, April 1957, p. 143; National Council on Crime and Delinquency, *Standards and Guides for Adult Probation* (New York, 1962), p. 57.

49. President's Commission on Law Enforcement and Administration of Justice, *Task Force Report: Corrections* (Washington, D.C.: Government Printing Office, 1967), p. 70; President's Commission on Law Enforcement and Administration of Justice, *The Challenge of Crime in a Free Society* (Washington, D.C.: Government Printing Office, 1967), p. 167.

50. Monachesi, for example, in the first probation prediction study, commented: "Human beings are usually characterized as highly variable and endowed with a mysterious 'free will.' Such a characterization assumes the impossibility of predicting human behavior under any given circumstances." He cited prior parole prediction studies, however, as contrary evidence and concluded prediction is not only possible but feasible. Monachesi, *supra* note 14 at 97. This, of course, did not end the debate; see, e.g., E. Reeves, "A Fresh Look at Prediction and Supervision," *Crime and Delinquency* 7:37 (1961).

51. L.T. Wilkins, "The Unique Individual," in M.E. Wolfgang et al., eds., *The Sociology of Crime and Delinquency* (New York: John Wiley and Sons, 1970), p. 144.

52. C. Kluckhohn and H.A. Murray, *Personality in Nature, Society, and Culture*, 2nd ed. (New York: Knopf, 1956), pp. 53–56.

53. See, for example, C.E. Sullivan, J.D. Grant, and M.Q. Grant, "The Development of Interpersonal Maturity: Applications to Delinquency," *Psychiatry* 20:373 (1957), for the initial statement of a well-known and influential typology that is further elaborated in a series of research reports on differential treatment—e.g., M.Q. Grant, "Interaction Between Kinds of Treatment and Kinds of Delinquents," in Board of Corrections Monograph Number 2 (Sacramento: State of California Printing Division, Documents Section, July 1961), pp. 5–13; M.Q. Warren, "Classification of Offenders as an Aid to Efficient Management and Effective Treatment," *Journal of Criminal Law, Criminology, and Police Science* 62:239 (1971). Other important perspectives from psychological theory include H.G. Gough and D.R. Peterson, "The Identification and Measurement of Predispositional Factors in Crime and Delinquency," *Journal of Consulting Psychology* 16:212 (1952); and D.R. Peterson, H.C. Quay,

and G.R. Cameron, "Personality and Background Factors in Juvenile Delinquency as Inferred from Questionnaire Responses," *Journal of Consulting Psychology* 23:399 (1959). For another perspective, see P.S. Venezia, "Delinquency as a Function of Intrafamily Relationships," *Journal of Research in Crime and Delinquency* 5:148 (1968). For a general overview of numerous additional perspectives from psychological theory, see M. Argyle, "A New Approach to the Classification of Delinquents with Implications for Treatment," in Board of Corrections Monograph Number 2 (Sacramento: State of California Printing Division, Documents Section, July 1961).

54. Examples include C.A. Schrag, "Social Types in a Prison Community," (M.A. thesis, University of Washington, 1944); G.M. Sykes, *The Society of Captives* (Princeton, New Jersey: Princeton University Press, 1958); W.B. Miller, "Some Characteristics of Present Day Delinquency of Relevance to Educators" (paper presented at the meetings of the American Association of School Administrators, 1959).

55. See, for example, A. Aichhorn, *Wayward Youth* (New York: Viking Press, 1938); H.A. Block and F.T. Flynn, *Delinquency* (New York: Random House, 1956); B.M. Cormier et al., "Presentation of a Basic Classification for Criminological Work and Research in Criminality," *Canadian Journal of Corrections* 1:34 (1959).

56. R. Hood and R.F. Sparks, *Key Issues in Criminology* (New York: McGraw-Hill, 1970), p. 193.

57. *Id.* at ch. 7: "Interaction Between Type of Treatment and Type of Offender," see esp. pp. 210-14.

58. R.N. Siu, "T-Thoughts," National Institute of Law Enforcement and Criminal Justice Pamphlet No. 4 (Washington, D.C.: Law Enforcement Assistance Administration, November, 1968), p. 3. Mimeograph.

59. J.H. Powell, "Critical Assessment of Revocation/Recidivism Statistics," in Gottfredson, Finckenauer, and Rauh, *supra* note 3 at ch. 5, pp. 183-243.

60. D.E. Frease, "Factors Related to Probation Outcome" (Tacoma: Washington State Board of Prison Terms and Paroles, April 1964).

61. J.R. Landis, J.D. Mercer, and C.E. Wolff, "Success and Failure of Adult Probationers in California," *Journal of Research in Crime and Delinquency* 6:34 (1969); P.H. Kusuda, "1974 Probation and Parole Terminations" (Madison: State of Wisconsin Division of Corrections, July 1976).

62. See, e.g., "How Effective is Probation?" in *State and County Probation: Systems in Crisis*, supra *note 40.*

63. G.F. Davis, "A Study of Adult Probation Violation Rates by Means of the Cohort Approach," *Journal of Criminal Law, Criminology and Police Science* 55:70 (1964).

64. M.G. Rector, "Factors in Measuring Recidivism as Presented in Annual Reports," *National Probation and Parole Association Journal* 4:218 (1958), as cited in Powell, *supra* note 59 at 196.

65. National Advisory Commission, *supra* note 4 at 528.

66. D. Glaser, *Routinizing Evaluation: Getting Feedback on Effectiveness of Crime and Delinquency Programs* (Washington, D.C.: National Institute of Mental Health, 1973), pp. 4-47.

67. J. Powell, *supra* note 59. In the ten studies reviewed, Powell found that, generally, factors associated with "failure" were previous criminal history, youthfulness, status other than married, unemployment, low income, low education, alcohol or drug abuse, and property offense.

68. L.T. Wilkins, "Perspectives on Court Decision-Making," in D.M. Gottfredson, ed., *Decision-making in the Criminal Justice System: Reviews and Essays* (Washington, D.C.: Government Printing Office, 1975), ch. V. Wilkins states:

> Judges, and indeed all persons in the criminal justice area as well as in many other areas, talk of making decisions about persons. We know, of course, what this phrase means, and it certainly does not mean what it says. Decisions cannot be made about individuals, but only about information about individuals. The individual may be put into prison, sent home, or other, as a result of a decision made with respect to him, but the basis for the decision can only be information which the court has about him, in some form or another. Obvious as this may seem, the consequences of this simple elaboration of the generally used language are seldom recognized. If we recognize that decisions are made about the information we have about a person, then we must accept that the information is limited in quantity and may have some deficiencies in quality. (At 68).

69. "Corrections in the United States," *Crime and Delinquency* 13:126 (1967). In some jurisdictions, e.g., New York State, certain presentence reports are required by law. See T. McCrea, and D. Gottfredson, *A Guide to Improved Handling of Misdemeanant Offenders* (Washington, D.C.: Government Printing Office, 1974).

70. R.M. Carter, *Presentence Report Handbook* (Washington, D.C.: Government Printing Office, 1978); for a discussion of historical development of the presentence report, see pages 3-9.

71. W. Healy, "The Individual Study of the Young Criminal," *Journal of the American Institute of Criminal Law and Criminology* 1:50 (1910), as quoted in Carter, *id.* at 3.

72. President's Commission, *Task Force Report: Corrections, supra* note 49 at 19, as quoted by Carter, *supra* note 70 at 5.

73. *Id.*, as quoted by Carter, *supra* note 70 at 5-6.

74. *Id.* at 11.

75. *Id.*

76. *Id.*

77. See generally, Wilkins, *supra* note 68 at 76-81.

78. L.T. Wilkins and A. Chandler, "Confidence and Competence in Decision-making," *British Journal of Delinquency* 5:22 (1965).

79. This was about two-thirds of the time in Carter's survey; see Table 7-1.

80. R.M. Carter and L.T. Wilkins, "Some Factors in Sentencing Policy," *Journal of Criminal Law, Criminology, and Police Science* 58:503 (1967).

81. Wilkins and Chandler, *supra* note 78.

82. R.M. Carter, "The Pre-Sentence Report and the Decision-Making Process," *Journal of Research in Crime and Delinquency* 4:203 (1967).

83. Gottfredson, Wilkins, and Hoffman, *supra* note 15 at 167–82. The study used a method adapted from Wilkins' "Information Board," using a variable access slide projector for information retrieval (rather than cards as in the original method). The authors reported, from results of a group exercise, that

Persons paroling, compared with persons not paroling, sought different information. Different items of information were generally considered important for different cases. The same decision often was made on entirely different bases; that is, different information was used by different people to arrive at the same conclusion. There was no unanimity among decision-makers as to the relative importance of information available to the decision. Finally, information may *reduce* confidence in the decision as well as increase it. (At 182).

84. Carter and Wilkins, *supra* note 80.

85. This section is adapted from Gottfredson, Finckenauer, and Rauh, *supra* note 3.

86. D. Lipton, R. Martinson, and J. Wilks, *The Effectiveness of Correctional Treatment: A Survey of Treatment Evaluation Studies* (New York: Praeger Publishers, 1975).

87. Gottfredson, Finckenauer, and Rauh, *supra* note 3.

88. Studies were identified from *Criminology Index;* the National Council on Crime and Delinquency Library and abstract files; abstracts from the National Criminal Justice Reference Service; the Library of the Center for Knowledge in Criminal Justice Planning; the libraries of Rutgers and Ohio State universities; and selected bibliographies and literature reviews. All studies located are listed in the bibliography of Gottfredson, Finckenauer, and Rauh, *supra* note 3.

89. R.C. Ford and S.R. Johnson, "Probation Prediction Models and Recidivism" (Geneva, Illinois: Kane County Diagnostic Center, 1976). Mimeograph.

90. "Probation in Missouri, July 1, 1968 to June 30, 1970: Characteristics, Performance, and Criminal Reinvolvement" (Jefferson City, Missouri: Division of Probation and Parole, 1976). Mimeograph.

91. D.V. Babst and J.W. Mannering, "Probation Versus Imprisonment for Similar Types of Offenders: A Comparison by Subsequent Violators," *Journal of Research in Crime and Delinquency* 2:60 (1965).

92. P.H. Kusuda, "Relationship of Adult Probation and Parole Experiences to Successful Termination of Supervision" (Madison, Wisconsin: State Department of Public Welfare, Bureau of Research, 1966), p. 2. Mimeograph.

93. C.C. Hopkinson and S. Adams, "The Specialized Alcoholic Caseload Project: A Study of the Effectiveness of Probation with Alcoholic Offenders" (Los Angeles: Los Angeles County Probation Department, 1964), p. iii. Mimeograph.

94. J.F. Irish, "Assessment of Adult Division Supervision Program Effectiveness" (Mineola, New York: Adult Probation Department, 1976), p. 11. Mimeograph.

95. K.J. Kavanaugh, "A Twelve-Month Probation Outcome Study: Examining the Effects of Employment on Probation Adjustment" (Columbus: The Ohio State University, 1975), p. 20. Mimeograph. See also Powell, *supra* note 59.

96. T.A. Kaput and M.E. Santese, "Evaluation of General Caseload Drug Unit" (Hartford, Connecticut: Department of Adult Probation, 1972), p. 7. Mimeograph.

97. J.S. Clarkson, "Probation Improvement Program" (Southfield, Michigan: 46th District Court, 1974), p. 7. Mimeograph.

98. D.J. Sheppard, "Denver High-Impact Anti-Crime Program: Intensive Probation and Parole" (Denver: State Judicial Department, 1975), p. 11. Mimeograph.

99. J.D. Lohman, A. Wahl, and R.M. Carter, "The Intensive Supervision Caseload: A Preliminary Evaluation" (Berkeley: University of California School of Criminology, 1966), p. 37. Mimeograph.

100. H.J. Vetter and R. Adams, "Effectiveness of Caseload Sizes: Review of the Empirical Literature," *Criminology* 8:335 (1971).

101. Gottfredson, Finckenauer, and Rauh, *supra* note 3.

102. A review of the many studies on this topic is beyond the scope of this book, but a substantial number of such studies in the area of probation are reviewed in Gottfredson, Finckenauer, and Rauh, *supra* note 3. For a discussion of various techniques for criticizing treatment evaluation research, not all of which may invariably be useful to incremental gains in knowledge about "what works," see M.R. Gottfredson, "Treatment Destruction Techniques," *Journal of Research in Crime and Delinquency* 16:39 (1979).

✳ *Chapter 8*

Correctional Decisions in Institutions

Decisions made in correctional institutions may be classed as program decisions (on program planning or resource allocation) or as individual decisions (affecting the placement of persons in differing institutions, custody levels, degrees of supervision, or treatment programs). As with correctional decisions in the community, these decisions are subject to a complexity of goals, alternatives, and information. Goals are diverse, and again, they may be apparently conflicting—a criminal justice problem not unique to correctional management. Alternatives, too, are found to have a great variety of forms; moreover, they are subject to wide variation in both resources and imagination. Information demonstrably relevant to correctional objectives, as in other areas of criminal justice decisionmaking, often is lacking, or evidence is conflicting, or questions of the reliability of potentially useful information must be weighed.

Yet as with the police officer, the prosecutor, the judge, or the probation administrator, decisions must be made daily. The complaint that "the data are not yet all in" hardly will be found satisfying to the jail or prison manager who is apt to be beset with decision problems demanding a prompt resolution.

In this chapter, the goals involved and some examples of alternatives and of information resources and needs will be examined. This is a large topic indeed: there is a wealth of relevant literature related to it, and only selected examples may be given. Our general aim is to develop a general strategy for improving information for correctional decisions.

The broad goals of correctional institutions have already been discussed in Chapter 7—reform, rehabilitation, reintegration, or restraint. With somewhat more specificity (but still at a very general level), we may identify goals at least of security, of treatment, of incapacitation, and of organizational maintenance.

These broad goals are closely related to sentencing aims and to those of community corrections, but here the context of decisionmaking differs substantially. The decisions are constrained in complex ways, a very large number of decisions per person is at issue, and generally, much more data about the individual offender typically are available to the decisionmakers. Burnham has described this context of special features of correctional decisionmaking as follows:

First . . . there is the very strong effect of system constraints and requirements. All prisons are, in several senses, run by their inmates, and a regular supply of these to essential jobs, such as kitchen and the laundry, must be maintained. Thus there are two types of decision usually collapsed into one. (1) "What is the appropriate disposition for that particular inmate?" (in terms of which institution, which work assignment, which training program, etc., is the most suitable for him), and (2) "Which inmates are to be used to provide the manpower for the following essential tasks?" The problem emerges in the collapsed form as (3) "Is this inmate suitable for what he requests, and does it suit system requirements for him to be so allocated?" or more simply (4) "Can we allow him to do what he wants?" In version (4), the factors involved in "allowing" refer to both the personal qualities of the inmate (e.g., offense, violence record, intelligence, aptitude test scores) and vacancies, either open to be filled or which must be filled. . . .

Second, the sheer number of decisions is different. For each passage through the system, each inmate usually is arrested once, tried once, sentenced once, paroled once, and so on. In the correctional stage, he is subject to frequent decisions which affect where he lives, what he does, and other issues which matter deeply to him. Thus in one respect correctional decisionmaking impinges more on an inmate's life. But in a more important way, it matters less—for most of these decisions are reversed with relative ease; and thus, as well as having less far-reaching implications for the subsequent system career path of the individual, they are not so final. . . .

The third main difference is in the amount and type of information available to the decisionmaker. The arresting police officer, the district attorney or whoever brings the charge, the court which tries, and the judge or jury who sentence will often have, or probably feel they have, a shortage of data upon which to base their decision. But what they do have is significant. Once an individual is in the correctional system, however, data about him are accumulated very rapidly, so that a great deal is known; but much of it is seemingly trivial and uninformative with regard to the particular decisions required.[1]

The security aim, in prisons as in jails, involves both institutional security (and this is related closely to the objective of institutional maintenance) and the personal security of individuals. In neither prisons nor jails has their been much research aimed at the classification of offenders for either purpose. This area has been a neglected one in which classification and prediction studies could provide needed assistance in decisionmaking.[2]

The treatment aim has been emphasized in a great deal of research, with conflicting results and the familiar questions of uncertainty about information concerning the information. There is an extraordinary diversity of "treatments" offered in some though not all prisons—for example, varieties of academic education, vocational education, individual psychotherapy, group psychotherapy, individual or group counseling, physical therapy, behavior modification programs, work assignments, or "on the job" training, to name only some of the most common.

In recent years it has become popular to express a complete disenchantment with the rehabilitative ideal that undergirded correctional reform in the earlier part of this century (based though it was on philosophical underpinnings of several thousand years). This abandonment of hope was based in large part on a series of widely cited reviews of correctional treatment evaluations.[3] These documented generally negative evidence on the effects of treatment and a rarity of promising leads that, when found, usually were based on small samples and on flawed research methods and were unreplicated.

Nevertheless, the evidence does not require or even support a policy of abandoning the goals of treatment. A panel from the National Research Council of the National Academy of Sciences in the most recent review of the evaluation research literature concluded: "there is not now in the scientific literature any basis for any policy or recommendations regarding rehabilitation of criminal offenders. The data available do not present any consistent evidence of efficacy that would lead to such recommendations. . . ."[4]

This conclusion does not state that nothing works, but neither does it state that anything does work. The emphasis is upon the lack of consistent evidence that could provide policy guidance. The National Research Council Panel also concluded, noting flaws in both the treatment interventions and the evaluation research methods, that "the quality of the work that has been done and the narrow range of options explored militate against any policy reflecting a final pessimism. . . . The magnitude of the task of reforming criminal offenders has been consistently underestimated."[5]

One of the panel members noted separately:

> In short, because there is so little evidence that credible treatments have been implemented with fidelity, and because much of the evaluation research done to date has been inefficient or defective in other ways, we have no compelling experimental evidence for the contention that powerful, theoretically defensible, and faithfully executed interventions hold no promise.[6]

Indeed, with respect to the effectiveness of treatment, the panel concluded: "The strongest recommendation that the Panel can make at this time is that the research on offender rehabilitation should be pursued more vigorously, more systematically, more imaginatively, and more rigorously."[7]

It is not our aim to undertake a thorough review of the treatment effectiveness literature. Several reviews are widely available. Instead, we devote our space in this chapter to some ideas about how decisionmaking within institutions can be made more rational. We start with a discussion of a specific example of the method we propose and then describe in some detail how data available to correctional decisionmakers can be structured to provide an evolutionary policy control model. Both of these discussions carry us deeply into the research data and, hence, also reveal some important patterns of much interest to correctional decisionmaking. Our example concerns estimating the relation between time served in prison and parole success.

TIME SERVED IN PRISON AND
PAROLE OUTCOMES

In a sense, commitment to prison itself is a "treatment," and arguments abound simply around the issue of whether or not the length of sentence (that is, time served in prison) is related to outcomes after the "treatment." The time actually served in prison as a result of conviction is an end result of a complex of decisions—by legislators, judges, correctional administrators, and others, as well as by the paroling authority (the latter are discussed in Chapter 9). Setting this complexity aside, it may be noted that debate is common about the relative merits of "long" or "short" terms of confinement not only in relation to desert but in regard to effectiveness in recidivism reduction. That is, unsupported claims often are heard that longer or shorter terms will reduce the likelihood of recidivism. Arguments for shorter terms, for example, often invoke the notion that prisons are schools of crime in which "prisonization" and increased commitment to criminal behavior may be enhanced by long terms.[8] On the other hand, it may be argued that a harsher punishment may enhance specific deterrence; or it may be suggested that since age is inversely related to recidivism, keeping the offender longer will decrease the chances of new offenses or recommitments.

A study bearing on these issues used data collected from paroling authorities across the United States in the Uniform Parole Reports Program.[9] The purposes of this study were to describe, for a large number of selected offenders, the lengths of time served in prison and to assess the relation of time served to parole outcomes. (All offenders included for study in this program were parolees.) The study is unusual in that a very large number of parolees was studied (more than 100,000) from a substantial number of jurisdictions (data from all adult parole boards in the United States are included in the data set used, though not with representative sampling) and with an attempt to control statistically for offense, age, and prior record variation (items found repeatedly to be related to parole violation).

Prior research had indicated that there was little or no effect of time served on recidivism rates. For example, an analysis of Washington State experience with a ten month reduction of median times served in prison reported little change in recidivism rates.[10] A California study of matched groups of parolees who committed misdemeanors on parole, some of whom were jailed and some who were returned to prison, reported no difference in recidivism rates of the two groups although the average time served by those jailed was seven months compared with twenty months by those reimprisoned.[11] A committee of the California Assembly reviewed data on time served and recidivism in California and concluded in 1968 that "no evidence can be found to support extended incarceration as a determinate element in the deterrence of crime. . . . Recidivism rates for offenders who had served comparatively long terms (compared to others of the same offense class) were higher than those who served comparatively short terms, if narcotics history and prior record are ignored."[12] Mueller studied 800 men paroled three months earlier than the usual parole date and found little difference.[13] Some studies have reported reduced recidivism observations along with reduced confinement periods, but it is difficult to sort out possible effects of marked changes in treatment;

examples are given by the well-known Highfields and Community Treatment projects.[14] In general, it has not been demonstrated that specific deterrence is enhanced by increasing the duration of imprisonment, nor has it been shown that recidivism increases with increased time served.

In the study of Uniform Parole Reports data, 104,182 male felons paroled for the first time from prison sentences were included. All were paroled between 1965 and 1970. (It should be noted that persons released by means other than parole, including discharge or mandatory conditional release, were not included. In 1970, perhaps 70 percent of all those released from prison were paroled.)[15] The criterion of "favorable outcome" used in this study was that within a one year follow-up period, the parolee was reported as having had "no difficulty or a sentence of less than 60 days" and had not absconded and that no adverse action had been taken by the paroling authority. All others, including those who absconded or were returned to prison with or without a new conviction, were classified as having "unfavorable" outcomes. Only offenders whose commitment offense could be classified into fourteen major offense categories were included (see Table 8-1).

Each offender was classified further in terms of the time-served pentile for his offense category into which he fell. That is, the distributions of time served for each offense were divided into five approximately equal parts—the 20 percent of cases in each offense category that served the shortest time before parole were classed in the first pentile, and so on.

Each offender was classified also according to age (at last admission to prison) and prior record. The indicant of prior record used was "one or more known prior sentences other than prison" (this attribute was found to be more closely related to the outcome criterion than the item "prior prison record"). The relations of offense classification and of prior record to the parole violation criterion used are shown, for the parolees of this study, in Table 8-1.

These associations are similar to those found in many prior studies.[16] Typically, as in this sample, the property offenses such as theft, burglary, check fraud, and vehicle theft have been found to be associated with higher violation rates; and person offenses such as homicide, assault, and sex offenses have been found to be associated with lower rates. Similarly, indicants of prior criminal record have been found consistently to be associated with parole violation criteria. In this sample, persons without any prior record other than prison had higher "favorable" rates in each offense

Table 8-1. Percent Favorable Parole Performance for Various Offense Groups, by Prior Record.

	Percent Favorable			Number of Cases		
Offense	*Priors*	*No priors*	*Combined*	*Priors*	*No priors*	*Total*
Homicide	88	93	90	4,738	3,311	8,049
Manslaughter	85	94	89	1,030	863	1,893
Other sex offenses	84	92	87	1,908	1,150	3,058
Statutory rape	82	89	84	572	306	878
Forcible rape	81	88	84	1,480	886	2,366
Aggravated assault	78	86	80	4,487	1,812	6,299
Narcotics offenses	76	86	78	3,916	1,051	4,967
Other fraud	75	84	78	673	335	1,008
Armed robbery	74	84	77	8,851	3,450	12,301
Unarmed robbery	72	83	75	3,050	1,119	4,169
Theft or larceny	71	80	74	7,448	2,755	10,203
Burglary	69	78	72	23,790	8,487	32,277
Check fraud	64	72	66	8,493	2,482	10,975
Vehicle theft	63	71	65	4,285	1,454	5,739
Total Number				74,721	29,461	104,182

Source: Adapted from D. Gottfredson, M. Neithercutt, J. Nuffield, and V. O'Leary, *Four Thousand Lifetimes: A Study of Time Served and Parole Outcomes* (Davis, California: National Council on Crime and Delinquency Research Center, 1973), p. 10.

classification. A similar result has been found when other indicants (for example, any prior arrest or sentence or conviction or confinement) are used; generally, the proportions that violate parole conditions or are returned to prison with new convictions increase with increased history of such "prior records."

Age has been found to be associated with parole violation criteria also, such that older offenders are more likely, in general, to be found in the "favorable" outcome category. Age and offense are themselves associated, however. Often, older offenders are found to have been convicted of person offenses such as homicide, manslaughter, or sex offenses that are associated with relatively high rates of favorable outcome. An exception is check frauds for which prison inmates tend to be older at prison admission and for which parole violation rates tend to be relatively high. Younger offenders in prison often have been convicted of burglary, theft, or auto theft, for which violation rates tend to be comparatively high.[17]

In view of these commonly found associations, and in order to exercise some degree of control for offense, prior record, and age, the analyses of the association of time-served pentile categories and parole outcome were done separately for offense classes and (within those) for the prior record classification. In addition, a statistical correction was made for age.[18]

Patterns of parole performance rates differed somewhat when offense classes were analyzed separately. Similarly, patterns from different jurisdictions were found to differ.[19] In general, however, it may be said that (1) observed differences in parole outcomes associated with the differing time-served classifications were relatively small, but (2) with some exceptions, offenders who served the longest terms in prison before their first parole, relative to others with similar offenses, tended to be classed more often as parole violators during the first year after release. When the entire sample was considered, which in effect collapsed the analyses over offense groups, the results of Table 8-2 were obtained.

Of course, if the poorer risks are selected to serve longer terms in relation to others of their offense classification and better risks are selected to serve shorter terms, and if this selection is based on information in addition to age and prior record (and in the offense-specific data to be described subsequently), then the comparison may test the risk classification rather than effects of time served. In any case, the differences are not large. Perhaps the main policy implication is found not in the slight trend shown but in the result that time served does not appear to have a substantial impact on parole violation rates. In the context of unsubstantiated arguments that increasing or decreasing time served will markedly affect recidivism, this finding of no substantial difference has a substantial practical significance. There is some small degree of

Table 8-2. Parole Performance Rates for all Offenses (104, 182 subjects) Across Time-served Pentiles, Age Adjusted, One Year Follow-up.

Percent Favorable Adjusted for Age	Percent Favorable Outcome by Time-served Pentile					Percent Differences 1st–5th Pentile
	First	Second	Third	Fourth	Fifth	
No priors	84.2	83.2	83.1	81.6	79.2	−5.0
Prior record	74.0	72.2	72.7	71.4	70.8	−3.2
Combined	77.7	75.7	75.3	73.7	73.1	−4.6

Note: Results reported in this table were obtained by combining subjects from each offense category based on their time-served pentile assignment for their respective offenses.

Source: Adapted from D. Gottfredson, M. Neithercutt, J. Nuffield, and V. O'Leary, *Four Thousand Lifetimes: A Study of Time Served and Parole Outcomes* (Davis, California: National Council on Crime and Delinquency Research Center, 1973), p. 10.

support for decreasing sentences; there is none whatever for increasing them.

Further caution in generalizing from the results of Table 8–2 is given, however, by examination of the similar analyses conducted separately for offense groups and for the prior record classification. These results can be summarized briefly.[20] In general, there was a tendency—although by no means a consistent one—for persons who served the most time, in relation to others with similar offenses, to more often be found in the parole violator group. Considering offenders against persons, the trend was slight at best, and there were several reversals of it. For property offenders the trend seemed usually apparent and somewhat more pronounced in both the "prior" and "no prior" record classifications. But when a narcotics offender group was considered alone the trend was opposite: those who served the most time, compared to others in their offense classification, tended to have the more favorable outcomes.

Speculative interpretations of these data are easily contrived but not easily tested. Considering the general trend, for example, various hypotheses may be advanced. It may result from parole board retention of "poor risks" in pursuit of incapacitative aims. The relatively small differences in outcomes associated with time served may result from constraints on parole decisionmaking—that is, it might be argued that a paroling authority unencumbered by legislatively or judicially set minima and maxima might then exercise a stronger incapacitative role. Alternatively, it could be argued that the fairly small differences observed may mask more pronounced differences to be observed when different jurisdictions are considered separately. (A related study of data from one jurisdiction only is discussed in the next section of this chapter.) Other hypotheses might call attention to the diversity of behaviors encompassed by such general offense classifications as used in this study. Paroling authority "sanctioning," for example (see Chapter 9), may result in more severe penalties for professional car theft as a business than for "joy riding"; or in generally more time for burglary of a home at night rather than of a business during daylight; or for "unarmed robbery" by a person actually, perhaps admittedly, armed who "plea-bargained" down from armed robbery. An alternative hypothesis about the general trend, of course, is that the prison experience is damaging, in general, to rehabilitative aims. Such hypotheses may be formulated in testable terms, and that will be needed to support speculations that raise issues that cannot be settled by these data. The results described do suggest that the arguments of those who perceive increasing (or decreasing) prison time as a ready panacea to reduction of recidivism should be viewed with a healthy dose of skepticism.

Results of a similar study of one jurisdiction (Ohio) were, in general, consistent with these.[21] Since the offenders serving different periods of time may not be comparable parole risks, all offenders in the study first were classified according to risk. Persons studied were a 10 percent random sample of all parolees in Ohio released between 1965 and 1972 (5349 men and 238 women). From study of a random half of the males in this sample (2726 persons), predictive classifications were developed on the basis of the method of predictive attribute analysis. (A similar procedure was used to study the female sample, but the limited numbers of cases did not permit confident statements of relations.) Nine risk categories were defined thereby, with proportions of "favorable" outcome (with one year follow-up) varying in the construction sample from a low of 63 percent to a high of 99 percent. When the other half of the sample was used for validation (N = 2623), there was substantial agreement in the success percentages for each category in both samples. (The overall "success" rate was, in each sample, 84 percent.)

Attributes taken into account in the risk classification included such items as type of offense, type of sentence, prior sentences, history of drug use or alcohol involvement, types of admission to prison, and age. Generally, with men not differentiated according to risk categories (that is, not controlling for attributes such as those just listed), the success rates decreased with increasing time served up to fifty months but increased somewhat thereafter. When the risk groups were studied, however, in order to control for the known associations of offender attributes and parole outcomes, a different picture was apparent. Either no relation was found (between time served and parole outcomes), as was the case in four groups, or no single pattern obtained (five groups). The study demonstrated that for men paroled (in Ohio) between 1965 and 1972, (1) for some specific classifications of offenders, time served is not related to parole outcome; (2) for some groups of offenders there are complex patterns of association between time served and parole outcomes; and (3) there clearly is no consistent pattern of increasing parole success with increased time served; rather, in general, success rates decrease or remain fairly constant with increased time served in prison. More generally, while pointing to the complexity of the question of the relations of time served to parole outcomes and suggesting that such relations, if they exist, may differ in important ways according to differences in inmate characteristics, the results mainly support the contention that there is no large positive relation between time served in prison and favorable parole outcome.

INFORMATION FOR CORRECTIONAL DECISIONS—A POLICY CONTROL MODEL

If more rational decisionmaking in corrections is to be achieved, data concerning offenders, treatments, and outcomes must be more systematically and reliably collected and analyzed than heretofore. In the remainder of this chapter, an outline for a general strategy of correctional study is proposed. A central feature of the system we advocate as a means toward an evolutionary correctional policy control model is that prediction issues occupy a central role. Therefore, some results of a parole prediction study from one jurisdiction (California) will be presented in some detail. It is believed that these results are informative of the general level of predictive ability obtainable from present knowledge and methods and of some of the complexities and limitations of such devices.[22]

The motivation for the development of the parole prediction device (called a base expectancy measure) was to provide, first, a possibly useful tool for treatment evaluations and, second, a device for aid in prison and parole management decisions. In the initial development of the measure, the relatively short follow-up study period of two years was used, and it was thought that an assessment of validity over a longer time of follow-up study could provide several kinds of needed information—on the validity of scales when parolees were studied years after their parole; on various categories of parole violation, concerning the nature of outcomes when a longer time frame is used; on whether predictive efficiency might be increased if longer follow-up periods are used; and on offender attributes related to the length of time offenders survived in the community without "major difficulty." Before examining the results of the longer follow-up study (eight years in duration), the original development and validation of the method will be described.

The prediction device was developed from study of the records of 873 men. They were selected by a procedure assumed to approximate random selection, from all men who were released from prison to California parole supervision in 1956. Items found related to parole outcomes were combined and weighted by a multiple regression analysis. The calculation of base expectancy raw scores according to Form 61B is shown in Figure 8-1.[23] The initial validation study of this prediction scale consisted in its application to a sample of 937 men, all of whom were (like the study sample

To Obtain Raw Scores:

If	*Add*	
A. Arrest free five or more years	16	_____
No history of any opiate use	13	_____
No family criminal record	8	_____
Not checks or burglary	13	_____
B. Age at commitment times 0.6		_____
21 is added for all persons		__21__
C. Subtotal: A + B		

D. Aliases: — 3 times number   — _____

E. Prior incarcerations: — 5 times number   — _____

F. Subtotal: D + E   —

G. Score: Subtract F from C

Figure 8-1. Base expectancy form 61B score calculation.

subjects) released from prison on parole in 1956. The validity of the method, judging from that test sample, may be seen in Table 8-3.

"Favorable parole adjustment" was defined, for the purpose of this study, as the completion of up to two years with no "major difficulty" after release to California parole supervision. A "major difficulty" was said to have occurred if the man was (1) awaiting trial or sentence at the end of two years; or (2) an absconder—that is, a parolee at large, with a felony warrant issued for his arrest; or (3) sentenced to jail for ninety days or more; or (4) returned to prison as a parole violator, either to finish the term as a technical violator or with a new prison commitment.

The further study in which offenders were followed for eight years after parole sought to obtain evidence of the validity of the scale over a longer time after parole by extracting data from arrest records over an eight year period after parole for each parolee. In coding both a "major difficulty" criterion and "new offenses," procedures devised for the national uniform parole reporting system were used.[24] The only source of follow-up data used was the arrest

Table 8–3. Base Expectancy Form 61B Scores and Parole Performance with Two Years Follow-up Study of a Validation Sample.

		Number			
				Percent	
Group	*Score*	*Favorable*	*Unfavorable*	*favorable*	*Total*
A	92–100	26	4	87	30
B	73– 91	90	29	76	119
C	62– 72	89	49	64	138
X	44– 62	183	162	53	345
D	34– 43	81	83	49	164
E	15– 33	39	95	29	134
F	0– 14	1	6	14	7
Total		509	428	54	937

	Parole Performance		
	Favorable	*Unfavorable*	*Total*
Mean score	57.36	46.79	52.53
Standard deviation	17.80	17.32	18.34

Difference between means	$=$	10.57
	$p <$	0.01
Biserial correlation coefficient		0.36
Point biserial correlation coefficient		0.29

records of these parolees. A major shortcoming of these data is that the court dispositions of arrests are not always known. (It may be noted also that deaths occurring after discharge from parole may not be expected to be identified from this source.)

The performance criterion is defined by eight categories (listed below). A more complete description of each is given in the publication cited.

No Difficulty—the subject has no convictions (except that convictions resulting in maximum sentences of less than sixty days confinement are ignored), and none of the remaining classifications is applicable.

Continued on parole after minor conviction(s)—the parolee has been continued on parole after one or more convictions (for one or more offenses after his parole) resulting in maximum sentences of at least sixty days confinement but less than one year.

Returned to prison, no violation—the parolee has been returned to prison for medical reasons or for other reasons not reflecting on his performance, or the parolee was returned to prison on a new commitment but the crime took place before his pa-role.

The above three classifications were not considered to constitute "major difficulty." Similarly excluded from the major difficulty criterion, and from the "minor difficulty" classification as well, were behavioral problems not resulting either in court convictions or paroling authority actions identified with the categories below. (Such problems would not be known from the arrest records.) Examples of other exclusions (described more fully in the report cited) are arrests not resulting in convictions, convictions resulting only in fines, and certain categories of detention. The latter include detention awaiting trial or execution of sentence, or confinement for suspicion or for investigation, or detention because of nonpayment of a fine.

If any of the following five classifications was applicable, then the subject was classified into the "major difficulty" (or "unfavorable") category:

Absconder—the whereabouts of the parolee is unknown and a warrant has been issued for his arrest.

Returned to prison as a technical violator with no convictions—the parolee has been adjudged by the paroling authority to be in violation of parole and returned to prison; however, no criminal convictions were related to the reason for his return to prison.

Returned to prison as a technical violator with minor or lesser conviction or in lieu of prosecution on a minor or lesser offense—the parolee has been adjudged by the paroling authority to be in violation of his parole and has been returned to prison after committing an offense punishable by confinement with a maximum sentence of greater than sixty days and less than one year.

Returned to prison as a technical violator on a "major offense" charge, punishable by a maximum sentence of one year or more, and returned to prison in lieu of prosecution—the parolee has been declared a parole violator by the paroling authority and has been returned to prison on the basis of a clear admission of guilt by the parolee of the commission of a crime that, if successfully prosecuted, would have resulted in a maximum sentence of one year or more.

Convicted and committed to prison with a new major conviction—the subject has been convicted, sentenced, and committed to prison in the same or any other jurisdiction for an offense committed since he was paroled with a new sentence of one year or more maximum.

It is clear that the arrest records do not provide, in every case, adequate information for correct classification of offenders into the above categories. The main interest in this study, however, was in the dichotomous classification provided by the "major difficulty" designation; and it was assumed to be safe to consider that those counted in the major difficulty category have absconded from parole or have been returned to prison either as a technical violator or with a new prison commitment.

When a new offense was committed and the offense was one punishable by a maximum sentence of one year or more, then that offense was recorded in terms of the offense categories used in the uniform parole reporting definitions. An offense was recorded if the subject was classified, for the performance criterion, either as "returned to prison as a technical violator on a 'major offense' charge" or "convicted and recommitted to prison with a new major conviction."

Before examining the relations of the prediction method classifications to later performance, this performance itself should be described in some detail. How many were again in trouble, of what kind, and when, during the eight years after parole? Thirty percent of the 1810 men were classified as having "no difficulty," meaning for each of these men that he was neither an absconder, nor convicted of offenses resulting in a maximum sentence of sixty days or more, nor returned to prison. Seventy percent, however, fell into the remaining categories, as shown in Table 8–4.

Fifty-eight percent were classified into the "major difficulty" category. Only twenty-two men were classed as absconders not returned to prison, and 56.5 percent of the sample were returned to prison either as parole violators or for new offenses. Forty percent of the parole sample committed new major offenses (in California or other states) and were again imprisoned before the eight years had elapsed.

One-fourth of all new major offenses were forgery or check frauds. Second most frequent were convictions and recommitments for burglary (one-fifth of all new major offenses), and third were violations of narcotics laws. New assaultive offenses against persons (not counting armed robbery) were found in 2.5 percent of all paroled. Armed robbery convictions were found in less than 4 percent of all paroled.

Table 8-4. Performance of Men with Minor Convictions, Absconding, or Prison Return Before Eight Years After Parole.

Performance	Number of Men	Percent of All Paroled Sample (1810)
Minor conviction	225	12.43
Absconding	22	1.22
Parole violator returned (no convictions)	214	11.82
Parole violator returned (minor convictions)	82	4.53
Major offense (California)	626	34.59
Major offense (elsewhere)	103	5.69
Total	1272	70.28

When these difficulties occurred may be seen in a general way in Table 8-5, which shows three classifications of unfavorable performance against the years after release from prison on parole. Thirty-five percent .of all with minor or major difficulty during the eight year period were so classified during the first year after parole. Sixty-one percent of these men had committed a new major offense, and about 10 percent had minor convictions or had absconded. The eighth year contributed only 2.5 percent of all with minor or major difficulty; of these, furthermore, 84 percent were those with minor convictions or absconding records, while about 16 percent were men with new major convictions. No "technical" parole violators were found after the fifth year following parole (when, of course, most have been discharged).

What proportions of parolees may be classified into the "no difficulty" category, bearing in mind that this includes all those with no record of absconding from parole, of sentences to confinement for sixty days or more, or of return to prison? The answer depends very much on the length of the follow-up study, as is apparent in Table 8-6 and shown more clearly in Figure 8-2. The proportion with "no difficulty" ranges from 75 percent if a one year criterion is used to 30 percent if the men paroled are followed for eight years.

It often is assumed that parole violations, if they occur, tend to occur soon after parole. A corollary is the belief that the longer a man goes without difficulty after parole, the greater is the likelihood that he will not be in further difficulty. Both contentions are supported by the data given in Table 8-7, although perhaps not so markedly as some would have expected. The percentage

Table 8-5. Performance of Men Classified According to Type of Difficulty and Year After Parole.

Year After Parole	Minor conviction or absconding		Parole violators (no major offense)		Parole violators (major new offense)		Total difficulties	
	Number	Percent[a]	Number	Percent[a]	Number	Percent[a]	Number	Percent[b]
1	44	9.76	132	29.27	275	60.98	451	35.46
2	48	14.81	109	33.64	167	51.54	324	25.47
3	38	20.99	45	24.86	98	54.14	181	14.23
4	27	25.96	7	6.73	70	67.31	104	8.18
5	21	29.17	3	4.17	48	66.67	72	5.66
6	22	37.29	0	—	37	62.71	59	4.64
7	20	40.82	0	—	29	59.18	49	3.85
8	27	84.38	0	—	5	15.62	32	2.52
Total	247	19.42	296	23.27	729	57.31	1272	100.00

aPercent of all difficulties for a given year.
bPercent of all difficulties for eight years.

263

Table 8–6. Numbers and Percent of Parolees with No Minor or Major Difficulty According to Various Lengths of Follow-up Study After Parole.

Parolees with No difficulty	Years of Follow-up Study							
	1	2	3	4	5	6	7	8
Number of men	1359	1035	854	750	678	619	570	538
Percent with no difficulty	75.08	57.18	47.18	41.44	37.46	34.20	31.50	29.72

column in that table has been calculated with only "surviving" parolees in the denominator. That is, these percents are the proportions of those in a given classification in relation to all those parolees who have not previously been classified according to some type of difficulty. Therefore, the percent given is that of men in difficulty among those who were still exposed to the risk of difficulty. As may be seen, the proportions with "no difficulty" increase, for a given year, with increasing time after parole. This is not true for all categories of difficulty—that is, the rates of minor convictions are nearly constant, while rates of major offenses decrease.

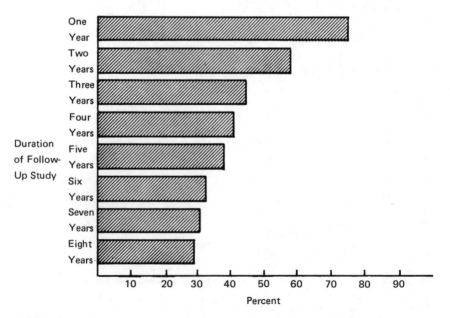

Figure 8-2. Percent of parolees with no minor or major difficulty according to various lengths of follow-up study after parole.

Table 8-7. Men with Various Types of Difficulty and No Difficulty as Percent of Parolees Remaining with No Difficulty and Exposed to Risk of Difficulty.

Year After Parole	Percent with Various Types of Difficulty			Percent with no difficulty	Remaining Total (1810 minus men with difficulty in prior years)
	Minor conviction or absconding	Parole violators (no major offense)	Parole violators (major new offense)		
1	2.43	7.29	15.19	75.08	1810
2	3.53	8.02	12.29	76.16	1350
3	3.67	4.35	9.47	82.51	1035
4	3.16	0.82	8.20	87.82	854
5	2.80	0.40	6.40	90.40	750
6	3.24	—	5.46	91.30	678
7	3.23	—	4.68	92.08	619
8	4.74	—	0.88	94.39	570
Total	13.65	16.35	40.28	29.72	1810

If a parolee has survived the first year after parole without difficulty, is he less likely to be in difficulty during the next year? The data of Table 8-7 give little support to this contention, since the percent with no difficulty in the second year (among those exposed to the risk of difficulty) is little different from the percent with no difficulty during the first year. Seventy-five percent were so classified during the first year and 76 percent in the second. Thereafter, however, the proportions with no difficulty tend to increase, so that in general (after two years without difficulty), there is less likelihood of difficulty the longer the man has been in the community without difficulty (minor convictions excepted). The number of men "surviving" without difficulty decreases quite rapidly in the first few years and continues to decrease more slowly up to eight years after parole. The percent of men with "no difficulty" in a given year after parole increases with the number of years after parole.

The accumulation of men with difficulties in three categories —minor convictions or absconding from parole, technical parole violation or minor convictions and prison return, and new major offenses with prison return—may be seen in Figure 8-3. The minor conviction (or absconding) category includes a fairly constant increment of men with these difficulties; the cumulative proportions of parolees in this category appear to be (after the first two and a half years) a linear function of the number of months since parole. The more rapid accumulation in this category during the first thirty months is associated with absconding not found later (when, of course, many have been discharged).

The category that includes men with technical parole violations or minor convictions and prison return accumulates men at a slightly decreasing rate until about thirty months after parole. After thirty-six months few are added, and after sixty-six months, none. The category that includes men convicted of major new offenses and men returned to prison accumulates men at a decreasing rate until ninety-six months—that is, until the end of the follow-up study. While the "typical" new offense and prison return (judging from the median) occurs less than eighteen months after release, the "average" (judging by the mean) occurs more than two years after parole.

The shapes of these distributions are shown in Figure 8-4. All are quite skewed to the right. They show that while the majority of difficulties occur during the first three or four years after parole, some are found up to eight years. There is in these distributions little support for limitation of follow-up study to two years (or less)

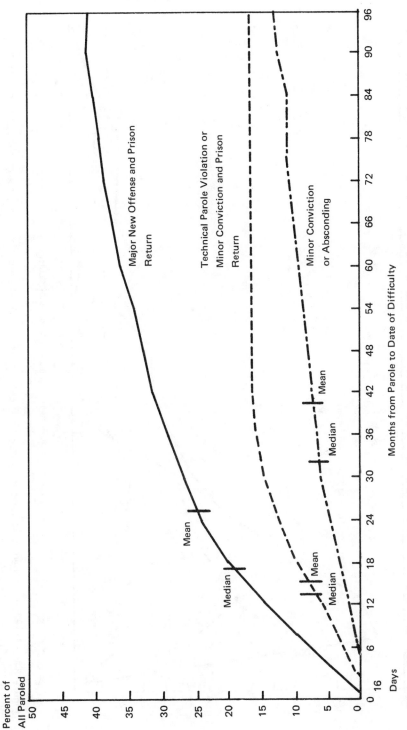

Figure 8-3. Cumulative percentages of parolees with various types of difficulty from month of parole to ninety-six months after parole, based on 1810 men paroled in 1956.

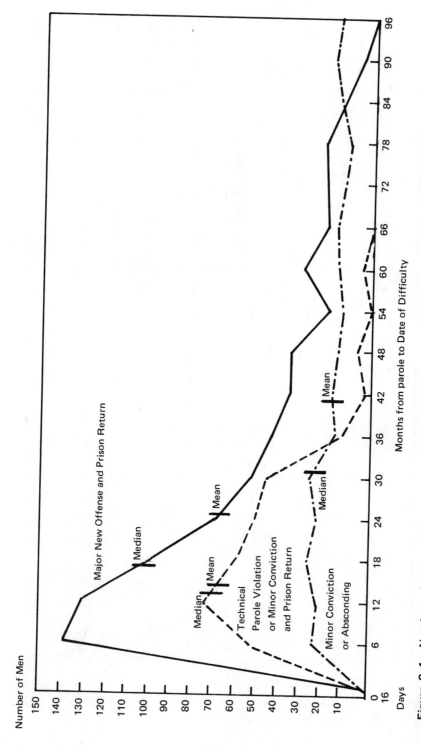

Figure 8-4. Number of men with various types of difficulty from month of parole to ninety-six months after parole, based on 1810 men paroled in 1956.

as in much current research in this field. Judging from this sample, a one year follow-up study can be expected to identify less than half the men in difficulty during eight years in any of the three categories included in Figure 8-4. Not until four or five years after parole can we expect to identify correctly the bulk of the parole sample that is classified into the "unfavorable" performance category.

After the first six months following parole, the cumulative percent of parolees who are returned to prison with major new offenses is a linear function of the logarithm of months since paroled. (This may be seen by plotting the data of Figure 8-3 on semilogarithmic graph paper.)

The best evidence of validity of this prediction instrument is the correlation coefficient describing the relation of the scores to the performance criterion in the validation sample of 937 men. This relation is about the same as that found in the same sample with the slightly different criterion and the two year follow-up study (Table 8-8). Figure 8-5 shows that for both a two year and eight year follow-up, the proportions of men in the favorable performance category increase with higher base expectancy 61B scores.

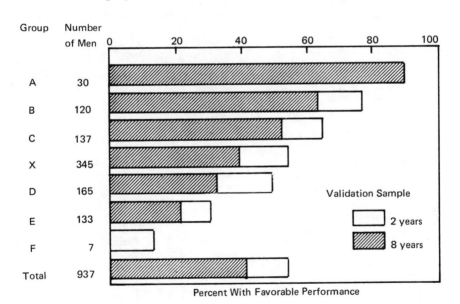

Figure 8-5. Base expectancy form 61B scores and percent with favorable performance when validation sample subjects were followed two and eight years after parole.

Table 8-8. Base Expectancy Form 61B Scores and Performance of Subjects in Validation Sample During Eight Years After Parole.

| Base Expectancy | | | Eight Year Performance | | | | | |
| | | | Number | | | Percent | | |
Group	Score	Percent of total	Favorable	Unfavorable	Total	Favorable	Unfavorable	Total
A	92-112	3.20	26	4	30	86.67	13.33	
B	73- 91	12.81	76	44	120	63.33	36.67	
C	63- 72	14.62	70	67	137	51.09	48.91	
X	44- 62	36.82	136	209	345	39.42	60.58	
D	34- 43	17.61	52	113	165	31.52	68.48	
E	15- 33	14.19	28	105	133	21.05	78.95	
F	0- 14	0.75	0	7	7	0.00	100.00	
Total		100.00	388	549	937	41.41	58.59	

	Favorable	Unfavorable	Total
Mean base expectancy score	60.39	48.32	53.32
Variance in BE scores	370.94	283.75	354.84
Standard deviation	19.26	16.84	18.84
Standard error	0.98	0.72	0.62
Difference between means			12.07

$F = 1.31$ $t = 10.18$ $p < 0.01$

Biserial correlation coefficient = 0.399

Point biserial correlation coefficient = 0.316

Note: Chi square, with 6 degrees of freedom, = 89.29 and is significant at the 1 percent level of confidence.

270

A further assessment of base expectancy form 61B was made to determine the relation of scores to a dichotomous criterion of "success" and "failure," counting as failure only those convicted of a new major offense and returned to prison during the eight year period of follow-up. The results indicated that the measure has some validity for prediction of new major offense convictions and for new major offenses against property. The measure gives no guidance, however, to prediction of new major offenses against persons or against narcotics laws. It may be noted that the base rate for failure by these two latter means is relatively low (8 percent in each case), while the base rate for new major offenses of any kind was 40 percent.

Much correctional folklore concerns the question of the proportions of parolees who are found later to be in difficulty, variously defined. This study demonstrates at least that the controversy regarding this issue, which cannot be resolved by debate, can be settled by systematic record keeping in order to account for later performance by persons paroled. The data of this study suggest further that the answer to such a question is closely dependent upon the length of the follow-up study.

Two widely held beliefs are not supported by the results presented here: One is the frequently heard contention that most parole violation behavior occurs soon after parole. The data presented here do indicate that parolee difficulty tends to occur early; however, 65 percent of the difficulties found in this study occurred after the first year, and 40 percent were found after the second. Difficulties occurred, though with decreasing rates, up to the end of the eight year study period. The second belief that may be questioned is that a two year follow-up study after parole is adequate for program evaluation studies. This may be a useful expedient, and it may provide useful information; but a substantial share of offenders back in trouble again with the law may be expected later than two years after release.

Use of a two year follow-up criterion was, however, supported in the case of the prediction method, in that the measure devised from a two year follow-up was found equally valid with an eight year study.

The base expectancy measure is predictive of major difficulty as defined for this study and predictive of new property crimes. It was not predictive, however, of new crimes against persons, new sex offenses, or new violations of narcotics laws. This result points to the need for development of methods for prediction of these more specific outcomes.

Classifications of offenders for a predictive purpose, as with the methods described, may, of course, have no relevance to the problem of classification for the purpose of assignments to differing treatments. On this problem, the whole literature concerning offender classifications with this purpose in view is relevant. Some of these issues have been discussed in relation to correctional decisions in the community (Chapter 7). But the general need, within any correctional agency, for an information system undergirding a continuous search for information related to correctional goals is apparent. The development and evaluation of programs aimed at reduction of recidivism, however defined, as well as improved individual assignment decisions, can be expected only when a reliable record-keeping, analysis, and feedback system has been established. The required classification studies and necessary assessments of relations of offender treatment or of environmental variables to the outcomes that define correctional objectives can be performed only after an adequate base of data on these variables has been established. Only in such a context can data now presumed pertinent to decisions be transformed into information demonstrably useful in efforts to make such decisions more rational.

STUDYING END PRODUCT DIFFERENCES

In a metal-working firm, where a polishing operation followed plating, the company had been bothered for years with a product quality problem.[25] Ninety percent of the items passed the final inspection; 10 percent were rejected. Too often the metal underneath was exposed by polishing. Supervisors were certain the trouble was due to differences in skill among the polishers or differences in the polishing cloths.

A study was then conducted which proved the polishers innocent by finding no significant differences among them when each used one polishing wheel and parts were randomly assigned. The supervisors' hypotheses, which had sounded reasonable, were not supported, and the problem remained.

The next step toward solving the problem made use of an important assumption commonly used in science: If variations in the end product are analyzed and related to their possible cause, one factor (or part of the total variation) may be expected to show up as being more important than the others, and the unknown cause may be associated with that particular factor. Based on this reasoning, a study of the total process was designed that made the reason for the unwanted deviation "tell on itself." Since the polishing operation had been shown not at fault, the engineer looked at the plating process. He divided plating thickness variations into that occuring (1) from time to time, (2) from plating tank to plating tank, and (3) within tanks.

A small variation in plating thickness was associated with hour-to-hour figures and with tank-to-tank figures. A large part of the total variation was found associated with the side of the tank in which plating was done. Something correlated with within tank variation was the "culprit."

> Discussion with the plating foreman brought forth no clues. . . . It seemed desirable to observe the plating procedure. The only nonsymmetrical feature seen was a hand valve on a pipe on the righthand side of each of the 14 tanks. This pipe carried steam along the length of the tank at the bottom on the right, across the front, and back on the left, rising up and out. The steam kept the plating solution warm, which was necessary for good results.[26]

A reason for the polishing problem became clear. The steam, hotter on entering the tank, set up a counterclockwise circulation of the plating solution. Plating particules were in a rising current on the right side of the tank, falling on the left, and articles on the left side were getting less thickness of plating.

The problem was solved by relocating the heating coils; it had "told on itself" when the engineer analyzed the variation in the "end product" and insisted on an objective approach, unbiased by what management "knew" to be the crucial factors.

This study illustrates the two main methods available for studying the relation of correctional practices to correctional goals—analyses of experiments and analyses of experience. The engineer used an experiment to test a specific hypothesis that the end product differences were associated with the polisher differences. He also used an analysis of experience—studying natural variation in the total system. The study points out that when variation in the "end product" is analyzed in terms of components of the system, the critical parts may "tell on themselves" to suggest either administrative action or further research to account for the special contribution to end product differences, or both.

Similarly, in corrections, the variance in the "end products" specified in terms of the objectives of the enterprise should be analyzed. That is, the variation in outcomes should be analyzed—both through experiments when feasible and through the systematic study of natural variation in the system when they are not—in order to identify relevant person or treatment differences accounting for that variation.

A STRATEGY FOR IMPROVING INFORMATION FOR CORRECTIONAL DECISIONS

The establishment of a data base of the character suggested by the illustrations of the previous sections is a requisite for the evolutionary system toward increased rationality and effectiveness that is required. Such a data base can undergird a systematic study both by experimentation and by careful analyses of "natural variation" in the system. Problems of improved predictive classification, of more useful treatment-relevant classifications, and of program evaluations are distinctly different; yet, they are closely related problems that can be addressed together in a systematic search for information for decisions.

This search requires, first, the collection of reliable data with potential predictive utility at each critical decision point in the processing of offenders in the correctional system. Studies of the relations of hypothesized indicants of probable outcomes then are required; and those found useful can be combined by various means to provide prediction methods. Repeated validation of such methods is needed. When the validity of such methods has been established, these may then be used in order to control statistically for known biases in treatment groups to be compared; and the comparisons of expected and observed outcomes—the "end products"—may at least give valuable clues as to the improvement of practice. Such clues may be followed and more rigorously tested by experimental designs.

A continuous cycle of data collection, information search, program development, and program evaluation is required. This is a large task, but if we are to learn from experience rather than merely repeat it, data that truly constitutes information useful in decision-making must be identified. An evolutionary system of analysis, program modification, test, feedback, and repetition of the cycle is the principal means available, using current knowledge, to increase the rationality of correctional decisionmaking. Some additional features of the model proposed will be described in the last chapter.

NOTES

1. R.W. Burnham, "Modern Decision Theory and Corrections," in D.M. Gottfredson, ed., *Decision-Making in the Criminal Justice System: Reviews*

and Essays (Washington, D.C.: Government Printing Office, 1975), pp. 93-94. The situation with respect to Burnham's last point is altogether common. Toch has described the problem well:

> The problem that arises in practice is that the diagnostic and classification centers that engage in the assessment of personal needs describe inmates in ways that carry no program implications or, to put it more fairly, are not easily converted into assignment options. Inmate folders contain MMPI and other test scores, social histories, and categorizations of mental health that are partly derived from previous classifications and are quoted by subsequent classifiers. . . . True, classifications affect a man's sentence and may delay or advance his parole date, and sometimes may bring a person mental health care if he has been classed as disturbed. But the man's prison life—the nature of his assignments—is apt to be uninfluenced by most data in his file.

H. Toch, *Living in Prison* (New York: The Free Press, 1977), pp. 286-87.

2. For a review and recommendations on specific research needs concerning psychological assessment in jails, including discussions of scientific, practical, and ethical issues, see E.L. Megargee, "Psychological Assessment in Jails: Implementation of the Standards Recommended by the National Advisory Commission on Criminal Justice Standards" (paper prepared for the Special National Workshop on Mental Health Services in Local Jails, Baltimore, Maryland, September 1978).

There are some major exceptions to the generalization that there is a lack of research aimed at improved classification of inmates in ways compatible with the goals of correctional decisionmaking. Toch, *supra* note 1 has investigated the relation between inmate concerns and aspects of the prison environment, developing a "Prison Preference Inventory" to aid the classification task. This instrument, derived on the basis of profile analysis of interviews with inmates, describes concerns that inmates may have with respect to such aspects of the environment as "safety," "privacy," and "freedom." The aims of the research were to develop classification tools to match inmates with institutional programs and to develop an instrument allowing the identification of persons in need of special attention. See also R. Moos, *Evaluating Treatment Environments: A Social Ecological Approach* (New York: John Wiley & Sons, 1974).

For a discussion of research and research needs concerning self-injury by jail inmates, see J.J. Gibbs, "Psychological and Behavior Pathology in Jails: A Review of the Literature" (paper prepared for the Special National Workshop on Mental Health Services in Local Jails, Baltimore, Maryland, September 1978).

3. These included notably, W.C. Bailey, "Correctional Outcome: An Evaluation of 100 Reports," *Journal of Criminal Law, Criminology and Police Science* 57:153-60 (1966); G. Kassebaum, D.A. Ward, and D.M. Wilner, *Prison Treatment and Parole Survival* (New York: Wiley, 1971); D. Lipton, R. Martinson, and J. Wilks, *The Effectiveness of Correctional Treatment: A Survey of Treatment Evaluation Studies* (New York: Praeger, 1975); and a summary, R.

Martinson, "What Works? Questions and Answers About Prison Reform," *Public Interest* 35:22 (1974). See also, J. McCord, "A Thirty-Year Follow-Up of Treatment Effects," *American Psychologist* 33:284–89 (1978), for a summary of evidence that the treatment groups of the Cambridge-Somerville Youth Project did worse, not better than the control group.

4. L. Sechrest, S.O. White, and E.D. Brown, eds., *The Rehabilitation of Criminal Offenders: Problems and Prospects*, Report of the National Research Council Panel on Research on Rehabilitation Techniques (Washington, D.C.: National Academy of Sciences, 1979), p. 34.

5. *Id.* at 34.

6. G.D. Gottfredson, "Penal Policy and the Evaluation of Rehabilitation" (remarks prepared for a symposium on Evaluating the Rehabilitation of Criminal Offenders, American Society of Criminology, November 1979). See also M. Gottfredson, "Treatment Destruction Techniques," *Journal of Research in Crime and Delinquency* 16:39, 1979).

7. Sechrest, White, & Brown, *supra* note 4 at 10.

8. See, for example, The President's Commission on Law Enforcement and Administration of Justice, *Task Force Report: Corrections* (Washington, D.C.: Government Printing Office, 1967), p. 47. For various discussions of potential impact of prison life and time served, see especially D. Clemmer, *The Prison Community* (Boston: Christopher Publishing Co., 1940); D.G. Garrity, "The Effects of Lengths of Incarceration Upon Parole Adjustment and the Estimation of Optimum Sentence" (Ph.D. dissertation, University of Washington, 1958); C. Schrag, "Social Types in a Prison Community," *Pacific Sociological Review* 4:12 (1961).

9. D.M. Gottfredson, M.G. Neithercutt, J. Nuffield, and V. O'Leary, *Four Thousand Lifetimes: A Study of Time Served and Parole Outcomes* (Davis, California: National Council on Crime and Delinquency Research Center, 1973); for a description of this program and definition of terms used, see D.M. Gottfredson, M.G. Neithercutt, P.S. Venezia, and E.A. Wenk, *A National Uniform Parole Reporting System* (Davis, California: National Council on Crime and Delinquency, 1970).

10. *Population Trends and Length of Prison Terms*, Research Monograph No. 27 (Olympia: State of Washington Department of Institutions, September 1967).

11. *Long Jail Terms and Parole Outcome* (Sacramento: California Department of Corrections, 1967).

12. S. Kolodney, *Parole Board Reform in California: Order Out of Chaos*, Report of the Select Committee on the Administration of Justice (Sacramento: Assembly of the State of California, 1970).

13. P. Mueller, *Advanced Release to Parole*, Research Report No. 20 (Sacramento: Department of Corrections, Youth and Adult Corrections Agency, 1965).

14. See H.A. Weeks, *Youthful Offenders at Highfields* (Ann Arbor: University of Michigan Press, 1958); J.D. Grant and M.Q. Warren, "An Evaluation of Community Treatment for Delinquents," *CTP Research Report* (Sacramento: California Youth Authority, August 1962).

15. U.S. Department of Justice, *National Prisoner Statistics: State Prisoners: Admissions and Releases, 1970* (Washington, D.C.: Federal Bureau of Prisons, 1970).

16. See, for example, for summary reviews and references, D.M. Gottfredson, "Assessment and Prediction Measures in Crime and Delinquency," in President's Commission on Law Enforcement and Administration of Justice, *Task Force Report: Juvenile Delinquency and Youth Crime* (Washington, D.C.: Government Printing Office, 1967); D. Glaser and V. O'Leary, *Personal Characteristics and Parole Outcome* (Washington, D.C.: U.S. Department of Health, Education and Welfare, Office of Juvenile Delinquency and Youth Development, 1966).

17. Gottfredson et al., "Four Thousand Lifetimes" *supra*, note 9 at table II.

18. The question of the relation of time served in prison to recidivism often is expressed in a quite simplistic fashion: Do persons who serve more time in prison do "better" or "worse" in terms of some criterion of performance after release? A somewhat more sophisticated version (since it does not assume a linear or any monotonic relation) asks what is the "optimal" time for release for lower "recidivism" or "parole violation" rates. In this study, both time served and parole violation were defined by the relevant operations performed in the Uniform Parole Reports Project. While it must be recognized that the study, therefore, was limited to persons released from prison on active parole and that other constraints upon generalization result from the specific definitions employed, the meanings of the terms "time served" and "parole violation" were reasonably clear. It is by no means assured, however, that any observed relation between time served and parole violation shows that differences in violation rates were a result of differences in time served.

It is known from much prior work that any comparisons—of differences in groups according to time served or of other differences in treatment—must take account of differences in the kinds of offenders who are paroled. Parole violation rates among or between different treatment groups cannot be compared with confidence unless relevant differences in parolees (in the treatment groups involved) are considered. That is, if different types of offenders are released following different periods of imprisonment and if some are better "risks" than others, this must be taken into account in any comparison of violations associated with the time served treatment groups. Thus, a simple comparison of violation rates associated with differing periods of incarceration does not necessarily indicate that parole violation rates are or are not due in whole or in part to variation in the length of incarceration.

As described in the text, the three variables believed, from much prior study, to be most important for inclusion in such analyses were offense, prior record, and age. In order to take account of these variables—that is, to remove their influence upon variation in parole violation—the analyses were performed separately for subgroups defined by offense and prior record, and in addition, a statistical correction was made for the effect of age.

The latter was accomplished by use of the method of analysis of covariance. In this analysis, the dependent variable was the parole outcome, scored zero or one, the covariate was age, and the time-served pentiles provided the subject classification.

Pentiles are theoretically defined (in a manner analogous to quartiles) as those values that are exceeded by 80, 60, 40, and 20 percent (respectively, for pentiles 1 through 4) of all scores in the sample. A rule for approximating a division into pentile groups with the data set used was formulated; it is described in D.M. Gottfredson et al. "Four Thousand Lifetimes", note 9, *supra.*

From the analysis of covariance, the adjusted means were calculated, and the significance of the differences among adjusted means was tested. In short, the intent was to allow a comparison of violation rates for the various classifications of offense and prior record while taking account of age—a third variable demonstrably related to the parole performance criterion.

The results of the analysis of covariance showed that the correction for age composition of the various pentiles made very little difference to the comparison of the violation rates. That is, the adjusted rates were only slightly different from the actual rates; indeed, the differences were trivial.

19. Gottfredson et al., "Four Thousand Lifetimes" *supra* note 9 at 25.
20. *Id.*

21. D.M. Gottfredson, M.R. Gottfredson, and J. Garofalo, "Time Served in Prison and Parole Outcomes Among Parolee Risk Categories," *Journal of Criminal Justice* 5:1 (1977).

22. This section is adapted from D.M. Gottfredson and K.B. Ballard, Jr., *The Validity of Two Parole Prediction Scales* (Vacaville, California: Institute for the Study of Crime and Delinquency, 1965). Two scales developed by multiple regression were devised, called forms BE 61A and BE 61B. They were, of course, highly correlated ($r = 0.85$ in the construction sample). Only form 61B will be described here; it is simpler and more reliable and is equally valid to 61A. Similar data concerning form 61A, which was widely used in the California Department of Corrections and adapted for use in some other jurisdictions, are given in the report cited. Also, the validity of a related but quite different method of classification was studied with the same data: this was an offender classification procedure based on the method of association analysis—see, W.T. Williams and J.M. Lambert, "Multivariate Methods in Plant Ecology, I. Association Analysis in Plant Communities," *Journal of Ecology* 47:83 (1959); L.T. Wilkins and P. MacNaughton-Smith, "New Prediction and Classification Methods in Criminology," *Journal of Research in Crime and Delinquency* 1:19 (1964).

23. Predictor items were selected from a larger pool of independent variables initially studied in order to measure both the reliability of coding information from case records and the relations of the item to the parole violation criterion. After calculating the correlation coefficients among all items including the criterion, the Gaussian multipliers were computed by the procedure given by Ostle, *Statistics in Research* (Ames: The Iowa State College Press, 1954). These were used to calculate the regression coefficients and other statistics shown. The proportion of variance attributable to including each additional regression term was calculated by the procedure given by C.A. Bennett and N.S. Franklin, *Statistical Analysis in Chemistry and the Chemical Industry* (New York: John

Wiley and Sons, 1954), app. 6A; and items failing to add 1 percent or more were arbitrarily dropped. The regression coefficients thus provided the basis for the weights applied to predictor items, but they were freely rounded in order to provide a simple method. That is, the weights used were roughly proportional to the unstandardized regression coefficients. Definitions of the items used are given in D.M. Gottfredson and J.A. Bonds, "A Manual for Intake Base Expectancy Scoring" (Sacramento: California Department of Corrections (April 1961). Mimeograph.

24. D.M. Gottfredson, K.B. Ballard, and V. O'Leary, *Uniform Parole Reports: A Feasibility Study* (New York: National Council on Crime and Delinquency, December 1965).

25. D. Shainin, "The Statistically Designed Experiment," *Harvard Business Review*, July-August 1957. This section is adapted from D.M. Gottfredson, "The Practical Application of Research," *Canadian Journal of Corrections* 5:212 (1963).

26. Shainin, *supra* note 25.

Chapter 9

Parole Decisions

In 1870, at the organizational meeting of what is now the American Correctional Association, Sir Walter Crofton was a featured speaker.[1] Crofton, who had been in charge of the Irish prison system, believed that the intent of the law was to make prisons "more than places of safekeeping" and that there should be programs of reform in prison with "tickets of leave" given only to those who evidenced a change in attitude. Thus, the idea of what now is called parole from prison initially was tied to the concepts of reformation and of indeterminacy in sentencing.

Tickets of leave had been used in England, along with quasi-indeterminate sentences (within a fixed range) since 1853; and they had been used first in 1840[2] in the program of transporting prisoners from England to America in accordance with English law of 1597.[3] The ticket of leave, as originated by Alexander Macanochie (who was in charge of the English penal colony at Norfolk Island in 1840), was part of a plan for passing convicts through several steps: first, strict imprisonment; second, chain gangs; then, freedom within a limited area; and finally, a ticket of leave resulting in a conditional pardon pending the full restoration of liberty.[4] Thus, the concept rested upon a system of progressive classification and assignment to increasingly lesser levels of supervision and custodial control, as discussed in Chapter 7, with increasing freedom while still under sentence.

The concept was related also to that of prediction. Under Crofton's system in Ireland, a prisoner received marks for good conduct and achievement in education and industry. Release under a ticket of leave was followed by supervision, either by the police in rural districts or by the Inspector of Released Prisoners in Dublin.

Earlier in Ireland there had been arguments for a fully indeterminate sentence. For example, the Archbishop Whatley of Dublin stated in a letter to Earl Grey in 1832 that

> It seems to me entirely reasonable that those who so conduct themselves that it becomes necessary to confine them in houses of correction should not be turned loose upon society again until they give some indication that they are prepared to live without a repetition of their offenses.[5]

The concept of systematic classification of prisoners by their characteristics and progress in correctional programs was included in a declaration of principles at that organizational meeting of prison administrators more than a century ago. Certain principles addressed the relation of such classification to the treatment aim of imprisonment (more specifically, to treatment concepts currently encountered under the rubric "behavior modification," including the implied theory that rewards are more effective than punishments). Among the principles were these three:

The progressive classification of prisoners based on characteristics and worked on some well-adjusted mark system should be established in all prisons above the common jail.

Since hope is a more potent agent than fear, it should be made an ever present force in the minds of prisoners by a well-devised and skillfully applied system of rewards for good conduct, industry, and attention to learning. Rewards, more than punishments, are essential to every good prison system.

The prisoner's destiny should be placed, measurably, in his own hands: he must be put into circumstances where he will be able through his own exertions, to continually better his condition. A regulated self-interest must be brought into play and made constantly operative.

The ticket of leave, of course, evolved into the concept of parole, gradually adopted over the next half century or so by all states and the federal government. In relation to the sentencing aims discussed in Chapter 6, the utilitarian goals of treatment and incapacitation both were clearly involved at the outset; and so were the concepts of classification and prediction.

These clearly are not the only goals that have provided the motivation for developing parole systems or that have given the basis for parole decisionmaking. However, all the goals of sentencing may be seen to be involved as well in decisions as to whether or not the prisoner will be paroled from prison.

The paroling decision thus provides another point at which critical decisions about the offender are made. In this chapter we seek to examine further the goals and objectives of these decisions, to discuss the diverse and often conflicting points of view that decisionmakers bring to bear on these decisions, to describe alternatives related to these goals and attitudes, to discuss the information needs of paroling authorities, to indicate potential avenues for improvement of the process, and to identify some prominent needs for research.

GOALS AND OBJECTIVES

It already has been asserted that the goals of paroling authorities in making parole decisions involve the sentencing aims heretofore discussed—treatment, incapacitation, deterrence, and desert. They may also involve aims related to the control of the prison and parole system; and they may reflect concerns for fairness and equity in treatment. Thus, for example, the four primary reasons for parole denial listed in the 1962 *Model Penal Code* of the American Law Institute bear upon most of these, if not all:

1. There is a substantial risk that he will not conform to the conditions of parole; or
2. His release at the time would depreciate the seriousness of his crime or promote disrespect for law; or
3. His release would have a substantially adverse effect on institutional discipline; or
4. His continued correctional treatment, medical care or vocational or other training in the institution will substantially enhance his capacity to lead a law-abiding life when released at a later date.[6]

The first, which requires prediction, is related to incapacitation and crime reduction. The second involves, if not desert, the reductionist purpose of deterrence. The third is an institutional control purpose, apparently also involving deterrence (that of unwanted behavior by other prisoners in confinement). The fourth clearly reflects a treatment purpose.

That paroling and sentencing aims are similar is not surprising, since in many jurisdictions the parole decision is actually more a deferred sentencing decision than a dichotomous decision as to whether or not to parole.[7] That is, the question often is when to parole, rather than whether, although this varies among jurisdictions[8] (as does the use of parole as one mode of release from prison). Further insight into the goals of paroling authorities, and their complexity, is given, however, by the conceptual development and discussion by O'Leary of six "frames of reference" or value systems commonly providing parole decisionmakers orientations to their task.[9] Each may be discussed in relation to the sentencing goals outlined in Chapter 6.

FRAMES OF REFERENCE IN PAROLING

Over a period of years, O'Leary and his colleagues developed, as part of a continuing program of National Parole Institutes for parole board members, a conceptual model and measuring instrument concerning general categories of concerns apparently important to such persons in arriving at paroling decisions. Six general areas of concern, expected to differ among jurisdictions and among individuals from the same jurisdiction but found to be important (and to some degree commonly shared by parole board members), have been included in the instrument. Although each "frame of reference" has been given a short word title, the authors suggest caution in ascribing common meanings to them. The meanings indicated below are adapted from their short summaries, except that we have tried to relate the frames of reference to the aims of sentencing as discussed previously.

The *jurist* value system "reflects an attitude that the parole process is part of the main stream of American criminal justice. It is sensitive to concepts such as due process, appeal, rules of evidence, impartiality, and the protection of individual rights."[10] In relation to sentencing, this parole decisionmaker orientation is related to concerns of fairness and equity.

The *sanctioner* value system also emphasizes exacting equitable penalties for criminal offenses. From this orientation, however, "the amount of time an offender serves should be linked closely to the relative seriousness of the offense committed. He should pay the penalty deserved, no more, no less."[11] The relation to the "desert" perspective in sentencing theories is apparent: penalties are to be assigned such that their severities are commensurate with the seriousness of the offense.

The remaining four frames of reference of paroling authorities outlined by O'Leary reflect utilitarian aims. In each case they are aimed ultimately at the reduction of crime. They are concerned with offender treatment, risk, maintenance of the social order, and maintenance of the prison and parole system.

The *treater* value system is a point of view that tends to emphasize "dealing with the offender in such a way as to lessen his propensity toward crime."[12] This is identical with the treatment aim of sentencing. The *controller* value system names an orientation for which "the risk posed by the offender is the major concern."[13] From this frame of reference the emphasis in decisionmaking is on maintaining external controls on the offender to prevent further criminal acts. It is apparent that this set is akin (or identical) to the sentencing aim of incapacitation or containment. The *citizen* value system "reflects itself in concern for the maintenance of community harmony and the preservation of social order" and in "a special sensitivity to the desires of citizens and officials and to their expectations regarding the appropriate handling of convicted persons."[14] This frame of reference seems to be related to the sentencing aim of deterrence. The *regulator* value system "reflects a concern about the effort of the parole board's decision on the prison and parole supervision system" and is "sensitive to the powerful influence of its decision on the treatment of inmates and the reaction of inmates to those decisions."[15]

The paroling objectives implied by the parole frames of reference conceptualized by O'Leary and colleagues may conflict, just as the purposes of sentencing may be in opposition. Particularly, the treatment orientation suggests aims that may lead to quite different decisions than the sanctioner, controller, citizen, or regulator, perspectives.

It seems reasonable that different objectives of the decisionmaker may be associated with different decision outcomes; but it is also the case that differect objectives may lead to the same outcome. Different information may be used by different people to arrive at the same conclusion.[16] Thus, the "sanctioner" may deny parole (or extend time in prison) after a conclusion that not enough time has been served to provide a commensurate desert for the seriousness of the crime; the "controller" may do the same from an opinion that there is a need for incapacitation; and the "citizen" may come to the same conclusion as a result of a belief that preservation of the social order requires this decision in order to support general deterrence or to assure the citizenry that crime is punished appropriately. The "treater" may believe that a denial of parole may be detrimental or counterproductive to rehabilitative aims in the particular case; and the "regulator" may conclude that a failure to parole will be detrimental to prison treatment programs in which the offender has been participating.

O'Leary and his colleagues do not assert that paroling authorities tend to be classified readily as to these orientations. On the contrary, they argue that paroling authorities generally share these concerns, although there are individual differences in the emphasis given to the various perspectives. It is clear that there is much room for conflict among parole board members; but there is also a likelihood of internal conflict for individual members as they struggle to reconcile the conflicting demands perceived to be placed on them by their roles.

EVALUATION CRITERIA

How is the performance of a parole board to be evaluated? At first glance, the answer may seem obvious and straightforward: persons paroled who subsequently commit new crimes or are returned to prison for violations of parole rules may be counted as "failures," and the more successful paroling authorities will have fewer cases in this category. Indeed, frequent criticisms of parole boards are seen in the press when such "failures" occur, especially when particularly heinous crimes are involved. The problem, however, is not that simple.

In some jurisdictions (for example, New Jersey, Michigan, and Utah), nearly all persons who leave prison do so as a result of placement on parole, while in others parole is the mode of release for a relatively small proportion (e.g., Louisiana, Arizona, Idaho). Although nearly all who are sent to prison are released sometime, they may be released by discharge when the sentence has expired or, in some jurisdictions, mandatorily released to supervision when certain criteria have been met. (In 1977, about 69 percent of prison releases were parolees; the range in the use of parole as a mode of release was, for fifty-two jurisdictions, from 24 (Wyoming) to 99 percent (New Hampshire, Washington).[17] Since the parole decision often involves not the decision whether to release but when to release and under what circumstances, it is apparent that recidivism measures may provide little information on the effective decisionmaking of a parole board.

The problem is, of course, complicated by the diversity of legal structures in various jurisdictions and by myriad influences other than the paroling authorities' decisions on the length of time that offenders serve in prison. Legislative, judicial, and administrative decisions all interact as a complex system to determine the time finally served in prison by inmates.[18] Moreover, as implied by the diversity of objectives associated with the various frames of reference already discussed, the assessment of risk for incapacitative purposes is only one of the aims of parole boards.

Consider, moreover, the shortcomings of a recidivism criterion even for evaluation of effectiveness from the incapacitation standpoint. Decisions to parole are not merely decisions to release from prison, nor are they concerned only with the time-setting function. Rather, they are placement decisions: parole release is linked to supervision in the community that otherwise may not be provided. In this circumstance, the parole board member, even from the "controller" perspective, may wish to release poor risks to supervision if a denial of parole will mean that the inmate otherwise will be released without such supervision and added control. Indeed, if the maximum sentence date is approaching, then discharge, rather then parole, may be imminent. Moreover, it often has been assumed that a function of the parole supervision process is to enable return to prison if parole rules are violated such that the parolee is judged to be in danger of committing new offenses. That is, there is presumed to be a crime prevention function of parole supervision. From this perspective, the return of a technical parole violator may—if new crimes were prevented—be viewed as a success of the parole decision–parole supervision system. (The demonstration that new crimes were prevented is of course another, different matter; so are the problems of fairness that arise in the circumstance, which always must be expected, of imperfect prediction).

How are sanctioning aims to be assessed? As shown later in this chapter, there is no doubt that in general, paroling decisions (as decisions elsewhere in the criminal justice system) operate to require more severe sanctions (if time served in prison is the measure) for offenses perceived generally as more serious or harmful. Again, however, the criteria are a result not only of parole board actions, but of myriad legislative, judicial, and administrative decisions. If careful study were able to isolate these factors, additional problems still would remain. In particular, there are serious problems of scaling of both the concepts of "seriousness of offense" and that of "severity of sanction." Once these are met reasonably by application of appropriate psychophysical scaling methods, a perhaps larger problem still will need to be confronted. This is the question of exactly what is meant by the term "commensurate" and by the popular and rather easy phrase "commensurate desert." How much punishment is deserved for a given offense is, of course, a matter of moral values; but at present we lack much systematic knowledge of these value judgments by the general public or even among various influential publics such as legislative bodies or the judiciary.

How are the "treater," "citizen," "jurist," or "regulator" aims to be assessed? Simply raising the question in this way, pointing as it does to the complexity of the problem of parole decision evaluation, is instructive as to the inadequacy of a simple recidivism criterion as a measure for evaluation. The decisions of parole board members, like those of judges, involve the aims of the whole of the criminal justice system.

Generally, the broad, unspecified question, How effective are parole boards?, is rather meaningless. When specific objectives of the paroling authority may be stated in advance, some evaluation tasks may be more straightforward, as illustrated in a later section of this chapter. But nearly any statement concerning parole in general is in danger of being shown to be a false generalization. The goals and objectives of parole boards are as diverse as the criminal justice system, the different state systems, the federal system, and the legal structures, procedures, and attitudes that obtain.

For similar reasons, the general question, How effective is parole?, is likely to be meaningless. This is not to say, of course, that the crime reduction purposes of parole supervision and treatment should not be rigorously addressed through empirical study. But such study is complicated; it involves the assessment of the two analytically distinct, yet difficult to separate, aims of incapacitation (supervision) and treatment. And the answers to this question also need to attend to variations in paroling policies, offenders, parole officers, form of treatment, level of supervision, and the like. Today, to the question, how effective is parole?, only one answer may be given—no one knows. The relevant research has not been undertaken.[19]

ALTERNATIVES

The alternatives available in parole decisionmaking also are so varied that the study of individual jurisdictions to identify decision options and constraints is needed before analysis very useful to individual boards can be accomplished. Factors affecting them, for example, commonly include the location of discretion concerning minimum and maximum terms (that is, in the legislature, the judiciary, or the parole board), systems for awarding "good time" credits or "time off" for "good behavior," the nature and degree of discretion for amending earlier decisions, and administrative rules adopted by the board itself.

Commonly, the legislature sets a maximum limit on sentence length for a given offense (or combination of offense and prior record). It is usual also, but not invariable, that judges may set a lesser maximum than that statutorily permitted. A prescribed maximum or a judicially fixed maximum will place a constraint on the board's decision; but in most instances some amount of "good time" may be deducted from the maximum. In some jurisdictions, a "minimum maximum" concept is used: the court may set a maximum sentence lower than that prescribed as an upper limit but not lower than a fixed amount (varied by crime class). Thus, in most but not all jurisdictions, minimum terms are also set, either by the legislature or by the courts. This constrains the boards' decisions as well, except that ordinarily prison and parole time both have been considered parts of the total sentence. Thus, if the prisoner is paroled, this constraint will apply not only to the term in prison but to the total term, including the length of parole supervision required by the board's decision. In a number of jurisdictions, the legislature has fixed a minimum term that may not be changed judicially or by the board; this usually is a fraction of the maximum term, commonly a third or a fourth. In at least one jurisdiction (Washington State) the court may set a minimum term, but this may be "waived" by the parole board. Another frequent model allows the judge to set a minimum but requires that this not exceed some fraction of the maximum term. In other jurisdictions, however, the judge may set the minimum and maximum terms at about the same length, leaving little discretion to the parole board. A still different common model has been one in which no minimum term is set by either the legislature or the judge. In these instances, the paroling authority commonly sets a date for first parole consideration, and this often is the decision outcome for initial hearings. In still other jurisdictions, the judge may have the authority, but may waive the setting of a minimum term, thus passing discretion to the parole board.[20]

The alternatives available to parole boards are thus exceedingly complex and varied. The decision outcomes may include such results as fixing the date for first parole consideration; fixing the date for subsequent hearings; fixing minimum terms; waiving minimum terms; modifying earlier decisions; fixing parole dates; denying further parole consideration; awarding good time credits; fixing the length of sentence to be served in prison and /or parole; or setting special conditions of parole, including requirements of supervision or treatment programs.

In order to understand better how parole decisions are made in practice, it is useful to consider in some detail the frames of reference identified by O'Leary and Hall. This classification can be used to structure our review of the research bearing on parole decisions and to help highlight gaps in our knowledge. As we shall see, O'Leary's classification also is useful for the explication of research models that tie together the concepts of goals, alternatives and information that are the focus of this book.

SANCTIONER FUNCTIONS

The time served in prison by offenders who have reached the stage of parole is not a function solely of parole board decisionmaking.

Table 9-1. Average Time Served in Months Before First Parole, by Offense Group, 1965-1970.

Offense	Number of Persons	Median Months	Mean Months	Standard Deviations
Homicide	8,049	58.6	79.3	72.3
Forcible rape	2,366	49.5	68.7	63.9
Armed robbery	12,301	33.1	44.4	40.2
Other sex offenses	3,058	25.4	34.4	32.6
Unarmed robbery	4,169	24.8	32.1	29.3
Statutory rape	878	22.6	34.9	36.0
Manslaughter	1,893	20.8	29.3	27.2
Narcotics offense	4,967	19.9	27.3	23.3
Burglary	32,277	16.2	22.3	23.0
Aggravated assault	6,299	15.4	22.7	24.4
Check fraud	10,975	14.7	18.9	15.4
Vehicle theft	5,739	13.8	18.0	16.2
Other theft, larceny	10,203	12.8	17.3	16.9
Other fraud	1,008	12.2	16.0	13.6

Source: Adapted from D. Gottfredson, M. Neithercutt, J. Nuffield, and V. O'Leary, *Four Thousand Lifetimes: A Study of Time Served and Parole Outcomes* (Davis, California: National Council on Crime and Delinquency Research Center, 1973).

Rather, it may reflect legislative, judicial, and correctional decisions as well, Nevertheless, there can be little doubt that one influence on the severity of the sanctions imposed by the criminal justice system operating as a whole—and including those legislative, judicial, and paroling decisions—is the sanctioner frame of reference or desert perspective. Consistently, persons convicted and sentenced for violent crimes serve, on the average, longer terms in prison before parole than do others sentenced for crimes not involving violence. The example given by Table 9-1 shows the average time served in prison before first parole for various offense classifications for 104,182 persons paroled between 1965 and 1970. Offenses involving violence (or the threat of violence) result generally in longer periods of incarceration. (The only exception in the table is the case of aggravated assault.)

Although the data of Table 9-1 include only paroled offenders, a similar ranking of crimes against persons versus property was obtained when the time served by persons discharged from prison, rather than paroled, was studied. In Table 9-2, the median number of months served in prison for four offense classifications were compared according to data on first paroles (from the National Uniform Parole Reports program) and on first paroles and discharges from a different data source (the National Prisoner Statistics Program). The offense rankings according to length of time served

Table 9-2. Median Time Served, in Months, Comparing Data from 1964 National Prisoner Statistics and from Uniform Parole Reports 1965-1970 Surveys.

Offense Category	National Prisoner Statistics 1964 First Releases to Parole and Discharge[a]		Uniform Parole Reports 1965-1970 First Releases to Parole Only	
	Number	Median in months	Number	Median in months
Homicide	3,686	48.5	9,943[b]	47.4
Robbery	7,318	36.1	16,470[c]	30.5
Burglary	10,760	20.1	32,277	16.2
Vehicle theft	3,077	17.9	5,739	13.8

[a]"State Prisoners: Admissions and Releases, 1964," *National Prisoner Statistics* (Washington, D.C., 1967).

[b]Includes both manslaughter and homicide, for comparability with the homicide category of NPS.

[c]Includes both armed and unarmed robbery, for comparability with the robbery category of NPS.

Source: Adapted from D. Gottfredson, M. Neithercutt, J. Nuffield, and V. O'Leary, *Four Thousand Lifetimes: A Study of Time Served and Parole Outcomes* (Davis, California: National Council on Crime and Delinquency Research Center, 1973).

were quite similar, although the national prisoner survey data include about 40 percent discharged, rather than paroled, offenders.

Offenders with a prior record generally may be expected to serve longer periods of confinement than those without. In Table 9-3 the median times served, in months, are shown for the same cases as included in Table 9-1. The generalization just made is supported in each instance except two—homicide and statutory rape. One may speculate on reasons for the reversal in these instances, but the study from which these data were derived did not provide a definite explanation. In any case, there is little doubt that the criminal justice system as a whole operates in such a way that more severe sanctions generally are imposed when the offender has a prior criminal record. (It should be noted that in Table 9-3 "prior record" means "one or more known sentences other than prison.")

Similar findings to these have been reported repeatedly on the basis of systematic empirical study of paroling decisions. For example, Heinz and associates, in a study of parole decisions in Illinois using multiple regression procedures and treating the parole decision as the dependent variable, found that the seriousness of the

Table 9-3.   Median Time Served, by Offense and Prior Record.

Number	Offense	Record	Median Time Served (months)
3,311	Homicide	No priors	60.5
4,738		Prior record	56.9
866	Forcible rape	No priors	44.0
1,480		Prior record	52.5
3,450	Armed robbery	No priors	29.2
8.851		Prior record	34.8
1,150	Other sex	No priors	23.9
1,908	offenses	Prior record	26.3
1,119	Unarmed	No priors	20.4
3,050	robbery	Prior record	26.1
306	Statutory rape	No priors	24.0
572		Prior record	22.3
863	Manslaughter	No priors	19.8
1,030		Prior record	22.3
1,051	Narcotics	No priors	15.1
3,916		Prior record	21.1
8,487	Burglary	No priors	13.8
23,790		Prior record	17.0
1,812	Aggravated	No priors	14.3
4,487	assault	Prior record	15.7
2,482	Check fraud	No priors	12.5
8,493		Prior record	15.3
1,454	Vehicle theft	No priors	12.9
4,285		Prior record	14.2
2,755	Other theft,	No priors	11.7
7,448	larceny	Prior record	13.5
335	Other fraud	No priors	11.3
673		Prior record	12.5

Source: Adapted from D. Gottfredson, M. Neithercutt, J. Nuffield, and V. O'Leary, *Four Thousand Lifetimes: A Study of Time Served and Parole Outcomes* (Davis, California: National Council on Crime and Delinquency Research Center, 1973).

inmate's commitment offense and the number of prior offenses were predictive of the decision.[21] And Scott studied parole release decisions in one midwestern state for 1968 and found that the seriousness of the crime (measured as the minimum sentence length) was the strongest correlate of the decision.[22]

If the desert perspective (sanctioner function) is accepted, then one must ask whether or not the severity of the sanctions is commensurate with the seriousness of the offense. These data, of course, cannot answer such broad questions adequately; but they raise other important ones that must be dealt with if we are to make progress toward such assessments. First, these data and the general question of commensurate desert call attention to the need for more adequate measurement of both "offense seriousness" and "penalty severity," obvious requisites to studying the question. Second, these data call attention to a critical issue from the perspective of "just desert": is the penalty that is deserved to be based on the present offense alone, or are more severe penalties to be required when there is a record of prior criminality? We return to both of these issues in the final chapter.

JURIST FUNCTIONS

The first discussed "frame of reference" in O'Leary's conceptualization (the jurist perspective) dealt not with the severity of the sanction, but with issues of procedure, fairness, and equity. Concern for these issues has accounted for much recent criticism of parole board decisionmaking.

In a recent review, Harris sorted the increasing criticism of parole systems into three categories:

> Many critics focus on procedural failings, contending that present parole procedures lack the safeguards necessary for fair and accurate decision-making. Other critics believe that the present parole system creates a level of anxiety and frustration among confined populations that is counterproductive in terms of institutional management and the correctional process. A smaller, but growing, number of critics are questioning the wisdom of having a parole system at all, contending that the system is not, and perhaps cannot be, effective in achieving its stated goals.[23]

The first concern focuses on issues of procedural due process but also on concerns for equity. It includes arguments that paroling decisions are arbitrary, capricious, or reflect the exercise of unfettered discretion without due care. The second criticism, that the parole process is counterproductive, asserts that it arouses a high level of tension and frustration in prisoners and "epitomizes for most inmates a system of whim, caprice, inequity, and nerve-wracking uncertainty."[24] Thus this criticism, related to the first, reflects either humanitarian concern or the rehabilitative ideal or both. The third criticism addresses the problem of effectiveness of treatment. In this section we can consider the first two criticisms (of unfairness and uncertainty). In a subsequent section we will consider the third.

The concept of "fairness" is not the same as the concept of "justice." There may be, however, reasonable agreement that justice requires fairness or that "justice includes fairness, but is more demanding."[25] Similarly, it seems that fairness includes the concept "equity," which may be taken to mean that similar persons are dealt with in similar ways in similar situations.

It is trite, but nevertheless may be assumed to be true, that equal injustice is no better than unequal justice; but if models of parole decisionmaking can provide increased equity—hence, fairness—at the same time providing explicit statements of policy and reducing uncertainty as to sentence length, these models would seem pertinent to the first two types of criticism about parole.

The concept of paroling "models" calls attention to the two general classes of decisions made about parole by paroling authorities—individual case decisions and policy decisions. The latter, which may be assumed to set the framework within which the former are made, generally are not stated explicitly.

As noted in our discussion of sentencing (Chapter 6), recent attention has been directed toward a guidelines model for articulating decision policy, aimed at providing a flexible and feasible method to structure discretion in several criminal justice contexts. The development of such models began in the field of parole.[26] At the time the studies leading to paroling guidelines began, there was considerable criticism of the United States Parole Commission (then the United States Board of Parole), including arguments that its decisionmaking practices were arbitrary, capricious, and disparate. The board began a pilot project in 1972 that included hearings by panels of hearing examiners, the providing of written reasons in cases of parole denial, an administrative review process, and the use of guidelines for decisionmaking. Previously, the board had no written general policy providing a framework within which its individual case decisions were made. The decisionmaking procedures developed were expanded in October 1974 to all federal parole decisions.

The guidelines developed by study of the decisions of the board in the prior year were designed to structure and control the board's discretion. They were developed in close collaboration with the board in a larger study of parole decisionmaking. These guidelines were based on the research finding that prominent considerations of the board were for the seriousness of the offense, the risk of recidivism if paroled, and the inmate's institutional behavior.

Table 9-4. Parole Guidelines Model of the Matrix Type Similar to That Used by the United States Parole Commission.

Offense Characteristics (seriousness)	Offender Characteristics (salient factor score categories)			
	Prognosis very favorable (11-9)	Prognosis favorable (8-6)	Prognosis fair (5-4)	Prognosis poor (3-0)
Least Serious Low Seriousness (e.g., minor theft)	6-10	8-12	10-14	12-16
Low-moderate seriousness (e.g., forgery, frauds; less than $1,000)	8-12	12-16	16-20	20-25
Moderate seriousness (e.g., theft, forgery, fraud; $1,000-$19,999)	12-16	16-20	20-24	24-30
High seriousness (e.g., theft, forgery, fraud; $20,000-$100,000)	16-20	20-26	26-32	32-38
Very high seriousness (e.g., robbery, weapon or threat)	26-36	36-45	45-55	55-65
Most Serious Highest seriousness (e.g., willful homicide)	(greater than above, but not specified due to limited number of cases for establishment of ranges)			

Source: Adapted from D. M. Gottfredson, L. T. Wilkins, and P. B. Hoffman, *Guidelines for Parole and Sentencing* (Lexington, Massachusetts: Lexington Books, 1978), pp. 24-26.

MATRIX MODELS

The guidelines now used by the parole commission are in the form of a two dimensional chart, or matrix, as illustrated in Table 9-4. On one dimension, the seriousness of the offender's commitment offense is considered. Six categories of offense seriousness are designated, and for each the commission has listed examples of common offense behaviors for that category, arrived at by consensus judgments of the commission members. On the other dimension, four categories of parole prognosis or "risk" (of parole violation) are defined. These classifications of offenders were established by an empirically developed parole prediction device, called a "salient factor score," used as an aid in making prognosis assessments.[27]

This decision range specifies the customary paroling policy in terms of the number of months to be served before release (subject to the limitations of the judicially imposed sentence) assuming that the prisoner has demonstrated good institutional behavior. After the offender is classified according to both offense seriousness and risk of parole violation if released, the parole board member or hearing examiner checks the table to determine the expected decision. The guidelines define the usual policy. A range of months is used in order to allow for some variation (discretion) within broad seriousness and risk categories. Should the decisionmaker wish to make the decision outside the expected range, then he or she is required to specify the factors that made that particular case unusual (such as particular aggravating or mitigating circumstances, unusually good or poor institutional adjustment, or credit for time spent in a sentence of another jurisdiction). Decisions outside the specified guideline ranges are not only permitted but *expected*, and they are taken in about 20 percent of the cases, with specific reasons given.

Since it was thought that use of the guidelines could induce rigidity, just as the absence of guidelines could produce disparity, the commission adopted two procedures for examining, modifying, and updating them. First, the commission may modify any guideline category at any time. Second, at six month intervals the board is given feedback from the decisionmaking of the previous six months and examines each category to see whether the average time served has changed significantly. At these policy meetings, the board is also provided feedback concerning the decisions that fall outside each guideline category and the reasons given for these decisions. This serves two purposes: the reasons for deviations from the guidelines may be examined to consider their appropriateness, and the percentages of decisions within and outside the guidelines for each category can be evaluated to determine whether the discretion range for the category is considered appropriate. That is, too high a percentage of decisions outside the guideline range without adequate explanation may indicate either that a wider range is thought necessary or that the hearing panels are exceeding inappropriately their discretionary limits. On the other hand, a very high percentage of decisions within the guidelines may indicate a mechanical, rigid application. The guidelines themselves cannot provide answers to these questions of policy. But by articulating the weights given to the major criteria considered, explicit decision guidelines permit assessment of the rationality and appropriateness of parole board policy. In individual cases they structure and control discretion—thus, it is hoped, increasing equity without eliminating that degree of discretion thought necessary.

A major advantage of this system is that its development requires the explicit description of paroling policy. Hence, it is open, public, and available for public review and criticism. Indeed, a central feature of the system is its provision for repeated review and revision. This allows for, and indeed, invites, subjecting parole decisionmaking criteria now in use to rigorous scrutiny with respect to both the moral and effectiveness issues raised. The moral issues may be debated more readily; the effectiveness issues can be tested.

Similar work was undertaken recently in a number of state paroling authorities; these were the parole boards in Washington State, of the California Youth Authority, and in New Jersey, Virginia, North Carolina, Missouri, and Louisiana. Also, the paroling authority in Minnesota has developed and is using similar guidelines.[28] Other states in which some form of guidelines are required, used, or being considered are Florida, Hawaii, Maryland, Michigan, New York, Ohio, Oregon, Pennsylvania, Rhode Island, South Carolina, West Virginia, and Wisconsin. California is reported to have guidelines for considering parole for persons on life terms.[29]

Does the use of such guidelines promise a reduction in unwarranted disparity? Numerous authorities have argued that one latent function of parole boards is to reduce unwarranted disparity; and the originators of the guidelines system posed that as one principal objective. According to the National Advisory Commission on Criminal Justice Standards and Goals:

> Though it is seldom stated openly, parole boards often are concerned with supporting a system of appropriate and equitable sanctions. This concern is reflected in several ways, depending upon a jurisdiction's sentencing system. One of the most common is through decisions seeking to equalize

penalties for offenders who have similar backgrounds and have committed the same offense but who have received different sentences.[30]

Similarly, Foote has argued that, despite their shortcomings, parole boards "are able to mitigate some of the abuses of discretionary sentencing."[31] His observational studies in California led him to believe that the parole board reduced some of the intercounty sentencing and plea-bargaining disparity.

Not all scholars are in agreement. A number doubt the existence of empirically demonstrated disparity reduction by the parole board. For example, although Dawson recognized the potential influence of parole decisions on sentencing disparity, his observational studies found that this goal typically was not deliberately or consciously undertaken in making release decisions.[32]

Recently, M. Gottfredson studied the disparity reduction issue in the federal jurisdiction (both before and after the implementation of the guideline system). In the first study, disparity was defined as dissimilar maximum sentence lengths (for judicial disparity) and dissimilar time served in prison (for parole board disparity) for persons of similar prior records and offense severity.[33] It was found that for the sample as a whole, the coefficients of variation for time served (parole board decision) and maximum sentence (judicial decision) were similar, despite a major difference in the standard deviations. (The coefficient of variation is a measure of variability standardized with respect to means.) Thus, rather than sharply reducing the variability in sentence lengths, the time served (that is, parole board) decision apparently moved the individual cases down the scale of months served, thus affecting the variance of the two samples, but much less substantially affecting the relative variability about the mean.

As an additional method of studying the disparity reduction question, Gottfredson classified all cases in the sample according to level of seriousness, type of sentence (simple versus concurrent and consecutive), and prior convictions (none versus at least one). The resulting subgroups consisted of cases fairly homogeneous with respect to offense, seriousness, sentence type, and prior record. For these subgroups overall, the differences in the coefficients of variation between sentence length and time served were not large; however, some significant subgroup differences did exist.[34] These data indicated therefore that overall there was little reduction in disparity as a result of parole board decisions, that some subgroup differences in the extent to which parole boards affect judicial disparity may exist, and that such reductions may vary in magnitude according to the particular offense under consideration. These results also indicate that such reductions are not consistent for all categories of offenses.

It should be noted that this study was conducted on data collected prior to the implementation by the U.S. Parole Commission of the guidelines system and thus the results could not be viewed as reflective of the current practices of that board. The second study, discussed in the next section, addresses the issue of disparity reduction in the context of the guideline system.

PAROLE GUIDELINES AND DISPARITY— A PRELIMINARY INQUIRY

The guidelines system adopted by the U.S. Parole Commission, in which time served decisions are made within categories of parole risk and offense seriousness, can indeed be viewed as an effort to raise the historically latent function of disparity reduction to a central decisionmaking concern. Given a recent interest in various U.S. jurisdictions in the abolition of discretionary release by parole boards, in part in order to enhance equity, and the strong claim by advocates of the guideline concept that by such means parole boards may reduce judicial disparity while simultaneously preserving individualized decisionmaking, it obviously is important to know whether time-served decisions made under the guideline model are, in fact, less disparate than are judicial decisions.

In any study of disparity it is necessary that two concepts receive operational definitions. Unwarranted disparity typically implies that "equally situated offenders" are not "treated equally." There is not a good deal of consensus surrounding the appropriate use of these terms. Thus, what is meant by "equally situated offenders" is difficult to operationalize in a satisfactory fashion. There are obviously numerous factors that may be considered by both judges and parole board members in setting length of confinement. Depending on the goals of incarceration that are being pursued by the decisionmaker (that is, general deterrence, incapacitation, retribution, or treatment) the offender's prior record, the seriousness of the conviction offense, the offender's family situation, and the prognosis for recidivism are but a few of the factors that may influence the disposition and, hence, be applicable in defining "equally situated offenders." The numerous potential aims of incarceration, with their corresponding differences in "legitimate" sentencing criteria, make the measurement of disparity hazardous at best. Difficulties also surround attempts to operationalize the concept "equal treatment."

In a study of incarceration disparity, place of commitment, custody level, job assignments, treatment services, and length of stay all may be relevant considerations.

Although any operational definitions of the concepts of "equally situated offender" and "equal treatment" are subject to controversy, some agreement may be reached about their minimum requirements. Thus, for example, there is a growing consensus that the seriousness of the behavior resulting in conviction and the extent and nature of prior criminal involvement are essential components to the term "equally situated offenders."[35] And although such concerns as the place of confinement might be important components to the idea of "equal treatment," the length of confinement in prison is probably the most important aspect in most cases. Therefore, for the purposes of an initial investigation into the problem of the effect of guidelines in reducing sentencing disparity, it would appear useful to define "equally situated offenders" on the basis of the seriousness of the offense serving as the basis for conviction and the extent and nature of the offender's prior criminal record and to define "equal treatment" on the basis of the length of institutional stay. When persons of similar offense and prior records receive similar lengths of confinement, then, there is no disparity in the sense that has been described.

These threshold elements for defining disparity are similar to the factors that define the U.S. Parole Commission's decision matrix. On one dimension, hearing examiners rate the "severity" (that is, seriousness) of the behavior resulting in conviction. These ratings were established by the parole commission on the basis of consensual judgments about specific offense behaviors.[36]

The items making up the salient factor score (providing the "prognosis" dimension) are essentially prior record data elements scaled in a variety of ways. In a sense, then, the cases that fall within the individual cells of the guideline matrix now in use the Parole Commission may be seen as fairly homogeneous with respect to prior record and current offense seriousness. Therefore, as a preliminary inquiry into the question of whether and to what extent that parole board may serve a disparity reduction function with the use of explicit decision guidelines, it should be useful to examine the time-served variability within the cells of the guideline matrix relative to the sentence length variability for the same cases.

In order to accomplish this objective, Gottfredson classified a sample of cases by salient factor score and offense severity. Specifically, judicially set sentence length data and parole commission set time-served data (presumptive sentence) were obtained for 4471 cases

Table 9-5. Length and Variability of Sentence and Presumptive Time to be Served, Federal Inmates, October 1977 to May 1978, Analyzed by Offense Seriousness and Salient Factor (Prognosis) Scores.

			Sentence Length		Time Served	
		Number	Mean	Standard Deviation	Mean	Standard Deviation
Low-Moderate Seriousness						
Salient	0-3	270	39.5	20.8	25.3	8.3
Factor	4-5	186	31.8	15.3	18.6	5.6
Score	6-8	121	28.7	14.0	14.9	4.3
	9-11	—	—	—	—	—
Moderate Seriousness						
Salient	0-3	307	43.3	22.3	27.4	8.9
Factor	4-5	220	37.1	17.2	23.0	7.9
Score	6-8	221	33.0	14.6	19.0	5.2
	9-11	130	30.1	13.3	13.8	4.0
High Seriousness						
Salient	0-3	177	48.8	26.8	32.7	11.7
Factor	4-5	217	44.0	23.0	28.0	9.7
Score	6-8	270	39.8	18.4	22.5	7.4
	9-11	338	39.5	23.3	18.4	6.1
Very High Seriousness						
Salient	0-3	201	80.1	52.3	46.2	18.6
Factor	4-5	231	78.1	51.0	42.4	15.6
Score	6-8	437	64.2	44.8	34.6	13.7
	9-11	701	53.8	37.5	26.7	10.4
Highest Seriousness						
Salient	0-3	50	95.4	71.4	58.7	23.9
Factor	4-5	—	—	—	—	—
Score	6-8	89	92.5	69.0	47.1	22.4
	9-11	183	67.4	42.5	36.5	14.2

appearing before the parole commission for the initial setting of release dates (between October 1977 and May 1978). In order to enhance the reliability of the results, only the most frequently occurring offenses (more than fifty during the time period studied) were selected for analysis.[37] These data, then, permit an examination of the disparity reduction hypothesis, under the specific conditions that (1) "equal treatment" is defined as equal maximum sentence lengths (for the judicial decision) and is defined as equal time served—as measured by presumptive release dates (for the parole commission decision)—and (2) "equally situated offenders" is defined as persons with similar offense severity ratings (defined by the consensual rankings of the parole commission itself) and similar prior records (as measured by the salient factor score categories).[38]

The results are presented as Table 9-5. The persons are classified by both offense seriousness and salient factor scores. For each classification, the mean maximum sentence length and standard deviation and the mean presumptive time served and standard deviation are presented. Also presented (in Figure 9-1) is a measure of the variability in each classification relative to the mean of the group—the coefficient of variation (the standard deviation divided by the mean). This statistic is useful for comparisons between groups with markedly different means, as is the case here. As can be seen in Table 9-5, the mean presumptive time served for each category is considerably smaller than is the mean for maximum sentence length, a finding reflective of the fact that most persons do not serve the maximum

Offender Characteristics

		Very Favorable (11-9)	Favorable (8-6)	Fair (5-4)	Poor (3-0)
	Prognosis				
Least Serious	Low Seriousness e.g., minor theft	/////	/////	/////	/////
	Low/Moderate Seriousness e.g., forgery, fraud (less than $1,000)	/////	49 / 29	48 / 30	53 / 33
	Moderate Seriousness e.g., theft, forgery fraud ($1,000–$19,999)	44 / 29	44 / 27	46 / 34	52 / 33
Offense Characteristics (Seriousness)	High Seriousness e.g., theft, forgery fraud ($20,000–$100,000)	59 / 33	46 / 33	52 / 35	55 / 36
	Very High Seriousness e.g., robbery, weapon or threat	70 / 39	70 / 40	65 / 37	65 / 40
Most Serious	Highest Seriousness e.g., willful homicide	63 / 39	75 / 48	/////	75 / 41

Source: Adapted from M.R. Gottfredson, "Parole Guidelines and the Reduction of Sentencing Disparity: A Preliminary Study," *Journal of Research in Crime and Delinquency* 16:218 (1979).

Figure 9-1. Coefficients of variation in sentence length (above diagonal) and in presumptive time served (below diagonal) for federal inmates, October 1977 to May 1978, by guidelines categories.

sentence but rather a portion of it (which emphasizes also the need to study issues such as disparity across various decision points). These data indicate that inmates serve, on the average, from 50 to 60 percent of their maximum sentences; that mean sentence lengths increase with offense seriousness; and that they increase with parole risk as well.

The most striking feature of these data is that *for every category* of "equally situated offenders" the coefficient of variation is markedly smaller for the time-served decisions than for the sentence length decisions. This is shown in Figure 9-1, which may be compared with the parole guideline matrix of Table 9-4. Thus, under the definitions set forth for this study, regardless of the category of prior record–offense seriousness examined, the parole commission decisions were less disparate. And the reductions in these coefficients of variation were sizeable, ranging from 26 to 46 percent.

These results are subject to one of two competing explanations. The first, of course, is that, for whatever reason (for example, use of guidelines), the parole commission substantially and consistently reduces judicial sentencing disparity. The other is that these parole commission decisions serve to homogenize disparate events. To the extent that it is agreed that the extent and seriousness of the offender's past criminal conduct and current offense severity are the critical dimensions relevant to the disparity question and to the extent that the salient factor score and the parole commission's offense severity ratings are seen as good proxy measures for these dimensions, then these data strongly suggest a considerable disparity reduction by the parole commission. If, on the other hand, these dimensions are not seen as critical or, perhaps more likely if these operational definitions are seen as inadequate, then the apparent disparity reduction may be an artifact of the parole commission's use of decision factors not employed by the judiciary (e.g., parole risk). This position, however, rests on the assumption that independently derived measures of offense severity and past criminal conduct would not be strongly related to those used in this analysis— an assumption that does not seem strong in light of the elements that heavily influence the salient factor score and the parole commission's severity ratings.

There is some suggestion in these data that for both the judicial and the parole board decisions, disparity as here defined is greater in the offense classifications of greater seriousness. This may be seen in Figure 9-2, which is an "inside out" figure of the data in Figure 9-1. Offense seriousness levels are plotted for each prognosis group against the coefficients of variation. Although there are some

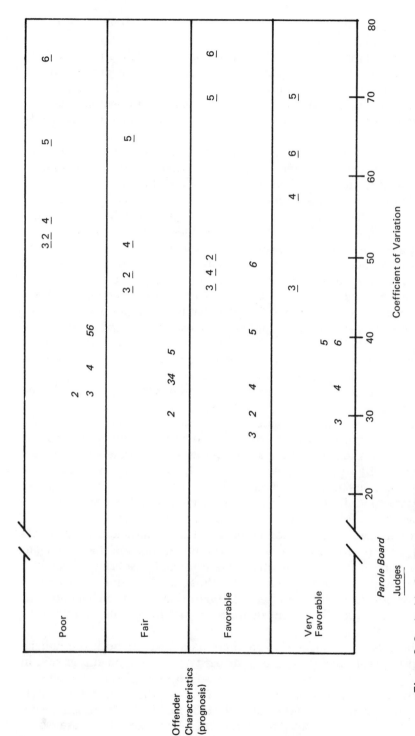

Figure 9–2. Inside Out Figure of Figure 9–1: Coefficients of Variation (in sentence length and presumptive time served) for Differing Levels of Offense Seriousness, Analyzed by Prognosis. ("Inside Out" figures have been suggested by Ramsey, J., "Inside-Out Displays and More.")

reversals, it appears that the variability increases as the offenses are classified in the more serious categories and that this obtains for both the judicial and parole board decisions.

These results might best be viewed as an examination of the maximum likely disparity reduction effect by the parole commission using current guidelines. That is, under the conditions that past conduct and current offense seriousness are the central dimensions defining "equally situated offenders" and that the factors employed by the parole commission are good measures of these dimensions, the disparity reduction effect of the parole commission's decisions may be smaller than these data indicate, but it is unlikely that it is larger.[39]

In the context of debate on the abolition of discretionary parole release decisionmaking, the question of the existence of a disparity reduction function for parole is one of a series of questions that need be raised and answered if the expected full effects of abolition are to be appreciated. It is, within the context of our discussion here, a question raised by the "jurist function." The data presented here strongly suggest that the decisionmaking structure of the U.S. Parole Commission does serve such a function. Significantly, this function is served without a substantial period of indeterminacy. That parole release decisionmaking can serve such a function does not, however, in itself argue against abolition; for once the empirical question has been addressed (and clearly this question needs considerably more attention), the question needs be asked whether it is desirable for the parole board to serve a jurist function or whether alternative mechanisms (for example, rigid constraints on judicial sentencing discretion) are preferable.

Given that with explicit decision guidelines the parole board can exert a substantial and consistent disparity reduction influence without lengthy indeterminacy, some benefits of such a sentencing system over the proposed alternatives merit note. The flexibility required to take consideration of individual variability is preserved both for the judiciary and for the parole board. The impracticality of the statutory precision required by some legislatively fixed determinate sentencing proposals is avoided, as is, perhaps, much of the unavoidable shift in discretion and power to the prosecutor inherent in such proposals.

The review of sentences under explicit guidelines with the clear aim of reducing inequities, a type of review that now characterizes the U.S. Parole Commission, has qualities that might recommend it over alternative systems. Some proposals, for example in recently advocated federal sentencing legislation, would place the entire authority for sentence review with the judiciary (such as the creation of a sentencing commission, with the elimination of parole release decisionmaking). It has been noted, however, that sole reliance on a sentencing commission for the production of guidelines for sentence equalization might leave equity problematic, given the larger number of individual judges who would be making the decisions and who would be interpreting the guidelines. For example, in the federal jurisdiction, regardless of the precision of the guidelines, it is difficult to believe that 550 district court judges would be able to apply and interpret decision guidelines with the apparent regularity achieved by the parole commission.[40]

Although these findings must be regarded as tentative due to the limitations heretofore outlined, they do suggest that when the task of disparity reduction is raised to a central correctional objective, parole boards may play a major role in the fairness of the criminal justice process. In a time of proposals profoundly altering the correctional role in the sentencing process, the extent to which this and other latent roles of the parole process are achieved needs empirical study, so that the full impact of the suggested reforms might be better understood.[41]

TREATER FUNCTIONS

Corresponding to the rehabilitative perspective in sentencing is the parole board frame of reference that involves a program placement function. The effectiveness of a parole board in decisionmaking from this perspective can not be assessed adequately from general studies of effectiveness of correctional treatment. Rather, as in the case of decisionmaking elsewhere in the criminal justice system, such assessment requires that the decisionmakers or others specify the objectives of the decisions to be considered in the evaluation. This is rare in the case of parole decisionmaking, just as it is in prosecution, sentencing, or other decisions affecting correctional placements. But an example of how this might be done and of how an assessment of the results may inform the decisionmakers can be described. Our description is based on an instance in which the parole board initiated a new program (including a decision policy) and did the rare thing—they specified objectives explicitly in advance.[42]

The new program (in California) was based upon the intended release, somewhat earlier than otherwise would be expected, of a group paroled to special treatment units with smaller than usual case loads. There was an objective of monetary savings that would result from a decrease in prison confinement time for the selected group of offenders. It was expected that the presumed reduction in prison costs would be achieved with no increase in parole violations. That is, the two objectives were (1) decreased confinement costs for the selected group and (2) no increase in parole violations.

In order to test (in the absence of an experimental design) whether these objectives were achieved, two prediction methods were devised:

1. Measures of parole violation expectancy, based on relevant information known at the time of the parole hearing; and
2. Measures of expected prison terms, set by the paroling authority under the then operant indeterminate sentence law.

These measures were needed in order to provide statistical controls for known biases in selection for the special parole program.

The parole expectancy measure, providing a parole violation prediction score for each individual, was similar to that described in Chapter 8. Information regarding the arrest and confinement history, psychological test scores obtained shortly before the parole hearing, and the offender's planned living arrangement were combined by multiple linear regression.[43] The device was based upon study of 581 men randomly selected from a larger number, and the items used were selected from a larger number of items studied according to their contribution to parole violation prediction. Applied to a validation sample of 572 men, a point biserial correlation coefficient of 0.32 was obtained with a dichotomous parole violation criterion, supporting the validity of the scale as comparable to those outlined in Chapter 8.

The devices shown in Figures 9-3 and 9-4, on the other hand, are intended for prediction of the behavior of the paroling authorities rather than of the parolee—that is, they provide for each individual a score that is the expected number of months to be served in prison. It was found that prediction was improved by development of separate scales for men previously in prison and for men never in prison before; when each scale is used with its appropriate subgroup, the expected sentence for each man in the sample was found.[44] The prediction method was based upon study of 1068 men randomly selected from a larger pool. It was tested with a validation sample of 1086 men released during the same year; the obtained validity coefficient of 0.67 indicated that about 45 percent of the variation in prison terms was associated with the weighted items included in the scales.

With this cursory review of the development and validation of

A. Add 7.4 for all cases

```
┌─────────┐
│         │ A
└─────────┘
```

B. If PV-TFT (Parole Violator to
   Finish Term) add 36.9

```
┌─────────┐
│         │ B
└─────────┘
```

C. Prior Prison Incarceration:

if	*add*
One	3.3
Two	6.6
Three	9.9
Four or More	13.2

```
┌─────────┐
│         │ C
└─────────┘
```

D. Legal Offense:

if	
Forgery or NSF checks	2.0
Grand theft, embezzlement, petty theft with prior, auto theft, attempt grand theft, fraud, receiving stolen property, burglary 2nd degree	4.0
Robbery 2nd degree, burglary 1st degree	8.0
Robbery 1st degree	10.0
Narcotics (possession or sale)	12.0
Assault	20.0
Homicide	24.0
Rape	26.0
Sex acts with child under 14	42.0

```
┌─────────┐
│         │ D
└─────────┘
```

E. *Add* A + B + C + D   (Sum A thru D)

```
┌─────────┐
│         │ E
└─────────┘
```

F. If PV-WNT (Parole Violator with
   New Term) subtract 4.0

```
┌─────────┐
│         │ F
└─────────┘
```

G. Expected number of months in prison:

E − F = Expected number of months after minimum eligible parole date

```
┌─────────┐
│         │   Expected
└─────────┘   Months
              After
              Minimum
```

Add months to minimum eligible parole date

```
┌─────────┐
│         │   Required
└─────────┘   Minimum
              Months
```

Expected Number of Months in Prison =

```
┌──────────┐
│          │   Total
└──────────┘   Expected
               Months in
               Prison
```

Figure 9–3. Calculation of Expected Number of Months in Prison for Those with Prior Prison History.

these prediction methods, we may return to the problem of the special parole program. It will be recalled that the aims of the program were a reduction in confinement time for selected offenders and no increase in the parole violation rate for the selected offenders.

Did the group assigned to the more intensive parole program serve, as intended, less time in the institutions before parole than did men not selected for this program? Table 9–6 shows that the men selected for the program served an average of thirty-four months in prison while the group not assigned this parole condition served more than

A. Add 19.2 for all cases   [____] A

B. Offense Severity
   if   add
   Minor theft, unplanned   0.0
   Normal sex, minor, 15 or over with mutual consent   2.2
   Walkaway   2.2
   Abnormal sex, adults, mutual consent   2.2
   Checks, unplanned   2.2
   Car theft, simple   2.2
   Possess marijuana   2.2
   Accidental death, negligence   4.4
   Minor theft, planned   4.4
   Attempt crime, no threat   4.4
   Theft, unplanned   4.4
   Checks, planned (4 or more and $60 or more each)   4.4
   Sell marijuana   4.4
   Theft, planned   4.4
   Burglary, 2nd degree   4.4
   Possess heavy narcotics   4.4
   Burglary, 1st degree   6.6
   Sell heavy narcotics to support habit   6.6
   Escape with force   6.6
   Abnormal sex, minor (age 15-18), with mutual consent   8.8
   Car theft, planned   8.8
   Criminal act, weapon, no injury   13.2
   Criminal act, involves fear   13.2
   Attempt crime with threat to harm   13.2
   Violence, spur of the moment   13.2
   Sell heavy narcotics for profit   15.4
   Criminal circumstances resulting in bodily harm   15.4
   Sex act with force or threat   15.4
   Sex act with child, no force or threat   15.4
   Criminal circumstances resulting in death   19.8
   Violence, planned, causing death or bodily harm   19.8
   Sex act with child, with force or threat   19.8
   Any act nor covered by above, including receiving stolen
       property, abortion, and bigamy   11.0   [____] B

C. If offense does not involve "illegal economic gain," then add 1.9   [____] C

D. Add A + B + C   [____] D
                                                            (Sum of A + B + C)

E. Number of prior incarcerations:
   if   add
   None   0.0
   One   1.2
   Two   2.4
   Three   3.6
   Four or more   4.8   [____] E

F. If no history of any opiate use, add 7.7   [____] F

G. Add E + F   [____] G

H. Subtract D − G   [____] H

I. Expected number of months in prison:

   Expected number of months
   after minimum eligible   [____]   Expected
   parole date   Months
                                             After
                                             Minimum

   Add months to minimum   [____]   Required
   eligible parole date   Minimum
                                             Months

   Expected number of   [____]   Total
   months in prison =   Expected
                                             Months in
                                             Prison

Figure 9-4. Calculation of Expected Number of Months in Prison for Those with No Prior Prison History.

Table 9-6. Means and Standard Deviations of Expected (predicted) and Observed (actual) Months Served, by Selection for Intensive Parole and by Prior Prison Record.

	Condition of Parole		
Months in Prison	*Intensive*	*Regular*	*Totals*
Prior prison			
Expected months			
Mean	43.29	49.52	46.81
Standard deviation	21.97	24.72	23.68
Observed months			
Mean	46.93	45.32	46.02
Standard deviation	30.99	32.66	31.84
Number of men	56	73	129
No prior prison			
Expected months			
Mean	30.43	33.56	31.82
Standard deviation	10.20	10.36	11.13
Observed months			
Mean	25.51	31.04	27.96
Standard deviation	14.34	16.56	15.45
Number of men	83	66	149
Totals			
Expected months			
Mean	35.61	41.94	38.78
Standard deviation	17.15	20.82	19.30
Observed months			
Mean	34.14	38.54	36.34
Standard deviation	24.82	27.09	26.03
Number of men	139	139	278

while the group not assigned this parole condition served more than thirty-eight months on the average. The group with which the selected men are compared was randomly selected from a large sample of men released on parole during the same year. Offhand, it would appear that the selected group did serve less time. Armed with this observed difference, it would have been easy to conclude that in the jurisdiction studied, it would represent savings estimated at nearly $80,000. It might be concluded further that continuation of the program, shortening terms by one-third of a year for an expected 138 men per year, would decrease the institution population by nearly fifty men, representing a savings in capital outlay for new institutional facilities of about half a million dollars. Estimates of this sort are quite often made by correctional agencies for budgetary planning on this sort of evidence.

Would these conclusions be justified? That they would not is seen by more careful study. Not only was the actual average number of months served by these selected subjects less that the actual average for those not selected; this was true also of the expected values. The men selected for the special program would be expected to serve less time in prison—with or without the new program.

The main question to be answered should be whether the groups differed after a correction was made for the expected sentences, based in turn upon the characteristics of the offenders selected or not selected for the program. When this was done through the use of an analysis of covariance, a quite different result was obtained. The covariate in the analysis was the expected sentences, calculated according to the procedure suggested by Figures 9-3 and 9-4. Differences in the adjusted means could be attributed reasonably to chance.[45] Thus, the selection bias would have to be considered in the analysis.

It was found, however, that the selected parolees who had not been previously in prison served less time (according to the adjusted means) than did the group released to regular supervision. Subjects who had prior prison records and who were assigned to the special program served more time, on the average, after the adjustment for the expected terms in the two groups. Neither the men with nor the men without prior prison terms considered separately could be said to differ in prison time according to whether or not they were selected for this special parole program, but the interaction of prior prison history with the program classification was significant.

This meant that the prison terms assigned for these subjects were associated not simply with the previous prison history nor with the designation for the special program; rather, they were associated with a combination of the two. Sentences were set consistently with the expressed aim of the program—that is, reduced, in the case of men not previously in prison— but the opposite was the case for men who had been in prison before, and only this interaction was significant. (It may be remembered that the paroling authorities intended to reduce time for all the selected group. Throughout the program they indicated that they believed this was being done.)

The net result of the interaction was that differences in prison terms associated with the program were not so large that we would expect from this sample to find them again. This must mean that one could not with confidence anticipate future savings from continuation of the program. Presenting merely the averages in terms served for the two groups, without any correction for the selection bias, would be to mislead the administrator to expect substantial monetary savings on insubstantial grounds. The second expected consequence of the program was that no differences in parole violation would be found for the inmates released earlier and then given more intensive supervision as compared with inmates released at the regularly expected time and assigned to regular parole caseloads.

Among the parole sample described above, 189 had been released a year or more previously, so that parole outcomes were known for this first year of release, and the data necessary for the parole expectancy scores were available. Of this group, 107 had been designated for the special parole program and 82 had not. Favorable parole performance was defined as completion of one year after release without return to prison as a parole violator, without absconding from parole, and without receiving a sentence of ninety days or more in jail.

How did the two groups compare in parole performance? The analyses of variance and covariance showed that the overall result supported the adminstrator's original hypothesis of no difference. Looking further, however, at the experience of men who previously had been in prison and those who had not, an interaction was again found. Men with no prior prison experience who were selected for the more intensive program were found in the favorable parole performance category three-fourths of the time; men with no prior prison experience who were not assigned the special program were found in the favorable category less than half the time. Men with prior prison incarcerations who were assigned to the special treatment program were found in the favorable outcome category only 46 percent of the time, while men with prior prison records not assigned to the special program were found in the favorable category in 57 percent of cases. The interaction between the prior prison classification and the treatment classification on parole performance was significant even when the expected parole performance (defined by the prediction method) was taken into account by the analysis of covariance.

The differences in parole violations must have been due to differences associated with (not necessarily "due to") the two types of parole supervision—that is, they must have been due to treatment or to unknown selective or ecological factors associated with it. More rigorous study by an experimental design with random allocation to the special program clearly must be suggested. Meanwhile, however, the correction administrators could at least be advised of the following points from the experience available:

1. Overall, men selected for the special parole program did not serve shorter prison terms, contrary to the expectation at the outset of program and of the decisionmakers themselves. First termers selected tended to serve less time, while recidivists selected tended to serve more time.
2. For the selected group on the whole, the orginal expectation of

no differences in parole violations was supported. However, first termers selected for the program tended to have markedly fewer violations in the first year on parole, while recidivists selected tended to have more.

It should be emphasized that these differences may not be ascribed with confidence to the two categories of parole supervision. The main point to be made here is that accounting procedures can provide data to test whether decisions have been made consistently with policy objectives. The first requirement is statement of the goal. Then, if comparisons of experimental and control groups randomly selected are not possible, we may still test the relationships of decisions to this goal with the aid of appropriate statistical controls. When decision policy objectives are stated clearly at the initiation of a new program accounting procedures can be devised to test whether decisions are made consistently with these aims.[46]

THE CONTROLLER FUNCTION

The orientation of the controller frame of reference, which is related to the sentencing aim of incapacitation, is a concern for the risk posed by the potential parole of the prison inmate. Such concern has been, as already noted, a part of the concept of parole since its inception as the "ticket of leave." There can be little doubt that although emphases vary, most parole board members perceive this function—in greater or lesser degree—to be one of the main functions of their role. The controller frame of reference refers to some weighing of the assets and liabilities of the person or his or her history and life situation. This consideration has a purpose: the aim is prediction of that person's future behavior or future status in the criminal justice system.

Specific outcomes that the parole board member wishes to predict may vary among parole board members and differ also when different offenders are considered. The decisionmaker may be interested in predicting outcomes of a quite general nature, such as parole violation, or return to prison, or conviction of new crimes. He or she might, however, wish to predict more specific behavior such as assault, sexual aggressiveness, drug use, alcohol abuse, or stealing. The decisionmaker may be more concerned with some of these outcomes than with others, some being considered in some sense more damaging or costly. If so, chances are that greater confidence in the accuracy of prediction would be required before deciding on release for these cases. That is, the board member may be more willing to take a chance with a relatively innocuous offender, more cautious when the potential harm is perceived to be greater. The parole board member's predictions may be still more complicated. They often have a sequential nature: if the person returns to his previous environment (or his family, or gets a certain job, or has close parole supervision, or receives outpatient psychotherapy), then. . . . Thus, the prediction made often is conditional upon the offender's expected life situation after release.

It must be remembered that these complex predictions are made within a more general context of the parole decision problem, with its conflicting demands from the other parole frames of reference. These demands may affect the perceived relevance of the risk assessment in arriving ultimately at a decision.

For example, consider these three aspects of decision problems—scarcity of resources, alternatives, and a desire to optimize. (It may be agreed that if none of these are present, there is no decision problem.) Usually, the paroling authority is confronted with a scarcity of resources. Although such scarcity—for example, of prison beds, of treatments of a given kind, or of parole supervision—may relate mainly to the regulator frame of reference, it may be relevant also to the controller perspective, since the extent of resources available may help determine the risks that must be taken. Similarly, a perceived good risk may not be paroled if it is judged that not enough time has been served to satisfy the sanctioner function. On the other hand, a perceived poor risk may be paroled if it is judged that parole to supervision is preferable to a longer stay in prison followed by outright discharge without the surveillance of parole.

The decisionmaker may grant or deny parole. Or, often the decisionmaker may continue the case—that is, postpone the decision—for a later consideration. (A decision not to decide is, of course, a decision; and in this case it constitutes a denial of parole at that time.) Each of these decisions may, of course, be regarded also as a decision as to the length of time the offender must remain in prison. The decision problem may be complicated, moreover, by the availability of alternatives within one or another of the major choices. It may thus be more appropriate to consider the parole decision not as a problem of selection (which may be the usual naive view) but as one of placement. If this analysis is correct, then the appropriate question may not be, How can offenders best be selected for parole? but, How can offenders best be placed in order optimally to achieve the goals of the agency? The former question usually would be associated with the idea that the parole board members' task is limited to (or consists principally in) selecting the best risks; the other, with the desire to optimize that and other competing ends.

What is desired to be optimized? The answer can be given only by the parole board member, by the board as a whole, or in statements of policy somehow derived within the legal framework. In general, however, it is safe to assert that parole boards generally are interested in optimizing "successful" parole outcomes (although debate about the operational definition of this term may be expected), in societal protection, and in releasing offenders at the optimal time with respect to both desert concerns and probable success on parole. At the same time, they may be interested in reducing costs and adverse reactions within prisons and in furthering general aims of sentencing such as deterrence.

It is clear that the nature of the parole decision problem may differ markedly among parole boards; so too, the roles that prediction methods might appropriately play may be expected to vary. Among parole boards legal constraints vary. So do resources. The latter help determine available alternatives. The choices available, together with goals and the information on hand, will determine the optimal decision.

A vast array of methods have been proposed to aid in the evaluation of risk. These range from interviews and subjective impressions through structured tests and statistical parole prediction devices. All these methods, however, may be regarded generally as of two types, each with special advantages but also with certain limitations.[47] These kinds of methods, which have been called "broad band" (low fidelity) and "narrow band" (high fidelity), both have strengths and weakesses for the risk evaluation task.

Procedures such as interviews and written evaluations prepared by institutional staff (the most frequently used basic data for parole decisionmaking) provide a wide variety of data that may or may not constitute information. All such "broad band" procedures are entirely unsatisfactory by usual, widely accepted standards of reliability and validity for prediction of parole behavior. This does not mean that these procedures are useless for other purposes. The special virtue of the interview is that because it has the potential for covering a broad range of data, it may provide information useful for many different decisions. It does not bear only on the issue of parole risk. Thus, the broad band methods are capable of covering a wide range of concerns, but they are undependable. Any specific predictions from this wide array of data are notoriously unreliable (different observers are not apt to agree), and they cannot be depended upon to be valid.

The narrow band procedures can provide more reliable and valid information in respect to specific outcomes, but they give no information at all concerning other outcomes. Among such methods, which would include objective psychological tests with demonstrable validity for predicting specific behavior, the parole prediction devices such as those described in this chapter and in Chapter 8 are perhaps most directly relevant to paroling authority objectives. Their virtue is generally more dependability (higher fidelity) than the interviews or other broad band methods in parole violation prediction. The main limitation (besides exhibiting only modest validity) of these devices is that such prediction covers only one aspect of the complex objectives of the decisions. That is, it is relevant only to that part of the decision process that is addressed to the specific question of the likelihood of parole violation. In arriving at a decision, the parole board member may be more concerned with predicting much more specific outcomes, such as assaultive behavior; and unless the method has been shown to be valid in prediction of such discrete behaviors, it provides no information for that purpose.

Thus, the narrow band procedures, including parole prediction devices, are generally more reliable and valid. (These issues, and accompanying research, are discussed at length in Chapter 7.) Narrow band procedures cover, however, only a limited area of interest to the decisionmaker. Compared with the broad band procedures, they have limited scope but comparatively high fidelity. When the paroling authority seeks an assessment of risk of parole violation in general, such devices can provide the best information available.

It should be noted here that predictive decisions related to the controller function raise important issues with respect to the accuracy of those predictions and the propriety of making time-served decisions on the basis of estimates of future illegal conduct (the so-called "false positive" issue). We have discussed those issues throughout this book (see especially Chapters 4 and 6) and will return to them again in our final chapter.[48]

One contemporary issue relating to the controller function is the degree to which the parole board is able to forecast illegal behavior on the basis of behavior within the institution. This issue is of current importance because the abolition of discretionary release by parole boards is being widely debated: such abolition is, of course, often urged for a variety of reasons (as noted earlier in this chapter). But many have argued that because no factors that are not known at the time of sentencing are predictive of postrelease behavior, there is no need for a body such as a parole board to consider postsentencing behavior in decisions about length of custody.[49] For example, Morris has argued that:

> Protracted empirical analysis has demonstrated. . . . that *predictions of avoidance of conviction after release are no more likely to be accurate on*

the date of release than early in the prison term (citations). Neither the prisoner's avoidance of prison disciplinary programs nor his involvement in prison training programs is correlated with later successful completion of parole or with later avoidance of a criminal conviction.[50] (Emphasis in original.)

Similarly, von Hirsch and Hanrahan write:

Some studies have measured how prisoners' behavior during confinement correlates with recidivism (citations). These studies generally find little correlation. This is not surprising, Given that living conditions in the institution are so different from those outside.[51]

Despite the claims that institutional misconduct is not predictive of postinstitutional success, few studies have examined the relation. The available research may be classified broadly for purposes of discussion into two groups. The first consists of implicit assessments of the predictive value of institutional variables. These studies have as their central aim the development of equations that optimize the predictability of parole success. The value of institutional misconduct for such a purpose is judged by whether it weighs heavily in such equations. The second are explicit studies of the bivariate association between some measure of institutional misconduct and parole success. Less frequent than the first category of research, these studies generally seek an association between the number of rule infractions while in the institution and some measure of recidivism.

There is considerable question as to whether either class of study is capable of directly determining the extent to which institutional misconduct is prognostic of future illegal involvement. With respect to the first class of studies, the extensive research on parole prediction does suggest that the most discriminating indicators of recidivism are known prior to incarceration—age, previous convictions, type of current offenses, and age at first conviction.[52] However, the fact that such equations as have been developed do not contain items relating to institutional behavior does not validate the assumption that it is unrelated to parole success. To begin with, institutional misconduct items may not have been studied as predictor items. Many of the equations that have been developed were designed to study the effects of treatment during incarceration and, as a logical consequence, the investigators explicitly ignored factors not known at the time of institutionalization. Furthermore, where institutional misconduct items have been studied, they may have been substantially correlated with other more powerful predictors. As these other predictors are selected for inclusion in prediction equations, a large portion of the information value of institutional behavior becomes redundant. In addition, the relative infrequency of serious institutional misconduct when correlated with the also relatively infrequent variable of parole failure may yield small correlation statistics. Thus, such items may not distinguish themselves in the commonly used multiple correlation methods of prediction, and the extent to which they are related or could, with other methods, bring about a gain in predictive efficiency is unknown.

The second class of study looks at the bivariate association between institutional misconduct and parole performance. O'Leary and Glaser present information of this type.[53] Drawing upon data from the federal system, they found a slight relation between the seriousness of an inmate's disciplinary record and the postrelease reimprisonment rate. In a second analysis of these federal data O'Leary and Glaser made a distinction between first time incarcerated offenders and those who had been incarcerated previously. This analysis revealed that the relation between prison conduct and recidivism was not significant for first time incarcerated offenders. But for those with a record of prior confinement, inmates with unsatisfactory prison conduct had a 58 percent reimprisonment rate, while those with satisfactory prison conduct had a 38 percent rate.[54]

The principal impediment to the use of such research findings to determine whether institutional misconduct is predictive of subsequent parole performance is the failure to control for *a priori* risk. That is, any association discovered between misconduct in prison and subsequent behavior may be accounted for by preprison factors that predict both.[55] This, of course, would then have implications for the issue of delayed penalty setting by parole boards; if *a priori* risk accounts for the relationship, the rationale for a delay in setting the prison term until after some period of observation in the institution loses credibility.

In a study designed to try to overcome some of these shortcomings, M. Gottfredson and K. Adams studied the relation of prison misconduct to release performance for a sample of federal releasees.[56] Three measures of institutional misconduct were studied (assaultive infractions, escape history, and prison punishments) in relation to release performance during a two year follow-up (follow-up data were collected from both the parole commission and the FBI). They discovered that at the bivariate level, each of the misconduct variables was related to performance in the follow-up period. But more importantly, they also studied the relation between misconduct and release performance, controlling statistically for *a priori* risk. Using the parole commission salient factor score as the measure of risk (see discussion earlier in this chapter), they discovered that even "holding risk constant," prison misconduct was often significantly related to release performance. For example, among "poor risks" they found that 68 percent of those with no prison punishments were "successful," whereas 47 percent of those with one or more prison punishments were "successful." Among "fair risks" the difference was 78 versus 60 percent; and among "good risks," 89 versus 66 percent. Each of these differences was significant according to the chi square statistic at the $p < 0.01$ level of probability. Among the "very good" risks there was no significant difference. Similar patterns were found for the other misconduct variables in the study.

Findings such as these certainly run against the conventional wisdom that postsentencing information is not predictive of postrelease performance. There are certainly limitations to the research, and considerably more study is needed about this topic.[57] And it is not clear that the ability to better forecast future illegal behavior by observation of institutional behavior should determine where the locus of sentencing authority should lie. But rational decision-making about sentencing policy needs to attend to the empirical answers to what are essentially empirical questions. Mere repetition of the conventional wisdom may help advance a point of view, but it may also simply obscure complex issues and difficult policy choices.

THE CITIZEN FUNCTION

If the analysis is correct that the citizen orientation of the parole decisionmaker, concerned with the preservation of the social order, is most closely related to the sentencing aim of general deterrence, then little relevant information to guide decisions may be expected to come from analyses within the correctional system itself. Since the aim of imposing sanctions is, in this case, the prevention of crime by others, the empirical questions to be answered must have to do with the behavior of persons not convicted, sentenced to prison, and considered for parole. In order to understand general deterrence, it will be necessary to study those who are deterred—not only those who are not.

THE REGULATOR FUNCTION

Although it is widely believed that the paroling practices of a board are related to inmate satisfaction or dissatisfaction, prison unrest, and the potential for prison disturbances, there has been little empirical study of such relations. Similarly, the role of the board's policy in possibly shaping inmate behavior toward desired program participation has been little studied.

THE NATIONAL UNIFORM PAROLE REPORTING SYSTEM

It has been nearly forty years since the Presidential Crime Commission study known as the Wickersham Report described accurate data as "the beginning of wisdom" and decried the lack of a statistical reporting system in criminal justice. It has been more than 12 years since the more recent President's Commission lamented that the situation was unchanged. The commission stressed the need for reliable statistical information on parole and its results, along with the same need for every other sector of criminal justice.[58] Long before, paroling authorities had expressed widespread concern with this problem—in 1956, for example, at a national conference on parole. The wheels of criminal justice statistics development, however, do grind slowly. In 1964, the Advisory Committee on Parole of the National Council on Crime and Delinquency called for an exploratory project to demonstrate procedures for compilation of comparable data on parole. As a result, in December of that year a feasibility study was started under the auspices of the National Parole Institutes.[59]

Collaboration by research workers and paroling authorities has resulted in the present system, in the development of which fifty-five paroling agencies in fifty states, the federal government, and Puerto Rico have participated. Data based upon agreed upon definitions, intensive deliberation, careful reliability studies, and systematic collection procedures now are available for more than a quarter of a million persons paroled in the various United States parole jurisdictions. All these persons have been followed to determine parole outcomes (all for one year, substantial numbers for two and three years, and some for four years). The present availability of data from this reporting program is unique in the criminal justice system. There are yet no comparable, offender-based national record-keeping systems, including individual follow-up procedures, for courts, jails, probation, or prisons.

This data resource has several important implications for parole decisionmaking study. One is that the Uniform Parole Reports can describe the extent of use of parole and the outcome of the process.[60] A fundamental point amply demonstrated by the data from this system is that parole is different in many ways among the various jurisdictions in the United States. The states and the federal system are extremely diverse in sentencing structures, paroling philosophies, paroling procedures, the use of parole as a mode of release, and kinds of persons paroled. A study of reports from this program should humble anyone prone to quick generalizations about parole—about its nature, its results, or the parole decisionmaking process.

We mention this data system here principally because it is transactional data systems of this type, systems designed to permit the acquisition of information relevant to the assessment of decision goals, that are among the first requisites for more rational decisionmaking in criminal justice. The identification of this and other requirements of enhanced rationality is a task to which we turn our attention in the next chapter.

NOTES

1. C.L. Newman, ed., *Sourcebook on Probation, Parole and Pardons*, 3rd ed. (Springfield, Illinois: Thomas, 1963), p. 29.
2. S. Rubin et al., *The Law of Criminal Correction* (St. Paul: West Publishing Co., 1963), p. 33.
3. Newman, *supra* note 1 at 19-20.
4. Rubin et al., *supra* note 2 at 33.
5. Quoted in E. Lindsay, "Historical Sketch of the Indeterminate Sentence and Parole System," *Journal of Criminal Law, Criminology and Police Science* 16:14 (1925-26).
6. American Law Institute, *Model Penal Code* (Philadelphia, 1962), ¶ 305.9, p. 290.
7. D.M. Gottfredson, L.T. Wilkins, and P.B. Hoffman, *Guidelines for Parole and Sentencing: A Policy Control Method* (Lexington, Massachusetts: Lexington Books, 1978), p. 15.
8. D.M. Gottfredson, C.A. Cosgrove, L.T. Wilkins, J. Wallerstein, and C. Rauh, *Classification for Parole Decision Policy* (Washington, D.C.: Government Printing Office, 1978), p. 29.
9. V. O'Leary and J. Hall, *Frames of Reference in Parole* (Hackensack, New Jersey: National Council on Crime and Delinquency Training Center, National Parole Institutes training document, n.d. [ca. 1976]).
10. *Id.* at 2.
11. *Id.* at 3.
12. *Id.*
13. *Id.*
14. *Id.*
15. *Id.*
16. Gottfredson, Wilkins, and Hoffman, *supra* note 7 at 182.

17. J.L. Galvin, C.H. Ruby, J.J. Galvin et al., *Parole in the United States: 1978* (San Francisco: National Council on Crime and Delinquency, July 1979), pp. 34-35.

18. D. Glaser, F. Cohen, and V. O'Leary, "The Sentencing and Parole Process" (Washington, D.C.: U.S. Department of Health, Education, and Welfare, Office of Juvenile Delinquency and Youth Development, 1966).

19. This is not to imply that no research has addressed the issue, but rather that the existing research is limited both in the variability in conditions that have been assessed (i.e., offender by treatment by supervision levels) and in the adequacy of design. With respect to the second issue, the most common problem is the absence of experimental designs with random allocation procedures or, lacking these, the absence of controls for risk. Most assessments are simple comparisons of recidivism rates (variously defined) for groups released to parole supervision and groups released without supervision. (See, e.g., R. Martinson and J. Wilks, "Save Parole Supervision," *Federal Probation* 41:23 [1977]). Such comparisons are problematic, of course, due to the fact that groups compared may not have been equivalent risks to begin with.

One study involving a two year follow-up of federal prisoners found that parolees did somewhat better than those discharged outright once statistical controls for risk were applied (17 versus 29 percent failures as measured by convictions). The interpretation of these results is complicated, however, by the fact that the periods at risk may not have been equivalent. See, D.M. Gottfredson, "Some Positive Changes in the Parole Process" (paper delivered at the annual meetings of the American Society of Criminology, Toronto, Canada, 1975). Somewhat different findings, however, were reported in a Canadian study. See, I. Waller, *Men Released From Prison* (Toronto: University of Toronto Press, 1974).

A recent study, taking advantage of a natural experiment, reported findings consistent with the hypothesis that parole supervision and/or treatment does reduce the recidivism, to some degree, of persons released from prison, at least for a certain class of offenders. See H. Sacks and C. Logan, *Does Parole Make A Difference?* (Storrs: University of Connecticut School of Law Press, 1979).

20. V. O'Leary and K.J. Hanrahan, *Parole Systems in the United States* (Hackensack, New Jersey: National Council on Crime and Delinquency, 1976), presents a summary of these structures.

21. A. Heinz, J. Heinz, S. Senderowitz, and M. Vance, "Sentencing by Parole Board: An Evaluation," *Journal of Criminal Law and Criminology* 67:1 (1976). Also strongly correlated with the parole decisions in this sample was the sociologist's prognosis concerning success on parole.

22. J. Scott, "The Use of Discretion in Determining the Severity of Punishment for Incarcerated Offenders," *Journal of Criminal Law and Criminology* 65:214 (1974). Among the other correlates identified by Scott, controlling for offense seriousness, were institutional record and age (older offenders served longer terms). Prior criminal record and demographic variables (sex, race, socioeconomic status) were not found to be related to these decisions.

Another recent study of parole decisions for youthful offenders in the federal system is largely compatible with those cited in the text. Elion and Megargee were interested in determining the extent to which race was a factor in these decisions. Although race did not emerge as a significant predictor, their analysis of several legal, social, and personal factors discovered that entry sentence, violence of the offense, and institutional adjustment were related to the parole decision. V. Elion and E. Megargee, "Racial Identity, Length of Incarceration, and Parole Decisionmaking," *Journal of Research in Crime and Delinquency* 16:232 (1979). Compare, L. Carroll and M. Mondrick, "Racial Bias in the Decision to Grant Parole," *Law and Society Review* 11:102 (1976).

23. M.K. Harris, "Disquisition on the Need for a New Model for Criminal Sanctioning Systems," *West Virginia Law Review* 77:263, 326 (1975).

24. R.W. Kastenmeier, and H.C. Eglit, "Parole Release Decisionmaking: Rehabilitation, Expertise, and the Demise of Mythology," *The American University Law Review* 22:477-88, reprinted in W.E. Amos and C.L. Newman, *Parole: Legal Issues, Decisionmaking, Research* (New York: Federal Legal Publications, 1975), p. 82.

25. L.T. Wilkins, "Some Philosophical Issues: Values and the Parole Decision," in Amos and Newman, *supra* note 24 at 154-58.

26. Gottfredson, Wilkins, and Hoffman, *supra* note 7.

27. For a discussion of the construction of the salient factor score and evidence concerning its validity, see *id.* at 41-68. For further data on validation, see P. Hoffman, B. Stone-Meierhoefer, and J. Beck, "Salient Factor Score and Release Behavior: Three Validation Samples," *Law and Human Behavior* 2:47 (1978).

28. See Gottfredson et al., *supra* note 8.

29. Galvin et al., *supra* note 17 at 11.

30. National Advisory Commission on Criminal Justice Standards and Goals, *Corrections* (Washington, D.C.: Government Printing Office, 1973). Portions of the following section are adapted from M. Gottfredson, "Parole Guidelines and the Reduction of Sentencing Disparity: A Preliminary Study," *Journal of Research in Crime and Delinquency* 16:218 (1979).

31. C. Foote, "Deceptive Determinate Sentencing," in National Institute on Law Enforcement and Criminal Justice, *Determinate Sentencing* (Washington, D.C.: U.S. Department of Justice, 1978), pp. 133-46.

32. R. Dawson, *Sentencing: The Decision as to Type, Length, and Conditions of Sentence* (Chicago: Little, Brown, 1968), p. 221.

33. M. Gottfredson, "Parole Board Decisionmaking: A Study of Disparity Reduction and the Impact of Institutional Behavior," *Journal of Criminal Law and Criminology* 70:77 (1979).

34. For cases involving forgery under $500 with simple sentences and at least one prior conviction, the standard deviation for sentence length was 61 percent of the mean, whereas for the identical cases, the standard deviation for time served was 52 percent of the mean, a reduction of 15 percent. For cases involving selective service violations with simple sentences and at least

one prior conviction, the standard deviation for sentence length was 35 percent of the mean, whereas for time served the standard deviation was 22 percent of the mean, a reduction of 37 percent.

35. See, e.g., A. von Hirsch, *Doing Justice* (New York: Hill and Wang, 1976); and N. Morris, *The Future of Imprisonment* (Chicago: University of Chicago Press, 1974).

36. P.B. Hoffman, J.L. Beck, and L. DeGostin, "The Practical Application of a Severity Scale," in Amos and Newman, *supra* note 4 at 169-87.

37. Also excluded were a small proportion of cases (4 percent) that did not have release dates determined within 120 days of admission, but rather were continued for a four year reconsideration.

38. The importance of these operational definitions for the critical elements of what is meant by disparity should be underscored, particularly with respect to the definition of "equally situated offenders." Under the significant assumption that past criminal conduct and the seriousness of the current offense tap the major dimensions relevant to the disparity issue, some major limitations of this design should also be noted. First, the offense severity ranking is derived from the decisionmakers themselves (although the coding of individual cases is done independently by research staff). It might be preferable, in a study of this type, to apply an independent severity rating as the classification variable, particularly if large discrepancies between a consensually derived judicial severity ranking and the parole commission ranking were suspected. A severity scale like the one employed, which classifies offense behavior and its constituent elements somewhat independently of legal classifications, would seem to be preferred to a simple hierarchy based only on statutory classification, due to the vast heterogeneity of behavior subsumed under statutory classifications (e.g., robbery). Apart from the question of whose notions of offense gravity are the relevant ones to be considered, there are also obvious measurement problems associated with the categorization of individual offenses by seriousness and the inevitable heterogeneity of conduct that will be subsumed in seriousness classes.

The second major limitation of this design concerns the use of the salient factor score as an operational definition of past criminal conduct. Optimally, what is desired is a measure of the frequency and seriousness of past criminal conduct. This is clearly incorporated heavily into the salient factor score, with such items as the number of prior convictions, the number of prior incarcerations, and parole revocation. These items do tap both the frequency and the seriousness (prior incarcerations) of the offender's past criminal record. However, the salient factor score includes other items (history of opiate addiction, employment in the community, and whether the instant offense involved either auto theft or check forgery) that are not central to this concept, although they are associated with parole risk. This is a lesser problem, of course, if it is determined that measures of risk (rather than only prior record) are considered relevant to the classifications used in an analysis of equity.

One further inadequacy of the model used here to study the disparity issue should be noted. The model implicitly assumes that if the coefficient of variation in a given classification were zero, then there would be no disparity. Clearly, given the crude classification variables used, such a result would not be desirable from the point of view of equity. Variability within these classes is to be expected; the difficult question, of course, is, How much is necessary and desirable? In the absence of a design in which all relevant factors bearing on the disparity issue are held constant (e.g., all cases falling within a seriousness class are identical with respect to seriousness), the question of how much variability is excessive will be problematic. Thus, clearly not all of the variability in the presumptive sentences reflected in Figure 9-1 should be regarded as disparity.

39. It should be noted that the question of the effect of guidelines on the disparity reduction question is one that requires an experimental design, with measurements taken both prior to and subsequent to the implementation of the decision guidelines, preferably with random allocation to a control group. These results suggest a "guidelines effect," but they do not demonstrate it.

40. See testimony of C. McCall, chairman, U.S. Parole Commission, before the Subcommittee on Criminal Justice, House Judiciary Committee, April 18, 1978, p. 9. It has been estimated that a district judge, on the average, imposes annually fewer than thirty sentences of imprisonment exceeding one year.

41. Another study relevant to the "jurist function" examined the extent to which variability in parole decisions could be attributable to differences in the decisionmaker rather than to the circumstance of the case. For a description see note 46 *infra*.

42. This section is adapted from D.M. Gottfredson, "A Strategy for Study of Correctional Effectiveness" (paper presented to the Fourth Section of the Fifth International Criminological Congress, Montreal, August 1965).

43. Some advantages and limitations of multiple regression for this purpose were discussed in Chapter 8.

44. D.M. Gottfredson and K.B. Ballard, Jr., *Estimating Sentences Under An Indeterminate Sentence Law* (Vacaville, California: Institute for the Study of Crime and Delinquency, June 1964).

45. The analyses discussed here and in the next section were done using the method of unweighted means according to procedures described in K.B. Ballard, Jr., and D.M. Gottfredson, *Analysis of Variance and Covariance With Unequal Treatment Groups* (Vacaville, California: Institute for the Study of Crime and Delinquency, 1965).

46. Similar logic and analytic methods may be used to test a variety of hypotheses about decisonmaking when the use of an experimental design is not feasible. An illustration is given by a study of variation in parole decisionmaking among decisionmakers of one parole board. D.M. Gottfredson and K.B. Ballard, Jr., "Differences in Parole Decisions Associated with Decisionmakers," *Journal of Research in Crime and Delinquency* 3:112 (1966). The study demonstrated that (1) there was variation among decisionmakers in the prison terms set; (2) there was variation in the expected terms of the inmates involved, when the measures described in Figures 9-3 and 9-4 provided the expected values (that is, the parole board members did not see comparable

groups of inmates); and (3) the analysis of covariance (to control for the expected values) showed that when the differences in groups of offenders considered by different members was taken into account, the variation in prison terms, by members, was not statistically significant. Thus, despite differences in parole board members' decisions that might at first glance appear disparate, a more careful analysis, taking account of biasing selection factors, showed that the decisionmakers tended to make similar sentencing decisions when the different kinds of offenders considered were taken into account. Similar methods could be used to provide feedback to paroling authorities (or judges, etc.) concerning differences in decisions for any subgroupings of offenders, treatment classifications, or decisions made under different policies.

47. L. Cronbach and G. Gleser, *Psychological Tests and Personnel Decisions* (Urbana: University of Illinois Press, 1957).

48. For discussions of the problems with predictive judgments with specific reference to parole, see D. Stanley, *Prisoners Among Us* (Washington, D.C.: Brookings Institution, 1976); A. von Hirsch and K. Hanrahan, *The Question of Parole* (Cambridge, Massachusetts: Ballinger, 1979).

49. Portions of the following discussion are adapted from M.R. Gottfredson and K. Adams, "Prison Behavior and Parole Performance: Empirical Reality and Public Policy" (Albany, New York: Criminal Justice Research Center, 1980). Mimeograph.

50. Morris, *supra* note 5 at 35.

51. Von Hirsch and Hanrahan, *supra* note 48 at 32.

52. See generally, V. O'Leary and D. Glaser, "The Assessment of Risk in Parole Decisionmaking," in D.J. West, ed., *The Future of Parole* (London: Duckworth, 1972); and D. Gottfredson, "Assessment and Prediction Methods in Crime and Delinquency," in President's Commission on Law Enforcement and Administration of Justice, *Task Force Report: Juvenile Delinquency and Youth Crime* (Washington, D.C.: Government Printing Office, 1967).

53. *Id.* at 157-58.

54. *Id.*

55. This problem, and the relevant literature prior to 1968, is discussed by D. Lipton, R. Martinson and J. Wilks, *The Effectiveness of Correctional Treatment* (New York: Praeger, 1975), page 87.

56. Gottfredson and Adams, *supra* note 49.

57. For a discussion of these limitations see *id.*

58. "Criminal Statistics—An Urgently Needed Resource," in President's Commission on Law Enforcement and Administration of Justice, *Task Force Report: Crime and Its Impact—An Assessment* (Washington, D.C.: Government Printing Office, 1967), ch. 10, p. 123; "Parole and Aftercare," in President's Commission on Law Enforcement and Administration of Justice, *Task Force Report: Corrections* (Washington, D.C.: Government Printing Office, 1967), ch.6, p. 60; P.P. Lejins, "National Crime Data Reporting System: Proposal for a Model," in President's Commission, *Task Force Report: Crime and Its Impact, supra* at App. C, pp. 178-206.

59. D.M. Gottfredson, M.G. Neithercutt, P.S. Venezia, and A. Wenk, *A National Uniform Parole Reporting System* (Davis, California: National Council on Crime and Delinquency, December 1970).

60. Over the last twelve years (1965-1977), the use of parole as a mode of release from prison in the various states fairly steadily but only gradually increased, from about 60 to 72 percent. The trend was not uniform across the country; see Galvin et al., *supra* note 17 at 18-19. The most recent data for parolees, a three year follow-up study (of persons paroled in 1970) show that of 17,654 persons studied, 71 percent were nonviolators; 8 percent (1415) were recommitted to prison with a new major conviction. See National Council on Crime and Delinquency, "Three-Year Follow-up Analyses—1970 Parolees," *Newsletter, Uniform Parole Reports* (Davis, California, n.d.).

Chapter 10

Toward More Rational Decisionmaking

At this point I cease trustworthy discourse and the thought about truth; from here on, learn the opinions of mortals. . . .[1]

Before outlining in a general way our ideas about how rationality might be enhanced in the criminal justice system, we should first pause and look back upon the preceding chapters to see whether any statements of a general nature might be made about the empirical work we have summarized. We have reviewed a large number of studies, united only by their focus on a decision point of interest to our analysis. Methodologies, statistical methods, and theoretical directions have varied considerably. The questions that the authors of these studies have asked of their data have been diverse. Can any general statements be made about the whole of the system on the basis of this impressive, yet quite heterogeneous, body of empirical research? Is there any consistency to be found in the ways that these various actors in the system—citizens, police, judges, correctional officials— made their decisions?

We think some general statements are possible and perceive a good deal of consistency. Of the several recurring themes and common issues that appear in the previous pages, three issues, each supported by ample empirical study, merit special comment. They transcend the complexity and contradiction so often seen in the process from the report of a crime to the release of an offender from state custody. We can state them first briefly and then elaborate their significance to our model in the rest of the chapter.[2]

Common Decision Correlates—The Two Systems of Justice

First, from the host of offender, offense, victim, decisionmaker, and situtational factors that potentially influence individual decisionmaking, three appear to play a persistent and major role throughout the system—the "seriousness of the offense," the prior criminal conduct of the offender, and the personal relationship between the victim of the crime and the offender. Other factors most surely are also influential (to a greater or lesser extent at various decision points), but none characterizes the process to a greater degree.

Given the widely observed conflicts over aims among the various components of the criminal justice system, it may surprise some to find considerable consistency with respect to major decisionmaking criteria. Yet perhaps because they so readily are perceived to be of service simultaneously to so many masters (for example, crime control, retribution, efficiency), the factors of offense seriousness, prior criminal record, and the personal relationship between the victim and the offender heavily influence nearly every decision in the process. In nearly every instance they are used as criteria to screen cases from further processing or for invoking more severe sanctions.

Although operationalized differently in various studies, offense seriousness, in the nature of bodily harm and property loss, has been shown to be a dominant factor in the decisions of victims, police, bail judges, sentencing judges, and parole boards.[3] The persistent finding is that, *ceteris paribus*, the more serious the event, the more likely the offender (or alleged offender) will be reported to the police, be arrested, be required to post cash bail, be sentenced to imprisonment, and be required to serve a lengthy prison term.

It is noteworthy that studies at each decision point report major effects for offense seriousness. After all, each successive stage in the process views only those cases passed on by the previous state—that is, only those cases that remain after "screening" for seriousness by earlier decisionmakers are required to be considered. Yet at each decision point the cases are sifted again on the basis of seriousness. The power of this factor is thus difficult to overestimate—it survives to be used again and again, despite continuous truncation of the seriousness distribution. At each stage, the gravest dispositions are reserved for those cases, among those that are passed on from earlier stages, that are the "most serious."[4]

The consequences of the centrality of offense seriousness are indeed many. One relates to the perceived inconsistency of aims among the components of the criminal justice system. Such inconsistency, we think, may be somewhat overstated given the empirically demonstrated regularity of some major decision criteria throughout the system. We discuss this in more detail in subsequent sections of this chapter. Another consequence has to do with the relationships among the various components of the system. Perhaps much of the animosity often reported on the part of the police toward the courts, for example, reflects the fact that the courts, in shunting cases from the sytem, use criteria that the police themselves believe have already been applied adequately.

A second decisionmaking factor that appears throughout the system, again with great regularity and importance, is the prior criminal conduct of the offender. It appears to operate both in conjunction with and independent of offense severity. That is, where an extensive prior record is present, even less serious offenses are, *ceteris paribus*, more likely to be given full processing and, when the offense seriousness is also great, to be given even greater attention. This influence is seen in relation to decisions to arrest, to require cash bail, to require incarceration, and to require lengthy prison terms.[5]

The persistence of this correlate of decision outcomes also raises numerous critical issues. Does it signify, for example, simply another measure of "legal seriousness," whereby not the act but the person is regarded as "more serious" and thus deserving of greater state intervention?[6] Or is the repeated use of this factor related primarily to predictive aims of incapacitation and treatment? What are the implications for fairness of compounding decision after decision on the basis of the same data about previous conduct? We can only raise these questions here, noting that they arise from the consistency of the empirical findings reviewed in this book.

The third strikingly consistent major correlate of the decisions we have reviewed is the prior relationship between the victim and the offender. The major pattern may be stated succinctly: it is preferred that the criminal justice process not deal with criminal acts between nonstrangers. Nearly every decisionmaker in the process seeks alternatives for criminal acts between relatives, friends, and acquaintances. The most grave dispositions are reserved continuously for events between strangers. Victims report nonstranger events less frequently, police arrest less frequently, prosecutors charge less frequently, and so on through the system.

Perhaps, as with prior record, the victim-offender relationship is simply another aspect of "legal offense seriousness." Some empirical evidence would suggest such an interpretation.[7] Nevertheless, the issues raised by these empirical patterns are complex.

Certainly, crimes among nonstrangers can be just as grave in their consequences to victims as stranger events—perhaps more so, given the increased opportunity for repetition. Yet the legal system shunts them away at every opportunity. Often it does so for obvious reasons—for example, it may be more difficult to obtain the required cooperation of the victim in prosecution of nonstranger crime.

One significance of this finding relates to the development and evaluation of decision alternatives throughout the system. Nonstranger crimes comprise a major classification of events for which decisionmakers repeatedly seek alternatives from full processing. We discuss this implication later in this chapter in conjunction with proposals toward a model for improved rationality in decisionmaking.

When the simultaneous influence of these correlates is considered, it appears to us that, in many respects, it is necessary to speak of two criminal justice "systems" rather than one.[8] The first is characterized by what may be considered to be consensually defined very serious events. Here we speak of grave offenses (such as homicide, rape, aggravated assault, and robbery) committed by strangers, but the list must include also crimes of lesser offense severity committed by persons with extensive or serious prior records. For events of these types there is very little discretion exhibited at any of the major criminal justice decision points. The decision virtually always is to proceed with full processing—to report the crime, to make an arrest, to charge, to require bail, to sentence to grave dispositions. Although the reason for full processing undoubtedly varies among decisionmakers from the victim's desire for retribution, to the bail judge's concern for incapacitation, to the sentencing judge's aim of general deterrence, the empirical result is the same—full processing, little decision variability.

The question immediately arises, therefore, for this "system," What difference it would make, as a matter of empirical reality, were a greater consistency of goals achieved among the decisionmaker components of this "system?" Would the strength of these correlates diminish if one or the other of the commonly asserted aims of treatment, desert, deterrence, or incapacitation were to achieve superiority throughout the process? We think not. Would a lessened conflict of goals have the empirical result of a change in the factors most influential in characterizing the decisionmaking of the whole of this "system?" We think not.

We think not, since it is precisely because offense seriousness, prior criminal conduct, and the personal relationship between the victim and the offender are seen to be central features of each of these major decision goals that they are so influential. The harm done by an offense is seen simultaneously (or alternatively) as indicating a more compelling need for treatment, as more deserving of punishment, as in greater need of deterrence, and as more urgently requiring incapacitation. This perception applies similarly to those with demonstrated previous extensive or serious criminal conduct. And criminal acts commited by strangers are at once perceived as more reprehensible and as creative of the fear necessary for invoking crime control aims. Thus, it may well be that for this "system," the endless debates alleging the primacy of one or another of the classic decision aims of desert, deterrence, treatment, or incapacitation could be summarized from the standpoint of empirical reality as "it don't make no nevermind." The ends may be the same despite diverse justifications of means.

But things are quite different in the second "system" that the empirical studies reveal. This system is characterized by offenses of relatively low seriousness (such as larceny, minor assault, forgery), crimes committed by first time offenders, and crimes between nonstrangers. Here the exhibition of discretion is vast. Here too, alternatives to full processing are sought continuously; effort is expended to rid the criminal justice system of these cases everywhere and any way that ingenuity can devise. Victims disproportionately fail to report them to the police; and police choose not to arrest, prosecutors not to charge, and judges to apply less severe sanctions.

It is within this "system" that factors other than the three mentioned so far play a larger role in decisionmaking. As the reviews of empirical studies in earlier chapters have shown, when the offense is less serious, characteristics of the decisionmaker (for example, attitudes) and of the situation (such as complainant's preference) and "extralegal" characteristics (including race and demeanor) have a greater influence on the decision.[9] No doubt a part of the influence of these variables is a result of the desire by some to pursue alternatives to full processing when possible. Part may be assumed to be inconsistency due to a lack of explicit guidelines designed to enhance evenhandedness among individual decisionmakers. Part may indeed result from the use of invidious decision criteria. It is within this second system that the challenge to control discretion is the greatest and for which the competition among the commonly held decision goals may be both most legitimate and most consequential.

We do not assert that the proper classification of cases into these two systems inevitably occurs. Which events or persons should be dealt with by full and formal processing in the criminal justice system and which events should be the object of a vigorous pursuit of alternatives is largely a matter of values. Nor do we believe that the first "system" is entirely devoid of decisionmaking on the basis of invidious criteria, a circumstance that should be relentlessly guarded against. Thus, we do not assert we have described an optimal state of affairs. Indeed, as we hope the following pages will amply demonstrate, we urge profound changes. What we do assert is that the data now available about the criminal justice process permit this analytical distinction. Although it results in a caricature, it has significant ramifications for conceptualization, research, and, we believe, for modifications of the process.

The Omnipresence of Prediction

Another common feature of every major decision in the criminal justice system is the ubiquitous centrality of prediction.[10] Often hidden, seldom verified, and increasingly denied justifiable relevance, the forecast of future behavioral states (of both persons and the system) is everywhere in evidence. It appears when the police decide that a person should be taken into custody, when the bail judge decides to release pending trial, when the prosecutor applies extra resources to "habitual offenders," when the judge sentences for incapacitation (or for treatment or deterrence), and when the parole board considers "parole risk" in determining length of institutional stay. Goals of these diverse decisionmakers may differ, but the evidence is compelling that they share the common problem of prediction.

Unfortunately, they share common problems *with* prediction as well. The requisites of prediction were discussed in Chapter 1, and therefore they need not be reviewed here. Suffice it to say that in elaborating a model for the enhancement of rationality one must take cognizance of the central role of predictive judgments throughout the system and include mechanisms by which they can be improved. (And it merits saying that those who seek to purge the justice process of predictive decisions scratch only the surface when they focus on sentencing or paroling decisions.) Utilitarian aims lie at the heart of every decision we have discussed. In the pages that follow we outline a defense of their inclusion and a method for their control and improvement.

The Absence of Feedback

The third recurring theme that we see emerging from the empirical literature that we have summarized concerns the acquisition of knowledge by criminal justice decisionmakers. At every decision point in the process, decisionmakers lack the feedback required for consistent decisions and for improvement of their rationality. Two critical forms of feedback are especially noteworthy by their nearly universal absence. The first is information about how colleague decisionmakers (and the individual decisionmakers themselves) have decided similar cases in the past. Police, prosecutors, judges, and parole boards make routine decisions without the systematic provision of such experience. Little else is required for inconsistency. The empirical evidence demonstrates that at every decisionpoint such inconsistency exists. Whenever researchers have attempted to define and measure the concepts of "equally situated offenders" and of "similar outcomes" and to relate them to one another, they repeatedly have found unwarranted variations in outcomes.

The second form of feedback routinely lacking is knowledge concerning the consequences of a decision choice. Given the goal of the decision in an individual case, was it achieved? Did the suspect appear for trial? Was the decision to *nolle prosequi* correct? Was probation an appropriate disposition? The evidence reviewed in this book reveals quite clearly that virtually nowhere are decisionmakers provided with information of this kind, as a routine matter, in order to assist them to improve their decisions. Without such feedback there can be no informed use of experience, which, after all, is the hallmark of learning.

None of these three themes—common decision correlates, the omnipresence of prediction, and the absence of feedback—will startle those familiar with the empirical literature we have summarized. To be sure, exceptions to each may readily be discovered, even within these pages. Yet each warrants reflection and discussion; and each weighs heavily in our proposed model toward the enhancement of rationality, to which we now turn.

TOWARD RATIONALITY

Ten requisites for increased rationality in criminal justice decisionmaking may be derived from the reviews and analyses of the previous chapters. They have to do first with the clarity and consistency of the aims of the criminal justice system. They also concern the adequacy of the available alternatives—that is, of the choices that criminal justice decisionmakers may make. These are matters of resources but also the imagination. Another requisite is that of relevant information on which to base the choices. As we stress repeatedly, mere data are not sufficient; to reduce uncertainty, information is required.

The decisionmaker, besides a clear conception of purposes and in addition to information relevant to their achievement, needs sufficient flexibility—that is, discretion—to use the information in a prudent and humane manner. Some discretion is necessary for the attainment of aims that relate actions in individual cases to actions in other cases. This requires, in turn, a differentiation of policy and case decisionmaking. Moreover, it calls for explicit statements of policy at each decision point, including standards, rules, and procedures for both policy and individual decisions. The next requisite is that of feedback systems, concerning the application of both general policy and individual decision rules, in order that modifications may be made rationally on the basis of experience. In relation to each of these requirements, there is a need for improved measurement and classification. The final requisite (of the ten proposed) is that of an evolutionary system of policy and case decisionmaking, monitoring, feedback, revision, and a repetition of this cycle—rather, a spiral of such cycles. The ten requisites will first be summarized briefly; then each will be reviewed in relation to some issues and evidence discussed in previous chapters. The requisites are:

- Clear, consistent aims,
- Adequate alternatives,
- Relevant information,
- Flexible decision structures,
- Controlled discretion,
- Differentiation of policy and case decisions,
- Explicit policy and decision rules,
- Feedback systems,
- Adequate measurement and classification, and
- Evolutionary processes.

Clear, Consistent Aims

Are the purposes of victims, police, judges, and correctional officials or of the citizenry as a whole so diverse and conflicting that an increased clarity of internally consistent aims, with adequate consensus, is beyond reach? We think not.

The increased conceptual clarity needed requires, ideally, the development of an adequate theory of criminal justice, integrating the diverse perspectives of the presently fragmented system into a philosophically sound, internally consistent, morally justifiable whole that would allow, and indeed enhance, the learning from experience that is the *sine qua non* of science. No such theory is available. None may be expected soon. Nonetheless, apparently contradictory purposes leap out to call for a resolution, and a start must be made. The research we have reviewed in the previous chapters is, we believe, a foundation for an attempt at such a resolution. The often apparently conflicting purposes of the victim, the police, the prosecutor, the judge, the warden, and the parole board member also have a good deal in common. Thus, we may identify shared or similar objectives; and if a sound means may be found for reconciling the fundamental points of conflict, a beginning will have been made.

The objectives of the victim in deciding whether or not to report a crime are of central interest for two reasons. First, we have stressed what seems to be an obvious but nevertheless often overlooked importance of the victim's decision: the victim is the principal gatekeeper of the system. Second, it may be assumed that the purposes of the victim may reflect general societal attitudes, beliefs, and values concerning criminal justice. Granted some probable distortion from personal investment, the victim's purpose still may reflect widely held citizen views of justice, of fairness, of equity, of incapacitation, of treatment, of deserved punishment, or of deterrence. Although these victim decisions have not been carefully studied to the extent deserved by their centrality, some evidence on victims' purposes is available.

We know, for example, that victims often decide not to report crimes, that there are marked differences in reporting by type of crime, and that the most commonly given reasons for not reporting have been that "nothing could be done" or that it was "not important enough." The first reason may be interpreted as a commentary on a perceived inefficiency and ineffectiveness of the system; the second is related to the concept of seriousness. Generally, the greater the gravity of the harm, the greater the likelihood that the victim will report the crime. Little is known (and what is known is largely from studies of particular types of crime) about the motivation or purposes of the victim when the crime is reported. But it appears from these studies that (in addition to personal utilitarian reasons) victims have many concerns similar to those expressed by later actors in the drama—for example, crime prevention (through deterrence or incapacitation, sometimes through treatment, or restitution or retribution) or the imposition of deserved punishment. Salient features of what is known about victims' purposes are thus that the gravity of the offense is a principal dimension of concern and that aside from personal (idiosyncratic) utilities, the major utilitarian and desert goals of the system appear to be reflected in decisions whether or not to report crimes.

The purposes of the police, when effecting an arrest, embody the utilitarian aims as well as that of desert. A principal concern in deciding to arrest is the need for custody, a need that certainly could encompass the goals of crime reduction. The arrest decision, it should be recalled, is one component of the order maintenance function of daily policing.

As with victim decisions, the research suggests that offense seriousness is a major determinant in police decisions to arrest. So too is the victim-offender relationship and the complainant's preference concerning arrest. It was argued in Chapter 3 that such criteria may reflect each of the common aims of treatment, deterrence, incapacitation, and desert, in alternative circumstances.

Certainly, it cannot be argued that an arrest should be made in the absence of desert consideration; the probable cause standard reflects such a concern. But given alternative mechanisms for invoking the criminal law—such as summonses and citations—neither can it be argued that desert considerations *per se* indicate any need for custody before trial. Rather, custody functions of arrest decisions are viewed appropriately as being in pursuit of utilitarian aims (for example, to ensure the availability for further processing or to facilitate investigatory activities). It was found also that the decision to arrest may be made to accomplish temporary incapacitative aims: the cessation of an ongoing victimization is an example. And arrests often are made with treatment aims; the chronic inebriate may be a case in point.

Prosecution decisions to charge are influenced greatly by the weight of the evidence against the accused. To a lesser extent, the seriousness of the offense plays a role, yet not as significant a role as does the victim-offender relationship, judging from the studies reviewed in Chapter 5.

Although the use of the factor "weight of the evidence" is clearly commensurate with the personal utilitarian goals of prosecutors (for example, establishing a "winning record"), it may clearly be suitable to desert aims as well. Repeatedly in Chapter 5 we found that prosecutors failed to prosecute unless they themselves were convinced of guilt. Beyond a concern for desert, however, the utilitarian aims of treatment, incapacitation, and deterrence were also in evidence in the charging decision. Emphasis on "habitual offenders" implies as much, as does the weight given to estimates of future crime risk in the emerging automated charging systems.

Pretrial release decisions by the courts highlight conflicting but widely supported goals of the entire system—namely, the preservation of liberty and community protection. Controversy in this area, like that concerning both sentencing and parole, centers especially on issues of prediction. The latter involves a fundamental issue of justice: May confinement be justified by what a person may do rather than what he has done?

In the case of the avowed purpose of pretrial decisions, one objective appears to be clear and uncontroversial. This is the purpose of ensuring the appearance of the accused at trial. A second implicit but often denied purpose, with questionable (but yet undecided) legality, is confinement before conviction for incapacitation. The use of pretrial detention for the purpose of punishment, however, is clearly unconstitutional. Thus, the salient aim of pretrial decisions is to provide assurance that the defendant is present for trial. The incapacitative aim raises numerous moral issues and is of doubtful legal justifiability; the punishment aim is not permissible. (If the incapacitative aim is found to be morally defensible and legally justifiable, this will not necessarily be inconsistent with the general model that we shall propose, as discussed in a later section.)

It was argued earlier that the purposes of the sentencing decision lie at the hub of the entire criminal justice system. The utilitarian aims of deterrence, of incapacitation, and of treatment have been contrasted with the morally based purpose of just desert. Are these two radically opposed orientations irreconcilable?

Morris, in a helpful discussion of sentencing aims, has distinguished among three types of principles of justice. He termed these defining, limiting, and guiding.[11] The limiting and guiding types of principle may be contrasted with the precisely fixed punishment that would stem from the application of a defining principle. Concerning limiting principles, he stated that he meant one that, "though it would rarely tell us the exact sanction to be imposed, . . . would give us the outer limits of leniency and severity which should not be exceeded. Desert, I will submit, is such a limiting principle."[12]

If this concept is accepted—that is, if the aims of just desert are considered to provide the justifiable lower and upper bounds of the severity of sanctions to be imposed, but only that—then utilitarian aims may be sought within those limits. As Morris went on to say:

The concept of "just desert" sets the maximum and minimum of the sentence that may be imposed for any offense and helps to define the punishment relations between offenses; it does not give any more fine tuning to the appropriate sentence than that. The fine tuning is to be done on utilitarian principles.[13]

By a guiding principle, Morris meant "only a general value which should be respected unless other values sufficiently strongly justify its rejection in any given case."[14] He asserted that equality is such a guiding principle. (Although he did not say so, we would submit that the use of sentencing guidelines models, so far as their purpose is achievement of greater equity within a system permitting of deviation, is consistent with this conception of equality as a guiding principle.)

According to utilitarian principles, how can the "fine tuning" suggested by Morris take place? A general model may be proposed in which this and other aims may be achieved. This model incorporates, however, the requisites for more rational decisionmaking that remain to be discussed. Its beginning point is to recognize that not all criminal justice functionaries (that is, police, prosecutors, judges, correctional administrators, and paroling authorities) must necessarily address the same aims, nor need it be assumed that they must given the same weight to the various systemwide goals.

Thus, the model proposed is based in part on the concept of a division of labor, especially among legislative decisionmakers, prosecutors, the judiciary, correctional administrators, and paroling authorities. Next, it assumes that a gradual reduction in discretion, as the offender is "processed" through the various stages of decisionmaking, may have merit. Third, it is based on the concepts of explicit policy, guidelines models, feedback systems, and evolutionary processes.

What is the appropriate "division of labor" suggested? Is a different emphasis on the various aims of the criminal law warranted at different stages?

Legislators may well be interested not only in the desert aims, but in those of deterrence, incapacitation, and treatment. But perhaps the emphasis given in prescribing sanctions ought to be on desert principles—employing this concept as a limiting principle. Thus, in this model a principal function of the legislative decisionmakers is to determine both the least penalty necessary in order that the gravity of the harm not be depreciated and the maximum sanction that may be imposed as deserved for the crime. This suggests, of course, a presumptive sentencing model, but one with some degree of "indeterminacy" at the legislative stage. If the legislature were to prescribe requirements for modification due to specific aggravating (for example, prior criminal record) or mitigating (for example, lessened culpability) factors, this would not be inconsistent, so long as these were related to the concept of deserved punishment. Neither would it be inconsistent if the least severe penalty perceived to be necessary were none.

Note that giving the emphasis to the aim of determining, within general bounds, the justifiable limits of deserved punishment does not in any way preclude the legislature from prescribing further procedures for the "fine tuning" necessary for utilitarian aims or from requiring the specific consideration of other factors later in the criminal justice decision process. Let us test whether the concept is sound in reference to the utilitarian purposes. Ought the legislature, in setting the limits of punishment, emphasize desert aims? Should they take account of treatment, incapacitation, and deterrence aims?

There seems to be widespread agreement that a person ought not to be sent to jail or prison for a treatment purpose. This view does not require any diminished efforts toward rehabilitation in confinement when incarceration is deemed to be required; it merely asserts that imprisonment is punishment no matter what it is called and that a perceived need for treatment does not justify punishment. Judge Marvin E. Frankel described this view in these terms:

> The court agrees that this defendant should not be sent to prison for "rehabilitation." Apart from the patent inappositeness of the concept to this individual, this court shares the growing understanding that no one should ever be sent to prison *for rehabilitation.* That is to say, nobody who would not otherwise be locked up should suffer that fate on the incongruous premise that it will be good for him or her. Facing that simple reality should help us to be civilized. It is less agreeable to confine someone when we deem it an affliction rather than a benefaction. If someone must be imprisoned—for other, valid reasons—we should seek to make rehabilitative resources available to him or her. But the goal of rehabilitation cannot fairly serve in itself as grounds for the sentencing to confinement.[15]

Thus, there may be no necessary conflict between the desert aim, if it is regarded as a limiting principle only, and the aim of voluntary, noncoercive treatment.

Similarly, there may be no necessary conflict between desert, considered as setting general bounds of deserved punishment, and the traditional aims of incapacitation and of deterrence. Many will argue that a person may not justifiably be punished for the sole purpose of deterring others. Similarly, many will assert that it is justifiable to punish only for that which has been done and therefore not permissible to punish solely to prevent expected offenses that may or may not occur. *But these arguments do not imply that these objectives are not justifiable if sought within the limits of deserved punishment.* This is merely to argue that few, we expect, would claim that a person may not be punished in order to deter others even if he deserves it; nor do we think many would argue that a person may not be confined for what he may do if the confinement is first regarded as deserved in any case.

This general argument suggests, in very broad outline, appropriate roles for the legislature, the judges, and the paroling authorities. The legislature, in prescribing sanctions for crime, may reasonably be expected to establish the limits of punishment, principally from a desert perspective. The legislature would state the penalties above and below which punishment is deemed too much or too little to meet the criteria of proportionality of crime seriousness and sanction. According to our assessment, this does not imply that they may not state, as general purposes to be served by sentencing, the utilitarian aims that we have discussed. Given these legislatively fixed parameters, both the courts and the paroling authorities may—and we believe should—develop explicit policy models utilizing guidelines in systems for more rational control and development of decisionmaking.

In such models, the aims of the judiciary, concerning both desert and utilitarian purposes, need not conflict. Even with respect to desert, the "fine tuning" suggested in the just cited statement by Morris may be done in part by the judges. In this respect, it should be noted that guideline models for sentencing have usually included the seriousness of the offense as a major dimension. When such models include elements of discretion in sentencing, either within the guidelines themselves or by virtue of an ability to sentence outside the usual or expected values or sanctions, then there seems to be no inconsistency in allowing consideration of utilitarian purposes. If the limits of desert have been set by the legislature, the judiciary cannot exceed them.

Purposes of corrections are, as we have seen, extremely diverse. It is in jails and prisons particularly that the hard face of desert confronts the utilitarian aim of treatment. According to our analysis, however, a sentence, whether to confinement or not, by itself satisfies the desert aim. It must, if it is within the limits prescribed as commensurate with the harm done. Within these limits, whatever is done with, for, or to the offender must be justified on other ethical principles and on the basis of the evidence with respect to utilitarian purposes. Thus, it is not necessarily inconsistent to seek, within the requirements of deserved punishment, either deterrence or incapacitation or treatment. In doing so, if rationality is desired, empirical evidence must be the guide.

In this framework, the correctional objectives of security are most directly related to the general goals of desert, incapacitation, and deterrence. All require secure custody when incarceration is the sentence. Thus, it is not surprising that correctional agency personnel ordinarily perceive this as a fundamental objective with a high (perhaps highest) priority. The responsibility for custody, however, stops at the fence of the institution. Beyond the fence there is a responsibility to the larger community, while within it the responsibility is to the welfare of the inmate body. This, of course, includes responsibilities for safety, but also includes a requirement of provision of services, whether medical, psychological, social, educational, or vocational. In part, these may be related to or justified by treatment purposes (that is, by the rehabilitation concept) when that is directed toward crime reduction goals. In part, however, such services may also be justified by objectives not necessarily related to crime reduction. If the desert aim is satisfied by incarceration and only incarceration (or other sentence), it may indeed be argued that a further deprivation of such services as are available to the free community goes beyond the limits of deserved punishment and therefore is unjust.

In addition, of course, it is clear that services offered in prison or jail need not be evaluated or assessed only in terms of crime prevention aims. If the purpose of educational programs is to promote learning, the evaluation of the program must be based principally on whether and to what extent learning occurs. If the education program were to reduce recidivism as well, then that clearly could be a welcome bonus. The evaluation of vocational training surely should be based, at least in large part, on the future work careers of persons exposed to the training. The evaluation of psychotherapy ought to rely mainly on measures of mental health. This is not to argue that linkages between such program objectives and the more general aims of crime reduction should not be sought; rather, it is to argue that that is not necessarily a sole concern or even a necessary one.

In community corrections, the emphasis on custody (now termed surveillance) is lessened by the very nature of the enterprise, and the treatment aim is paramount. Indeed, were the surveillance functions of probation and parole to be turned over to the police, whose objectives clearly include the detection of crime as a central feature, this would not be inconsistent. Similar to correctional programs in confinement, the services provided probationers and parolees may be evaluated in part by crime reduction considerations but also in terms of other objectives of similar social services.

The aims of paroling authorities and those of the judiciary are strikingly similar, although different terms for central concepts tend to be used. Judges assign deserved punishments or exact retribution; parole boards apply sanctions. Judges seek rehabilitation; parole boards seek treatment. Judges seek due process, procedural regularity, equity; so do parole boards. Judges seek incapacitation; parole boards are also concerned with estimation of risk and seek to apply controls to prevent further criminal acts. The judge seeks deterrence; the parole board member may adopt in part a "citizen" frame of reference concerned with maintenance of the social order. The judge is concerned with equity, in part persuaded by the potential effects of unwarranted disparities on the populations of prisons; the parole board member, part "regulator," may have the same concerns.

Generally, then, a set of purposes of the criminal justice system may be outlined within a framework in which much of the apparent inconsistency of aims of the various parts is eliminated or at least reduced. The principal difficulty heretofore has been the assumption that desert is a defining principle. If it is not, but rather can only set limits to the punishments that must be exacted, then within those limits there is still considerable potential for the achievement of utilitarian purposes.

When general goals have been defined adequately, then it may be expected that specific objectives en route to them may be defined as well. Much work remains to be done to more adequately specify such objectives and operational definitions of them, and these concerns are discussed in a later section of this chapter. No matter how clear the objectives, however, and no matter how informative in relation to them the data, there is no decision problem without alternative courses of action available to the decisionmaker. We turn next to an examination of alternatives.

Adequate Alternatives

The alternatives that are available to decisionmakers in the criminal justice system have one outstanding feature—one that gives excitement and challenge to the entire decisionmaking fabric. It is the feature that calls out for creativity and the one that reveals the philosophical bent, attitudes, and beliefs of decisionmakers. This notable feature is that alternatives are invented.

The whole system, of course, has been invented in a rather chaotic and haphazard process of evolution as society's leaders have sought to provide a system of justice and to control crime. Thus, police, courts, and jails came into being—and more recently parole and probation. These are major structures, and it may appear that they are now relatively fixed, setting the parameters within which criminal justice decisionmaking must henceforth be expected to take place. Not so: these structures themselves are still in a process of evolution. Much current debate, for example, centers upon issues of the appropriate role of legislation in prescribing the operation of the rest of the system; on the best division of labor of the courts in respect to criminal trials versus other mechanisms for dispute resolution; on concepts of neighborhood justice centers to deal with disputes by means other than the criminal law and the courts; on the role of the police between service and law enforcement functions; and on whether the paroling function should be retained.

Although we quote Parmenides at the start of this chapter to warn the reader that we now offer more mere opinion than in earlier chapters, it is Heraclitus' concept of change we now discuss. Parmenides, it may be recalled, denied the existence of change: only the present exists. In sharp contrast, Heraclitus believed in perpetual change: the world is a wonderful, enormous process in which "You could not step twice in the same river; for other and yet other rivers are flowing on."[16]

Fortunately for science, we may assume that change occurs slowly. If not, we could not find relations sufficiently stable over time that they may reasonably be depended upon. In the cases of decisionmaking structures, we could not identify stable relations among goals, alternatives, and information. Thus, we must expect change but we may expect also to find reasonably stable relations. At the same time we must be alert to system change, be prepared to evaluate rigorously the consequences of change, and regard what is "known" with a healthy skepticism.

Within the criminal justice system as now structured, even without major design changes (such as the abolition of paroling decisions), there is ample room for creation of alternatives to decisions. Examples of recent ones abound at every criminal justice decision point discussed in earlier chapters.

Assistance center programs for victims and witnesses and police community relations efforts may increase the tendency of citizens to report crimes or to seek police assistance in their problems without the invocation of the criminal justice system. The alternatives of the police were markedly changed when, largely through the efforts of one judge in New York City, a policy decision that drunks who were not disorderly would no longer be arrested was made by the police commissioner.[17] An alternative was invented: a shelter and voluntary detoxification unit was established.[18]

Expanded use of the summons and of citations, in lieu of arrest, provide further examples of new alternatives. The recent development and expanded use of release on recognizance, discussed in Chapter 4, which markedly changed judicial pretrial release decision options, provides a dramatic example of change alternatives available for those decisions.

If probation as an alternative sentence available to the judge does not exist for misdemeanor offenders, as is the case in about two-thirds of the nation's lower courts,[19] it is possible that the availability of this alternative disposition may become more common. An expanded use of restitution and of community service as sanctions explicitly permissible might increase similarly the diversity of sentences that judges may select. Alternatively, the range of alternatives available to the prosecutor—as with pretrial intervention and supervision programs in some jurisdictions—may be increased.

The nature of alternatives available to corrections administrators is directly related to the degree of creativity exercised by them in program planning and development. Within institutions, a great variety of educational, vocational, work, counseling, and therapy programs have been developed in some settings; in others, work may be the only program provided. The development of halfway house programs, of school and work furlough programs, and of other placement alternatives designed to assist in the transition from confinement to life in the wider community provide other examples.

Thus, the development of alternatives may provide essential steps toward a more rational criminal justice system; but clearly, the invention of such alternatives is not enough. Providing other choices does not ensure progress. The police officer, the prosecutor, or the judge may have a wider selection of optional decision outcomes, but this does not yet mean that anything has been learned and does not give assurance of more effective decisions. If the choices are to be made rationally, that implies the presence of information such that the selections increase the likelihood of movement toward goals. This suggests, of course, the need for rigorous evaluations of the consequences of the new alternatives when they are put into place. In order for such evaluations to be most useful, new programs must be accompanied by a clear, explicit statement of the program's objectives; clear descriptions of the programs themselves not only as designed or intended but as actually implemented in practice; and the use of careful procedures to test whether and to what extent the integrity of the plan was maintained and the objectives were achieved.

Thus, our use of the term "adequate alternatives" as a requisite toward more rational decisionmaking implies not only the need for choices but of provision for informative evaluations of the consequences of selection of that option. Without this provision, we are not likely to increase the information available to the decisionmaker.

Relevant Information
A fundamental thesis of this book is that knowledge that an alternative choice exists does not by itself provide the decisionmaker with information. That is, the availability of the alternative does not reduce his or her uncertainty about the probable consequences of the selection; that requires knowledge also of the relation of the choice to the decision objective. This is a principal reason for the need for program evaluation at each stage in the criminal justice processes, and it is why such research is critical to the improvement of individual decisionmaking.

The general problem of program evaluation is a very large and complex one. Generally, however, it may be said that either experimental or quasi-experimental (statistical) designs are used with the aim of determining how much, if any, of the variance in outcomes (that is, consequences related to objectives) may be attributed reasonably to the program under study. This is the kind of information needed by the decisionmaker, and each available alternative should be assessed in this way.

This circumstance exists at each stage of the criminal justice system. The victim of crime must assess the likely consequences of reporting it, and on this assessment rests the principal trigger event for activating the rest of the process. The police officer needs to know the expected consequences of arrest versus citation versus summons, and the estimate should be based on systematic study rather than guesswork. The judge needs to know, from empirical study, the likelihood that the offender will appear for trial if released on his or her own recognizance. The juvenile judge needs to know, from the evidence after follow-up study, whether detention versus foster home placement makes any difference in the probability of later delinquency. The prosecutor needs to know, from examination of prior cases, how assessments of offense seriousness, of the weight of the evidence, of the probability of winning the case, and of prior criminality may best be used in setting priorities for prosecution. The judge of the criminal court needs to know empirically whether placement on probation, in jail, or a combination changes the probabilities of future crimes, compared with other alternatives. The probation officer needs to know whether persons placed in treatment category A will respond better or worse than persons placed in category B. The classification committee in the prison reception center needs to be aware, from follow-up study, of the probable consequences of their placements.

These examples only hint at the complexity of the general problem. Before much progress can be made in rigorously examining the interrelated decisions along the continuum from arrest of offenders to their final discharge, we will need reliable, comparable data about the persons involved, the decisions made about them, and a wide range of consequences of these decisions. Thus, there is a pressing need for data that are uniformly collected along this continuum. Then we can begin to examine consequences of decisions in one sector upon other justice areas and to provide administrators with the tools necessary for their policies and programs.

In order to make a start toward dealing adequately with this complexity and begin to improve the information available to guide decisions, systems are needed that meet three fundamental requirements:

1. Agency information systems are needed, with sufficient sophistication to permit program evaluation feedback routinely.
2. Since it is not feasible to provide such feedback routinely from experimental designs for all alternatives of concern, the systems developed must provide for statistical control of nontreatment variables related to outcome.
3. The integrated nature of the criminal justice system is such that the necessary feedback can be obtained only by the coordination of each agency's components.

In developing such systems, the interrelated nature of the concepts of diagnosis, classification, and prediction must be recognized (as discussed in Chapter 1). Diagnostic data must be assessed to determine their utility for classifications demonstrably relevant to treatment placement. The criterion of relevancy is the proportion of variance in outcomes that is associated with treatment for specific groups of persons. Prediction methods must be developed and tested to provide the means for statistical control of nuisance variables in the feedback-reporting system.

Such a system would have much potential for both scientific and practical contributions. It could provide a general framework for adding to knowledge about the relative effectiveness of programs in achieving specified objectives for various classifications of offenders. At the same time, the decisionmakers could be advised routinely, from experience, of the probable outcomes of their alternative decision choices. It also could provide a basis for feedback from parts of the system that deal with a later phase of the process to those that occur earlier. The police need information on the results of their decisions: these data must be obtained from prosecutors, judges, and corrections. The judge needs feedback on the results of sentencing: these data must come from the probation, prison, and parole agencies.

These arguments are related to issues of efficiency and effectiveness with respect to utilitarian goals. What of other justice concerns? Such a system cannot define justice, but it can provide information necessary for addressing concerns such as desert and equity. Throughout the justice system, the data should be available to permit fairness comparisons for various classifications of offenders.

Simple decision processes or rules that fail to deal with the complexity of behavior are inadequate. Hence, some flexibility in decision processes (that is, some discretion for the decisionmaker) is needed. Can discretion be controlled, or is that a contradiction in terms? We assert that both flexibility and control are additional requisites toward more rational decisions.

Flexibility

A problem frequently encountered with specific decisionmaking policy is that it does not always fit the individual case. Indeed, the arguments against any general policy often have invoked the concept of the uniqueness of the individual, with the argument that such uniqueness implies that no general institutional policy can be formulated to specify adequately the "best" choice in individual cases. The argument overlooks, of course, that no individual case is entirely unique and also that in dealing with the unique factors of the individual case there can be no experience to guide in making the decision. Some persons who argue forcefully against any classifications of persons on grounds of uniqueness often also argue that for case decisionmaking, it is experience that counts—and fail to perceive the error in logic. Yet the diversity of cases—in nature and circumstances of offenses, in offenders, and in resources available—is indeed extensive. Decisionmaking structures are needed that are sufficiently flexible to permit reasonable responsiveness to this diversity. The policy control methods using guideline models, as discussed in Chapters 6 and 9, appear to be useful because they permit deviation and indeed because it is the deviations that enable the system to provide a learning process.

Discretionary Control

Even though some discretion (that is, flexibility) is required in the decisions discussed in this book, adequate mechanisms for control of the exercise of that discretion is also a requisite for more rational decisionmaking. If discretion implies a lack of control—that is, the freedom to choose from among available alternatives completely unfettered by constraints of law or policy—then the idea of "controlled discretion" may seem to be a self-contradiction. But discretion can be limited, depending upon circumstances, in such a way as to provide considerable freedom within constraints of policy—and this is what is meant here by "controlled discretion."

Consider the paroling and sentencing policy and guidelines models as described in Chapters 6 and 9. In each, there are two levels at which discretion may be (and is expected to be) exercised consistently with an articulated policy. First, the parole hearing examiner, commission member, or judge has some limited discretion within the guidelines themselves. For example, the judge considering the sentence for a Felony 4 offense, using the guidelines shown as Figure 6-3, may find that the offense score (for seriousness) is five and the offender score is nine. The guidelines indicate the policy position that the usual sentence is confinement, with an indeterminate minimum and a three to four year maximum. The guidelines have set some constraints within the bounds of the legislatively prescribed sentence, which in the case of the jurisdiction in question has set the maximum sentence at ten years for Felony 4 sentences. The structure does not include the setting of a minimum sentence by the court. Therefore, in the absence of guidelines or similar court policy, the judge might select any maximum sentence between no incarceration and ten years in confinement. The constraint provided by the guidelines, however, is twofold. First, the judge is made aware that the policy of the court, for cases similar to this one (on the factors considered by the court to be most commonly relevant), is that incarceration be required and, further, that the maximum be fixed between three and four years. Second, although the judge may deviate from the usually expected sentence, if that is done, then explicit written reasons are required. Thus there are the two levels of discretion: The first is a limited degree of choice within the guidelines. The second is within the legislatively prescribed boundaries, but outside the guidelines. In the second level there is a further control—that of requiring reasons for deviation. It is this feature that permits, and indeed may enhance, the judges' ability to learn from experience in application of the guidelines. The deviations and reasons are important elements in the feedback system that is essential to the rational review and assessment of the guidelines system.

If unfettered discretion is an ill, but some discretion is a value, then perhaps the decisionmakers involved may thus fetter their own area of discretion. This could occur in a reasonable way that does not completely bind them within a smaller scope of choices than permitted by the appropriate legal structure. Indeed, "fettered" is too strong a word for the constraints of the guidelines as described here; they do not shackle, but they do add a degree of constraint.

Differentiation of Policy and Case Decisions

Implicit in much of the discussion in this book is the need for a clear distinction between decisions of general institutional policy and individual case decisionmaking. Some decisions are made, in any agency, that provide a general framework within which decisions about persons are made. Examples of policy decisions would include decisions to develop or to implement decision guidelines of the type discussed in the previous section. Similarly, the structure of the guidelines, the admissible information for consideration within the model, and the permissible ranges of decision outcomes all are matters of policy. They are not directed specifically with respect to any individual person. The police commissioner may set rules for the use of citations versus arrest; the prosecutor may issue directives to prosecutorial staff as to the selection of cases for prosecution; the administrative office of the courts may establish guides for bail amounts; the jail superintendent may require screening procedures to identify inmates for suicide prevention; the director of corrections may define criteria for differential assignment to levels of custody; the probation officer may devise rules for assignment of probationers to differing levels of supervision. These policy decisions establish the context within which the individual decisions are made.

Although this distinction may seem obvious, it is clear that it is not apparent to all and that, indeed, decisionmakers may not always readily agree that a general policy exists concerning their decisions. They may assert not only that no general policy exists but that this is a value. This may be expected particularly when the concept of a general policy is seen as in conflict with an aim of individualized decisionmaking within which each decision is assumed to be made on the merits of each individual (and unique) case. As shown by the reviews in the previous chapters, however, experience demonstrates that analyses of decisions may be expected to reveal an implicit policy even in such instances. It may be asserted that the implicit policy, if made explicit, may afford a greater degree of control and, hence, an increased opportunity for attaining a greater degree of rationality. Individual uniqueness may not be denied, but the fact of uniqueness should not be a straw man set up to hide either unwritten, merely implicit policy or sloppy procedures conducive to bias and unfair treatment in decisionmaking. People are, in some respects, all different; and in some ways they are similar to others and may be classified into groups; and in other ways, they are all alike. The establishment of general policies requires use of the facts of similarities—that is, the use of classification. Individual differences, even after such classifications have been established, require some opportunity for the exercise of discretion.

Thus, it may be assumed that neither the language of the law nor general policy statements can differentiate persons and criminal acts to such a degree that the infinite variety of offenders and offenses will be described adequately for all decision situations. *No matter how clear the law, no matter how explicit the policy, some interpretive functions are required in decisionmaking by the complexity and variety of the persons and behaviors concerned.* At some point there must be provision for consideration of the individuality of the offender and the idiosyncratic nature of the criminal act.

Explicit Policy

Discretion is needed in order to provide an opportunity for the diverse response that is required by the variety of persons, acts, alternatives, and objectives of a given criminal justice decision. The improved rationality in decisionmaking that is sought, however—as well as fairness—requires clear statements of established policy within which that discretion is to be exercised. Otherwise, there is no general guide for examination of the consequences of the decisions made and no avenue toward increased effectiveness of the general pattern of decisionmaking. Thus, there is no mechanism for utilization of information discovered to be relevant to the achievement of the criminal justice goals.

Examples have been provided in this book, in the areas of sentencing and paroling, of the development of more explicit policy. It is not asserted that these examples suggest the only means for development of decision policy models. It may be claimed, however, that there are values present in the decisionmaking processes of the jurisdictions studied that were not present before the development of policy guidelines. The procedures are more clear, and the nature of the information used is revealed. Hence they may be debated on ethical or scientific grounds; the process is more open to review and criticism; and the increased articulation of the bases for decisions sets the stage for assessment with respect to the decision objectives. In order that such assessment may be accomplished, feedback systems are needed to inform the policymakers of the actual use of the model.

Feedback Systems

The development of adequate feedback systems, which are also claimed to be a requisite to more rational planning, policy formulation, policy review, and individual case decisionmaking, requires coordinated research and management operations. Models for decisionmaking (for example, the guidelines systems previously discussed) may be developed through a collaboration of research workers and those responsible for and actively engaged in the decisions. The collaboration is initially important at the first step of problem formulation and analysis.

We have seen in this book that the objectives of decisions may not always be readily defined and that they may vary over differing points in the criminal justice decision process and over jurisdictions (or among decisionmakers in one jurisdiction). Furthermore, they may be in conflict. A first step in research and operational collaboration is to clarify the objectives of the decision and to define how these are to be measured. This, of course, is critical to the later assessment of both the policy model to be devised and the individual decisions taken, with or without the model.

Similarly, we have seen that available alternatives differ among jurisdictions, legal structures, and available resources. These too need to be defined, from observations of the decisions or from discussions with the decisionmakers. Also, the data resources providing information relevant to the decisions may vary markedly among criminal justice decision problems. These need to be identified as well—or possibly, they need to be created.

Either a descriptive analysis of the decisions or hypothesis testing about them requires a research function that may enable the invention, guided by the empirical results, of a tentative model of the decision. This calls for further collaboration by the decision-makers themselves and the research staff, possible revision, and a test of the model in order to determine how well it "fits" as a description of the present decision processes. The policy model may be implemented in practice when it is acceptable to the decisionmakers. The research operation may proceed to examine the implications of the model, while the operational monitoring of its use sets the stage for further examination and possible revision.

Thus, a policy development, implementation, examination, and revision cycle may be established in which a process of repeated examination and revision is a central feature. An evolutionary process has been designed that is a requisite to more rational policy development.

A second evolutionary process, distinct from that just described but related to it, is also essential. It has to do with the utilitarian aims of the criminal justice system and the central issues of effectiveness in achieving those crime control purposes.

We have found it necessary to assert repeatedly throughout this book that demonstrably relevant information with respect to the utilitarian aims of treatment, deterrence, and incapacitation is simply not available to guide decisions toward greater rationality. This lack is not a function of unavailable technology; procedures for assessing relevance are available. It is not a result of inability to conceptualize the problem adequately: the utilitarian aims are reasonably clear and may be readily defined. It is not due to inadequate funding of the criminal justice system: large sums are spent annually to detect, arrest, convict, confine or supervise offenders against the law. It is not due to a lack of caring: the public and criminal justice functionaries alike decry the ineffectiveness of present crime control measures. Rather, it is due to a lack of data, information systems, and analyses adequate to the task of informing decisionmakers, through feedback systems. Only with such feedback systems can there be an increase in the rationality of decisionmaking.

Decisionmakers throughout the criminal justice process have in common that they all make decisions about offenders against the law. What they share in addition is a frustrating lack of feedback on the consequences of their decisions. Although it has been known for half a century that learning does not occur in the absence of knowledge of the results of one's actions, adequate information systems have not yet been developed to provide such feedback.

Individual-based tracking systems are needed to enable the adequate follow-up and analyses of offenders and of decisions affecting their placement, from start to finish, in the criminal justice process.

Some good starts toward such a system have been made, and we have described some of them elsewhere.[20] But the necessary integrated system of accounting that could provide a sound basis in reliable data to permit the needed analyses has not yet been developed.

When the decisionmaking processes discussed in this book are viewed in the context of a system, the importance of the critical concepts, discussed by Klein, of system rates and system determinants are apparent.[21] System rates may refer, in part, to objectives of decisions at each of the major decision points we have discussed. System determinants are the data elements that provide information in the sense used in this book. Only with a unified, interfaced system of data collection throughout the process can we measure system rates and conduct the analyses needed to identify system determinants. Only on the basis of such a system can policymakers and individual case decisionmakers be informed adequately of the likely consequences of their decisions with respect to the objectives of the decisions. Such a system, in order to be most useful, must deal also with some critical problems of measurement that as yet have been addressed only crudely in the criminal justice system.

Adequate Measurement

A first illustration of the yet unshaped state of the measurement art in criminal justice may be given by pointing to the concept of offense seriousness. The idea that criminal acts vary in seriousness has appeared in each of the chapters of this book as a concept that provides an important dimension to many critical criminal justice decisions. Variation in seriousness of the offense seems to be an important factor for understanding the gatekeeping decisions of victims as to whether or not to invoke the criminal justice process. It appears to be a key consideration in the decisionmaking of police, judges, corrections administrators, and parole boards. Yet only crude measures, based on assumptions that may be questioned, are available for its assessment. It is true that a reasonable consensus may be obtained at least to provide a simple ordinal scale of judged seriousness. Work from scaling efforts to provide a weighted linear scale also may be applied. But the unidimensionality of the seriousness concept may be questioned; and the assumptions of linearity and additivity present in available scales may not be supported if examined critically.[22] The point to be stressed here is simply that, considering the apparent central importance of the concept, the best and the most careful application of available psychophysical methods should be applied to improve the needed tools of measurement.

A related concept, equally important to decisionmaking in criminal justice (and especially sentencing and paroling), is that of severity of sanctions. In the case of this concept, measurement is still more primitive than that concerning the seriousness of offense. Until more adequate measures are available, the lofty concepts and high ideals of requiring sanctions commensurate with the gravity of harm done may gain philosophic acceptance but are certain to be frustrated in application. How can harms and punishments be evaluated adequately if the measurement of both is flawed or primitive?

These are but striking examples. The general problems of measurement, even of key concepts, call for research at every stage of decisionmaking in the criminal justice process. Given the importance and complex purposes of these decisions, it is remarkable that the objectives must still be so crudely measured.

Similarly, the need for development of more useful procedures for offender classifications is apparent. The general problems of what works for deterrence, incapacitation, or treatment may not be solved for decisionmaking until the requisite classification methods have been developed, shown to be demonstrably relevant, and incorporated into routine agency information systems. Work toward improvement of classification for predictive purposes must continue as well. Besides adding potentially relevant information for both policy and individual decisions, such classification tools are needed in order to aid in evaluations of the effectiveness of decisions.

Thus, two types of feedback systems are required: the first to inform policy development and to provide guidance for individual decisions; the second to provide input to the process from a systematic study of the policy decisions and of agency effectiveness. In combination, they can provide the evolutionary process of learning that is needed.

Evolutionary Processes

Both science and criminal justice management must proceed toward a greater rationality by successive approximations. The increased rationality desired is not apt to come by revolution; it can be achieved by evolution. This requires, however, attention to establishing a framework within which acceptable decision processes may evolve and from which gains in knowledge can be made. The process envisioned is a dynamic one, with no firm answers and only partial, perhaps temporary, gains. Its central features are the articulation of problems and of policies, procedures to structure and control decisionmaking while assessing the consequences of alternative actions, repeated analysis of the relations of the alternative choices to the purposes of the decisions, and a continuous search for knowledge to inform those responsible for the entire process.

FRAIL WAND, PROFOUND SPELL

These aspirations toward greater rationality may, at this stage of our ignorance, seem at worst grandiose and at best unfeasible. The requisites listed are easy to recite but exceedingly difficult to achieve. Yet we have asserted (amidst considerable mere opinion) the need mainly for application of scientific methods to the analysis of decisions throughout the criminal justice process. In a world of values and ethics, science may play only a part, but that part may be profound.

PARADOX

Not truth, nor certainty. These I foreswore
In my novitiate, as young men called
To holy orders must abjure the world.
"If . . . , then . . . ," this only I assert;
And my successes are but pretty chains
Linking twin doubts, for it is vain to ask
If what I postulate be justified,
Or what I prove possess the stamp of fact.
Yet bridges stand, and men no longer crawl
In two dimensions. And such triumphs stem
In no small measure from the power this game,
Played with the thrice-attenuated shades
Of things, has over their originals.
How frail the wand, but how profound the spell! [23]

NOTES

1. Parmenides, "On Opinion," cited in M.C. Nahm, ed., *Selections From Early Greek Philosophy* (New York: F.S. Crafts & Co., 1934), p. 117.

2. The empirical support for the assertions that follow is to be found throughout the earlier chapters, to which the reader is referred. To recite all here would be excessively cumbersome.

3. As discussed in Chapter 5, the prosecutor's decision to charge may stand in contrast to the general finding that offense seriousness is a persistent major decisionmaking criterion.

4. As we discuss subsequently, one consequence of the centrality of this empirical finding is that both conceptual and measurement studies with respect to seriousness are a pressing need in future research agendas.

5. The influence of known prior criminal conduct has not been studied in relation to victims' decisions to report a crime.

6. Several desert theorists, most notably von Hirsch, argue that prior criminal conduct does indeed make an offense more blameworthy and thus, from a purely desert point of view, can be a factor legitimately used to increase penalties. This position has been criticized on the grounds that prior record is a characteristic of persons, not acts, and thus is antithetical to the desert perspective. Also, it has been noted that von Hirsch's position to let prior record enhance penalties could provide simply a rationalization for the use of the best predictive data while eschewing any role for prediction in sentencing. See V. O'Leary, M. Gottfredson, and A. Gelman, "Contemporary Sentencing Proposals," *Criminal Law Bulletin* 11:55 (1975); G. Newman, *The Punishment Response* (New York: Lippincott, 1978); A. von Hirsch, *Doing Justice* (New York: Hill and Wang, 1976).

7. See P. Rossi *et al.*, "The Seriousness of Crimes: Normative Structure and Individual Differences," *American Sociological Review* 39:224 (1974).

8. For a comparable distinction predating our own, see J. Vorenberg, "Narrowing the Discretion of Criminal Justice Officials," *Duke Law Journal* 4:65 (1976).

9. We suspect that the controversy in the sociological literature that argues the relative importance of "legal" versus "extralegal" attributes in criminal justice decisions may be resolved by the distinction made here.

10. For insightful discussion of the many issues raised by predictive judgments in the law, see B. Underwood, "Law and the Crystal Ball: Predicting Behavior With Statistical Inference and Individualized Judgment," *Yale Law Journal* 88:1408 (1979).

11. N. Morris, "Punishment, Desert and Rehabilitation," in U.S. Department of Justice, *Equal Justice Under Law*, Bicentennial Lecture Series (Washington, D.C.: Government Printing Office, 1976), pp. 136-65.

12. *Id.* at 141-42.

13. *Id.* at 159.

14. *Id.* at 142.

15. M.E. Frankel, Sentencing Memorandum 75 Cr. 785, U.S. District Court, Southern District of New York, June 17, 1976, as cited in N. Morris, *supra* note 11 at 142-43.

16. Heraclitus, fragment, as quoted in Nahm, *supra* note 1 at 91.

17. L.T. Wilkins and D.M. Gottfredson, *Research, Demonstration and Social Action* (Davis, California: National Council on Crime and Delinquency, 1969), pp. 130-32.

18. *Id.* at 124-25.

19. President's Commission on Law Enforcement and Administration of Justice, *Task Force Report: The Courts* (Washington, D.C.: Government Printing Office, 1967), p. 32.

20. D.M. Gottfredson and M.R. Gottfredson, "Data for Criminal Justice Evaluations: Some Resources and Pitfalls," in M. Klein and K. Teilman, eds., *Handbook of Criminal Justice Evaluation* (Beverly Hills: Sage, 1980).

21. M. Klein, S. Kobrin, A. McEachern, and H. Sigurdson, "System Rates: An Approach to Comprehensive Criminal Justice Planning," *Crime and Delinquency* 17:355 (1971).

22. S. Gottfredson, K. Young, and W. Lauter, "Additivity and Interaction in Offense Seriousness Scales," *Journal of Research in Crime and Delinquency* 17:26 (1980).

23. C. Wylie, Jr., "Paradox," *Scientific Monthly*, 67:63 (1948). Reprinted by permission.

Bibliography

Abrams, N. "Internal Policy: Guiding the Exercise of Prosecutorial Discretion." *U.C.L.A. Law Review* 19:1 (1971).

———. "Prosecutorial Charge Decisions Systems." *University of California Law Review* 21:1 (1975).

Adams, S. "Some Findings From Correctional Caseload Research." *Federal Probation* 31:48 (1967).

Aichhorn, A. *Wayward Youth.* New York: Viking Press, 1938.

Albanese, J.S. "Predicting Probation Outcomes: An Assessment of Critical Issues." In D.M. Gottfredson, J.O. Finckenauer, and C. Rauh, *Probation on Trial,* ch. IV. Newark, New Jersey: School of Criminal Justice, Rutgers University, 1977.

Alexander, G.; M. Glass; P. King; J. Palermo; J. Roberts; and A. Schury. "A Study of the Administration of Bail in New York City." *University of Pennsylvania Law Review* 106:685 (1958).

American Bar Association. *Standards Relating to Pretrial Release.* New York: Institute of Judicial Administration, 1968.

———. *Standards Relating to the Prosecution and the Defense Function.* Approved Draft. New York: Institute for Judicial Administration, 1971.

———. *Standards Relating to the Urban Police Function.* Approved Draft. Chicago, 1973.

American Law Institute. *Model Penal Code.* Philadelphia, 1962.

Angel, A.; E. Green; H. Kaufman; and E. Van Loon. "Preventive Detention: An Empirical Analysis." *Harvard Civil Rights–Civil Liberties Law Review* 6:301 (1971).

Ares, C.; A. Rankin; and H. Sturz. "The Manhattan Bail Project: An Interim Report on the Use of Pre-Trial Parole." *New York University Law Review* 38:67 (1963).

Argyle, M. "A New Approach to the Classification of Delinquents With Implications for Treatment." In Board of Corrections Monograph 2, Sacramento: State of California Printing Division, Documents Section, July 1961.

Asher and Orleans. "Criminal Citation as a Post-Arrest Alternative to Custody for Certain Offenses." Paper cited in M. Berger, "Police Field Citations in New Haven." *Wisconsin Law Review*, 2:382 (1972).

Babst, D.V., and J.W. Mannering. "Probation Versus Imprisonment for Similar Types of Offenders: A Comparison by Subsequent Violators." *Journal of Research in Crime and Delinquency* 2:60 (1965).

Bailey, W.C. "Correctional Outcome: An Evaluation of 100 Reports." *Journal of Criminal Law, Criminology, and Police Science* 57:153–60 (1966).

Ballard, K.B., Jr., and D.M. Gottfredson. *Analysis of Variance and Covariance With Unequal Treatment Groups.* Vacaville, California: Institute for the Study of Crime and Delinquency, 1965.

Banks, E. "Reconviction of Young Offenders." *Current Legal Problems* 17:74 (1964).

Barnes, H. and N. Teeters. *New Horizons in Criminology.* New York: Prentice-Hall, 1950.

Bard, M. *Family Crisis Intervention: From Concept to Implementation.* Washington, D.C.: Government Printing Office, 1974.

_____. *Training Police as Specialists in Family Crisis Intervention.* Washington, D.C.: Government Printing Office, 1970.

Beccaria, C. *On Crimes and Punishments.* 1764; Rpt. Indianapolis: Bobbs-Merrill, 1963.

Beeley, A. *The Bail System in Chicago.* Chicago: University of Chicago Press, 1927.

Bennett, C.A., and N.S. Franklin. *Statistical Analysis in Chemistry and the Chemical Industry.* New York: John Wiley and Sons, 1954.

Bercal, T. "Calls for Police Assistance: Consumer Demands for Governmental Service." *American Behavioral Scientist* 13:681 (1970).

Bernstein, I.; E. Kick; J. Leung; and B. Schulz. "Charge Reduction: An Intermediary Stage in the Process of Labelling Criminal Defendants." *Social Forces* 56:363 (1977).

Bernstein, I.; W. Kelly; and P. Doyle. "Societal Reaction to Deviants: The Case of Criminal Defendants." *American Sociological Review* 42:743 (1977).

Bittner, E. "Florence Nightingale in Pursuit of Willie Sutton: A Theory of the Police." In H. Jacob, ed., *The Potential for Reform in Criminal Justice.* Beverly Hills: Sage, 1974.

_____. *The Functions of the Police in a Modern Society.* Chevy Chase, Maryland: Center for Studies in Crime and Delinquency, Public Health Service Publication No. 2059, 1970.

_____. *The Functions of the Police in Modern Society.* New York: Aronson, 1975.

_____. "The Police on Skid-Row: A Study of Peacekeeping." *American Sociological Review* 32:699 (1967).

Black, D. "The Social Organization of Arrest." *Stanford Law Review* 23:1087 (1971).

Black, D., and A. Reiss. "Patterns of Behavior in Police and Citizen Transactions." In *Studies of Crime and Law Enforcement in Major Metropolitan Areas,* §1. Washington, D.C.: Government Printing Office, 1967.

_____. "Police Control of Juveniles." *American Sociological Review* 35:63 (1970).

Bloch, R. "Why Notify the Police?: The Victim's Decision to Notify the Police of an Assault." *Criminology* 11:555 (1974).

Block, H.A., and F.T. Flynn. *Delinquency.* New York: Random House, 1956.

Bock, E., and C. Frazier. "Official Standards versus Actual Criteria in Bond Dispositions." *Journal of Criminal Justice* 5:321 (1977).

Brosi, K. *A Cross-City Comparison of Felony Case Processing.* Washington, D.C.: Institute for Law and Social Research, 1979.

Bruce, A.A.; E.W. Burgess; and A.J. Harno. *The Working of the Indeterminate Sentence Law and the Parole System in Illinois.* Springfield: Illinois Parole Board, 1928.

Bruce, A.A.; A.J. Harno; E.W. Burgess; and J. Landesco. *Parole and the Indeterminate Sentence.* Springfield: Illinois Parole Board, 1928.

Burdman, M. "Increased Correctional Effectiveness Progress Statement." Memorandum from the California Department of Correction to the California Senate Finance Subcommittee and the California Assembly Ways and Means Subcommittee. January 1, 1963. Unpublished.

Burnham, R.W. "Modern Decision Theory and Corrections." In D.M. Gottfredson, ed. *Decision-Making in the Criminal Justice System: Reviews and Essays,* ch. VII. Washington, D.C.: Government Printing Office, 1975.

Bynum, T. "An Empirical Exploration of the Factors Influencing Release on Recognizance." Ph.D. dissertation, Florida State University, 1976.

Cameron, M. *The Booster and the Snitch.* New York: The Free Press, 1964.

Caplovitz, D. *The Poor Pay More.* New York: The Free Press, 1967.

Carroll, L. and M. Mondrick. "Racial Bias in the Decision to Grant Parole." *Law and Society Review* 11:102 (1976).

Carter, R.M. "The Pre-Sentence Report and the Decision-Making Process." *Journal of Research in Crime and Delinquency* 4:203 (1967).

_____. *Presentence Report Handbook.* Washington, D.C.: Government Printing Office, 1978.

Carter, R., and M. Klein. *Back on the Street—The Diversion of Juvenile Offenders.* Englewood Cliffs, New Jersey: Prentice-Hall, 1976.

Carter, R.M., and L.T. Wilkins. "Some Factors in Sentencing Policy." *Journal of Criminal Law, Criminology and Police Science* 58:503 (1967).

Chambliss, W. "A Sociological Analysis of the Law of Vagrancy." *Social Problems* 12:67 (1969).

Chiricos, T., and G. Waldo. "Socioeconomic Status and Criminal Sentencing: An Empirical Assessment of a Conflict Proposition." *American Sociological Review* 40:753 (1975).

Chute, C.L. "Probation and Suspended Sentence." *Journal of the American Institute of Criminal Law and Criminology* 12:558 (1922).

Clarke, S. *The Bail System in Charlotte: 1971–1973.* Charlotte-Mecklenburg Criminal Justice Pilot Project. Chapel Hill, North Carolina: Institute of Government, 1974.

Clarkson, J.S. "Probation Improvement Program." Southfield, Michigan: 46th District Court, 1974. Mimeograph.

Clemmer, D. *The Prison Community*. Boston: Christopher Publishing Co., 1940.

Cohen, L., and J. Kluegel. "Determinants of Juvenile Court Dispositions: Ascriptive and Achieved Factors in Two Metropolitan Courts." *American Sociological Review* 43:162 (1978).

———. "Selecting Delinquents for Adjudication." *Journal of Research in Crime and Delinquency* 16:143 (1979).

Cohen, L., and R. Stark. "Discriminatory Labeling and the Five-Finger Discount." *Journal of Research in Crime and Delinquency* 11:25 (1974).

Cole, G. "The Decision to Prosecute." *Law and Society Review* 4:313 (1970).

Comment. "Prosecutorial Discretion in the Initiation of Criminal Complaints." *Southern California Law Review* 42:518 (1969).

Comptroller General of the United States. *The Federal Bail Process Fosters Inequities*. Report to the Congress, GGD-78-105. October 18, 1978.

Conklin, J., and D. Meagher. "The Percentage Deposit Bail System: An Alternative to the Professional Bondsman." *Journal of Criminal Justice* 1:299 (1973).

Cormack, R. "A Review of Classification." *Journal of the Royal Statistical Society* 3:321 (1971).

Cormier, B.M., et al. "Presentation of a Basic Classification for Criminological Work and Research in Criminality." *Canadian Journal of Corrections* 1:34 (1959).

Cronbach, L., and G.C. Gleser. *Psychological Tests and Personnel Decisions*. Urbana: University of Illinois Press, 1957.

"Corrections in the United States." *Crime and Delinquency* 13:126 (1967).

Cumming, E.; I. Cumming; and L. Edel. "Policeman as Philosopher, Guide, and Friend." *Social Problems* 12:276 (1965).

Cureton, E.E. "Recipe for a Cookbook." *Psychological Bulletin* 54:494 (1957).

———. "Validity, Reliability, and Baloney." In D. Jackson and S. Messick, eds., *Problems in Human Assessment*. New York: McGraw-Hill, 1967.

Davis, G.F. "A Study of Adult Probation Violation Rates by Means of the Cohort Approach." *Journal of Criminal Law, Criminology and Police Science* 55:70 (1964).

Davis, K. *Discretionary Justice*. Baton Rouge: Louisiana State University Press, 1969.

———. *Police Discretion*. St. Paul: West Publishing Co., 1975.

Dawson, R. *Sentencing: The Decision as to Type, Length and Conditions of Sentence*. Chicago: Little, Brown and Company, 1969.

Dershowitz, A. "Imprisonment by Judicial Hunch: The Case Against Pre-trial Prevention Detention." *Prison Journal* 1:12 (1970).

———. *Fair and Certain Punishment: Report of the Twentieth Century Fund Task Force on Criminal Sentencing*. New York: McGraw-Hill, 1976.

———. "The Law of Dangerousness: Some Fictions About Prediction." *Journal of Legal Studies* 23:24 (1970).

"Determinate Sentencing: Making the Punishment Fit the Crime." *Corrections Magazine* 3:3 (1976).

Diamond, S., and H. Zeisel. "Sentencing Councils: A Study of Sentencing Disparity and Its Reduction." *University of Chicago Law Review* 43:1 (1975).

Dill, F. "Bail and Bail Reform: A Sociological Study." Ph.D. dissertation, University of California at Berkeley, 1972.

Dunbar, W. "Provision of Base Expectancy Information to the Adult Authority." *California Department of Corrections Administrative Bulletin* 61/115. Sacramento: Department of Correction, December 1961.

Dunford, F. "Police Diversion: An Illusion?" *Criminology* 15:335 (1977).

Ebbesen, E., and V. Konecni. "Decisionmaking and Information Integration in the Courts: The Setting of Bail." *Journal of Personality and Social Psychology* 32:805 (1975).

Elion, V., and E. Megargee. "Racial Identity, Length of Incarceration, and Parole Decisionmaking." *Journal of Research in Crime and Delinquency* 16:232 (1979).

Ennis, P. *Criminal Victimization in the United States.* Field Surveys II, President's Commission on Law Enforcement and Administration of Justice. Washington, D.C.: Government Printing Office, 1967.

Fabricant, N. "Bail as a Preferred Freedom and the Failures of New York's Revision." *Buffalo Law Review* 18:303 (1969).

Feeley, M., and J. McNaughton. "The Pre-Trial Process in the Sixth Circuit." New Haven, 1974. Mimeograph.

Feeney, F. "Citation in Lieu of Arrest: The New California Law." *Vanderbilt Law Review* 25:36 (1972).

Feinberg, J. *Doing and Deserving: Essays on the Theory of Responsibility.* Princeton, New Jersey: Princeton University Press, 1970.

Ferry, J., and M. Kravitz. *Issues in Sentencing: A Selected Bibliography.* Washington, D.C.: National Institute on Law Enforcement and Criminal Justice, 1978.

Fielding, H. *The History of Tom Jones.* Book III, ch. X. Garden City, New York: International Collector's Library. n.d.

Finckenauer, J. "Some Factors in Police Discretion and Decisionmaking." *Journal of Criminal Justice* 4:29 (1976).

Fogel, D. *We Are the Living Proof: The Justice Model for Corrections.* Cincinnati: Anderson, 1975.

Foote, C. "The Coming Constitutional Crisis in Bail." *University of Pennsylvania Law Review* 113:959 (1965).

_____. "Deceptive Determinate Sentencing." In National Institute on Law Enforcement and Criminal Justice, *Determinate Sentencing.* Washington, D.C.: U.S. Department of Justice, 1978.

Foote, C.; J. Markle; and E. Woolley. "Compelling Appearance in Court: Administration of Bail in Philadelphia." *University of Pennsylvania Law Review* 102:1031 (1954).

Ford, R.C. and S.R. Johnson. "Probation Prediction Models and Recidivism." Geneva, Illinois: Kane County Diagnostic Center, 1976. Mimeograph.

Forst, B., and K. Brosi. "A Theoretical and Empirical Analysis of the Prosecutor." *Journal of Legal Studies* 6:177(1977).

Forst, B.; J. Lucianovic; and S. Cox. *What Happens After Arrest?*, Institute for Law and Social Research. Washington, D.C.: Government Printing Office, 1977.

Frankfurter, F., and R. Pound. *Criminal Justice in Cleveland.* 1922; rpted., Montclair, New Jersey: Patterson Smith, 1968.

Frease, D.E. "Factors Related to Probation Outcome." Tacoma: Washington State Board of Prison Terms and Paroles, April 1964.

———. "Probation Prediction for Adult Offenders in Washington." Olympia, Washington: Department of Institutions, 1965. Mimeograph.

Freed, D. "The Imbalance Ratio." *Beyond Time* 11:25 (1973).

Freed, D., and P. Wald. *Bail in the United States: 1964.* Washington, D.C.: U.S. Department of Justice and the Vera Foundation, 1964.

Friedrich, R. "The Impact of Organizational, Individual, and Situational Factors on Police Behavior," Ph.D. dissertation, University of Michigan, 1977.

Galvin, J.L.; C.H. Ruby; J.J. Galvin et al. *Parole in the United States: 1978.* San Francisco: National Council on Crime and Delinquency, 1979.

Garofalo, J. *The Police and Public Opinion.* National Criminal Justice Information and Statistics Service. Washington, D.C.: Government Printing Office, 1977.

Garrity, D.G. "The Effects of Lengths of Incarceration Upon Parole Adjustment and the Estimation of Optimum Sentence." Ph.D. dissertation, University of Washington, 1958.

Gaudet, F.; G. Harris; and C. St. John. "Individual Differences in the Sentencing Tendencies of Judges." *Journal of Criminal Law and Criminology* 23:811 (1933).

Geason, D., and F. Hangren. "Predicting the Adjustment of Federal Probationers." *National Probation and Parole Association Journal* 4:265 (1958).

Gibbs, J.J. "Psychological and Behavioral Pathology in Jails: A Review of the Literature." Paper prepared for the Special National Workshop on Mental Health Services in Local Jails, Baltimore, Maryland, September 1978.

Glaser, D. *Routinizing Evaluation: Getting Feedback on Effectiveness of Crime and Delinquency Programs.* Washington, D.C.: National Institute of Mental Health, 1973.

Glaser, D.; F. Cohen; and V. O'Leary. "The Sentencing and Parole Process." Washington, D.C.: U.S. Department of Health, Education, and Welfare, Office of Juvenile Delinquency and Youth Development, 1966.

Glaser, D., and V. O'Leary. *Personal Characteristics and Parole Outcome.* Washington, D.C.: U.S. Department of Health, Education and Welfare, Office of Juvenile Delinquency and Youth Development, 1966.

Goldfarb, R. *Ransom.* New York: Harper and Row, 1965.

Goldkamp, J. *Two Classes of Accused: A Study of Bail and Detention in America.* Cambridge, Massachusetts: Ballinger Publishing Company, 1979.

Goldkamp, J., and M. Gottfredson. "Bail Decisionmaking and Pretrial Detention: Surfacing Judicial Policy." *Law and Human Behavior,* 3:227 (1979).

Goldstein, H. "Administrative Problems in Controlling the Exercise of Police Authority." *Journal of Criminal Law, Criminology and Police Science* 58:160 (1967).

_____. *Policing A Free Society*. Cambridge, Massachusetts: Ballinger, 1977.

_____. "Setting High Bail to Prevent Pretrial Release." In *Proceedings*. National Conference on Bail and Criminal Justice, Washington, D.C., 1964.

Goldstein, J. "Police Discretion Not to Invoke the Criminal Process: Low Visibility Decisions in the Administration of Justice." *Yale Law Journal* 69:543 (1969).

Gottfredson, D.M. "Assessment and Prediction Methods in Crime and Delinquency." In President's Commission on Law Enforcement and Administration of Justice, *Task Force Report: Juvenile Delinquency and Youth Crime*. Washington, D.C.: Government Printing Office, 1967.

_____. "Comparing and Combining Subjective and Objective Parole Predictions." *Research Newsletter* 3. Vacaville: California Medical Facility, California Department of Corrections, September–December 1961.

_____. "One Approach to Social Agency Self-Study." *Canadian Journal of Corrections* 5:271 (1965).

_____. "The Practical Application of Research." *Canadian Journal of Corrections* 5:212 (1963).

_____. "The Role of Base Expectancies in the Study of Treatment." Paper presented as part of the Symposium on Methods for the Study of Effectiveness of Treatment, Western Psychological Association meeting, San Diego, California, April 1959.

_____. "Sentencing Trends in the United States: Implications for Clinical Criminology." Paper presented at the Sixth International Seminar on Clinical Criminology, Santa Margharita, Italy, May 1975.

_____. *A Shorthand Formula for Base Expectancies*. Research Report No. 5. Sacramento, California: Department of Correction, December 1961.

_____. "Some Positive Changes in the Parole Process." Paper delivered at the annual meetings of the American Society of Criminology, Toronto, Canada, 1975.

_____. "A Strategy for Study of Correctional Effectiveness." Paper presented to the Fourth Section of the Fifth International Criminological Congress, Montreal, August 1965.

Gottfredson, D.M., and K.B. Ballard, Jr. "Differences in Parole Decisions Associated with Decisionmakers." *Journal of Research in Crime and Delinquency* 3:112 (1966).

_____. *Estimating Sentences Under an Indeterminate Sentence Law*. Vacaville, California: Institute for the Study of Crime and Delinquency, June 1964.

_____. *The Validity of Two Parole Prediction Scales*. Vacaville, California: Institute for the Study of Crime and Delinquency, 1965.

Gottfredson, D.M., and J.A. Bonds. "A Manual for Intake Base Expectancy Scoring," Sacramento: California Department of Corrections. Mimeograph.

Gottfredson, D.M., and M.R. Gottfredson. "Data for Criminal Justice Evaluations: Some Resources and Pitfalls." In M. Klein and K. Teilman, eds., *Handbook of Criminal Justice Evaluation*. Beverly Hills, California: Sage Publications, 1980.

Gottfredson, D.M., and B. Stecker. "Sentencing Policy Models." Newark, New Jersey: School of Criminal Justice, Rutgers University, 1979. Manuscript.

Gottfredson, D.M., K.B. Ballard, and V. O' Leary. *Uniform Parole Reports: A Feasibility Study.* New York: National Council on Crime and Delinquency, December 1965.

Gottfredson, D.M.; J.A. Bonds; and J.D. Grant. "La Combinazione Della Previsione Clinica e di Quella Statistica Nelle Decisione Penitenziare." *Quaderni di Criminologia Clinica.* Roma: Tipografia della Mantellate, Gennaio-Marzo 1962.

Gottfredson, D.M.; C.A. Cosgrove; L.T. Wilkins; J. Wallerstein; and C. Rauh. *Classification for Parole Decision Policy.* Washington, D.C.: Government Printing Office, 1978.

Gottfredson, D.M.; J.O. Finckenauer; and C. Rauh. *Probation on Trial.* Newark, New Jersey: School of Criminal Justice, Rutgers University, 1977.

Gottfredson, D.M.; M.R. Gottfredson; and J. Garofalo. "Time Served in Prison and Parole Outcomes Among Parolee Risk Categories." *Journal of Criminal Justice* 5:1 (1977).

Gottfredson, D.M.; M.G. Neithercutt; J. Nuffield; and V. O'Leary. *Four Thousand Lifetimes: A Study of Time Served and Parole Outcomes.* Davis, California: National Council on Crime and Delinquency Research Center, 1973.

Gottfredson, D.M.; M.G. Neithercutt; P.S. Venezia; and A. Wenk. *A National Uniform Parole Reporting System.* Davis, California: National Council on Crime and Delinquency, December 1970.

Gottfredson, D.M.; L.T. Wilkins; and P.B. Hoffman. *Guidelines for Parole and Sentencing: A Policy Control Method.* Lexington, Massachusetts: Lexington Books, 1978.

Gottfredson, G.D. "Penal Policy and the Evaluation of Rehabilitation." Remarks prepared for a Symposium on Evaluating the Rehabilitation of Criminal Offenders, American Society of Criminology, November 1979.

Gottfredson, M.R. "The Classification of Crimes and Victims." Ph.D. dissertation, State University of New York at Albany, 1976.

———. "An Empirical Analysis of Pre-Trial Release Decisions." *Journal of Criminal Justice* 2:287 (1974).

———. "Parole Board Decisionmaking: A Study of Disparity Reduction and the Impact of Institutional Behavior." *Journal of Criminal Law and Criminology* 70:77 (1979).

———. "Parole Guidelines and the Reduction of Sentencing Disparity: A Preliminary Study." *Journal of Research in Crime and Delinquency* 16:218 (1979).

———. "Treatment Destruction Techniques." *Journal of Research in Crime and Delinquency* 16:39 (1979).

Gottfredson, M.R., and K. Adams. "Prison Behavior and Parole Performance: Empirical Reality and Public Policy." Albany, New York: Criminal Justice Research Center, 1980. Mimeograph.

Gottfredson, M.R., and M. J. Hindelang. "A Study of the Behavior of Law." *American Sociological Review* 44:3 (1979).

———. "Theory and Research in the Sociology of Law." *American Sociological Review* 44:27 (1979).

———. "Trite But True." *American Sociological Review* (April 1980).

Gottfredson, S.; K. Young; and W. Laufer. "Additivity and Interaction in Offense Seriousness Scales." *Journal of Research in Crime and Delinquency* 17:26 (1980).

Gough, H.G. "Clinical Versus Statistical Prediction in Psychology." In L. Postman, ed., *Psychology in the Making.* New York: Alfred A. Knopf, 1962.

Gough, H.G., and D.R. Peterson. "The Identification and Measurement of Predispositional Factors in Crime and Delinquency." *Journal of Consulting Psychology* 16:212 (1952).

Grant, J.D., and M.Q. Warren. "An Evaluation of Community Treatment for Delinquents." CTP Research Report. Sacramento: California Youth Authority, August 1962.

Grant, M.Q. "Interaction Between Kinds of Treatments and Kinds of Delinquents." In Board of Corrections Monograph Number 2, Sacramento: State of California Printing Division, Documents Section, July 1961.

Green, E. *Judicial Attitudes in Sentencing.* London: MacMillan, 1961.

Greenwood, P.; S. Wildhorn; E. Poggin; M. Strumwasser; and P. DeLeon. *Prosecution of Adult Felony Defendants in Los Angeles County: A Policy Perspective.* Washington, D.C.: U.S. Department of Justice, 1973.

Hagan, J. "Extra-Legal Attributes and Criminal Sentencing: An Assessment of a Sociological Viewpoint." *Law and Society Review* 8:357 (1974).

Hall, J. *Theft, Law, and Society.* 2nd ed. New York: Bobbs-Merrill, 1955.

Hamilton, W., and C. Work. "The Prosecutor's Role in the Urban Court System: The Case for Management Consciousness." *Journal of Criminal Law and Criminology* 64:183 (1973).

Hanley, C. "The Gauging of Criminal Predispositions." In H. Toch, *Legal and Criminal Psychology.* New York: Holt, Rinehart and Winston, 1961.

Harris, M.K. "Community Service by Offenders." Submission draft prepared for the American Bar Association's Basics Program, January 1979.

_____. "Disquisition on the Need for a New Model for Criminal Sanctioning Systems." *West Virginia Law Review* 77:263 (1975).

Harris, M., and F. Dunbaugh. "Premise for a Sensible Sentencing Debate: Giving Up Imprisonment." *Hofstra Law Review* 7:417 (1979).

Hart, H.L.A. *Punishment and Responsibility: Essays in the Philosophy of Law.* New York: Oxford University Press, 1968.

Havel, J. *Special Intensive Parole Unit, Phase IV: A High Base Expectancy Study.* Sacramento: California Department of Correction, June 1963.

Hawkins, R. "Determinants of Sanctioning Initiations for Criminal Victimization." Ph.D. dissertation, University of Michigan, 1970.

Healy, W. "The Individual Study of the Young Criminal." *Journal of the American Institute of Criminal Law and Criminology* 1:50 (1910).

Heinz, A.; J. Heinz; S. Senderowitz; and M. Vance. "Sentencing by Parole Board: An Evaluation." *Journal of Criminal Law and Criminology* 67:1 (1976).

Hemple, W.E.; W.H. Webb, Jr.; and S.W. Reynolds. "Researching Prediction Scales for Probation." *Federal Probation* 40:34 (1976).

Hindelang, M.J. *Criminal Victimization in Eight American Cities: A Descriptive Analysis of Common Theft and Assault.* Cambridge, Massachusetts: Ballinger, 1976.

————. "Decisions of Shoplifting Victims to Invoke the Criminal Justice Process." *Social Problems* 21:580 (1974).

————. "On the Methodological Rigor of the Bellamy Memorandum." *Criminal Law Bulletin* 8:507 (1972).

Hindelang, M., and M. Gottfredson. "The Victim's Decision Not to Invoke the Criminal Process." In W. McDonald, ed., *Criminal Justice and the Victim.* Beverly Hills: Sage Publications, 1976.

Hindelang, M.; M. Gottfredson; and J. Garofalo. *Victims of Personal Crime: An Empirical Foundation for a Theory of Personal Victimization.* Cambridge, Massachusetts: Ballinger, 1978.

Hirschi, T. "Labelling Theory and Juvenile Delinquency: An Assessment of the Evidence." In W. Gove, ed., *The Labelling of Deviance.* New York: Halsted Press, 1975.

Hoffman, P.; B. Stone-Meierhoefer; and J. Beck. "Salient Factor Score and Release Behavior: Three Validation Samples." *Law and Human Behavior* 2:47 (1978).

Hogarth, J. "Alternatives to the Adversary System." In Law Reform Commission of Canada, *Studies on Sentencing.* Ottawa: Information Canada, 1974.

————. *Sentencing as a Human Process.* Toronto: University of Toronto Press, 1971.

Hood, R. "Research on the Effectiveness of Punishments and Treatments." In *Collected Studies in Criminological Research* I. Strasbourg: Council of Europe, 1967.

Hood, R., and R.F. Sparks. *Key Issues in Criminology.* New York: McGraw-Hill, 1970.

Hopkinson, C.C.; and S. Adams. "The Specialized Alcoholic Caseload Project: A Study of the Effectiveness of Probation with Alcoholic Offenders." Los Angeles: Los Angeles County Probation Department, 1964. Mimeograph.

"How Effective is Probation?" *State and County Probation: Systems in Crisis.* Report to the Congress by the Comptroller General of the United States. Washington, D.C.: Government Printing Office, 1976.

Hruska, R. "Preventive Detention: The Constitution and Congress." *Creighton Law Review* 3:36 (1969).

Humphreys, L. *Tearoom Trade.* Chicago: Aldine, 1970.

Institute for Law and Social Research. *Curbing the Repeat Offender: A Strategy for Prosecutors.* Institute for Law and Social Research Publication Number 3. Washington, D.C.: Government Printing Office, 1977.

————. *Uniform Case Evaluation and Rating.* INSLAW Briefing Paper Number 3. Washington, D.C.: INSLAW, 1976.

Irish, J.F. "Assessment of Adult Division Supervision Program Effectiveness." Mineola, New York: Adult Probation Department, 1976. Mimeograph.

Jackson, R. "The Federal Prosecutor." *Journal of American Judicature Society* 24:18 (1940).

Jacoby, J. *The Prosecutor's Charging Decision: A Policy Perspective.* Washington, D.C.: Government Printing Office, 1977.

Kadish, S. "Legal Norm and Discretion in the Police and Sentencing Process." *Harvard Law Review* 75:904 (1962).

Kant, I. *The Philosophy of Law, Part II.* Trans. W. Hastic. Edinburgh: T.T. Clar, 1887.

———. *Rechtslehre* (1797). Cited in H. Gross, *A Theory of Criminal Justice.* New York: Oxford University Press, 1979.

Kaplan, J. "The Prosecutorial Discretion—A Comment." *Northwestern University Law Review* 60:174 (1965).

Kaput, T.A., and M.E. Santese. "Evaluation of General Caseload Drug Unit." Hartford, Connecticut: Department of Adult Probation, 1972. Mimeograph.

Kassebaum, G.; D.A. Ward; and D.M. Wilner. *Prison Treatment and Parole Survival.* New York: Wiley, 1971.

Kastenmeier, R.W., and H.C. Eglit, "Parole Release Decisionmaking: Rehabilitation, Expertise, and the Demise of Mythology." *The American University Law Review* 22:477-88 (1975).

Kavanaugh, K.J. "A Twelve-Month Probation Outcome Study: Examining the Effects of Employment on Probation Adjustment." Columbus: The Ohio State University, 1975. Mimeograph.

Kelling, G.; T. Pate; D. Dieckman; and G. Brown. *The Kansas City Preventive Patrol Experiment.* Summary Report. Washington, D.C.: The Police Foundation, 1974.

Kittrie, N. *The Right to be Different: Deviance and Enforced Therapy.* Baltimore: The Johns Hopkins Press, 1971.

Klein, M., S. Kobrin, A. McEachern, and H. Sigurdson. "System Rates: An Approach to Comprehensive Criminal Justice Planning." *Crime and Delinquency* 17:355 (1971).

Klein, M.; K. Teilman; J. Styles; S. Lincoln; and S. Labin-Rosensweig. "The Explosion in Police Diversion Programs: Evaluating the Structural Dimensions of a Social Fad." In M. Klein, ed., *The Juvenile Justice System.* Beverly Hills: Sage, 1976.

Kluckhohn, C., and H.A. Murray. *Personality in Nature, Society, and Culture.* 2nd. ed. New York: Knopf, 1956.

Kolodney, S. *Parole Board Reform in California: Order Out of Chaos.* Report of the Select Committee on the Administration of Justice. Sacramento: Assembly of the State of California, 1970.

Kress, J.; L. Wilkins; and D. Gottfredson. "Is the End of Judicial Sentencing in Sight?" *Judicature* 60:216 (1976).

Kusuda, P.H. "1974 Probation and Parole Terminations." Madison: State of Wisconsin Division of Corrections, July 1976.

———. "Relationship of Adult Probation and Parole Experiences to Successful Termination of Supervision." Madison, Wisconsin: State Department of Public Welfare, Bureau of Research, 1966.

LaFave, W. "Alternatives to the Present Bail System." Conference on Bail and Indigency, 1965.

———. *Arrest: The Decision to Take A Suspect Into Custody.* Boston: Little, Brown, and Co., 1965.

———. "The Police and Nonenforcement of the Law." *Wisconsin Law Review* 104 (1962).

———. "The Prosecutor's Discretion in the United States." *The American Journal of Comparative Law* 18:532 (1970).

Landes, W. "The Bail System: An Economic Approach." *Journal of Legal Studies* 2:79 (1973).

———. "Legality and Reality: Some Evidence on Criminal Procedure." *Journal of Legal Studies* 3:287 (1974).

Landis, J.R.; J.D. Mercer; and C.E. Wolff. "Success and Failure of Adult Probationers in California." *Journal of Research in Crime and Delinquency* 6:34 (1969).

Lejins, P.P. "National Crime Data Reporting System: Proposal for a Model." In *Task Force Report: Crime and Its Impact—An Assessment*, app. C. Washington, D.C.: Government Printing Office, 1967.

Lindsay, E. "Historical Sketch of the Indeterminate Sentence and Parole System." *Journal of Criminal Law, Criminology and Police Science* 16:14 (1925-26).

Lipton, D.; R. Martinson; and J. Wilks. *The Effectiveness of Correctional Treatment: A Survey of Treatment Evaluation Studies.* New York: Praeger Publishers, 1975.

Locke, J.; R. Penn; R. Rock; E. Bunten; and G. Hare. *Compilation and Use of Criminal Court Data in Relation to Pretrial Release of Defendants: Pilot Study.* Washington, D.C.: Government Printing Office, 1970.

Lohman, J.D.; A. Wahl; and R.M. Carter. "The Intensive Supervision Caseload: A Preliminary Evaluation." Berkeley: University of California School of Criminology, 1966. Mimeograph.

Long Jail Terms and Parole Outcome. Sacramento: California Department of Corrections, 1967.

Lundman, R. "Routine Police Arrest Practices: A Commonweal Perspective." *Social Problems* 22:127 (1974).

———. "Shoplifting and Police Referral: A Re-examination." *Journal of Criminal Law and Criminology* 69:395 (1978).

Lundman, R.; R. Sykes; and J. Clarke. "Police Control of Juveniles: A Replication." *Journal of Research in Crime and Delinquency* 15:74 (1978).

Mannheim, H., and L.T. Wilkins. *Prediction Methods in Relation to Borstal Training.* London: Her Majesty's Stationery Office, 1955.

Martinson, R. "What Works? Questions and Answers About Prison Reform." *The Public Interest* 35:22 (1974).

Martinson, R., and J. Wilks. "Save Parole Supervision." *Federal Probation* 41:23 (1977).

Mattick, H. "The Contemporary Jails of the United States: An Unknown and Neglected Area of Justice." In Daniel Glaser, ed., *Handbook of Criminology.* Chicago: Rand McNally, 1974.

McCall, C. Chairman, U.S. Parole Commission. Testimony before the Subcommittee on Criminal Justice, House Judiciary Committee, 1978.

McCarthy, D., and J. Wohl. "The District of Columbia Bail Project: An Illustration of Experimentation and a Brief for Change." *Georgetown Law Journal* 55:218 (1965).

McCord, J. "A Thirty-Year Follow-Up of Treatment Effects." *American Psychologist* 33:284 (1978).

McCrea, T., and D. Gottfredson. *A Guide to Handling of Misdemeanor Offenders.* Washington, D.C.: Government Printing Office, 1974.

McGarry, A., et al. *Competency to Stand Trial and Mental Illness, Final Report on NIMH Grant R01-MH 18112.* Boston: Harvard Medical School, Laboratory of Community Psychiatry, 1972.

McIntyre, D., ed. *Law Enforcement in the Metropolis.* Chicago: American Bar Foundation, 1967.

McIntyre, D., and D. Lippman. "Prosecutors and Early Disposition of Felony Cases." *American Bar Association Journal* 56:1154 (1970).

McKechnie, J., ed. *Webster's New Twentieth Century Dictionary of the English Language.* 2nd ed. Collins-World, 1975.

Meehl, P.E. *Clinical Versus Statistical Prediction.* Minneapolis: University of Minnesota Press, 1954.

Meehl, P.E., and A. Rosen. "Antecedent Probability and the Efficiencies of Psychometric Signs, Patterns, or Cutting Scores." *Psychological Bulletin* 52:215 (1955).

Megargee, E.L. "Psychological Assessment in Jails: Implementation of the Standards Recommended by the National Advisory Commission on Criminal Justice Standards." Paper prepared for the Special Workshop on Mental Health Services in Local Jails, Baltimore, Maryland, September 1978.

Messer, A. *Immanuel Kants Leben and Philosophie.* Stuttgart: Streaker and Schroder, 1924.

Miller, F. *Prosecution: The Decision to Charge a Suspect With a Crime.* Boston: Little, Brown and Co., 1970.

Miller, F.; R. Dawson; G. Dix; and R. Parnas. *Criminal Justice Administration and Related Processes.* Mineola, New York: The Foundation Press, 1971.

Miller, W.B. "Some Characteristics of Present Day Delinquency of Relevance to Educators." Paper presented at the meetings of the American Association of School Administrators, 1959.

Mills, R. "The Prosecutor: Charging and 'Bargaining'." *Illinois Crim. Proc.* 1966:511 (1966).

Mitchell, J. "Bail Reform and the Constitutionality of Pretrial Detention." *Virginia Law Review* 55:1223 (1969).

Monachesi, E.D. *Prediction Factors in Probation.* Minneapolis: The Sociological Press, 1932.

Moos, R. *Evaluating Treatment Environments: A Social Ecological Approach.* New York: John Wiley & Sons, 1974.

Morris, N. *The Future of Imprisonment.* Chicago: University of Chicago Press, 1974.

_____. "Punishment, Desert and Rehabilitation." In U.S. Department of Justice, *Equal Justice Under Law*, Bicentennial Lecture Series. Washington, D.C.: Government Printing Office, 1976.

Morse, W., and R. Beattie. *Survey of the Administration of Criminal Justice in Oregon.* New York: Arno Press, 1974.

Mueller, G. *Sentencing: Process and Purpose.* Springfield, Illinois: Charles E. Thomas, 1977.

Mueller, P. *Advanced Release to Parole.* Research Report No. 20. Sacramento: Department of Corrections, Youth and Adult Corrections Agency, 1965.

Muir, W. *Police: Streetcorner Politicians.* Chicago: University of Chicago Press, 1977.

Nahm, M.C., ed. *Selections From Early Greek Philosophy.* New York: F.S. Crafts, 1934.

National Advisory Commission on Criminal Justice Standards and Goals. *Corrections.* Washington, D.C.: Government Printing Office, 1973.

_____. *Police.* Washington, D.C.: Government Printing Office, 1973.

National Association of Pretrial Services Agencies. *Performance Standards and Goals for Pretrial Release and Diversion, Pretrial Release.* Washington, D.C., 1978.

National Center for State Courts. *Policymaker's Views Regarding Issues in the Operation and Evaluation of Pretrial Release and Diversion Programs: Findings from a Questionnaire Survey.* Denver, 1975.

National Commission on Law Observance and Enforcement. *Report on Criminal Procedure.* Washington, D.C.: Government Printing Office, 1931.

National Council on Crime and Delinquency. *Standards and Guides for Adult Probation.* New York, 1962.

_____. "Three-Year Follow-Up Analyses—1970 Parolees." *Newsletter, Uniform Parole Reports.* Davis, California, n.d.

National Research Council. *Deterrence and Incapacitation: Estimating the Effects of Criminal Sanctions on the Crime Rate.* Washington, D.C.: National Academy of Sciences, 1978.

Neithercutt, M.G., and D.M. Gottfredson. *Caseload Size Variation and Difference in Probation/Parole Performance.* Pittsburgh: National Center for Juvenile Justice, 1973.

Neithercutt, M., and W. Moseley. *Arrest Decisions as Preludes to?: An Evaluation of Policy Related Research.* Vol. III. Davis, California: National Council on Crime and Delinquency Research Center, 1974.

Nettler, G. *Explaining Crime.* 2nd ed. New York: McGraw-Hill, 1978.

"The New Techniques of Decision Making." *Acme Reporter.* New York: Association of Consulting Management Engineers, Inc., January 1955.

Newman, C.L., ed. *Sourcebook on Probation, Parole and Pardons.* 3rd ed. Springfield, Illinois: Thomas, 1963.

Newman, D. *Conviction: The Determination of Guilt or Innocence Without Trial.* Boston: Little, Brown and Co., 1966.

_____. "Role and Process in the Criminal Court." In D. Glaser, ed., *Handbook of Criminology,* ch. 15. Chicago: Rand McNally, 1974.

Newman, G. *The Punishment Response.* New York: Lippincott, 1978.

Nicholson, R.C. "Use of Prediction in Caseload Management." *Federal Probation* 32:54 (1968).

Note. "Preventive Detention Before Trial." *Harvard Law Review* 79:1489 (1966).

Ohlin, L.E. *Selection for Parole: A Manual of Parole Prediction.* New York: Russell Sage Foundation, 1951.

Ohlin, L., and F. Remington. "Sentencing Structure: Its Effects Upon Systems for the Administration of Criminal Justice." *Law and Contemporary Problems* 23:495 (1958).

O'Leary, V. *Correctional Policy Inventory.* Hackensack, New Jersey: National Council on Crime and Delinquency, n.d.

O'Leary, V., and D. Glaser. "The Assessment of Risk in Parole Decision-making." In J.D. West, ed., *The Future of Parole.* London: Duckworth, 1972.

O'Leary, V., and J. Hall. *Frames of Reference in Parole.* Hackensack, New Jersey: National Council on Crime and Delinquency Training Center, National Parole Institutes training document, n.d. (ca. 1976).

O'Leary, V., and K.J. Hanrahan. *Parole Systems in the United States.* Hackensack, New Jersey: National Council on Crime and Delinquency, 1976.

O'Leary, V.; M. Gottfredson; and A. Gelman. "Contemporary Sentencing Proposals." *Criminal Law Bulletin* 11:55 (1975).

Ostle, B. *Statistics in Research.* Ames: The Iowa State College Press, 1954.

Packer, H. "Two Models of the Criminal Process." *University of Pennsylvania Law Review* 113:1 (1964).

Palmer, T. "Martinson Revisited." *Journal of Research in Crime and Delinquency* 12:133 (1975).

———. "The Youth Authority's Community Treatment Project." *Federal Probation* 38:3 (1974).

Parkinson, C.N. *The Law of Delay.* 2nd ed. Boston: Houghton Mifflin, 1971.

Parnas, R. "Police Discretion and Diversion of Incidents of Intra-Family Violence." *Law and Contemporary Problems* 36:539 (1971).

———. "The Police Response to Domestic Disturbance." *Wisconsin Law Review* 1967:914 (1967).

Parole and Community Services Division. *The Work Unit Parole Program: 1969.* Sacramento: California Department of Correction, December 5, 1969.

Petersen, D. "Police Disposition of the Petty Offender." *Sociology and Social Research* 56:320 (1972).

Peterson, D.R.; H.C. Quay; and G.R. Cameron. "Personality and Background Factors in Juvenile Delinquency as Inferred from Questionnaire Responses." *Journal of Consulting Psychology* 23:399 (1959).

Piliavin, I., and S. Briar. "Police Encounters With Juveniles." *American Journal of Sociology* 70:206 (1964).

Pope, D. "The Influence of Social and Legal Factors on Sentence Dispositions: A Preliminary Analysis of Offender-Based Transaction Statistics." *Journal of Criminal Justice* 4:203 (1976).

———. *Offender-Based Transaction Statistics: New Directions in Data Collection and Reporting.* Washington, D.C.: National Criminal Justice Information and Statistics Service, 1975.

———. "Postarrest Release Decisions: An Empirical Examination of Social and Legal Criteria." *Journal of Research in Crime and Delinquency* 15:35 (1978).

————. "Sentence Dispositions Accorded Assault and Burglary Offenders: An Exploratory Study in Twelve California Counties." *Journal of Criminal Justice* 6:151 (1978).

Population Trends and Length of Prison Terms. Research Monograph No. 27. Olympia: State of Washington Department of Institutions, September 1967.

President's Commission on Law Enforcement and Administration of Justice. *The Challenge of Crime in a Free Society.* Washington, D.C.: Government Printing Office, 1967.

————. *Task Force Report: Corrections.* Washington, D.C.: Government Printing Office, 1967.

————. *Task Force Report: The Courts.* Washington, D.C.: Government Printing Office, 1967.

————. *Task Force Report: Crime and Its Impact—An Assessment.* Washington, D.C.: Government Printing Office, 1967.

————. *Task Force Report: The Police.* Washington, D.C.: Government Printing Office, 1967.

"Probation in Missouri, July 1, 1968 to June 30, 1970: Characteristics, Performance, and Criminal Reinvolvement." Jefferson City, Missouri: Division of Probation and Parole, 1976. Mimeograph.

Ramsey, J. "Inside-Out Displays and More." Presentation at a symposium on Multivariate Data Display, Psychometric Society Meeting, Iowa City, Iowa, 1980 (personal communication from Howard Wainer).

Rankin, A. "The Effect of Pretrial Detention." *New York University Law Review* 39:641 (1964).

Rawls, J. *A Theory of Justice.* Cambridge, Massachusetts: Belknap Press of Harvard University Press, 1971.

Rector, M.G. "Factors in Measuring Recidivism as Presented in Annual Reports." *National Probation and Parole Association Journal* 4:218 (1958).

Reed, H.P. "Caseloads." *National Probation and Parole Association Journal* p. 143, (April 1957).

Reeves, E. "A Fresh Look at Prediction and Supervision." *Crime and Delinquency* 7:37 (1961).

Reiss, A. *The Police and the Public.* New Haven: Yale University Press, 1971.

Reiss, A., and D. Bordua. "Environment and Organization: A Perspective on the Police." In D. Bordua, ed., *The Police: Six Sociological Essays.* New York: John Wiley, 1967.

Remington, F.; D. Newman; E. Kimball; M. Melli; and H. Goldstein. *Criminal Justice Administration.* Indianapolis: Bobbs-Merrill, 1969.

Robison, J., and G. Smith. "The Effectiveness of Correctional Programs." *Crime and Delinquency* 17:67 (1971).

Rosett, A., and D. Cressey. *Justice By Consent.* Philadelphia: Lippincott, 1976.

Rossi, P., et al. "The Seriousness of Crimes: Normative Structure and Individual Differences." *American Sociological Review* 39:224 (1974).

Roth, J., and P. Wice. "Pretrial Release and Misconduct in the District of Columbia." PROMIS Research Project Publication 16. Washington, D.C.: INSLAW, 1978.

Rubin, S., et al. *The Law of Criminal Correction.* St. Paul: West Publishing Co., 1963.

Russell, B. "An Outline of Intellectual Rubbish." In *Unpopular Essays.* New York: Simon and Schuster, 1962.

_____. *The Scientific Outlook.* New York: W.W. Norton, 1962.

Sacks, H., and C. Logan. *Does Parole Make A Difference?* Storrs: University of Connecticut School of Law Press, 1979.

Sarbin, T. "On the Futility of the Proposition that Some People Be Labelled as 'Mentally Ill'." *Journal of Consulting Psychology* 31:447 (1967).

Schneider, A.; J. Burcart; and L. Wilson. "The Role of Attitudes in the Decision to Report Crimes to the Police." In W. McDonald, ed., *Criminal Justice and the Victim.* Beverly Hills: Sage, 1976.

Schrag, C.A. "Social Types in a Prison Community." M.A. thesis, University of Washington, 1944.

_____. "Social Types in a Prison Community." *Pacific Sociological Review* 4:12 (1961).

Scott, J. "The Use of Discretion in Determining the Severity of Punishment for Incarcerated Offenders." *Journal of Criminal Law and Criminology* 65:214 (1974).

Sebba, L. "Some Explorations in the Scaling of Penalties." *Journal of Research in Crime and Delinquency* 15:247 (1978).

Sechrest, L., S. White, and E. Brown, eds. *The Rehabilitation of Criminal Offenders: Problems and Prospects.* Washington, D.C.: National Academy of Sciences, 1979.

Sellin, T., and M. Wolfgang. *The Measurement of Delinquency.* New York: John Wiley, 1964.

Shainin, D. "The Statistically Designed Experiment." *Harvard Business Review* (July–August 1957).

Sharma, S.L., ed. *The Medical Model of Mental Illness.* Woodland, California: Majestic, 1970.

Sheppard, D.J. "Denver High-Impact Anti-Crime Program: Intensive Probation and Parole." Denver: State Judicial Department, 1975. Mimeograph.

Sherman, L. "Causes of Police Behavior: The Current State of Quantitative Research." *Journal of Research in Crime and Delinquency* 17:69 (1980).

_____. "Execution Without Trial: Police Homicide and the Constitution." *Vanderbilt Law Review* 33:71 (1980).

Simon, F.H. *Prediction Methods in Criminology.* London: Her Majesty's Stationery Office, 1971.

Single, E. "The Unconstitutional Administration of Bail: *Bellamy v. the Judges of New York City." Criminal Law Bulletin* 8:459 (1972).

Siu, R.N. "T-Thoughts." National Institute of Law Enforcement and Criminal Justice Pamphlet No. 4. Washington, D.C.: Law Enforcement Assistance Administration, November 1968. Mimeograph.

Skolnick, J., and J. Dombrink. "The Legalization of Deviance." *Criminology* 16:193 (1978).

Smith, A., and D. Maness. "The Decision to Call the Police." In W. McDonald, ed., *Criminal Justice and the Victim.* Beverly Hills: Sage Publications, 1976.

Sparks, R. "Types of Treatment for Types of Offenders." In *Collected Studies in Criminological Research* III. Strasbourg: Council of Europe, 1968.

Sparks, R.; H. Genn; and D. Dodd. *Surveying Victims: A Study of the Measurement of Criminal Victimization.* New York: John Wiley and Sons, 1977.

Spencer, H. *The Study of Sociology.* New York: D. Appleton and Co., 1924.

Sperlak, D. "Bail: A Legal Analysis of the Bond-Setting Behavior of Holiday Court Judges in Chicago." *Chicago-Kent Law Review* 51:757 (1974).

Stanley, D. *Prisoners Among Us.* Washington, D.C.: Brookings Institution, 1976.

Steele, E. "Fraud, Dispute, and the Consumer: Responding to Consumer Complaints." *University of Pennsylvania Law Review* 173:1107 (1975).

Stevenson, B. *Handbook of Quotations.* New York: Dodd, 1967.

Suffet, F. "Bail Setting: A Study of Courtroom Interaction." *Crime and Delinquency* 12:318 (1966).

Sullivan, C.E.; J.D. Grant; and M.Q. Grant. "The Development of Interpersonal Maturity: Applications to Delinquency." *Psychiatry* 20:373 (1957).

Sullivan, D., and L. Siegal. "How Police Use Information to Make Decisions." *Crime and Delinquency* 18:253 (1972).

Sutherland, H. *Principles of Criminology.* Philadelphia: J.B. Lippincott Co., 1934.

Sutton, L. *Federal Sentencing Patterns: A Study of Geographical Variations.* Washington, D.C.: National Criminal Justice Information and Statistics Service, 1978.

Sutton, L. *Variations in Federal Criminal Sentences: A Statistical Assessment at the National Level.* Washington, D.C.: National Criminal Justice Information and Statistics Service, 1978.

Swanson, C. "A Comparison of Organizational and Environmental Influences in Arrest Policies." In F. Meyer and R. Baker, eds., *Determinants of Law-Enforcement Policies.* Lexington, Massachusetts: Lexington Books, 1979.

Sykes, G.M. *The Society of Captives.* Princeton, New Jersey: Princeton University Press, 1958.

Sykes, R., and J. Clarke. "A Theory of Deference Exchange in Police-Citizen Encounters." *American Journal of Sociology* 81:58 (1975).

Sykes, R.; J. Fox; and J. Clarke. "A Socio-Legal Theory of Police Discretion." In A. Niederhoffer and A. Blumberg, eds., *The Ambivalent Force*, 2nd ed. Hinsdale: Dryden Press, 1976.

Szasz, T. *The Manufacture of Madness.* New York: Harper and Row, 1970.

———. *The Myth of Mental Illness.* New York: Harper and Row, 1961.

———. *Psychiatric Justice.* New York: Macmillan, 1965.

Talarico, S., and C. Swanson. "Styles of Policing: An Exploration of Compatibility and Conflict." In F. Meyer and R. Baker, eds., *Determinants of Law-Enforcement Policies.* Lexington, Massachusetts: Lexington Books, 1979.

Taylor, G. "An Evaluation of the Supervised Pretrial Release Program." Sacramento, California: American Justice Institute, 1975. Manuscript.

Thomas, W. *Bail Reform in America.* Berkeley: University of California Press, 1976.

Tiffany, L.; Y. Avichai; and G. Peters. "A Statistical Analysis of Sentencing in Federal Courts: Defendants Convicted After Trial, 1967-68." *Journal of Legal Studies* 4:369 (1975).

Toch, H. *Living in Prison.* New York: The Free Press, 1977.

Tribe, L. "An Ounce of Detention: Preventive Justice in the World of John Mitchell." *Virginia Law Review* 56:371 (1970).

Underwood, B. "Law and the Crystal Ball: Predicting Behavior With Statistical Inference and Individualized Judgment." *Yale Law Journal* 88:1408 (1979).

U.S. Bureau of the Census. *National Crime Survey: National Sample Survey Documentation.* Washington, D.C.: U.S. Department of Commerce, 1975.

U.S. Department of Justice. *National Prisoner Statistics: State Prisoners: Admissions and Releases, 1970.* Washington, D.C.: Federal Bureau of Prisons, 1970.

Van Alstyne, D., and M. Gottfredson. "A Multidimensional Contingency Table Analysis of Parole Outcome." *Journal of Research in Crime and Delinquency* 15:172 (1978).

Van den Haag, E. *Punishing Criminals: Concerning A Very Old and Painful Question.* New York: Basic Books, 1975.

Venezia, P.S. "Delinquency as a Function of Intrafamily Relationships." *Journal of Research in Crime and Delinquency* 5:148 (1968).

———. "Delinquency Prediction: A Critique and a Suggestion." *Journal of Research in Crime and Delinquency* 8:108 (1971).

———. "Pretrial Release With Supportive Services for 'High Risk' Defendants; Evaluation Report Number 3." Davis, California: NCCD, 1973.

Vera Institute of Justice. *Felony Arrests: Their Prosecution and Disposition in New York City's Courts.* New York, 1977.

Vetter, H.J., and R. Adams. "Effectiveness of Probation Caseload Sizes: A Review of the Empirical Literature." *Criminology* 8:33 (1971).

von Hirsch, A. *Doing Justice: The Choice of Punishment.* New York: Hill and Wang, 1976.

———. "Prediction of Criminal Conduct and Preventive Confinement of Convicted Persons." *Buffalo Law Review* 21:717 (1972).

von Hirsch, A., and K. Hanrahan. *Abolish Parole?* Washington, D.C.: Government Printing Office, 1978.

———. *The Question of Parole.* Cambridge, Massachusetts: Ballinger, 1979.

Vorenberg, J. "Narrowing the Discretion of Criminal Justice Officials." *Duke Law Journal* 4:651 (1976).

Wald, P. "Pretrial Detention and Ultimate Freedom: A Statistical Study." *New York University Law Review* 39:631 (1964).

———. "The Right to Bail Revisited: A Decade of Promise Without Fulfillment." In S. Nagel, ed., *Rights of the Accused in Law and Action.* Beverly Hills: Sage, 1972.

Waller, I. *Men Released From Prison.* Toronto: University of Toronto Press, 1974.

Walters, A.A. "A Note on Statistical Methods of Predicting Delinquency." *British Journal of Delinquency* 6:297 (1956).

Warren, M.Q. "Classification of Offenders as an Aid to Efficient Management and Effective Treatment." *Journal of Criminal Law, Criminology, and Police Science* 62:239 (1971).

Weeks, H.A. *Youthful Offenders at Highfields.* Ann Arbor: University of Michigan Press, 1958.

Weiler, P.C. "The Reform of Punishment." In Law Reform Commission of Canada. *Studies on Sentencing.* Ottawa: Information Canada, 1974.

Welsh, J., and D. Viets. *The Pretrial Offender in the District of Columbia.* Washington, D.C.: District of Columbia Bail Agency, 1977.

Wice, P. *Bail and Its Reform: A National Survey.* Washington, D.C.: Government Printing Office, 1973.

———. *Freedom for Sale.* Lexington, Massachusetts: Lexington Books, 1974.

Wilkins, L.T. *Evaluation of Penal Measures.* New York: Random House, 1969.

———. "Perspectives on Court Decision-making." In D.M. Gottfredson, ed., *Decision-making in the Criminal Justice System: Reviews and Essays,* ch. V. Washington, D.C.: Government Printing Office, 1975.

———. *Social Deviance.* Englewood Cliffs, New Jersey: Prentice-Hall, 1964.

———. "Some Philosophical Issues: Values and the Parole Decision." In W.E. Amos and C.L. Newman, eds., *Parole: Legal Issues, Decision-making and Research.* New York: Federal Legal Publications, 1975.

———. "The Unique Individual." In M.E. Wolfgang et al., eds., *The Sociology of Crime and Delinquency.* New York: John Wiley and Sons, 1970.

———. "What is Prediction and Is It Necessary in Evaluating Treatment?" In *Research and Potential Application of Research in Probation, Parole, and Delinquency Prediction.* New York: Citizens Committee for Children of New York, Research Center, New York School of Social Work, Columbia University, July 1961.

Wilkins, L.T., and A. Chandler. "Confidence and Competence in Decision-making." *British Journal of Delinquency* 5:22 (1965).

Wilkins, L.T., and D.M. Gottfredson. *Research, Demonstration and Social Action.* Davis, California: National Council on Crime and Delinquency, 1969.

Wilkins, L.T., and P. MacNaughton-Smith. "New Prediction and Classification Methods in Criminology." *Journal of Research in Crime and Delinquency* 1:19 (1964).

Wilkins, L.T.; J. Kress, D.M. Gottfredson, J. Calpin, and A. Gelman. *Sentencing Guidelines: Structuring Judicial Discretion.* Washington, D.C.: Government Printing Office, 1978.

Williams, K. *The Role of the Victim in the Prosecution of Violent Offenses.* Institute for Law and Social Research, Publication Number 12. Washington, D.C.: Government Printing Office, 1978.

Williams, W.T., and J.M. Lambert. "Multivariate Methods in Plant Ecology, I. Association Analysis in Plant Communities." *Journal of Ecology* 47 (1959).

Wilson, J. *Varieties of Police Behavior.* Cambridge, Massachusetts: Harvard University Press, 1965.

Wilson, J.Q. *Thinking About Crime.* New York: Basic Books, 1975.

Wylie, C., Jr. "Paradox." *Scientific Monthly*, 67:63 (1948).
Zalman, M. "A Commission Model of Sentencing." *Notre Dame Lawyer* 53:266 (1977).

Author Index

Subject Index

About the Authors

Michael R. Gottfredson teaches in the School of Criminal Justice at the State University of New York at Albany. Formerly he was the director of the Criminal Justice Research Center in Albany, New York. He has co-authored (with Michael Hindelang and James Garofalo) *Victims of Personal Crime: An Empirical Foundation for a Theory of Personal Victimization* (Cambridge, Massachusetts: Ballinger Publishing Company, 1978) and is co-editor of the annual *Sourcebook of Criminal Justice Statistics* (Washington, D.C.: U.S. Government Printing Office). He has been engaged in research projects involving victimization surveys, parole decisionmaking, and pretrial release decisionmaking. His current research project is a feasibility study of bail decision guidelines. He is an associate editor of the *Journal of Research in Crime and Delinquency.*

Don M. Gottfredson is the dean of and professor in the School of Criminal Justice at Rutgers University. Previously, he was the director of the National Council on Crime and Delinquency Research Center, and earlier he was a project director for the Institute for the Study of Crime and Delinquency. A psychologist, he was a visiting professor of sociology at the University of Hawaii and a distinguished visiting professor at the National College of Juvenile and Family Court Judges of the University of Nevada, Reno.

Currently, he is a member of the Advisory Council of the National Institute of Law Enforcement and Criminal Justice and a fellow of the National Center for Juvenile Justice. He has been the vice president of the American Society of Criminology and he was the first president of the Association for Correctional Research and Statistics. Recently, he was a member of the Task Force on Research and Development, National Advisory Commission on Criminal Justice Standards and Goals, and he was a consultant to the Task Force on Juvenile Delinquency and Youth Crime and a consultant and advisor to the Task Force on Corrections for the President's Commission on Law Enforcement and Administration of Justice. He has been the executive editor of the *Journal of Research in Crime and Delinquency* and an editorial consultant or advisor for various other professional journals. He co-authored (with Leslie T. Wilkins and Peter B. Hoffman) *Guidelines for Parole and Sentencing: A Policy Control Method* (Lexington, Massachusetts: Lexington Books, 1978) and (with Leslie T. Wilkins and others) *Sentencing Guidelines: Structuring Judicial Discretion* (Washington, D.C.: U.S. Government Printing Office, 1978). His current research addresses problems in sentencing.